The Autobiography of Arthur Young

You are holding a reproduction of an original work that is in the public domain in the United States of America, and possibly other countries. You may freely copy and distribute this work as no entity (individual or corporate) has a copyright on the body of the work. This book may contain prior copyright references, and library stamps (as most of these works were scanned from library copies). These have been scanned and retained as part of the historical artifact.

This book may have occasional imperfections such as missing or blurred pages, poor pictures, errant marks, etc. that were either part of the original artifact, or were introduced by the scanning process. We believe this work is culturally important, and despite the imperfections, have elected to bring it back into print as part of our continuing commitment to the preservation of printed works worldwide. We appreciate your understanding of the imperfections in the preservation process, and hope you enjoy this valuable book.

THE AUTOBIOGRAPHY

OF

ARTHUR YOUNG

Miniature in the possession of Alfred Morrison Esqre

THE AUTOBIOGRAPHY

OF

ARTHUR YOUNG

WITH

SELECTIONS FROM HIS CORRESPONDENCE

'That wise and honest traveller'—JOHN MORLEY

EDITED BY

M. BETHAM-EDWARDS

WITH PORTRAITS AND ILLUSTRATIONS

LONDON
SMITH, ELDER, & CO., 15 WATERLOO PLACE
1898

[All rights reserved]

Young, Arthur.   Autobiography, with selections from his correspondence ; edited by M. Betham-Edwards.

London *Smith, Elder* 1898.   10+[1]+480 p. illus. portrs. plates, fac-sim. O. 12s. 6d

An abridged autobiography of the eminent English agriculturalist and political writer. 1–1820; *from* 7 packets of MS. and 12 folio volumes of correspondence; *contains* correspondence with Dr. Priestley, Dr. Burney, Bentham, etc.; little about his writings, less about his travels; of *value* for the history of the Board of Agriculture and Commerce (supplementing the memoir of Sir John Sinclair), and of political thought during the last years of the 18th century. There is a good biography of Young as agriculturalist by John Donaldson 1854; a Young bibliography by J. P. Anderson in Young's Tour in Ireland (A. W. Hutton, editor) 2:349–374 (1892).

Econ. J. 8:367 (Henry Higgs); Eng. Hist. R. 13:797 (Jas. Bonar); Ed. R. 188:78. Ath. 1:176; Sat. R. 85:498.

W. Dawson Johnston, Feb. 1899

ALA E53

INTRODUCTORY NOTE

AN apology for these Memoirs is surely not needed. Whilst Arthur Young's famous 'Travels in France' have become a classic, little is known of the author's life, a life singularly interesting and singularly sad. Whether regarded as the untiring experimentalist and dreamer of economic dreams, as the brilliant man of society and the world, or as the blind, solitary victim of religious melancholia, the figure before us remains unique and impressive. We have here, moreover, a strong character portrayed by himself, an honest piece of autobiography erring, if at all, on the side of outspokenness. In his desire to be perfectly frank, the writer has laid upon his editor the obligation of many curtailments, the Memoirs from beginning to end being already much too long. From seven packets of MS. and twelve folio volumes of correspondence I have put together all that a busy public will probably care to know of Arthur Young—his strength and weakness, his one success and innumerable failures, his fireside and his friends. One striking and instructive feature in this man's history is his cosmopolitanism, his affectionate relations with Frenchmen, Poles, Russians, Danes, Italians, Scandinavians. Never

Englishman was more truly English; never Englishman was less narrow in his social sympathies.

The religious melancholia of his later years is explicable on several grounds: to the influence of his friend, the great Wilberforce; to the crushing sorrow of his beloved little daughter 'Bobbin's' death; lastly, perhaps, to exaggerated self-condemnation for foibles of his youth. Few lives have been more many-sided, more varied; few, indeed, have been more fortunate and unfortunate at the same time.

The Memoirs, whilst necessarily abridged and arranged, are given precisely as they were written—that is to say, although it has been necessary to omit much, not a word has been added or altered. Whenever a word or sentence needed explanation or correction, the editorial note is bracketed. The foot-notes, unless when otherwise stated, are all editorial.

For the use of Memoirs and letters, &c., I am indebted to Mrs. Arthur Young, widow of the late owner of Bradfield Hall, the last of Arthur Young's race and name, a gentleman alike in his public and private life well worthy of his distinguished ancestry.

Mr. Arthur Young, who died last year, is buried beside the author of the 'Travels in France,' in the pretty little churchyard of Bradfield, near Bury St. Edmunds.

M. B.-E.

CONTENTS

CHAPTER I

CHILDHOOD AND YOUTH, 1741–1759

PAGE

Ancestry—Anecdotes—Childhood—School life—Inoculation—The paternal character—Mrs. Kennon—Letters to a schoolboy—A mercantile apprenticeship—A youthful love affair—Family troubles—A gloomy outlook . . . .

CHAPTER II

FARMING AND MARRIAGE, 1759–1766

The gay world—A call on Dr. Johnson—A venture—Offer of a career—Farming decided upon—Garrick—Marriage—Mr. Harte—Lord Chesterfield on farming—Literary work—Correspondence—Birth of a daughter 26

CHAPTER III

IN SEARCH OF A LIVING, 1767–1775

Home travels—A move—Anecdote of a cat—Disillusion—'A Farmer's Letters'—Another move—'In the full blaze of her beauty'—Hetty Burney and her harpsichord—'Scant in servants'—Maternal solicitude—Money difficulties—More tours—Lord Sheffield—Howard the philanthropist—Correspondence 4

CHAPTER IV

IRELAND, 1776-1778

The journey to Ireland—Characteristics—Residence at Mitchelstown—Intrigues—A strange bargain—Departure—Letter to his wife—A terrible journey 66

CHAPTER V

FARMING AND EXPERIMENTS, 1779-1782

Corn bounties—A grievance—Reading—Hugh Boyd—Bishop Watson—Howlett on population—Irish Linen Board—Experiments—Correspondence 83

CHAPTER VI

FIRST GLIMPSE OF FRANCE, 1783-1785

Birth of Bobbin—Ice baths—'The Annals of Agriculture'—A group of friends—Lazowski—First glimpse of France—Death of my mother—The Bishop of Derry—Fishing parties—Rainham 110

CHAPTER VII

FIRST FRENCH JOURNEY, 1786-1787

Death of my brother—Anecdotes of his character—Dr. Burney on farming—Greenwich *versus* Eton—Blenheim—Correspondence with Dr. Priestley—County toasts—French projects—First French journey 138

CHAPTER VIII

TRAVEL AND INTERNATIONAL FRIENDSHIPS, 1788-89-1790

The Wool Bill—Sheridan's speech—Count Berchtold—Experiments—Second French journey—Potato-fed sheep—Cost of housekeeping—Chicory—Burnt in effigy—Correspondence—Third French journey—With Italian agriculturists—Bishop Watson and Mr. Luther—Correspondence—Literary work—Illness—The state of France 163

CHAPTER IX

PATRIOTIC PROPOSALS, 1791-92

Illness—Correspondence with Washington—The King's gift of a ram—Anecdotes—Revising MSS.—Patriotic proposals—Death of the Earl of Orford—Agricultural schemes—Correspondence 189

CHAPTER X

THE BOARD OF AGRICULTURE, 1793

The Board of Agriculture—Secretaryship—Residence in London—Twenty-five dinners a month—The King's bull—The Marquis de Castries—'The Example of France'—Encomiums thereof—Correspondence 219

CHAPTER XI

THE SECRETARYSHIP, 1794-95-1796

The Secretaryship and its drawbacks—Social compensations—Illness and death of Elizabeth Hoole—Letters of Jeremy Bentham and others—A visit to Burke—Home travels—Enclosures . . 241

CHAPTER XII

ILLNESS AND DEATH OF BOBBIN, 1797

Illness of Bobbin—Letters of Bobbin and her father's replies—Dress minutes at the opera—Hoping against hope—Bobbin's death—Seeking for consolation—Retrospection—Beginning of diary—Correspondence 263

CHAPTER XIII

DIARY AND CORRESPONDENCE, 1798, 1799, 1800

Assessed taxes—Society—Mr. Pitt and the Board of Agriculture—A foolish joke—Dinners to poor children—Interview with the King—Royal farming—Correspondence—Bradfield—Incidents of home travel—Portrait of a great lady—Correspondence. . 312

CHAPTER XIV

DIARY CONTINUED, 1801–1803

Public affairs and prophecy—The divining rod—The appropriation of waste lands—The word 'meanness' defined—South's sermons—Projected theological compendia—Correspondence—Journalising to 'my friend'—Anecdote of Dean Milner and Pitt—Death of the Duke of Bedford—Napoleon and Protestantism . 347

CHAPTER XV

APPROACHING BLINDNESS, 1804–1807

A great preacher—Arthur Young the younger goes to Russia—Cowper's letters—Mrs. Young's illness—Dr. Symonds—Novel reading—Skinner's 'State of Peru'—Death of Pitt—Burke's publishing accounts—Literary projects—Approaching blindness   391

CHAPTER XVI

LAST YEARS, 1808–1820

Gradual loss of sight—Illness and death of Mrs. Oakes—Daily routine—A disappointment—Riots—Death of Mrs. Young—Anecdotes of Napoleon—A story of the Terror—National distress—Close of diary—The end 441

INDEX 475

LIST OF ILLUSTRATIONS

PORTRAIT OF ARTHUR YOUNG . . . . *Frontispiece*

BRADFIELD HALL AS IN ARTHUR YOUNG'S TIME . . . *to face p.* 127

FACSIMILE OF LETTER FROM ARTHUR YOUNG TO MISS
    YOUNG . . . . „ 188

PORTRAIT OF 'BOBBIN' (MARTHA YOUNG) . . . . „ 265

ARTHUR YOUNG'S TOMB AT BRADFIELD . . . . „ 472

AUTOBIOGRAPHY
OF
ARTHUR YOUNG

CHAPTER I

CHILDHOOD AND YOUTH, 1741-1759

Ancestry — Anecdotes — Childhood — School life — Inoculation — The paternal character—Mrs. Kennon—Letters to a schoolboy—A mercantile apprenticeship—A youthful love affair—Family troubles—A gloomy outlook.

I WAS born at Whitehall, London, on September 11, 1741, many years after my brother John and my sister Elizabeth Mary. In examining the family papers from which the following detail is drawn, I should observe that difficulties often occurred by reason of the ancient hand-writing of many documents, and from several being written in the Latin language not easily deciphered; but the circumstances relative to the following dates were clearly ascertained as far as they are noted. The principal object is the possession of the Manor of Bradfield Combust, which is traced in the family of Canham till it came by marriage into that of Young. Bartholomew Canham the elder had two sons and two daughters. In 1672 he transferred Bradfield Hall, manor and lands to Arthur Young, married to Elizabeth, his daughter. The Young shield bears a Field Argent, three Bends sable and a Lyon rampant; that of Canham a Field Gule, Bend Argent charged with a cannon ball sable, the Bend cotised with Or. The estate had been purchased in 1620 by my ancestor of Sir Thomas, afterwards Lord Jermyn of Rushbrooke, being part of the great possessions of that family. The steward who acted for Sir Thomas was Martin Folkes, ancestor of the present Sir Martin Folkes. And here it is curious to observe the different results affecting the posterity of the private gentleman who purchases, and of the steward of the great man who sells—I am a poor little gentleman, and Sir Martin Folkes owner of an estate not far short of 10,000l. a year. My father, Dr. Arthur Young, inherited Bradfield from my grandfather, Bartholomew Young, Esq., called Captain from a command in the Militia, and it is remarkable that with only a part of the present Bradfield estate he lived genteely and drove a coach and four on a property which in these present times just maintains the establishment of a wheelbarrow.

Dr. Arthur Young, my father, was educated at Eton and admitted to Pembroke Hall, Cambridge, in 1710, afterwards settling at Thames Ditton, Surrey. He was so much liked by the inhabitants that they elected him, against a violent opposition of the inferior classes, minister of that parish. Whether the ladies of the place had a particular influence I know not, but he was a remarkably handsome man and six feet high. It was here he became acquainted with Miss Anne Lucretia de Cousmaker, to whom he was afterwards married. She was the daughter of John de Cousmaker, Esq., who came to England with King William III., bringing with him a fortune of 80,000*l*., the greater part of which he was deprived of by the imprudence of one or two of his sons. If ever there existed in human form an Israelite without guile, it was this worthy man; and it gives me great pleasure to reflect on the extreme respect and affection which were always felt for him and my dear mother. Mr. de Cousmaker, my maternal grandfather, was executor and residuary legatee to a Mrs. Keene, on which account he could have legally possessed himself of an estate left by her. With an honesty unexampled he would not take one penny of it, but exerted himself with incredible industry to discover some distant relation to whom he might transfer the property. He did find one who had no legal claim, and he gave him the estate. This Mr. Keene dying without issue, his widow told my grandfather that out of gratitude she would provide for two of his children. To a daughter she left an annuity of 300*l*. a year, to a son an estate which passed on to his descendants.

My mother brought a fortune to my father, the amount I know not, but it was sufficient to demand the settlement of the Bradfield estate upon her for life. She was of a very amiable, cheerful disposition, loved conversation, for which she had a talent, and read a great deal on various subjects. The residence at

Thames Ditton resulted in a friendship with the Onslow family, which proved highly advantageous to my father. General, then Colonel Onslow, appointed him chaplain to his own regiment, and the General's brother, Speaker of the House of Commons, also named him chaplain, a step which afterwards led to the prebendaryship of Canterbury. Mr. Speaker Onslow and the Bishop of Rochester were my godfathers. Colonel, afterwards General Onslow, was in the estimation of the world a highly respectable character, in the formation of which it may easily be supposed that religion formed no part from the following anecdote. One Sunday morning his wife obtained his permission to read a chapter of the Bible, but he first bolted the door lest the servants should witness the performance. He was afraid that the matter might reach the ears of his Commander-in-Chief, the Duke of Cumberland, who to much brutality of character added the abhorrence of a soldier troubling his head about religion.

In 1734 my father published his 'Historical Dissertations on Idolatrous Corruptions in Religion,' a very learned work which is quoted by Voltaire. In 1742 he was in Flanders acting as chaplain to Colonel Onslow's regiment, and I have found among his papers the journal of a tour made through Brabant, Flanders, and a part of Picardy; on the whole, it is interesting, and the cheapness of living therein described is remarkable. The following letter is from my father to his relation, his Excellency Governor Vassy, relating to the conduct of General Ingoldsby (who married my mother's sister) at the battle of Fontenoy, and which throws a little additional light upon that transaction, though at the expense of the Commander-in-Chief.

'Bradfield Hall: July 22, 1745 (O.S.).

'Dear Sir,—My last, which I wrote some time before our Parliament broke up, was of such a length as I suppose has tired you of my correspondence, since which I, having been here in the country, have had nothing of news worth troubling you with. I make little doubt but that our friend Ingoldsby's behaviour has made much the same figure in your publick papers as your Appius's has done in ours. But I can assure you, Sir, that, notwithstanding the account published in our Gazette, he behaved like a good and a brave officer. A court-martial has set upon him, but what the result of it is we know not as yet. But fear the worst, since the clearing of him must reflect upon a King's son who has the command of an Army. I have enclosed his case, which contains as much of the truth as he could have leave to print, at the bottom of which you will find something wrote which his Royal Highness commanded particularly to be left out. But if you, Sir, who are nearer to the Army than we are, desire a more particular account of this affair, your nephew Everet, who will continue here with us for more than a month longer, shall give you the full detail of it.

'If, dear Sir, the gentleman who is the bearer of this shall want your protection, I recommend him to it; he is going to the Army as my substitute. His name is Gough, and is nephew to Captain Gough, who is a member of the House of Commons and director of, and the great manager in, our East India Company. All that I particularly ask in behalf of him is that you will give him your directions how to find our Army, and, if it be necessary, to halt in your garrison.

'I am, dear Sir,
  'Your Excellency's kinsman and servant,
      'T. YOUNG.'

Ingoldsby was cruelly used at the battle of Fontenoy by the Duke of Cumberland, who had sent him orders to put himself at the head of a detachment to attack a temporary redoubt which the French had thrown up, but gave him no directions to take cannon; and when Ingoldsby arrived at the spot he saw the necessity. He instantly dispatched his Aide-de-camp to demand cannon, but before they came the position of the troops changed, and an order came to draw off. No consequences attended this business, nor had it any effect on the loss of the battle; but an opportunity was taken to throw the whole blame on Ingoldsby, and to attach to him all the consequences of that defeat. Ingoldsby complained of this, and Ligonier himself came to him from the Duke to assure him that the D. knew his bravery, and highly valued him, but advised him by all means to be quiet, and everything would blow over, and the business be forgotten. Nothing had been said on the affair, but to save the reputation of the Duke. Mrs. Ingoldsby, losing all patience at his not being promoted according to promise, never let him rest till he published his case, which put an end to all hope of promotion in the Army, and he was obliged to retire. He was in all the Duke of Marlborough's campaigns, and served with great reputation to the moment of the battle of Fontenoy.

When I was of a proper age to be placed at school, a choice had to be made between those of Bury St. Edmunds and Lavenham [1]; no possible motive could induce any one to think of the latter, except the circumstance of my father having been there himself. The master of the former school, Mr. Kinsman, was one of the finest scholars of his age, and is mentioned with much respect by Cumberland in his memoirs.[2] Whilst the matter was in abeyance the Rev. M. Coulter, Master of Lavenham School, came to Bradfield, and my mother, unfortunately for me, was so much pleased with the extreme good temper manifested in his countenance that she persuaded my father to entrust me to his care. I was accordingly sent to that wretched place. I was to learn Latin and Greek, with arithmetic, but whether from being a favourite or from the diversion of frequent visits home, I afterwards found myself so ill-grounded in the above languages that for some time before I left the school I found it necessary to give much attention to them in order to recover the lost time. It is easy to suppose how much I was indulged from one instance among many others. At dinner the first dish the boys were helped to was pudding, which I disliked, and was excused from eating—the case of no other pupil. As to correction, I have no recollection of receiving any thing of the

[1] Lavenham is a very pretty village, with splendid church, lying between Sudbury and Whelnethan, whilst Bury St. Edmunds is the second town in Suffolk.
[2] *Memoirs of Richard Cumberland*, 1806.

sort.¹ I had, however, a sufficient awe of the Master. During the last years of my stay I had a pointer and gun, and often went out with Mr. Coulter, he with a partridge net and I with my gun. I had a room to myself and a neat collection of books. I remember beginning to write a history of England, thinking that I could make a good one out of several others. How early began my literary follies! I seemed to have a natural propensity for writing books. The following bill for a year's schooling and board must in the present period (about 1816) be considered a curiosity:—'The Rev. Dr. Young to John Coulter, Xmas 1750, to Xmas 1751. A year's board, &c. 15*l.* Sundries 2*l.* 4*s.* 4*d.* Total 17*l.* 4*s.* 4*d.*' I find from a memorandum book of my mother's that in 1746 beef was 3*d.*, veal 3*d.*, and mutton 3½*d.* per pound at Bury.

About the year 1753 I was inoculated. This was a scheme of my mother's which she had more than once proposed, but my father would not consent to it. Taking, however, the opportunity of his visit to Cambridge, she ventured on the experiment. At this period inoculation was so little understood that it is utterly astonishing how anyone could escape; instead of the cool regimen afterwards prescribed by Sutton,² the practice was to

---

¹ Elsewhere Arthur Young mentions a severe flogging 'very properly' administered by his father for an act of cruelty, adding, 'It was the only time that I ever received any correction at his hands, yet he was a remarkably passionate man.'

² Robert Sutton, physician and inoculist, 1757, *Dict. of Biography*, Sampson Low. Dr. Guy's *Public Health* has the following: 'The Suttons were noted for their success in inoculation, but Dr. Gregory gives more credit to diet and exposure to air than to the antimonial and mercurial medicines they extolled.'

keep the patient's chamber as close and hot as possible, the shutters were kept up, and the door never opened without being shut speedily. I suffered much, and Dr. Kerrich, the physician at Bury, for some time attended every day. It pleased the Almighty that I should recover, one of many instances in which His providence preserved a wretch who was to sin against Him by a multitude of offences. When my father returned and I ran out to meet him, my mother exclaimed in a triumphant tone, 'There! I have had Arthur inoculated, and you enjoy the comfort of knowing that your boy has had that terrible disorder.' My father looked at me, but neither spoke a word on the subject then nor ever after. This was his way—resolute in rejecting all proposals touching upon novelty, and cool after their accomplishment. In an inferior circumstance he showed the same temper, as I will relate. The family pew at church was a wretched hole, lined with ragged cloth and covered with dust; the pulpit also was tumbling with age and rottenness. On my father's going to London and leaving my brother at Bradfield, he begged permission to have a new pew and pulpit. This was refused. 'Good enough, Jack!' said my father. But Jack attacked his mother, and set the carpenter to work, who made a spacious pew, with one for the servants, new pulpit and reading desk. The first Sunday my father went to church, on approaching the place, he stopped short, surveyed all three with great attention, said nothing, and on joining the family party home never opened his lips, nor ever after mentioned the subject. He was inwardly pleased, but not gracious enough to confess it. There was in Dr. Young a strong mixture of obstinacy and *sang-froid*, as the preceding anecdotes prove.

In 1753 I went to London, and find by an old pocket-book that I saw Mr. Garrick in 'Archer,'[1] heard the Oratorio, 'The Messiah,' spent an evening at Ranelagh, and viewed the Tower and St. Paul's. I also remember visiting the widow of General Ingoldsby, who opened her house every evening to all comers, nor was the number of fashionable people inconsiderable. John Wilkes, afterwards so well known, I met there more than once; he was then considered a wit. Mrs. Ingoldsby made a point of going to Court at least twice a year, but I never heard her repeat any other conversation with the King than complaining to him how much she was afflicted with rheumatism.

In 1754 died Mrs. Sidney Kennon, a lady highly respected and well known as the midwife to the Princess of Wales; she also brought into the world my brother, sister and myself, and was a very old friend of my father's, and him she left executor and residuary legatee. That her professional emoluments were of some consideration was proved by the fact of a gentleman after her decease presenting her executor with fifty guineas as her fee for having delivered his wife. By her will all her furniture and a great collection of medals, bronzes, shells, curiosities, books on natural history, &c. with money in the funds, came into his possession, to the amount of nearly five thousand pounds. By a codicil she had ordered that her

[1] Hero of *The Beaux' Stratagem*, G. Farquhar.

servants should be retained and the house kept for six months after her death, in consequence of which our family moved into her residence in Clifford Street. It was, of course, to be expected that my father would sell all the curiosities, but that a clergyman, a man of learning, having a son of my brother's attainments should dispose of such a collection, was not looked for; my maternal Uncle, de Cousmaker, dining one day at the house enquired as to my father's intentions. On being informed that everything would go to an auction, he asked the price. My father replied that the articles had not been valued, but he supposed that they would fetch fifty or sixty pounds. Mr. de C. at once offered sixty guineas, the bargain was struck, and the books departed next day, to our great mortification; the price was preposterous, as the collection contained many curious and scarce publications, and my Uncle afterwards sold many of the duplicates for a greater amount than he had given for the whole, yet retaining a most valuable number. As a proof of the worth of what might be called Mrs. Kennon's Museum, I insert a letter to her from Sir Martin Folkes, President of the Royal Society.

'Madame,—I am sorry I had not the happiness of seeing you when I was last to wait on you, but will take another opportunity of paying my respects. The worms you were pleased to send seem to me the very same I received from Holland, and which I was in the utmost distress for, being quite out, and my Polypes in great want, so that a word of instruction, how I may

get at some of these worms, will be a great obligation. When I had the honour of leaving you a Polype, I had never a one by me with a young one fairly put out, so here was one beginning. I now beg leave to send you such a one; and when you are disposed to cut one will wait on you, and show it you in a microscope, if you have not yet seen it. I beg leave to return very many thanks for the favour of seeing your noble collection of rarities, and have hardly talked of anything else since.
'I am, Madam, with the sincerest respect,
'Your ladyship's most obedient humble servant,
'M. FOLKES.
'May 6, 1743.'

Doddington, in his diary, under the date of June 28, 1750, mentions supping at this lady's house, in company with Lady Middlesex, Lord Bathurst, and Lady Torrington; and in the 'World' (No. 114) there is a humorous paper on the distinctions between noble birth, great birth, and no birth, in which the writer says, 'I never suspected that it could possibly mean the shrivelled tasteless fruit of an old genealogical tree. I communicated my doubts, and applied for information to my late, worthy, and curious friend, Mrs. Kennon, whose valuable collection of fossils and minerals, lately sold, sufficiently prove her skill and researches in the most recondite parts of nature. She, with that frankness and humanity which were natural to her, assured me that it was all a vulgar error, in which, however, the nobility and gentry prided themselves; but that, in truth, she had never observed the children of the quality to be wholesomer and stronger than others, but rather the contrary, which difference she imputed to certain causes which I shall not here specify.' I possess several letters written to this lady by the Governor of Bermuda, Mr. Popple, in 1739 and 1740, in which he considers her of sufficient importance to request that she would speak a good word for him in behalf of his being removed to a better Government, or some other employment at home, and concludes a letter with saying, 'I believe your present power to assist your absent friends is now as great as I have always thought your inclination was.'

When my father returned to Bradfield, after passing the winter in London, he pulled down the old part of the house, a wretched lath and plaster ill-contrived building; then, to the astonishment of every one, he employed a hedge carpenter to rebuild exactly on the old foundations. Thereby was constructed a mansion which had not a single room free from every fault that could be found, whether as to chimney, doors, windows, or connecting passages, and this at a larger expense than need have cost an excellent house. The new stables, with coach-house, brew-house and offices, were built of brick, and cost 500*l*. It was rather whimsical to give his horses, carriage, and brewery [1] the warmth of solid walls, and to house himself in lath and plaster; but in fixing his new farmery,[2] a sad error was committed. The whole interposed between the dwelling,

[1] Till the last generation it was the fashion to brew one's own beer in Suffolk.

[2] 'The buildings and yards necessary for the business of a farm.'—*Webster*.

and four acres of turf dotted with beautiful oaks. My poor father, however, did not live to enjoy his improvements, for he was very soon seized with a dropsy, and which—as will be seen—terminated his life. During one of his journeys to London in order to consult a doctor, occurred a circumstance so whimsical that I must mention it. Several sleepless nights made him take it into his head that anything would be better than a bed; as an experiment at one inn he ordered that a hole should be cut in a haystack, in which he passed the night. But it is time to return to myself. During all these years I was at Lavenham School reading Cæsar, Sallust, Homer and the Greek Testament, when a sudden whim seized my father, and he ordered Latin and Greek to be discarded and algebra to take their place. I thus became absorbed in Saunderson.[1] But what commanded more of my attention at this time was a very different branch of learning, namely, the lessons of a dancing master; he came once a week from Colchester to teach the boys, also some young ladies of the neighbourhood, two of whom made terrible havoc with my heart. The first was Miss Betsy Harrington, a grocer's daughter, admitted by all to be truly beautiful; the second of my youthful flames was Miss Molly Fiske, a clergyman's sister. For one or two years we corresponded, but afterwards I went away, and she married the Rev. M. Chevalier, of Aspall. Long after her marriage she told me that she had accepted that gentleman on finding that I did not

[1] Nicholas Saunderson, D.D., author of the *Elements of Algebra*, in ten books, 1740.

come forward with the proposal. Her fortune was 4,000*l*.

Arthur Young, from his Sister Elisa Maria
'1755.

'Dear Brother,—I acknowledge it's very long since I last wrote to you, but I enclose you my excuses, and what was I assure you the occasion of my delay. I designed making you a present of lace for a pair of ruffles, and the weather had been so bad that it was too dirty for me to go out and get them. I hope they will engage your approbation, which is all I desire, and you'll do me honor in wearing them. I've not yet seen Miss Aspin, and believe I shall not till Monday, when we propose going to Gen¹ Onslow's, and calling upon her in our way. We have had so much rain lately that there has been no stirring, or I would have made her a visit long ago.

'I believe I told my Mother my Uncle was disappointed of his company which were to be here on Saturday last by Miss Turner being ill, but she recovering we are to have the same party next week, and a very grand concert it is to be, because we are musical people.

'Ranelagh is to be opened on the 8th with a rural carnival. I vastly wished for you at Mrs. Cibber's benefit. The play was "Tancred and Sigismunda," the plan of which you and I have often weep'd over together in "Gil Blas." It was most inimitably acted by Garrick and Mrs. Cibber; you would have been vastly entertained. The play I was at before, but went purposely to see the

Princess of Wales and her family. The Prince and Prince Edward were in one box, and the Princess, Lady Augusta, Elizabeth, and Louisa in the other. Upon my word, they are a fine parcel of children; only poor Elizabeth is, unhappily, almost a dwarf, but the rest make very good figures.

'Monday your Aunt and I were in the House of Commons from one o'clock at noon till nine at night; it was the Mitchell Election,[1] when the great ones were setting themselves in combat against each other; it was a most hard-fought battle. The[2] Duke espousing our party against the Duke of Newcastle in support of the other, but the Tories most of them going with the D. of N. gave him the majority. Though he lost it at the Committee. There was much speaking, which was very entertaining; Mr. Fox talked a great deal with great vehemence, for this loss frustrates his schemes, as he finds the strength of the D. of N.'s party though he had all the Army and the Duke's Court people with him. And now, Mr. Arthur, you being a very good polititian, I shall proceed to entertain you with some more Parliamentary affairs. Tuesday last the Message was brought from the King to the House. It imparted little; nothing to be collected from it of either peace or war. Only desiring the Parliament would support him in the armaments he might have occasion for by sea and land, &c. &c. General Onslow

[1] The Mitchell Election, a petition brought by Lord Orwell and Colonel Wedderburn against undue election and return for borough of Mitchell, in Cornwall. See *Commons' Journals*, xxii., xxiv. and xxxii.

[2] The Duke of Cumberland.

says during the eight and twenty years he has sat in that house he never saw, or could have conceived it to be so unanimous in the acclamations of the King. Every one striving who should in the strongest terms express their confidence in him, Tories and all. Even Sir John Phillips declared he would vote the King twenty shillings in the pound, for that their lives and *whole* fortunes were not too much for him, and the House rung with their *confidence* in the King, without any one of the Ministers saying a syllable. They were the silentest people. The General says he would have given any money Miripoix[1] had been in the House to have heard the Parliament of England's hearty affection for their King. I should have much liked to have been there, but the ladies' privilege extends no farther than elections. Lady Crosse sent to us on Monday morning at ten o'clock to let us know she would call on us at eleven, and we had to dress in gowns and petticoats and eat our breakfasts, which last was not to be omitted, for it was certain we were to have no dinner. And by much hurry we did get ready for her ladyship, but waited at her house for Sir John till near one, frighted to excess, fearing we should not get in. This Mitchell Election so famous an affair that all the town wanted to hear it, and evidently the gallery would hold a small part of them. However, we had the luck to get excellent places, having a chair for one of us brought out of the Speaker's chamber. The elections for this year are now all over except the Oxfordshire, and whether they will be able to finish

[1] M. de Miripoix, then French Ambassador at St. James's.

that no one can tell. In answer to this long letter I shall hope to hear very soon from you, and am,

'Your most affectionate
'E. M. YOUNG.

'Friday Good (sic).'

'August 26, 1755 (from Bristol Hot Wells).

'Dear Arthur,—I was in hopes you would have given me the pleasure of hearing from you. I should have wrote to you before now, but have so many letters perpetually upon my hands that no clerk to an attorney has more pen exercise. I want much to have a particular account of the Bury Assizes; I suppose you will go to an Assembly, and therefore pray you to send me intelligence of who and who are together, who dresses smartest, looks best, and seems most pleased with themselves and those about them. The balls here are vastly disagreeable. I dance French dances constantly, but none of the people of fashion dance country dances; there are such numbers of Bristol people that do, and they are such an ordinary set that it prevents the fine folks. The rooms of another night are much cleverer; there is a lottery table which we play at from eight till half an hour after nine most nights. My Aunt and I have both hitherto played with great success. The principal support of our table we lose to-day, Mr. Brudenell, member for Rutlandshire, an extreem good-natured, pretty kind of man; the company is going off so fast and the place is so thin, that I fear we shall miss him very much. My Aunt sends her love to you. She says she made you a promise of giving you a pair of lace ruffles or a guinea, which ever you chose, and desires you will consult with your mother which you will have, and if the lace, let her know it; for it's sold here as well as at Bath. I should advise the money; for you have two pair of lace ruffles which I am sure is as much as you can possibly have occasion for; those you have must be taken off the footings, for the fine men weer them extreemly shallow; they should not be near a nail of a yard deep.

'Pray make my compliments to everybody that enquires after me, and let me have a very long letter from you very soon. I have nothing to add to your entertainment, heartily wish I was at Bradfield, and beg you to tell me all you can that is doing there; and
  'Believe me with great sincerity,
    'Your most affectionate
      'ELISA MARIA.

'Be sure don't speak before my father of my playing at lottery.'

Extracts from further letters

'My Uncle Ingoldsby I think looks very well. He asked after you, and so did my Aunt. He goes out of town for a fortnight next Monday, and Mr. and Miss go then. Dr. In. has made a new coach. Yesterday was the second day of using it, cost him 82l.; it's very handsome, all but being painted in a mosaic, which all the smart equipages are. Miss Joy's mother has made one this spring, cost 147l. There is hardly such a thing seen as a two-wheeled post-chaise;

nobody uses anything but four-wheeled ones, and numbers of them with boxes put on and run for chariots, and vastly pretty they are.

'Now I must give you some account of the masquerade at Mrs. Onslow's; Lady Onslow was there, Mr. and Mrs. Onslow, the Mr. Shelley we met at the Speaker's, and Miss Freeman. Lady Onslow was in a Venetian domino white lustring trimmed with scarlet and silver blonde. Mrs. Onslow's dress we thought not at all pretty nor becoming; she had no jewels on, but was ornamented with mock pearl. Mr. Onslow was in a domino, as was Mr. Shelley; the first was very genteel and handsome, white lustring trimmed with an open shining gold lace and little roses of purple with gold in the middle of them. I never saw anything prettier. Miss Freeman was the sweetest figure I ever saw. Her dress, a dancer, blue satin trimmed with silver in the richest genteelest taste and very fine jewels. They say Fenton Harvey was the best figure there amongst the gentlemen, with his masque; on his dress was a domino which was reckoned the genteelest dresses.

'Lady Coventry, amongst the ladies, was the best figure; Lady Peterson another much admired. The Town said beforehand that she was to be Eve and wear a fig leaf of diamonds; however, this was not true.'

Mrs. Tomlinson (née Elisa Maria Young) to her Father

'Honoured Sir,—Mr. Tomlinson and myself are your urgent petitioners for a favour which, if granted, will give us very great pleasure. It is that you will give my brother Arthur leave to make us a short visit; my mother (who we found safe and well at Chelmsford and have conducted hither) rejoins in the request; she desires you to determine in what manner is best for him to come hither on horseback, the joiner with him or in the stage coach, but either way, we beg to see him Tuesday at farthest, but on Monday if he comes on horseback. Be pleased to direct him to have his linnen washed, stocking (*sic*) mended, &c., and in case he comes on horseback, it may not be amiss to hint to him that he is not to reach London on one gallop, for his impatience may outrun his prudence. It was a great pleasure to hear a pretty good account of your health, and hope we shall hear often from Bradfield during my mother's stay here.

'Beg my love with Mr. T.'s to my brother. He desires to present his duty to you.

'And I am, honoured Sir,
'Your most affectionate and most dutifull daughter,
'E. M. TOMLINSON.

'Bucklersbury: Tuesday night, 10 o'clock (1757).'

Whilst at school I made in the playground a famous fortification, and then besieged it with mines of gunpowder, nearly blowing up two boys and an old woman selling pies. A better example was my habit of reading, which became a sort of fashion. I was thought to be of an uncommon stamp, and when the pupils returned home their parents became desirous of seeing the lad to whom they thought themselves indebted.

My own acquisitions received a mortal shock on the marriage of my sister with Mr. Tomlinson, of the firm of Tomlinson & Co. The opportunity of introducing me into their counting-house was thought advantageous by my father, and in consequence orders came that I should receive immediate instruction in mercantile accounts; as a further preparation the sum of 400*l.* was paid to Messrs. Robertson, of Lynn, Norfolk, for a three years' apprenticeship.

In February 1758 I took my last farewell of Lavenham, and paid a visit to my married sister in London. I remember nothing more of this visit than several performances of Mr. Garrick. When I took leave of my sister, who was far advanced in her pregnancy, she wept and said she might never see me more. This proved to be the case, as she died during her lying-in. She was a remarkably clever woman, with much beauty and vivacity of conversation, combined with much solidity of judgment. My mother grieved so much for her loss that she could never be persuaded to go out of mourning, but mourned till her own death, nor did she ever recover her cheerfulness. This had one good effect, and that a very important one for me; she never afterwards looked into any book but on the subject of religion, and her only constant companion was her Bible, herein copying the example of her father.

Every circumstance attending this new situation at Lynn was most detestable to me till I effected an improvement. This was done by hiring a lodging, surrounding myself with books, and making the acquaintance of Miss Robertson, daughter of my employer's partner. She was of a pleasing figure, with fine black expressive eyes, danced well, and also sang and performed well on the harpsichord; no wonder, as she received instructions from Mr. Burney.[1] He was a person held in the highest estimation for his powers of conversation and agreeable manners, which made his company much sought after by all the principal nobility and gentry of the neighbourhood. Here I must reflect, as I have done many times before, on the unfortunate idea of making me a merchant. The immediate expense absolutely thrown away differently invested would have kept me four years at the University, enabling my father to make me a clergyman and Rector of Bradfield. This living he actually gave to my Lavenham schoolmaster. The whole course of my life would in such a case have been changed. I should have known nothing of Lynn, and have taken a wife from a different quarter. I should probably have been free from all attraction to agriculture, and that circumstance alone would have changed the whole colour of my existence. I might never have been of any use to the public, but my years would have passed in a far more tranquil current, escaping so many storms and vicissitudes which blew me into a tempest of activity and involved me in great errors, great vice, and perpetual anxiety. This was not to be the case, and what I thought an evil star sent me to Lynn. In this place monthly assemblies were held, a mayor's feast

[1] Dr. Charles Burney, author of the *History of Music*, father of Madame d'Arblay.

and ball in the evening, a dancing master's ball and assemblies at the Mart. It was not common, I was told, for merchants' clerks to frequent these, a suggestion I spurned, and attended them, dancing with the principal belles. I was complimented by the dancing master, who assured me that he pointed out my minuet as an example to his scholars. But pleasure alone would not satisfy me; I was by nature studious, and from my earliest years discovered a thirst for learning and books. These, the smallness of my allowance (I think not more than 30*l.* per annum), with my great foppery in dress for the balls, would not permit me to purchase and supply me with what I so much needed. Accordingly in 1758 I compiled a political pamphlet named ' The Theatre of the Present War in North America,' for which a bookseller allowed me ten pounds' worth of books; as he urged me to another undertaking I wrote three or four more political tracts, each of which procured me an addition to my little library. My first year's apprenticeship had not expired before the death of my sister overthrew the whole plan which had sent me to Lynn. As 400*l.* had been paid for the agreed period of three years, I was kept there from no other motive. Under such circumstances it may be supposed that the counting-house and the business received not an atom more of attention than could be dispensed with. I was twenty years old on leaving Lynn, which I did without education, profession or employment. In June of this year (1759) my father died, and as he left debts, my mother thought it necessary to take an exact account of his effects. The following is the result:—

	£	s.
Household goods	674	1
Farming stock	226	4
Plate	149	13
Books	57	0
Total	£1,106	18

I am sorry to add that money or money due to him made no part of the estimate. The fact was that my father died much in debt, and it was two years before my mother found herself tolerably free.

CHAPTER II

FARMING AND MARRIAGE, 1759-1766

The gay world—A call on Dr. Johnson—A venture—Offer of a career—Farming decided upon—Garrick—Marriage—Mr. Harte—Lord Chesterfield on farming—Literary work—Correspondence—Birth of a daughter.

IN 1761 I was at the Coronation, had a seat in the gallery of Westminster Hall, and being in the front row above the Duke's table, I remember letting down a basket during dessert, which was filled by the present Duke of Marlborough. On this visit to London I had a mind to see everything, and ordered a full dress suit for going to Court. This was in September. In December I was again in London figuring in the gay world.[1] In January 1762 I set on foot a periodical publication entitled 'The Universal Museum,' which came out monthly, printed with glorious imprudence on my own account. I waited on Dr. Johnson, who was sitting by

---

[1] The following notes are taken from a small memorandum-book appended to memorials :—

'1761. July 23.—Leak in full (meaning debts), 5*l*. 5*s*.
  ' Sept. 22.—Coronation.
  ' „   28.—To Court.
  ' Oct. 9.—Blackheath ; cards.
  ' Dec.   —To London with Ed. Allen.
  ' „   31.—Debts 62*l*.
  ' (My) History of the War published.'

the fire so half-dressed and slovenly a figure as to make me stare at him. I stated my plan and begged that he would favour me with a paper once a month, offering at the same time any remuneration that he might name. 'No, sir,' he replied, 'such a work would be sure to fail if the booksellers have not the property, and you will lose a great deal of money by it.' 'Certainly, sir,' I said; 'if I am not fortunate enough to induce authors of real talent to contribute.' 'No, sir, you are mistaken, such authors will not support such a work, nor will you persuade them to write in it; you will purchase disappointment by the loss of your money, and I advise you by all means to give up the plan.' Somebody was introduced, and I took my leave. Dr. Kenrick,[1] the translator of Rousseau, was a writer of a very different stamp; he readily engaged to write for me; so did Collier[2] and his wife, who between them translated the 'Death of Abel.'[3] I printed five numbers of this work, and being convinced that Dr. Johnson's advice was wise and that I should lose money by the business, I determined to give it up. With that view I procured a meeting of ten or a dozen booksellers, and had the luck and address to persuade them to take the whole scheme upon themselves. I fairly slipped my neck out of the yoke—a most fortunate occurrence, for, though they continued it under far more favourable circumstances, I believe no success ever attended it.

[1] Dr. Kenrick, critic of the *Monthly Review*, attacked Dr. Johnson, who said, 'I do not think myself bound by Kenrick's rules.'

[2] Joseph and Mary Collier; the first, author of a *History of England*.

[3] Gesner Solomon, born at Zurich, 1730.

In September of the following year I broke a blood-vessel and was attended by a Lynn physician, who ordered me to Bristol Hotwells, as I was in a very consumptive state. I accordingly went, boarding and lodging in a house where I met very intelligent and agreeable society; amongst the number was one gentleman with whom I had many arguments concerning Rousseau and his writings, I, like a fool, much admiring both, my new acquaintance abusing them with equal heat. But the principal acquaintance I made at the Hotwells was Sir Charles Howard, K.B., then an old man. Being informed that I was a chess-player, he introduced himself to me in the pump-room and invited me to coffee and a game of chess. After some time and various conversations he made enquiries relating to my family and destination. I took it into my head that he seemed more affable when he was informed (for his enquiries were numerous) that Mr. Speaker Onslow and the Bishop of Rochester were my godfathers. On understanding that I was not bred to any profession and was without hope of any settlement in life, he asked me if I should like to enter the Army. I answered in the affirmative, but added that it could only be matter of theory, as I had not lived with any officers. He often recurred to the idea, and at last told me that he would give me a pair of colours in his own cavalry regiment, and bade me write to my mother for her approval.

This I did, and was not at all surprised by her reply. She begged and beseeched me not to think of any such employment, as my health and strength

were quite inadequate to the life. I loved my dear
mother too much to accept an offer against her consent.
I also became acquainted with an officer in the Army,
Captain Lambert, who visited the Countess of B. at
B. Castle. She was esteemed a demirep, handsome
and fascinating. A little before I left Bristol I was
introduced to her, and had my stay been longer should
have made one in the number of her many slaves. On
returning from Bristol to my mother at Bradfield, I
found myself in a situation as truly helpless and forlorn
as could well be imagined, without profession, business, or pursuit, I may add without one well-grounded
hope of any advantageous establishment in life. My
whole fortune during the life of my mother was a copyhold farm of twenty acres, producing as many pounds,
and what possibility there was of turning my time to
any advantage did not and could not occur to me; in
truth, it was a situation without resource, and nothing
but the inconsiderateness of youth could have kept me
from sinking into melancholy and despair. My mother,
desirous of fixing me with her, proposed that I should
take a farm, and especially as the home one of eighty
acres was under a lease expiring at Michaelmas. I
had no more idea of farming than of physic or divinity,
but as it promised, at least, to find me some employment, I agreed to the proposition, and accordingly
commenced my rural operations, which entirely decided the complexion of all my remaining years. My
connections at Lynn carried me often to that place,
and my love of reading proved my chief resource. I
farmed during the years 1763-4-5-6, having taken also

a second farm that was in the hands of a tenant. I gained knowledge, but not much, and the principal effect was to convince me that in order to understand the business in any perfection it was necessary for me to continue my exertions for many years. And the circumstance which perhaps of all others in my life I most deeply regretted and considered as a sin of the blackest dye, was the publishing the result of my experience during these four years, which, speaking as a farmer, was nothing but ignorance, folly, presumption, and rascality. The only real use which resulted from those four years was to enable me to view the farms of other men with an eye of more discrimination than I could possibly have done without that practice. It was the occasion of my going on the southern tour in 1767, the northern tour in 1768, and the eastern in 1770, extending through much the greater part of the kingdom, and the exertion in these tours was admitted by all who read them (and they were very generally read) to be of most singular utility to the general agriculture of the kingdom. In these works I particularly attended to the course of the farmer's crops, the point perhaps of all others the most important, and the more so at that period, because all preceding writers had neglected it in the most unaccountable manner. They relate good and bad rotations with the same apathy as if it was of little consequence in what order the crops of a farm were put in provided the operations of tillage and manuring were properly performed.

It has been very justly said that I first excited the agricultural spirit which has since rendered Britain so famous; and I should observe that this is not so great a compliment as at first sight it may seem, since it was nothing more than publishing to the world the exertions of many capital cultivators and in various parts of the kingdom, and especially the local practice of common farmers who, with all their merit, were unknown beyond the limits of their immediate district, and whose operation wanted only to be known to be admired.

In December 1762 I was again in London, and, as usual, constantly at the theatre. The parts in which Mr. Garrick acted to my great entertainment were, Macbeth, Benedict, Lear, Posthumus, Oakely,[1] Abel Drugger,[2] Sir J. Brute,[3] Sir J. Dorrimant,[4] Bayes,[5] Carlos,[6] Felix,[7] Ranger,[8] Scrub,[9] Hastings.[10] I must once for all remark that this astonishing actor so much exceeded every idea of representing character that the delusion was complete, Nature, not acting, seemed to be before the spectator, and this to a degree a thousand times beyond anything that has been seen since. The tones of his voice, the clear discrimination of feeling and passion in the vast variety of characters he represented, surpassed anything one could imagine, and raised him beyond competition. I have often reflected on the principal personages who figured in England during this age, and I am disposed to think that Garrick was by far the greatest, that is to say, he excelled

[1] *The Jealous Wife.* [2] *The Alchemist.* [3] *The Provoked Wife.*
[4] *The Man of Mode.* [5] *The Rehearsal.* [6] *Love Makes a Man.*
[7] *The Wonder.* [8] *The Suspicious Husband.*
[9] *The Beaux' Stratagem.* [10] *She Stoops to Conquer.*

This last play seems to have been first acted in 1773. See Brewer's *Reader's Handbook.*

all his contemporaries in the art he professed. Few men have been able to laugh at their own foibles with as much wit as Garrick. A striking instance was his little publication called 'An Ode to Garrick on the Talk of the Town,' in which we find this stanza :

> Two parts they readily allow
> Are yours, but not one more they vow,
>   And they close their spite.
> You will be Sir John Brute [1] all day,
>   And Fribble [2] all the night.

In 1765 the colour of my life was decided. I married. My wife [3] was a daughter of Alderman Allen, of Lynn, and great-granddaughter of John Allen, Esq., of Lyng House, Norfolk, who, according to the Comte de Boulainvilliers,[4] first introduced the custom of marling in the above-named county. We boarded with my mother at Lynn.

This year (1765) I was in correspondence with the Rev. Walter Harte,[5] Canon of Windsor, and author of

---

[1] 'The coarse pot-house valour of Sir John Brute, Garrick's famous part, is finely contrasted with the fine lady airs and affectation of his wife.'—*Chambers's English Literature.*

[2] 'All the domestic business will be taken from my wife's hands. shall make the tea, comb the dogs, and dress the children myself.'— Fribble, in *Miss in her Teens* (Garrick).

[3] Mrs. Young was sister to Fanny Burney's stepmother. The marriage proved unhappy from the beginning.

[4] See his work, *Les Intérêts de la France mal entendus*, Henri, Comte de Boulainvilliers, voluminous author on French history, 1658–1722.

[5] Rev. W. Harte, poet, writer on rural affairs, historian, 1700–1774. Dr. Johnson much commended Harte as a scholar and a man of the most companionable talents he had ever known. He said the defects in his history (Gustavus Adolphus) arose not from imbecility, but from foppery. His *Essays on Husbandry* is an elegant, erudite, and valuable work (Lowndes).

the 'Essays on Husbandry' and the 'Life of Gustavus Adolphus.' He advised me to collect my scattered papers in the 'Museum Rusticum,' and, with additions, to publish them in a volume. This I did under the title of 'A Farmer's Letters.' I visited Mr. Harte at Bath; his conversation was extremely interesting and instructive. I have rarely received more pleasure than in my intercourse with this amiable and deeply learned man. It is well known that he was tutor to Mr. Stanhope, natural son of Lord Chesterfield, to whom so many of that nobleman's letters were addressed.[1]

To Mr. Harte

'Blackheath: August 16, 1764.

'Sir,—I give you a thousand thanks for your book, of which I've read every word with great pleasure and full as great astonishment. When in the name of God could you have found time to read the ten or twenty thousand authors whom you quote, of all countries and all times, from Hesiod to du Hamel?[2] Where have you ploughed, sowed, harrowed, drilled, and dug the earth for at least these forty years? for less time could not have made you such a complete master of the practical part of husbandry. I can only account for it from the Pythagorean doctrine of the transmigration of souls, and the supposition that Hartlib's soul has animated your body with a small alteration of name; seriously, your book entertains me exceedingly, and has made me

---

[1] The accompanying letter is included in Arthur Young's correspondence of this year, and is given, although not addressed to himself.

[2] Duhamel du Monceau, botanist and *agronome*, contributor to the *Encyclopédie*, 1700–1781.

quite a *dilettante*, though too late to make me a *virtuoso*, in the useful and agreeable art of agriculture. I own myself ignorant of them all, but am nevertheless sensible of their utility, and the pleasure it must afford to those who pursue them. Moreover, you've scattered so many graces over them that one wishes to be better acquainted with them, and that one reads your book with pleasure most exquisite. It is the only prose Georgic that I know, as agreeable, and I dare say much more useful, in this climate than Virgil. Why have you not put your name to it? for though some passages in it point you out to be the author here, they will not do it so in other countries, and as I am persuaded that your book will be translated into most modern languages and be a polyglott of husbandry, I could have wished your name had been to it. How goes the Havabilious complaint: has not the Bath waters washed it away yet? I heartily wish it was, as I sincerely wish you whatever can give you ease or pleasure.

'For I am with great truth your
  'Faithful friend and servant,
    'CHESTERFIELD.

'P.S.—Though I can be as partial as another to my friends, I cannot be quite blind to their omissions; for though you have enumerated so many sorts of grass, with a particular panegyrick on your dear Lucern, you have not described, nor so much as mentioned, that particular sort of grass *which while it grows the steed starves.*

'Your Elève is very well at Dresden. I will send him his book when I can find a good opportunity.'

The following letters Mr. Harte was so good as to address to me:—

'Bath: February 3, 1765.

'Dear Sir,—That I am obliged to trouble you with a letter, purely on my own account, I balance not a moment within myself, between interrupting a friend and being thought ungrateful. The kind mention you have been pleased to make of my Essays on Husbandry in the last number of the Museum Rusticum deserves my warmest thanks and acknowledgements: and though your good opinion of me as *bonus agricola, bonus civis* may be a little partial, yet sure I am that your favourable report is the overflowing of a generous mind, and under that medicament I must with modesty and diffidence arrange it, feeling at the same time that inward pleasure which Tacitus describes *Dulce est laudari a laudato Viro*. For my own part, my ill health, as I greatly fear, will make me unable to continue much longer on the theatre of agriculture; but if it pleases God that this nation is ever touched with a true vital sense of the uses of husbandry in *their full extent* (and runs not mad with the visionary notions of Colonies), there will soon be a succession of younger and abler genius's to perfect *that*, which I have had the honor and satisfaction of suggesting to my beloved but mistaken country. I may say as old Dryden did to Congreve. (You will put aside the vanity of naming Dryden in the same paragraph with myself.)

'So, when the States one Edward did depose,
A greater Edward in his room arose,
But now not I but husbandry the curst,
And Tom the Second writes like Tom the First.

'And now, Sir, give me leave to assure you that I am extremely pleased with your last published performance, and the rather as the idea is useful and new. In order to send abroad a truly qualified person, as you have most judiciously characterised him, you do well to address yourself to noble-spirited individuals. Kings and ministers look upon agriculture as only *physical* means of supplying mankind with food; nor does one glimpse of an idea ever enter their heads or hearts concerning the circulation of profit from the highest to the lowest resulting from thence; nor of the national strength, health, population, and, I may say, the sobriety of getting money which results from that art when it is exercised and maintained in full activity. France might till this time have languished for her enclosure of waste land and exportation of superfluous corn if a shrewd and artful foreigner had not flattered a fair lady into a passion for agriculture; the man I mean is M. Patulle.[1] And indeed, since the times of Augustus and Mæcenas (which latter loved agriculture, before he loved poetry, but lavishly united both in Virgil) and since the time of Constantine IV. to the present hour I can recollect no Princes and Prime Ministers who understood the national advantages of husbandry in their full extent but Henry IV. and Sully.' [*Letter breaks off here.*]

'Windsor: May 1, 1765.

'Dear Sir,—Your last kind pacquet was conveyed to me here by our much esteemed friend Mrs. Allen, whom I hope to see at Bath in about twelve days. I am now

[1] Patulle. A French writer on agriculture.

to thank you for entertaining me with so much and so good matter relating to Harrows, and look upon your improvement to be a most sensible and most ingenious one at the same time. This is the happy perfection in writing which Horace mentions:

'Omne tulit punctum qui miscuit utile dulci.

'In the same manner I have also read with delight and improvement your remarks upon broad-wheeled waggons, in the Museum for last March: but why, my good friend, do you bury such dissertations as yours in blue-paper Periodical Essays? Or why rather do you not throw them together in one book, or large pamphlet? I return you my best thanks for your Technical Terms of Art in the Suffolk Husbandry, and the provincial words, which latter, one time or other, shall be considered by me in a more extensive and critical view respecting the English language in general. Many of these provincial words[1] are the truly classical words of our nation. Some of them are elegant and musical, and most of them in general express the sense in their sound. In one word, from a thorough knowledge of the provincial words of our language, one might venture to explain Shakespear, B. Jonson, Beaumont and Fletcher, &c., better and safer than all his editors and conjectural critics. If you have a friend tolerably

---

[1] Here is an illustration. The Suffolk husbandman's afternoon collation is invariably called 'beaver.' In Nares' *Glossary* we find, 'Bever, from the Sp. and It.: an intermediate refreshment between breakfast and dinner.' 'Without any prejudice to their bevers, drinkings, and suppers.'—*B. and Fletcher*, '*The Woman Hater*.'

skilled in husbandry, who lives in any part of England except the southern and western, be so obliging to me as to solicit his assistance, and convey the list of words to me; for by what I have before suggested, you see I have views that extend beyond husbandry.

'When you go to London, will you not be tempted to make a flying excursion to Bath? 'Tis a digression, but it can hardly be called an episode. If I have any skill, or knowledge of the world, Mrs. Allen's conversation alone will indemnify you for your trouble, and that most amply. He also who subscribes his name to this letter has a private ambition to be better known to you than upon paper.

'I am, dear Sir, your most obedient and most humble servant,

'W. HARTE.'

'Kintbury, Berks: May 7, 1765.

'Dear Sir,—If gratitude did not operate strongly upon me (and that towards a friend whom I never saw but hope to see, know, and cultivate his friendship) I should not trouble you with another letter so quick upon the heels of my last from Windsor; but finding by chance here, in a lone village, the Museum Rusticum, I see you have done justice to the Essays on Husbandry. I wish they had half the merit which your partiality to the author fancies they have.

'In the main particular you have spoken exactly my private sentiments. When I write for the instruction and amusement of *Cuddy* and *Lobbin* and *Clout* in matters of husbandry I will also publish a supplemental essay on the art of push-pin,[1] stylo puerili. Who would write for farmers, who perhaps cannot read, or who, I am sure, will never try to read? Were I condemned to this punishment I would desire my footman to hold the pen—and even *then* what would such critics say? They would find fault with inelegance and want of propriety in the work. They bring to my mind an anecdote which de Voltaire once told me of his father (by the way, Voltaire put the incident into a farce, and was disinherited for it). The peevish old gentleman said one morning when his son rose from bed at about 11 o'clock: "Young man, you were drunk last night; you will sleep away your senses, neglect your studies, and die a beggar." Piqued at this reproach, Voltaire got up at 4 next morning, and by the by it was in winter. "Son," said his father at breakfast, " you will ruin us in the expenses of fire and candle. All your draggle-tailed Muses will never indemnify us with the wood-merchant and chandler." This is a just picture of a reviewing Critic or a Mago.

'Quo teneam vultus mutantem Protea noto?

'As to the Museum Rusticum (your writings in it excepted) I know nothing of the authors, but look upon it (as I am now speaking to you *sub sigillo silentii*) as a blue-paper job. Books in this age are a manufacture as much as hats or pins. The bookseller chooses a subject and the author writes at 10*s.* a sheet. It is probable that one man in a garret, who does not know a blade of wheat from a blade of barley, writes

---

[1] 'A child's game, in which pins are pushed alternately.'—*Webster.*

half the letters from the 'Kentish man,' 'Yorkshire man,' 'Glocester man,' &c. And perhaps the same hand, in the notes, signs with all the letters in the alphabet. Perhaps this very man Rocque (I speak only from conjecture), for I observe the whole work has a tendency to favour this avanturier in agriculture. I declare to you seriously that I know nothing of its authors, you excepted. Might it not be better if you kept your admirable tracts by you, and to those you have already published, so much to your honour, you may add such occasional pieces as you shall afterwards write, and let them all appear together in a volume which might be entitled SYLVAE,[1] or occasional tracts on husbandry and rural economics. I would have all books on husbandry, if possible, pocket volumes, that one may read in the fields, &c. In short, I would print it in a beautiful duodecimo as du Hamel does; you have written enough already to make one such volume, or nearly. However, there must be some new things in this work; doubtless you have the plan of more tracts by you. If you read French I would recommend a charming idea to you in this enclosing age, namely a little 12mo. called "L'amélioration des Terres," by Patulle. In that work are plans, and also the manner of throwing a square tract of ground of three or four hundred acres, &c., into an ornamented farm, or, as the French call it, *ferme ornée* : the house and buildings in the centre; the fields are square, the hedges quick set, and the owner may command with his eye, and almost with his voice, everybody and thing he is

[1] Included in *A Farmer's Letters*.

concerned with. If you cannot get the book (though you certainly may at Vaillant's) I will send you mine.

'Adieu, dear Sir,
   'Your most affectionate and obliged friend,
        'WALTER HARTE.'

        'Barton Street, Bath : Oct. 16, 1766.

'Dear Sir,—My wretched state of health must be my just excuse for being so bad a correspondent. I owe you an answer to a letter of yours which was equally kind and long, and that answer is now of near a quarter of a year's standing ; not but that I think of you and my honoured friend at Lynn almost every day of my life. Pray inform me in your next how your husbandry lucubrations go on in point of progress and advancement? I will be responsible for their good taste and accuracy. You are like the Matinian bee mentioned by Horace, which gathers more fragrance from a few sprigs of thyme than others can do from the stately lilac and larch trees. You gave me some hopes that my ever honoured friend at Worcester should convey to me, from you, some manuscript dissertations on agriculture, but I have been so unhappy as to know no more of them than of the lost books of Livy. In the course of the winter you will see an octavo volume of religious poems intituled the "Amaranth," adorned with very fine sculptures from the designs of the greatest masters, and executed by an artist of my own forming, who never appeared before in a public capacity, except on my Essays on Husbandry. The poetry I hope will prove that I have been bred up in the school of Pope, and I hope the disciple will retain something at least of the manner of the master. When you see Mrs. Allen you will impart this little anecdote to her, because I am not yet quite clear whether I shall prefix my name or not.

'I am, dear Sir, &c., &c.,

'WALTER HARTE.

'P.S.—I have just had a visit from my old friend the Marquis of Rockingham, who (to say truth) loves husbandry as much as you or I do, and is, besides, an excellent judge of it speculatively and practically.'

'Bath: Nov. 24, 1766.

'Dear Sir,—I received safely by coach your manuscript, which shall be perused with all the accuracy of friendship, after having turned partiality out of doors. My impatience about whatever concerns you has already made me read a part of your work, and enables me to prophesy well concerning it. Pray be not fearful about the execution of your plan, which seems to me a good one; authors must be careful but not fearful; we have a proverb in husbandry (as old, I think, as Henry VII.'s time), which deserves to be written in letters of gold: "He that's afraid of a blade of grass must not sleep in a meadow."

'I like one part of your manuscript exceedingly; it is in truth the only thing wanted, and yet the only thing too often omitted, I mean the idea and calculation of the outgoing expenses. M. Patulle felt this as fully as you do, and as good wit will jump, hit upon a part of your plan. You therefore must see that book, as the French say, *coûte que coûte*; I have, I believe, almost the only copy in England, which shall be conveyed to you in a week's time.

'I am, dearest Sir,
'Your affectionate friend,
'WALTER HARTE.'

Mr. Harte published a volume of religious poems called 'Amaranth,' which he sent me. He took great pains about the decoration of this book by a young artist of his own forming, but it had no success.

In 1766 my daughter Mary was born, and I remained at Bradfield, with the exception of several journeys to Lynn.

CHAPTER III

IN SEARCH OF A LIVING, 1767-1775

Home travels—A move—Anecdote of a cat—Disillusion—'A Farmer's Letters'—Another move—'In the full blaze of her beauty'—Hetty Burney and her harpsichord—'Scant in servants'—Maternal solicitude—Money difficulties—More tours—Lord Sheffield—Howard the philanthropist—Correspondence.

DURING this year I executed that journey, the register of which I published under the title of a 'Six Weeks' Tour,' in which, for the first time, the facts and principles of Norfolk husbandry were laid before the public, and which have since become famous in the agricultural world. Till my work appeared nothing of that husbandry was known beyond the county. The publication excited great interest, and became unquestionably the origin of many and great improvements in various parts of the kingdom. I scarcely went into any company in which it was not mentioned. Had I better understood the art of husbandry it might, perhaps, have been well for me. Finding that a mixture of families was inconsistent with comfortable living, I determined to quit Bradfield, and advertised in the London papers for such a house and farm as would suit my views and fortune, that is to say, one thousand pounds which I received with my wife, the remainder being settled upon her. I fixed upon a very fine farm in Essex called Samford Hall; there I worked with incredible avidity both in the agricultural and literary department. I remember once to have written a quire of foolscap in one day! The work was entitled 'Political Essays on the Present State of the British Empire.'

And here I may mention a singular instance of animal sagacity. The gentleman who gave up the house to me was a Mr. Farquharson. His wife had a favourite cat which, upon their removal, was put into a sack and carried away with the furniture from Essex to Yatesby Bridge in Hampshire. I was surprised in about five or six days to see poor puss again at Samford Hall; nearly at the same time a letter was received from Mrs. Farquharson lamenting her loss, but doubting the possibility of the cat having returned to its original home. The circumstance is astonishing, and shows an instinct almost incredible, for the animal must have travelled seventy miles and threaded the Metropolis.

My landlord, a Mr. Lamb, was a King's messenger. He had formerly been, I believe, butler or *valet de chambre* to the Duke of Leeds, and gave me many accounts of the journeys he had made to Petersburg, Constantinople, Naples, &c., profiting by every journey very considerably, as he expended much less in travelling than was allowed by Government. I write from memory, but I think he said that a journey to Petersburg or Constantinople paid him a neat profit of a hundred guineas.

This speculation turned out a bitter disappointment.

I trusted to the promise of a relative to lend me some money, making, with what I possessed, sufficient for the undertaking. But he was himself disappointed of the money, and I clearly foresaw that an insufficient capital would infallibly cramp me in such a manner as to render all my efforts very uncomfortable and perhaps vain. I determined to make a short cut and get rid of it immediately, which I did at the end of six months at no further loss than of 100*l.* This was a lesson of some use to me at subsequent periods of my life, and taught me early to distinguish between certainty and probabilities.

Arthur Young to his Wife

'Tuesday: 1767.[1]

'My Dearest,—I am much in hopes I shall have a letter from you to-morrow; if I have not it will be a great disappointment; for when you don't write in huffs your letters are my only comfort. I went to Yeldham's this morning, but he, according to custom, was out, and will not be home of some days; it will be Saturday before I can see him. How this terrible affair will end I cannot conjecture, nor what I am to do. The most miserable circumstance of all is the being in such suspense and anxiety. It absolutely stupefies me, and I am forced to pin myself down to writing without the soul for anything but mere copying. I would give my right hand that I had never seen this place, but such reflections only make one the more miserable; and the

---

[1] 'We were married more than two years.' [Note by A. Y.]

thoughts at the same time of what you feel with a
young child to suckle hurt me more than I can express
in a word; we shall both be capitally miserable till we
are fixed somewhere on a certainty, and when that will
be Heaven knows. I had infinitely rather live in a
cottage upon bread and cheese than drag on the
anxious existence I do at present. Whichever way I
turn my thoughts I see no remedy, nor know who can
advise me what step to take. I know not which is best
myself, I am sure, for everyone depends so on con-
tingencies that sagacity itself cannot foresee the consequences of all. An ill star rose on my nativity; had I
never been born it would have been just so much the
better for me, for you, and our wretched children. If
anybody was to knock me on the head it would
be a trifling favour done to you all three, for most
assuredly no good will ever come from my hands.

'Adieu! I have scribbled out the paper to but little
purpose.

'A. Y.'

The gentleman who assisted me in getting rid of
this nuisance was a Mr. Yeldham. I am sure the
reader will peruse with gratification the following
letter (given in part):—

'Saling: Dec. 10, 1768.

'Dear Sir,—Your obliging present of lampreys and
more obliging letter of the 7th came safe to my
hands, as did your books and Westphalia ham. I assure
you I thought myself amply rewarded for the service
I did you in Essex by the present of your work on

agriculture, and everything beyond that was unnecessary and the result of your generosity. Give me leave to return you my respectful thanks, and to assure you that in the twenty-six years I have had transactions with mankind, and whenever in my power have endeavoured to assist as many as I could, I have scarce ever met with so much gratitude as you have shown. It will not be in my power ever again to do you any acceptable service, but for your sake I shall be more ready to do a kind office than ever; so if I mended your fortune by helping you off a hurtful contract, you will mend my heart by making me more in love with mankind, and more ready to seek opportunities of being useful.

'I have often heard of the fine husbandry of the North. If such things as you speak of are to be had every day, why are North Country farmers so poor? Here we give from ten to fifteen shillings per acre for lands not a whit better than you can have in the North for a penny. We get estates and live like gentlemen; North Country farmers are poor and live worse than our labourers. These are allowed truths, but utterly irreconcilable to the small share of reason I possess. All our good farmers can lay up from one to two years' rent of their farms in common years, after paying the landlord, the parson, the poor, servants' wages, &c. &c. Were the North Country farms in the least comparable should not we hear of it? Would not some of us get farther from the capital for the sake of profit? Our mercantile people ramble all over the world for gain, so would the farmer could he find it; and any distance would be agreeable. There must, I think, be something in the distant counties' prices which counterbalances the cheapness of the land and labour. I heartily wish you success and comfort in all your undertakings, and that Bradmore Farm may produce corn, wine, and oil in abundance.

'Mrs. Yeldham joins in compliments to you and Mrs. Young.

'I remain, dear Sir, &c. &c.,

'JOHN YELDHAM.'

My correspondence with Mr. Harte continued. It gave me pain to find that his health greatly declined. He was a cripple at Bath, but the disorders of his body seemed little to affect the vigour of his mind. He spoke very flatteringly of the reception of my 'Farmer's Letters.' 'I am amazed,' he writes, 'that you have so soon and so easily acquired the hardest point in all writing—namely, perspicuity and ease of style.' And elsewhere, 'Your letter addressed to my Lord Clive on an experimental farm is new, spirited and pleasing, but I fear he has not a spark of the *divina aura* in him. I have shown your pamphlet to the best judge in England, my Lord Chesterfield, who is now here. He likes it extremely, and vows if he was young and rich enough he would carry your scheme into execution.'

From Samford Hall I moved, in 1768, to another farm at North Mimms, in Hertfordshire. I had scarcely settled here before my bookseller united with many correspondents in urging me to take another tour. I accordingly travelled through the north of England, registering so many observations, and noting the experiments of such a number of gentlemen, that the record of the whole, with the necessary remarks, filled four octavo volumes, and enabled me to present the public with interesting agricultural details never before published. I may assert this without vanity, because the real merit belonged to those who furnished me with the information; and the success of the work was so great that the first edition was sold almost as soon as it appeared. In the 'Six Weeks' Tour' I visited but few gentlemen, and consequently witnessed but few experiments. On the 'Northern Journey' the case was very different, and the number of trials reported on a variety of soils were great and interesting. I spent some time with my friend, Mr. Ellerton, of Risby, in the East Riding; he accompanied me to York races and on a visit of several days to the Marquis of Rockingham, who had previously to the journey invited me to see him, and pointed out a number of persons proper for me to visit. Amongst the company at Wentworth was Mr. Danby, of Swinton, and his daughter,[1] then in the full blaze of her beauty. My Lord Rockingham overheard her speaking to me and using the expression 'amazingly fine turnips.' 'So, so, Mr. Young,' said his lordship, 'you are getting farming intelligence of Miss Danby; the lady must let us hear more of those fine turnips.'[2] His lordship ordered me into an apartment, in a closet

---

[1] 'The Mashamshire Molly,' afterwards Countess of Harcourt.

[2] It must be remembered that turnips were a comparative novelty at this date, not being cultivated as food for cattle till the latter part of the last century.

of which was a considerable collection of ancient and curious books on agriculture, which he pointed out for my amusement when I had time to consult them. There was one circumstance which seemed very awkward to me at Wentworth, the necessity of every person always having his hat under his arm, a hint of which Lord R. gave me on my arrival, and I saw the want of it in one or two new comers, who, when the horses were brought to the door, had a journey to make through the house before they could find their hats. From Wentworth I went to the Duke of Portland's and others, and afterwards examined a great part of the county of York with much attention, everywhere being received in a very flattering manner.

This year I made many visits to my friend, Dr. Burney, in Poland Street, to whom my wife's sister was married, and whose daughter Hester (by a former marriage) entertained, or rather, fascinated me, by her performance on the harpsichord and singing of Italian airs. I was never tired of listening to the 'Ah, quelli occhi ladroncelli,' and 'Alla larga,' of Piccini,[1] and it is marvellous to me now to recollect that I was thus riveted to her side for six hours together.

During this year my daughter Bessy was born, and the second edition of my 'Farmer's Letters' published.

1769.—My son Arthur born. The whole of this year I passed at North Mimms, very well received and visited in that thronged neighbourhood. The Duke of Leeds, who lived in the parish, condescended to make

---
[1] Nicolo Piccini, 1728–1800, composer of the opera *Zénobie*, &c.

overtures with a view to my acquaintance. Sir Charles Cocks, afterwards Lord Somers, if I do not mistake the year, did the same, and often drank tea with me; also Dr. Roper and his wife Lady Harriet. He was a man of great learning, and she a most amiable woman, free from all pride and affectation. I also often met Lady Mary Mordaunt at two or three houses, and her sister Lady Frances Bulhely, with whom she lived; with the former I had something of a flirtation and lent her many books; she was rather handsome and very agreeable. I was elected member of a dining club at Hatfield, and became acquainted with Samuel Whitbread, Esq. M.P.,[1] and Mr. Justice Willes from East Barnet. I was very well received by Mrs. Willes, a fine lady, and rather fantastical. They were both vain people, and I remember one day at dinner Judge Willes saying to his wife, 'My dear, I think we are rather scant in servants'—yet there was one to every chair and some to spare. She was making an ornamental path round the homestead, and asked my advice in several difficulties. During this year Prince Massalski, Bishop of Wilna, wrote me a long French letter on the agricultural prosperity of England. He afterwards passed two days with me in Hertfordshire, an agreeable, well-instructed man, who much lamented the miserable state of his own country.

1770.—What a year of incessant activity, composition, anxiety and wretchedness was this! No carthorse ever laboured as I did at this period, spending like an

[1] Samuel Whitbread, son of a great brewer, distinguished in Parliamentary life as a vigorous assailant of Pitt; committed suicide 1815.

idiot, always in debt, in spite of what I earned [1] with the sweat of my brow and almost my heart's blood, such was my anxiety; yet all was clearly vexation of spirit. Well might my dear mother write to me as she did. I trusted in an unparalleled industry, but not in God; and see how He brought it all to nought, as if to convince me of my supreme folly and infatuation. My old Suffolk bailiff was the channel through which I ran into debt to the Bury banker by a series of drawing bills, one to pay another, till the plan became so obvious that he cut short and refused to accept any more. I had run near a thousand pounds into his debt, and it was necessary for me to go over directly to Bury to see what could be done to pacify him. He was at his country seat at Trosston. Thither I followed him, and, with great difficulty, persuaded him to have patience, under a promise that I would make arrangements to pay him very speedily. This I did with difficulty, and I scarcely recollect how. I shall, in the first place, note that the Eastern Tour was accomplished, the journal of which was afterwards published in four volumes. In the preface I returned thanks to those who contributed to my information, and in the number were many most distinguished personages amongst the nobility and gentry in the counties through which I travelled, with numerous distinguished farmers.

It is necessary here to pause a little in order to examine the object and the effect of the three tours I made and published. They have, by the very best

[1] Entry in memorandum-book of this year: 'The year's receipts, 1,167*l.*'

judges, been esteemed highly useful to practical agriculturists, and unquestionably they are equally so for the information they afford in political economy : they have accordingly, in these views, been celebrated [1] in almost every language of Europe. When a work appears, the object and execution of which are equally novel and unexampled, it is not surprising that a certain measure of success should attend such a work. Nothing in the least similar to it had before appeared in the English language ; for though there had been a tour of Great Britain, and other tours through great part of the kingdom, yet all these works agreed in one circumstance—that of the authors confining their attention absolutely to towns and seats, without paying any more thought to agriculture than if that art had no existence between the towns they visited. Indeed my work was admitted on all hands to be perfectly original. In regard to the practical husbandry of the farmers, and the experimental observations of the gentlemen I visited, the utility of these could not be doubted. When a Lord Chancellor of England, amusing himself with husbandry, read the English works on that subject for information, and burnt them as affording him nothing but contradictions, without doubt he complained that these writers did not describe the common management of the farmers, and on that management founding their propositions of improvement. But the fact was, and it must be, in the nature of things, writers confined to their closets, or, at most, to a single farm, could not describe what it was impossible for them to know ; and before the appearance

---

[1] *Sic* in author's MS. ; 'translated' would seem to be the word.

of my tours there was scarcely a district in the kingdom described in such a manner as to convince the reader that the authors had any practical knowledge of the art; for a man to quit his farm and his fireside in order to examine the husbandry of a kingdom by travelling above four thousand miles through a country of no greater extent than England was certainly taking means sufficiently effective for laying a sure basis for the future improvement of the soil. To understand well the present state of cultivation is surely a necessary step prior to proposals of improvement. This I effected; and in the opinion of some very able agriculturists now living, the greatest of the subsequent improvements that have been made during the last forty years have, in a great measure, originated in the defects pointed out by me in the detail of these journeys.

I shall venture to insert one anecdote which occurred in the Northern Tour. At Mr. Danby's, at Swinton in Yorkshire, I met a very uncommon instance of extraordinary industry in a collier, who improved some waste moors by the labour of his own hands beside his common hours of working in the colliery. He had so animated a spirit of improvement that I thought it a great pity that he should be left without better support; and therefore I proposed a subscription for him, which raised in all about 100*l*., and Mr. Danby, his landlord, releasing him from his colliery, he was enabled to extend his improvements with much more comfort to himself. After a few years he died, leaving his farm for the benefit of his family. He shortened his life, poor fellow, by his industry.

This year I was obliged to decline an invitation

from Lord Holdernesse to accompany him to Hornby Castle. Upon informing my mother of the refusal, she, with her ever watchful kindness concerning my interests, wrote thus: 'I am extremely sorry that you refused Lord Holdernesse's invitation; it was an opportunity you may never have again, for when favours that great people offer are refused, they seldom, if ever, make a second; it is very extraordinary indeed if they do. He is as likely to be one in the Administration as any other, for since Lady H. is one of the Ladies of the Queen's Bedchamber it is not likely that he [Lord H.] will be long out of post; and who knows? you might have found favour in his sight. I fear as long as my poor eyes are open I shall never want for something relating to your welfare to vex me extremely, which I must own is a great weakness. As to the regard of this world, thank God I do often reflect on the shortness of every earthly felicity, a misery compared with the duration of hereafter, and I am fully convinced that on God all events depend. I can't help transcribing a few lines out of a book you know little of. [*Here follow scriptural texts.*] Thank God, I don't owe five pounds in the world, not that I brag of being free from debt as owing to any merit to me, for I am far from thinking anything like it; no, it is to the mercy and goodness of God who has given me a comfortable provision for the situation I am in, and in a better I don't desire to be, for a little with God's blessing goes much farther than a great deal without it. You may call all this rubbish if you please, but a time will come when you will be convinced whose notions are rubbish, yours or mine.'

I here insert another letter from my mother, at the risk of being taxed with personal vanity :—

'I had a letter yesterday from your brother, in which was a paragraph that I think will give you a little pleasure. It is as follows: "I find that Arthur has printed lately a pamphlet on the 'Exportation of Corn.' A gentleman who came from the Drawing Room yesterday told me that the King asked him whether he had read Mr. Young's pamphlet on the subject, and commended it." Oh, dear! how pleasing it is to have the approbation of a King, even though we never get sixpence by it. And yet how few are desirous of the approbation of the King; yet they may be sure of it if they sincerely try, and can never fail of being well rewarded, both in this world and the next. Oh! Arthur, with what capacities are you endowed—with what advantages for being greatly good! But with the talents of an angel a man may be a fool if he judges amiss on the supreme point.'

1771.[1]—The same unremitting industry, the same anxiety, the same vain hopes, the same perpetual disappointment. No happiness, nor anything like it.

This year I published the third edition of the 'Farmer's Letters,' the second edition of the 'Northern Tour,' the 'Farmer's Calendar,' my 'Proposals for Numbering the People'—the occasion of which was the Earl of Chatham's words: 'When I compare the number of our people—estimated highly at seven[2]

[1] In a memorandum-book occurs the following entry: '1771.—Receipts, 697*l*.; expenses, 360*l*.—I know not how.'

[2] Estimated population of England and Wales in 1770, 7,428,000.—*Haydn's Dictionary of Dates.*

millions—with the population of France and Spain, usually computed at twenty-five millions, I see a clear, self-evident possibility for this country to contend with the united powers of the House of Bourbon merely upon the strength of its own resources.' I conceived that to draw such political principles for the national conduct from a mere supposition of population was a doctrine tending to very mischievous errors. I therefore was convinced that an actual enumeration of the people ought to take place. Nothing, however, was done at the time, but thirty years afterwards [1] the Legislature was of the same opinion, and not till then were the numbers ascertained.'

This year I began my correspondence with Mr. John Baker Holroyd,[2] afterwards so well known for his literary productions as Lord Sheffield. In his first letter, dated March 1771, he mentions his wish that I should forward some cabbage seed, and hopes that I may be the means of introducing the culture of cabbages into that neighbourhood (Sussex), but adds—what must now appear singular—that the very extraordinary scarcity of hands cramps him very much. 'All the lively, able young men are employed in smuggling. They can have a guinea a week as riders and carriers without any risk; therefore it is not to be expected that they will labour for eight shillings a week until some more effectual means are taken to prevent smuggling.'

I had also a letter from the deservedly celebrated

[1] The first census was taken in 1801.
[2] 1740–1821. The friend and editor of Gibbon.

philanthropist, John Howard, with a basket of his American potatoes, afterwards known under the name of 'the Howard and cluster potatoes.' He added: 'Permit me, sir, to offer my thanks for the entertainment of your very ingenious and useful labours, and the honour you did me in the mention of my name.'

1772.—Published 'Political Essays on the British Empire,' 'Present State of Waste Lands.' A third edition of the 'Six Weeks' Tour' was also published.

This year I attended very much the meetings of the Society for the Encouragement of Arts,[1] Manufactures and Commerce, as well as the Committee of Agriculture,[2] of which I was Chairman. In a letter from Mr. Butterworth Bayley, he lamented the want of a respectable publication by the Society of Arts, and called on me to think of some means of remedying the misery (sic). When I became Chairman of the Committee of Agriculture, I was the first to propose that annual publication which afterwards took place. This proposition was at once acceded to, and Valentine Green, the engraver, had the impudence to assert that it originated with him.

This year I visited Samuel Whitbread, Esq., at Cardington, in Bedfordshire, and as Mr. Howard, who afterwards became so celebrated for his philanthropy, lived in the same parish, Mr. W. took me to call upon him one morning. He was esteemed a singular character, but was at that time quite unknown in the

[1] Founded 1754, mainly owing to the efforts of Mr. Shipley and Lord Folkestone.
[2] This evidently depended on the Society of Arts.

world. He was then only famous for introducing a new series of potatoes into cultivation. We found him in a parlour, without books or apparently any employment, dressed as for an evening in London—a powdered bag wig, white silk stockings, thin shoes, and every other circumstance of his habiliments excluding the possibility of a country walk. He was rather pragmatical in his speech, very polite, but expressing himself in a manner that seemed to belong to two hundred years ago. I asked Mr. Whitbread if Mr. Howard was usually thus dressed and confined to his room, for he was as intimate with Whitbread as with anybody. He had never seen him otherwise, he said, but added that he was a sensible man and a very worthy one.

At this time I published my 'Political Essays on the Present State of Affairs in the British Empire,' also the third edition of the 'Six Weeks' Tour.' Comber's 'Real Improvements in Agriculture on the Principles of A. Young, Esq.,' was likewise printed. Comber was afterwards deeply engaged in the 'Monthly Review,' and belaboured me with all the abuse he could accumulate. I published also a tract entitled 'The Present State of Waste Lands in Great Britain.'

In March, Mr. Allen, my wife's brother, an alderman of Lynn, applied to the Earl of Orford to procure for me an establishment in some public office, and his Lordship wrote to Lord North on the subject. In his reply the latter spoke of me as one 'whose very ingenious and useful writings point out as a very proper object of notice and reward.' It was an application for a King's waiter's [1] place, a sinecure.

At this time I was so distressed that I had serious thoughts of quitting the kingdom [2] and going to America. Surely the three last years ought to have convinced me, had I not been worse than an idiot, of the vanity and folly of my expenses, and how utterly all comfort and happiness must fly such pursuits. Feeling a force and vigour of mind in myself erroneously, I trusted in them. As to God, I lived without Him in the world, and had not a companion that could bring me to Him. But my mother, my ever dear mother, wrote in vain to me; her advice was not listened to. She tried to bring me to a right sense of religion, which would have conferred that peace and content which flew before my vain pursuits.

Dr. Hunter,[3] of York, wrote to me this year on the Georgical Essays, and on carrots and their conversion into a confection for the use of seamen, of which he entertained great expectations. 'I received much pleasure,' he wrote, 'from the perusal of your Eastern Tour, and could not help expressing uneasiness at the rancorous treatment of the monthly reviewers. We are all open to fair and candid criticism, but when

[1] King's waiter. I have not been able to discover the precise nature of this sinecure.

[2] 'Mr. Young is not well, and appears almost overcome with the horrors of his situation; in fact, he is almost destitute. This is a dreadful trial for him, yet I am persuaded he will find some means of extricating himself from his distress—at least, if genius, spirit, and enterprise can prevail.'—*Early Diaries of Fanny Burney.*

[3] Dr. Alexander Hunter, died 1809, editor of Evelyn's *Sylva*, and author of *Georgical Essays*, 'an able and esteemed work' (Lowndes).

there is the least spark of resentment seen it then ceases to be criticism, and deserves another name. I propose to finish the Georgical Essays, with two more volumes, in 1773. My own natural avocations will not permit me in future to be anything but an editor; I wish I had leisure to prosecute so agreeable a study. I have, however, some satisfaction in seeing the art (of agriculture) improve under your hands, and hope that nothing will prevail upon you to withdraw yourself from the public. I have, this year, a large experiment with onions and carrots. These vegetables have not hitherto been cultivated in the field in this country. Besides the application of carrots for horses and hogs, I am persuaded that they may be converted by a cheap process into a confection for the use of seamen. This, and the last year's experiments, convince me of the practicability of the scheme, and next year I propose to ship a considerable quantity for the above purpose. The expense is small, and my expectations are great.'

1773.—Here began a new career of industry, ill-exerted, of new hopes and never-failing disappointments, labour and sorrow, folly and infatuation, which it is scarcely possible for a man, turned into the world without business or profession, to escape, and it affords a most impressive lesson to all parents to be almost as ready to hang their children as to bring them up without a regular profession. If I had been a country curate with 50*l*. a year, in addition to the income I possessed, and had lived in a quiet parsonage, the probability of happiness would have been far greater. The business of my farm at North Mimms was insufficient to keep me employed, and the intercourse I constantly had with London I considered as a means which should be turned to some account in the increase of a most insufficient income; in fact, I was in a most uncomfortable state, which induced me to listen to the proposals of a gentleman I met with—I have quite forgotten whom—who informed me that the 'Morning Post' proprietors were in great want of some person to report the debates in Parliament. In consequence of this information I applied at their office, and they very readily engaged me for a trial, to see if I was able to perform the business they required. This was done, and as they were well satisfied with the manner in which the work was executed, I continued it at a salary, as well as I can recollect, of five guineas a week. Every Saturday I walked seventeen miles to my farm, and back again on the Monday morning. This year I published my observations on the present state of waste lands, which contained a new idea of extreme importance in the mode of working any great and effective improvement. In most of the attempts that have been made by individuals to accomplish these meritorious works, there generally appeared a weakness of effort and insufficiency of means, which prevented anything considerable being effected, and the cause I justly explained to be, a want of proportion between the means and the end, not so much in a want of money as in a most erroneous method of applying it. To raise a set of buildings for a farm, with gradual additions to the whole, and enclosing from the waste, field after field for improvement, with views merely of forming a large farm, and keeping the whole in hand, demands so large a capital that the succeeding languor of the exertions has been evidently owing to want of money, the capital being insufficient for the two distinct objects of farming and improving. The novel idea struck me that the whole capital in such cases should be appropriated to improvements alone; that no other buildings should be raised than exactly sufficient for such a small farm as lets most readily in the district— and this, usually, is little more than a cottage, and ten or twenty acres of grass round it. Hence I proposed that an entire new farm should, after one course of crops, be formed, and let, sold, or mortgaged every year. In this mode of proceeding the farming would be entirely subservient to the improvement, and the capital would be constantly moving to fresh land. I showed that a small sum of money, thus employed, would gradually improve a great and increasing breadth of waste; whereas, if the same money was employed in the common manner of farming and occupying a larger farm, the space improved, after fifteen or twenty years, would be trifling, and the profit very inferior. My explanation of this system carries conviction with it; but the work appearing at a period when the rapidity of my publications satiated the world, little or no attention was paid to it.

1774.—I, this year, published on my own account my political arithmetic, one of my best works, which was immediately translated into many languages, and highly commended in many parts of Europe. Judges of the subject here, as well as abroad, have considered it as abounding in valuable information and the justest views; but, unfortunately, as in the case of my work on waste lands, it followed so many other of my publications that little attention was paid to it, except by the *few* who saw the importance of the subject, or who were able to judge of the merit of the work.

The winter was passed in London in the same employment as the preceding; but I had become known to so many men of science that several hinted to me the propriety of my being a candidate for election as a Fellow of the Royal Society, and my recommendation as such being garnished with some respectable names I was accordingly elected, which adds the F.R.S. to my name. Once in conversation with Dr. Burney on these elections, he said, 'No matter, for that we have got our *ends* of them.' This year I was elected an honorary member of the Palatine Society of Agriculture established at Mannheim, also of the Geographical Society of Florence.

1775.—This winter I spent in London. From 1766 to 1775 being ten years, I received 3,000*l*., or 300*l*. a year.

CHAPTER IV

IRELAND, 1776-1778

The journey to Ireland—Characteristics—Residence at Mitchelstown—Intrigues—A strange bargain—Departure—Letter to his wife—A terrible journey.

THE events which followed the close of this year carried a better complexion than the preceding period, and therefore I shall in general remark that the last four or five years of my life had been detestable, my employments degrading, my anxiety endless, every effort unsuccessful, exertion always on the stretch, and always disappointed in the result, uneasy at home, unhappy abroad, existing with difficulty and struggling to live, never out of debt, and never enjoying one shilling that was spent. What would not a sensible, quiet, prudent wife have done for me? But had I so behaved to God as to merit such a gift?

The only pleasant moments that I passed were in visits to my friend Arbuthnot[1] at Mitcham, whose agriculture so near the capital brought good company to his house. He was upon the whole the most agreeable, pleasant and interesting connection which I ever

---

[1] Appears to have been brother to the Hon. Robert Arbuthnot, third son of John, Viscount Arbuthnot, whose death is recorded in the *Annual Register* of 1801.

made in agricultural pursuits. He was brother of the present Rt. Honorable.

I had in 1775 determined on making the tour of Ireland, to which the Earl of Shelburne [1] much instigated me, and I corresponded with several persons on the subject, who urged me much to that undertaking, but I was obliged to postpone it to the following year. The following is a note from Mr. Burke on the subject:—

'Mr. Burke sends the covers with his best compliments and wishes to Mr. Young. He would be very glad to give Mr. Young recommendations to Ireland, but his acquaintance there is almost worn out, Lord Charlemont and one or two more being all that he thinks care a farthing for him. However, if letters to them would be of any service to Mr. Young, Mr. B. would with great pleasure write them.'

On June 19 of this year 1776 I embarked at Holyhead for Ireland, and in consequence of this journey through every part of the kingdom, produced in 1780 that tour which succeeded so well, and has been reckoned among my best and most useful productions; and I have reason to believe had considerable effect in enlightening the people of that country. I took with me many letters of introduction, from the Earl of Shelburne, Mr. Burke, and other persons of eminence in England; and on landing at Dublin, was immediately introduced to Colonel Burton, afterwards Lord Cunningham, aide-de-camp to the Earl of Harcourt, at that time Lord Lieutenant, and well known to the whole

[1] First Marquis of Lansdowne; took part in Lord Chatham's Ministry.

kingdom. Colonel Burton, to whom I was more indebted for letters of introduction than to any other man in England, was a most remarkable character. He had great care and elegance united with a measure of roughness, which may be attributed to a sort of personal courage which was apt to boil over. This led him into many quarrels, and not a few duels, one of which was fought across a table of no great length from end to end, and, not strange to tell of in Ireland, several of the party stood near enjoying the sport. He was a true friend to the interests of Ireland, and far more enlightened upon it than the greater part of well-informed people to be found there. He made immense exertions to improve the fisheries on his estate at Donegal, but they were unsuccessful. He was respectable [1] for general knowledge, and possessed a great flow of animated conversation. He carried me to Lord Harcourt's villa at St. Woolstans, with whom I spent some days; and the Colonel arranged the plan of my journey, giving me a multitude of letters to those who were best able to afford valuable information. I kept a private journal throughout the whole of this tour, in which I minuted many anecdotes and circumstances which occurred to me of a private nature, descriptive of the manners of the people, which, had it been preserved, would have assisted greatly in drawing up these papers; but, unfortunately, it was lost, with all the specimens of soils and minerals which I collected throughout the whole kingdom. On returning to England, I quitted my whisky [2] at Bath, and got into a

---

[1] This use of the word as respectworthy is noticeable.
[2] Whisky: a light carriage built for rapid motion.—*Webster.*

stage, and sent a new London servant, the only one I had, thither to bring the horse and chaise to London, and the trunk containing these things. The fellow was a rascal, stole the trunk, and pretended that he had lost it on the road; in addition to the loss was the torment of hunting him out (for he went away directly) through London for punishment. With great difficulty I found him, and serving a warrant upon him, carried him to Bow Street, where Fielding the magistrate at once dismissed the complaint, it being only a breach of trust, as the robbery could not be proved; and all I got for my pains was abuse from the fellow.

This was a very great loss to me, as the specimens I brought of soils would have been of great use to me in the course of experiments which I soon after began in the object of expelling gases from earths. In my journey through Ireland I was received with great hospitality, which characterises the nation, and with that particular attention which my peculiar object excited in so many persons who rendered agriculture either their profit or amusement.

I travelled four hundred miles *de suite* without going to an inn. Amongst those who were most desirous of my calling upon them was Sir James Caldwell, of Castle Caldwell, on Lough Erne. One anecdote will give some idea of his character.

The Marquis of Lansdowne, then Earl of Shelburne, being in Ireland, and intending to call on Sir James, he, with an hospitality truly Irish, thought of nothing night or day but how to devise some amusement to entertain his noble guest, and came home to breakfast one morning with prodigious eagerness to communicate a new idea to Lady Caldwell. This was to summon together the hundred labourers he employed, and choose fifty that would best represent New Zealand savages, in order that he might form two fleets of boats on the Lough, one to represent Captain Cook and his men, the other a New Zealand chief at the head of his party in canoes, and consulted her how it would be possible to get them dressed in an appropriate manner in time for Lord Shelburne's arrival. Lady C., who had much more prudence than Sir James, reminded him that he had 200 acres of hay down, and the preparations he mentioned would occupy so much time that the whole would now stand a chance of being spoiled. All remonstrances were in vain. Tailors were pressed into his service from the surrounding country to vamp up, as well as time would permit, the crews of men and fleets. The prediction was fulfilled: the hay was spoiled, and what hurt Sir James much more, he received a letter from Lord S. to put off his coming till his return from Kilkenny, and that uncertain. To add to the mortification, after some weeks, Sir James being on business at Dublin, Lord S. arrived without giving notice, and Lady C., not presuming to exhibit the intended battle, but wishing to amuse his Lordship as well as the place would afford, told him at breakfast that the morning should be spent in fishing. Lord S. replied, 'My dear Lady C., you look upon a fine lake out of your windows; but I have often remarked—from the ocean to the pond—that where at the first blush you have reason to expect most fish you are sure to find least.' This made Lady C. exert herself—boats, nets, and all were collected, and they caught such an immensity as really proved a most gratifying spectacle to his Lordship, who confessed that his maxim failed him for once. His stay was too short for Sir James's return.

At Lord Longford's I met a person of some celebrity at the time for adventures not worth reciting, Mr. Medlicott. Lord L. and he gave me an account of a gentleman of a good estate in that neighbourhood, but then dead, whose real life, manners and conversation far exceeded anything to be met with in 'Castle Rackrent.' His hospitality was unbounded, and it never for a moment came into his head to make any provision for feeding the people he brought into his house. While credit was to be had, his butler or housekeeper did this for him ; his own attention was given solely to the cellar that wine might not be wanted. If claret was secured, with a dead ox or sheep hanging in the slaughter-house ready for steaks or cutlets, he thought all was well. He was never easy without company in the house, and with a large party in it would invite another of twice the number. One day the cook came into the breakfast parlour before all the company : ' Sir, there's no coals.' 'Then burn turf.' ' Sir, there's no turf.' 'Then cut down a tree.' This was a forlorn hope, for in all probability he must have gone three miles to find one, all round the house being long ago safely swept away. They dispatched a number of cars to borrow turf. Candles were equally deficient, for unfortunately he was fond of dogs all half starved, so that a gentleman walking to what was called his bed-chamber, after making two or three turnings, met a hungry greyhound, who, jumping up, took the candle out of the candlestick, and devoured it in a trice, and left him in the dark. To advance or return was equally a matter of chance, therefore groping his way, he soon found himself in the midst of a parcel of giggling maid-servants. By what means he at last found his way to his 'shakedown' is unknown. A 'shakedown' when I was in Ireland meant some clean straw spread upon the floor, with blankets and sheets, in what was called the barrack room, one containing several beds for single men.

At Mr. Richard Aldworth's, in the county of Cork, I met with an instance, both in that gentleman and lady, of elegant manners and cultivated minds. He had made the grand tour, and she had been educated in that style which may be imagined in a person nearly related to a Lord Chief Justice and an Archbishop. But it was evident that patriotic motives alone made them residents in Ireland. A sigh would often escape when circumstances of English manners were named, and they felt the dismal vacuity of living in a country where people of equal ideas were scarce. Mrs. Aldworth had in her possession one original manuscript letter of Dean Swift, entrusted to her under a solemn promise that she would permit no copy to be taken, nor ever read it twice to the same people. It was without exception the wittiest and severest satire upon Ireland that probably ever was written, and it was easy to perceive by the manner in which it was read that the sentiments were not a little in unison with those of the reader. This letter was equally hostile to the nobility, the gentry, the people, the country, nay the very rivers and mountains; for it declared the Shannon itself to be little better than a series of marshes, that carried to the ocean less water than flows through one of the arches of London Bridge.

From various other instances, as well as from this, I was inclined to think that that degree of a polished and cultivated education, which suits well enough for London or Paris, or a country residence in a good neighbourhood of England, was ill-framed for a province in Ireland. Persons of equal attainments may now and then come across them, but they are compelled to associate with so many who are the very reverse that a more certain provision of misery can scarcely be laid.

The preceding observation is in a measure applicable to Mr. and Mrs. Jefferys and Mr. and Mrs. Trant, who lived in the vicinity of Cork. The two former when I was there were actually embarking for France, after great speculations in building a town and establishing manufactures, which probably had proved too expensive. They were well informed and cultivated, and spoke most modern languages. Mr. Trant was an instance of a singularly retentive memory. It was never necessary for him to consult the same book twice. All that he ever read in a variety of languages was at his tongue's end, and he applied these uncommon stores with great judgment and propriety. The most beautiful description of Kilkenny was written by him. It gave me pleasure to hear not long afterwards that Mr. and Mrs. Jefferys were at Paris but a few days, and then returned to England. The motive of the journey was reported to be to get rid of a much too numerous establishment of servants, as they started again on a much more moderate and comfortable plan.

As a feature of Irish manners, I may mention another circumstance which astonished me. When upon my tour I spent a day or two with the Right Hon. Silver Oliver, who had at that time much company in his house. The table was well appointed, and everything wore an air of splendour and affluence. Afterwards when I resided at Mitchelstown—Mr. Oliver was either dead or absent, and everything in the house was advertised to be sold by auction—I went over to that auction, which gave me an opportunity of examining the whole house. I desired to be shown into the kitchen, as I could not find it of myself. When pointed out I was in utter amazement. There never was such a hole. I insisted upon it that it could not be the kitchen, as I had myself partook of dinners which could never have been dressed in such a pig-stye; but they assured me there was no other. It was about eight feet wide and ten long. Scarcely any light, and the walls black as the inside of the chimney. The furniture was no better than the fitting up; dressers, tables, and shelves seemed to have been laid aside as superfluous luxuries. It must have been an effort of uncommon ingenuity to cook at a turf hearth, in such a cave as this, the ample dinners I had seen in this house, and Etna or Vesuvius might as soon have been found in England as such a kitchen. Its existence for a single instant in the house of a man of fortune would be a moral impossibility. No English farmer would submit to it for a week. This strongly shows the manners of the people.

A family with whom I resided for some time, while waiting for the Waterford packet, was that of Mr. Bolton, in a beautiful situation, commanding the finest views. Mr. Bolton, the elder, was a respectable man; but his son, the present proprietor of the estate, then in Parliament, was a man of singular and genuine patriotism, and of so mild and pleasing a temper that I much regretted I had him not for a neighbour at Bradfield. I had the pleasure of sending him from Suffolk many implements &c. for assisting him in his improved husbandry; and he has proved to the present day one of the most enlightened friends that Ireland has to boast, making an equal figure in my tour, and in the very able work of Mr. Wakefield [1] published within an interval of thirty years.

Among the persons who received me in the most agreeable and hospitable manner I may be permitted to name the following: Earl of Harcourt (Lord Lieutenant), Earl of Charlemont, Lord Chief Baron Forster, his Grace the Lord Primate, the Archbishop of Tuam, Sir James Caldwell, &c.

1777.—This was the first favourable turn that promised anything after ten years' anxiety and misery, yet how little did I deserve from that Providence I had so long neglected. The year was a remarkable one in the events of my life.

[1] Edward Wakefield, *An Account of Ireland: Political and Statistical*, 1812.

Mr. Danby, of whom mention has already been inserted, was this spring in London, and as Lord Kingsborough, son of the Earl of Kingston, was intimately acquainted with Mr. D., and at that time there also, his Lordship often complained of the sad state of neglect in which his property remained in the hands of an Irish agent, who never saw an acre of the estate but merely on a rapid journey once, or at most twice, a year to receive the rents. For this purpose a clerk resided at Mitchelstown, having a summer house in the Castle garden for his office, and here the tenants came to pay their rents in a constant succession of driblets the whole year round. His Lordship observed that it would be of much importance to him to have a respectable resident agent who understood agriculture, and might greatly contribute to the improvement of the property. Mr. Danby entirely coincided in this opinion, and told his Lordship that he knew a gentleman who possessed the unquestionable knowledge and management of estates, and as he had known me for several years he had every reason to believe in my integrity. He then named me. Lord K. begged him to make the application to me immediately, which Mr. Danby did, and invited me to meet Lord and Lady K. to dinner. I had a good deal of conversation with Lord K., and the next day Mr. Danby made an agreement with his Lordship for me to become his agent at an annual salary of 500*l.*, with an eligible house for my residence, rent free, and a retaining fee, to be paid immediately, of 500*l.* more.

In consequence of this arrangement, to which I

readily agreed, I disposed of the lease of my farm in Hertfordshire, and sent my books and other effects which I might want to Cork by sea, going myself to Dublin, where I resided some time in a constant round of Dublin dinners, till I was informed by Lord Kingsborough that the house at Mitchelstown was ready in which I was to reside, whilst a new one was building on a plan and in a situation approved of myself. In September I left Dublin for Mitchelstown—130 miles off—making a detour through those counties which I had not sufficiently seen the preceding year. And here I cannot avoid inserting the following excellent advice from my ever affectionate mother: 'My memory begins to fail me, but no wonder at 72. That is not the cause of yours doing so, but the multiplicity of business you are engaged in. I attribute it also to being overburthened with your affairs. I can get neither ploughman nor footman to go over to Ireland, so you must see what you can do when you come yourself, which, I am sorry to hear, is not till (next) September. God only knows if I shall live so long as to see you once more. However, to hear you are well and happy is a great comfort to me, and the only one I have left, for it is my lot to be deprived of all those who to me are dearest. I hate now to do anything but sit by the fire and write to you. . . . But the happiness of this world, Arthur, is but of a short duration; I therefore wish you would bestow some thoughts on that happiness which will have eternal duration.'[1]

[1] Entries in memorandum-book 'The year's receipts, 1,145*l*. Wrote *Alcon and Flavia*, a poem.'

1778.—The opening of this year found me at Mitchelstown, where Mrs. Young joined me. On my arrival I busied myself incessantly in examining and valuing the farms which came out of lease, and was so occupied several months. I was most anxious to persuade Lord K. into the propriety of letting his lands to the occupying cottar as tenant, and dismissing the whole race of middlemen. I adhered steadily to this, and had the satisfaction to find that Lord K. was well inclined to the plan. But a distant relation of Lady K.'s, who had one farm upon the estate as middleman, Major Thornhill, feeling the sweets of a profit rent upon that one farm, was exceedingly anxious to procure from Lord K. the profits of others upon the same terms, and in this respect I was placed in an awkward situation. It was impossible for me, consistently with the interest of Lord K., in any measure whatever to promote the success of designs which struck at the very root of all my plans, as the Major had his eye upon several of the most considerable farms. Lady K. had a high opinion of the Major, who was a lively, pleasant, handsome man, and an ignorant open-hearted duellist; she had of course favoured his plans, and I as carefully avoided ever saying anything in favour of them. Thus from the beginning it was not difficult to see an underground plot to frustrate schemes commencing very early, but things in the meantime carried a fair outward appearance. I dined very often at the Castle, and generally played at chess with Lady Kingsborough for an hour or more after dinner, and I learned by report that her Ladyship was highly pleased with me, saying that I was one of the most lively, agreeable fellows. Lord Kingsborough was of a character not so easily ascertained, for at many different periods of his life he seemed to possess qualities very much in contradiction to each other. His manner and carriage were remarkably easy, agreeable, and polite, having the finish of a perfect gentleman; he wanted, however, steadiness and perseverance even in his best designs, and was easily wrought upon by persons of inferior abilities. Mrs. Thornhill, the wife of the Major, was an artful designing woman, ever on the watch to injure those who stood in her husband's way, and never forgetting her private interest for a moment. I saw a fixed plan in her mind for dispossessing me of the agency and procuring it for the Major, and I conceive it was by her misrepresentations that a decisive use was made of an opportunity which soon after offered for effecting her plan.

Lady K. had a Catholic governess, a Miss Crosby, relative to whom Mrs. T. had inspired Lady K. with sentiments of jealousy, insomuch that she was discharged, and I was employed to draw up an engagement to grant her an annuity of 50*l.* per annum. This transaction and others connected with it occasioned me to be much at the Castle, and in situations which were converted by Mrs. Thornhill into proofs that I was in league with Miss C. for securing the affections of Lord Kingsborough at the expense of his wife, and, at the same time, it was carefully impressed into his Lordship's mind that I was in love with Lady K. Thus by a train of artful intrigues and deceptions the ladies brought Lord K. to the determination of parting with me, after which nothing remained but to settle our accounts. This was done, and a balance being due to me of about 600*l.* or 700*l.*, I informed his Lordship that I waited only to be paid in order to set off for England. Here was a demur, and Major Thornhill came to inform me that his Lordship had not the money to pay me; several days passed in which I was in a very awkward state of uncertainty. It occurred to me as I saw no sign of payment to propose that he should give me an annuity for life, which he at once agreed to. What that annuity should be I was perfectly ignorant, but there was an advertisement in a London paper offering terms, which I sent to his Lordship, with a note, informing him that if he would give me an annuity on the terms there specified I would agree to it and free him for the present from all payment. This his Lordship at once acceded to, and signed a bond granting me an annuity for life of 72*l.*,[1] according to the terms specified in the advertisement. This business being settled to the satisfaction of both parties, and my books packed up and sent to Cork, I stepped into my post-chaise, and, with a pair of Irish nags, set off on a journey to Waterford on a visit to my excellent friend, Cornelius Bolton, Junr. Esqr. M.P., where I waited for the packet to sail for Milford Haven long enough to have gone round by Dublin and have reached Rome or Naples. I had a miserable passage of three days and nights, a storm blowing us almost to Arklow, but through the providence of God we escaped the threatened dangers and landed safely in the desired

---

[1] This curious arrangement seems to have been faithfully kept, as will be seen later on.

haven. I travelled post to London, and thus ended one of the greatest speculations of my life, and I remember observing that in all probability the providence of God was exerted to remove me from a kingdom in which no unconnected motives could induce me to remain. The transaction was not absolutely free from circumstances in a measure favourable to my future ease and repose. I had received 500*l*., which took me out of some difficulties, and had the addition of 72*l*. per annum to my income, which was to me an object of some consideration. It also removed me entirely from the farm in Hertfordshire, a most unprofitable one, and, what was better, from a winter residence in London. It also took me back to Bradfield to my aged mother, whose health was daily declining, and whose memory, being much impaired, subjected her to imposition by tenants and servants.

To his Wife

'Haverford West : Oct. 23.

' My Dearest,—It pleases God that I am once more to embrace you and my children—a passage that is common in eight hours was from Sunday morn eight o'clock till one o'clock this morning Wednesday, thirty-six hours of which, a raging storm ; we talk of them at land, but those who have not seen them at sea know not what the very elements are. Pent up in the Irish Channel, the ship ran adrift, wearing [1] to keep free from rocks and sands—the wind did not blow, it was like volleys of artillery ; part of the sails were torn into

---

[1] Wear : sea-term, to bring a ship on.—*Bailey's Dictionary*.

fritters; the waves were mountains high, while the ship was perfectly tossed on end of them; the cabin window burst open, and deluged everything afloat; the horses kicked and groaned, the dogs howled; six passengers praying, shrieking, and vomiting; every soul sick but myself; the sailors swearing and storming; and the whole—such a scene! The Captain, who has been many voyages, and the pilot thirty-six years, never saw such a storm—to last so long.

'It has worried and starved the horses so that I know not what I am to do—shall go with them as far as I can, and if they knock up must leave them and take some fly to be by you thirty-first; of which send immediate notice to B.

'I know not if Bath be my nearest way, so let me have a letter at Nicoll's in case I am not in Town, to the same purport as that to Bath, to inform me what I am to do and when to go.

'Adieu,
' Most truly yours,
' A. Y.

'Thank God for me. Peter would not come over with me. My passage has cost me between 7*l.* and 8*l.*, which is the very devil, so that I shall come home without a shilling, and the thoughts of coming full swing upon poverty again make me miserable. Two ships were lost in the storm.'

Note in memorandum-book.—' Note of my being thirty-eight, and poetry in my head.'

CHAPTER V

FARMING AND EXPERIMENTS, 1779-1782

Corn bounties—A grievance—Reading—Hugh Boyd—Bishop Watson—Howlett on population—Irish Linen Board Experiments—Correspondence.

1779.—QUITTING Ireland and coming again to Bradfield occasioned a great pause and break in my life and pursuits, and had I made a proper use of it might have fixed a quiet destiny, so far as a heart not renewed could be happy and content; but I wanted religion, and that want includes all others. I arrived at Bradfield on the first of January, and had then full time to reflect upon what should be the future pursuit of my life, and upon what plan I could devise for that fresh establishment of myself, which should, at the same time, prevent any relapse into those odious dependencies upon uncertainties, which from 1771 to 1778 had been the perpetual torment of my life. While I was hesitating what plan to follow, an emigration to America arose in my mind and much occupied my thoughts. But the advanced period of my mother's life and her persuasions against any scheme of that sort prevailed, and with some reluctance I relinquished it. I had also to consider, how far it would be prudent to yield to her earnest entreaties to return to farming at Bradfield and live with her. To stock a farm of any size would have been to me a matter of difficulty, but, at the same time, to get free from all London engagements, and to secure the tranquillity of a retired life after all the stormy perplexities through which I had passed, was an object full of attraction, and it prevailed. A small farm contiguous to the old family mansion was to be vacant at Michaelmas, and notice was accordingly given to the tenant to quit. Thus was I once more engaged in husbandry, with a prospect of gradually increasing my business according as my capital should enable me. Relative to my farm, it may here be proper once for all to observe, that as the leases of the estate fell vacant I gradually enlarged my occupation, till I had between three and four hundred acres in hand, most amply stocked, and conducted with such an expense of labour as enabled me to support the credit of my husbandry. I remained at Bradfield the whole year, and the only literary pursuit I engaged in was a correspondence with Mr. Wight upon some points in the Scotch system of farming; it was published in his 'Present State of the Husbandry of Scotland.'[1] I had reason to believe that his letters were written under the eye of Lord Kames,[2] the author of the well-known work called, 'The Gentleman Farmer,' and much better known book, 'Elements of Criticism.'

[1] In memorandum-book [occurs this note: 'Correspondence with Wight printed in his reports.' This seems to be Alexander Wight, author of 'An Enquiry into the Rise and Progress of Parliament, chiefly in Scotland.'

[2] Henry Home, a Scotch judge, better known by the title of Lord Kames, author of several legal and other works, among them 'Introduction to the Art of Thinking.' Died 1782.

About this period I was elected a member of the Imperial Œconomical Society of Petersburg.

The first event of the year 1780 was the publication of my Irish Tour in one volume quarto. It was so successful and popular in both kingdoms that it is unnecessary to expatiate upon it; thus much, however, I trust I may say without vanity, that it has stood the test of examination, and received from the best judges the highest commendation. But there is one circumstance which appears never to have been sufficiently understood, or at least the *effect* properly attributed to this work. Perhaps the most novel, instructing, and decisively useful part of the publication was the attack made upon the bounty paid on the land carriage of corn to Dublin.[1] I therein proved beyond the possibility of doubt the gross absurdity of the measure. The whole kingdom, however, without exception, considered this bounty as the great palladium of their national agriculture, and in conversation upon that subject with the most able men then living there, I found them so strongly prejudiced in its favour that they were not very willing to hear anything spoken against it. But it appeared to me so manifestly absurd that I exerted my industry to examine the measure on its very foundation. When I was a complete master of the subject and stated the result in conversation to the warmest friends of the measure, I had the satisfaction

[1] Corn bounty in Ireland, 1780. This was granted by the Irish Parliament. The Lord Lieutenant, in his speech at the close of the session, said: 'Ample bounties on the export of your corn, your linen, and your sail-cloth have been granted.' See *Annual Register*, 1780, p. 338.

to find that the documents thus produced were utterly unknown to all, and they were fairly beat[1] out of their prejudices in favour of the measure; at least their *argument* entirely failed on the occasion. But the event proved that the conviction was real. For in the very first session after the publication of my book the bounty was reduced by half, as appears by Mr. Henry Cavendish's publication on the revenue and national expenses of Ireland. It was afterwards gradually reduced, and at last gave up entirely. The saving to the nation occasioned palpably by this publication amounted to 40,000*l*. per annum immediately, and as the expense of the bounty had been constantly increasing, the saving was of course in reality much greater. Long after, in conversation with Lord Loughborough, he told me that he had read that part of my work relative to the bounty, &c., with particular attention, and that he thought the arguments most unanswerable, adding, 'Ireland ought to have rewarded you for that.' When the whole was given up it was a saving of 80,000*l*. a year to the nation. This was much for one individual to effect; and some reward for such services would not have been much for the nation to grant.

I cannot on such an occasion name Ireland without remarking that though the Irish are certainly a generous people, and liberal sometimes almost to excess, yet not a ray of that spirit was by any public body shed on my labours.

After I had left the kingdom and published the tour, I received the following letter:—

[1] Beat: participial adjective.—*Webster*.

'Dublin: Sept. 16, 1780.

'Sir,—With great pleasure I take up the pen in obedience to the commands of the Dublin Society, to communicate to you their thanks for the late publication of your tour in Ireland, a treatise which, in doing justice to this country, puts us in a most respectable view; for which reason we consider you to have great merit. But what particularly gained the attention of the Society were your just and excellent observations and reasoning, in the second part of that work, relative to the agriculture, manufactures, trade, and police of the kingdom. And gentlemen thought the publication of that part, particularly so as to fall into the hands of the generality of the people of this country, might be of great benefit and use; and we wish you would let us know your sentiments relative to the preparing a publication of that kind, and in what mode you would think it most proper, and would answer best, and what you would judge a reasonable amends for all this trouble, that we may lay the same before the Society at our next meeting, the beginning of November. There are a great many useful observations and hints interspersed in many parts of your tour which may be of great use to throw into the hands of the public.

'I am, Sir,
'Your most obedient servant,
'RED. MORRES.'

In answer to this letter, I returned sincere thanks for the honour of the vote; and assured them that I should be ready either to publish any part of the work separately, or to make an abridgment of the whole, reduced in such a manner as to be diffused at a small expense over all the kingdom. In a few posts I received, under the Dublin post-mark, an envelope, enclosing an anonymous essay, cut out of a newspaper, which referred to the transactions of the Society relative to me, and condemning pretty heavily my whole publication; and in this unhandsome manner the business ended.

In a Society which disposed of 10,000*l*. a year of public money, granted by Parliament chiefly with a view, as the Act expresses, to encourage agriculture, but which patronised manufacturers far more, there will necessarily be an agricultural party and a manufacturing one. According as one or the other happens to prevail, such contradictions will arise. All that is to be said of my case now is, that it was not so bad as that of poor Whyman Baker, who settled in Ireland as their experimenter in agriculture—lived there in poverty ten or twelve years—and broke his heart on account of the treatment which he met with. But while their Societies acted thus, the Parliament of the kingdom paid my book a much greater compliment than any Society could do; for they passed more than one Act almost directly, to alter and vary the police of corn, which I had proved was vicious, but which till then had been universally esteemed as the chief pillar of their national prosperity, and I had thus the satisfaction to see the Legislature of the kingdom improving the policy of it from the known and confessed suggestions of a work that, in other respects, had proved to the author a mere barren blank. I have, however, since

'Dublin: Sept. 16, 1780.

'Sir,—With great pleasure I take up the pen in obedience to the commands of the Dublin Society, to communicate to you their thanks for the late publication of your tour in Ireland, a treatise which, in doing justice to this country, puts us in a most respectable view; for which reason we consider you to have great merit. But what particularly gained the attention of the Society were your just and excellent observations and reasoning, in the second part of that work, relative to the agriculture, manufactures, trade, and police of the kingdom. And gentlemen thought the publication of that part, particularly so as to fall into the hands of the generality of the people of this country, might be of great benefit and use; and we wish you would let us know your sentiments relative to the preparing a publication of that kind, and in what mode you would think it most proper, and would answer best, and what you would judge a reasonable amends for all this trouble, that we may lay the same before the Society at our next meeting, the beginning of November. There are a great many useful observations and hints interspersed in many parts of your tour which may be of great use to throw into the hands of the public.

'I am, Sir,
'Your most obedient servant,
'RED. MORRES.'

In answer to this letter, I returned sincere thanks for the honour of the vote; and assured them that I should be ready either to publish any part of the work separately, or to make an abridgment of the whole, reduced in such a manner as to be diffused at a small expense over all the kingdom. In a few posts I received, under the Dublin post-mark, an envelope, enclosing an anonymous essay, cut out of a newspaper, which referred to the transactions of the Society relative to me, and condemning pretty heavily my whole publication; and in this unhandsome manner the business ended.

In a Society which disposed of 10,000$l.$ a year of public money, granted by Parliament chiefly with a view, as the Act expresses, to encourage agriculture, but which patronised manufacturers far more, there will necessarily be an agricultural party and a manufacturing one. According as one or the other happens to prevail, such contradictions will arise. All that is to be said of my case now is, that it was not so bad as that of poor Whyman Baker, who settled in Ireland as their experimenter in agriculture—lived there in poverty ten or twelve years—and broke his heart on account of the treatment which he met with. But while their Societies acted thus, the Parliament of the kingdom paid my book a much greater compliment than any Society could do; for they passed more than one Act almost directly, to alter and vary the police of corn, which I had proved was vicious, but which till then had been universally esteemed as the chief pillar of their national prosperity, and I had thus the satisfaction to see the Legislature of the kingdom improving the policy of it from the known and confessed suggestions of a work that, in other respects, had proved to the author a mere barren blank. I have, however, since heard from many most respectable gentlemen of that nation, as well as from the correspondence of others, that the book is even now esteemed of some value to Ireland, and that the agriculture of the kingdom has been advanced in consequence. But it is time to dismiss a subject upon which I have dilated too much, and spoken perhaps with an unguarded vanity and self-love which would ill become me.

I was the chief part of this year at Bradfield, but I' had bought at London a pair of roan mares for drawing a post-chaise, and having the small farm in hand, I made myself by practice no bad ploughman, and could finish the stetches[1] neatly, and execute everything except the rivalling the Suffolk ploughman in drawing straight furrows to a mark set for that purpose; yet I overcame this difficulty in a manner that would have been commended in any other county.

The Society for the Encouragement of Arts, Manufactures, and Commerce voted me their Honorary Medal for some experiments I had communicated to them on the culture of potatoes.

According to custom, part of my time was occupied in reading, and among other works was highly entertained with Gray's letters, and particularly with the following passage, which displays so much knowledge of the human mind, and, at the same time, much sterling sense: 'To find oneself business I am persuaded is the great art of life, and I am never so angry as when I hear my acquaintance wishing they had been bred to

[1] Stetch: as much land as lies between one farm and another.—*Prov. Eng., Halliwell.*

some poking profession, or employed in some office of drudgery, as if it were pleasanter to be at the command of other people than at one's own, and as if they could not go unless they were wound up. Yet I know and feel what they mean by this complaint; it proves that some spirit, something of genius (more than common) is required to teach a man how to employ himself—I say a man, for women, commonly speaking, never feel this distemper, they have always something to do. Time hangs not on their hands (unless they be fine ladies), a variety of small inventions and occupations fill up the void, and their eyes are never open in vain' (vol. ii.)

Thank heaven, I have so much of the woman in me as to possess this faculty of employing myself. The day is never too long, for I think time spent in reading is always well employed, unless a man reads like an idiot, that is, equally removed from instruction and entertainment. Now the general occupation of my life—agriculture—has the happy circumstance of giving much employment, and with it exercise, at the same time that it naturally leads into a course of reading, to which it gives the air and turn of a study, and consequently renders it more interesting, an advantage I shall be solicitous to preserve, by persisting, at all events, to be much interested in farming, even though I should not continue an actual farmer. Gray felt the advantage of country pursuits. 'Happy they that can create a rose tree or erect a honeysuckle, that can watch the brood of a hen, or see a fleet of their own ducklings launch into the water; it is with a sentiment of envy I speak it, who never shall have even a thatched roof of my own, nor gather a strawberry but in Covent Garden.'

I read also Roberts' 'Map of Commerce,'[1] and find the following extract about the spot where should be the ruin of Troy: 'Anno Domini, 1620.—I hardly saw the relics of this mighty fabric (Troy), though I traced it for many miles, and gave ear to all the ridiculous fables of those poor Grecians that inhabit thereabouts in many villages within the compass of her ancient walls, from Mount Ida to the River Scamander, now only a brook not two feet deep, so that what Ovid said of old I found by experience verified, "jam seges est ubi Troja fuit."' There is a melancholy which attends such reflections that with me makes a deep impression; the idea that what was once the seat of power, arts, literature and elegance is now in the most miserable situation which Turkish oppression and Mahometan superstition can inflict, that not a trace of a once mighty city is now to be found, is depressing to the human mind. In an equal series of time what will become of the cities which are now the pride of Europe? what obscure farmer of futurity shall plough the ground whereon that House of Common stands in which a Hampden, a Bolingbroke, a Pitt, and a Mansfield have delighted the most celebrated assembly now in the world?[2]

My visit to London was, part of it, very agreeable,

[1] Lewis Roberts, *The Merchant's Map of Commerce*, London, 1638. 'The first systematic writer upon trade in the English language' (Lowndes).

[2] Had this sentence appeared in print anterior to Macaulay's famous passage, the latter might have been deemed a plagiarism.

my whole intercourse with Arbuthnot entirely so. At Dr. Burney's, while it lasted, the same; the opera, parties, the Royal Society, with some of the attendance on Parliament, add to this being in the world and on the spot for whatever happened, were all so many opportunities for pleasure and amusement, which, however, I did not make the most of. Against these I must now rank ease in my circumstances. Let it fly, and the change has been a bad one, indeed. But I think I have resolution enough to take special care of the greatest of all man's chances. I do not remember when my acquaintance with Mr. Hugh Boyd [1] began, but I was acquainted with him in London, met him in many companies in Dublin, and travelled with him from thence to London. It has been supposed that he was the author of 'Junius,' and I must give it as my opinion that there was much probability in the supposition. I have been many times at his house, at breakfasts, morning calls and dinners, and never without seeing the *Public Advertiser* and remarking that they were blanks, that is to say, without being stamped. All writers in newspapers are allowed a copy gratis, and these are never stamped. His company was so much sought after in Dublin that I was scarcely at a great dinner without his being present. A very striking circumstance in his character was a memory in some points beyond example; he would multiply nine figures by eight entirely in his head, and would give the result

[1] Hugh Boyd, a writer whose real name was Macaulay, author of two political tracts now forgotten. Died at Madras in 1791, having dissipated his wife's fortune and his own.

with the most perfect accuracy. When it is considered that such an operation demands the recollection not merely of the figures, but of their position in order for the final addition, it must be admitted to be a stupendous one. He was on all occasions and in every circumstance a most pleasing, agreeable companion. His wife was a woman of very good understanding, and appeared to be sensible of her husband's extraordinary talents. One morning at breakfast Mr. Burke's son came in, and as his father had made a very celebrated speech the day before in the House of Commons which he intended to publish, but had, in the conclusion, departed from his notes in a very fine strain of eloquence, knowing the great memory of Boyd, he sent his son to request some hints for that conclusion. We set to work to recollect as much as possible his own words, and furnished young Burke much to his satisfaction. Mr. Boyd's letters, of which I have preserved several, are written in a most pleasing, lively style.

'Norfolk Street: August 16, 1780.

'My dear Sir,—You have an excellent physician, but I should be glad to know what right the patient has to become his own apothecary? The doctor's prescription consists of such rare ingredients as require no common skill to discover and use, *Cuivis in suâ arte*. If it had been your inferior fate to wield the pestle instead of the ploughshare and the pen, I should subscribe to the judgment of the apothecary as fully as I do to the author's genius and the farmer's knowledge. "A friend who can enliven the dulness of the country." Well said, doctor. Macbeth himself might take your advice, for there is little difference between a dull mind and "a mind diseased;" but my good friend has neither. His mistake, therefore, in making up your prescription, and shaking me up as the aforesaid ingredient, is of little consequence. To convince him, however, that he is mistaken—for I love to set your clever men right—I shall make my appearance, first in the county of Cambridge, and next in the county of Suffolk—or ere the amorous Phœbus shall have twice resorted to his evening assignation to take an oyster with Miss Thetis. By the bye, we have had very good [entertainment] in town for some days—though as to days I can only answer for one and a half; being no longer returned from a Western Tour, which I have had the pleasure and trouble of making—for everything is mixed, you know, pleasure and pain—rose and thorns—man and wife; I ask Mrs. Young ten thousand pardons.

'I have had hopes sometimes of tempting Mrs. B. to a country excursion, and she has almost agreed to make it with me to Cambridge, where I wish to call for half a day, and perhaps longer, soon; the hopes of seeing her friends at Bradfield Hall are a strong inducement.

'Believe me,
'Very sincerely yours,
'H. Boyd.'

'August 17, 1780.

'My good friend will be at least just in this instance, when he is in every other so partial to his friends; and

with the most perfect accuracy. When it is considered
that such an operation demands the recollection not
merely of the figures, but of their position in order for the
final addition, it must be admitted to be a stupendous
one. He was on all occasions and in every circumstance a most pleasing, agreeable companion. His wife
was a woman of very good understanding, and appeared
to be sensible of her husband's extraordinary talents.
One morning at breakfast Mr. Burke's son came in, and
as his father had made a very celebrated speech the day
before in the House of Commons which he intended to
publish, but had, in the conclusion, departed from his
notes in a very fine strain of eloquence, knowing the
great memory of Boyd, he sent his son to request some
hints for that conclusion. We set to work to recollect
as much as possible his own words, and furnished young
Burke much to his satisfaction. Mr. Boyd's letters,
of which I have preserved several, are written in a most
pleasing, lively style.

'Norfolk Street: August 16, 1780.

'My dear Sir,—You have an excellent physician, but
I should be glad to know what right the patient has to
become his own apothecary? The doctor's prescription
consists of such rare ingredients as require no common
skill to discover and use, *Cuivis in suâ arte*. If it had
been your inferior fate to wield the pestle instead of
the ploughshare and the pen, I should subscribe to the
judgment of the apothecary as fully as I do to the
author's genius and the farmer's knowledge. "A friend
who can enliven the dulness of the country." Well

said, doctor. Macbeth himself might take your advice, for there is little difference between a dull mind and " a mind diseased ; " but my good friend has neither. His mistake, therefore, in making up your prescription, and shaking me up as the aforesaid ingredient, is of little consequence. To convince him, however, that he is mistaken—for I love to set your clever men right—I shall make my appearance, first in the county of Cambridge, and next in the county of Suffolk—or ere the amorous Phœbus shall have twice resorted to his evening assignation to take an oyster with Miss Thetis. By the bye, we have had very good [entertainment] in town for some days—though as to days I can only answer for one and a half; being no longer returned from a Western Tour, which I have had the pleasure and trouble of making—for everything is mixed, you know, pleasure and pain—rose and thorns—man and wife ; I ask Mrs. Young ten thousand pardons.

'I have had hopes sometimes of tempting Mrs. B. to a country excursion, and she has almost agreed to make it with me to Cambridge, where I wish to call for half a day, and perhaps longer, soon ; the hopes of seeing her friends at Bradfield Hall are a strong inducement.

'Believe me,
'Very sincerely yours,
'H. Boyd.'

'August 17, 1780.

'My good friend will be at least just in this instance, when he is in every other so partial to his friends ; and you'll believe that it is no small disappointment to me *quod* inclination, though the cause will probably be very advantageous, *businessly* speaking, that I am obliged to postpone my Suffolk trip. Observe I establish a credit by the term postpone, and I sincerely hope it will not be a long term. I have at present only another half minute to say fifty things. But not being able to think, speak, or write the fiftieth part as quick as certain persons of my acquaintance (my love to Mrs. Young), I must confine myself to one subject—which I have too much at heart to omit—the assuring you and her of my being very sincerely yours,

'H. BOYD.'

'September 2, 1780.

'My dear Friends,—You'll excuse coarse paper, and coarse writing in every sense, I'm afraid, " in matter, form, and style," according to Milton's divisions, when you know that I sit down to this delectable epistle in a City coffee-house, in the midst of Bob-wigs and worsted stocking knaves, Turks, Jews, and brokers, infidels, and merchants. *Nunquam, si quid mihi credis, amavi Hos homines.* O dialect of Babel! "Who calls for coffee?"—"This policy, sir"—"Strong convoy, a very good thing"—"Pen, ink, and wafer"—"I'sh would be rejoished to *do* for you, shur"—"Was Mr. Shylock here this morning?"—"Yesh, just gone to Jerusalem." O blessed race! I wish you were all there, with all your adopted brethren of Jewish Christians from this holy land.

'I have continued in much disappointment—at least,

suspense—since I wrote to you last, when I hinted the sudden occurrence of some business preventing the pleasure of my proposed trip. Depending on the pleasures not only of some three or four different persons, but of great ones, too, who think themselves *personages,* you will not wonder that the said business has been like Sisyphus's Stone, or Ixion's Cloud, or Tantalus's Apple, or anything else that's infernally troublesome. But it may, and, notwithstanding their greatness, probably it will, be very consequential. In the meantime I must deny myself both Suffolk and Cambridge. The former, indeed, is the self-denial; for Cam. I had more at head than at heart. Besides, wishing to establish my Mastery of Arts by a little residence near them, I had a little reading and writing also in contemplation, near the walks locally —*perlongo intervallo* in every other sense—of old Erasmus.

'I should have been happy in being at Bradfield Hall; I long to hear my friend refute himself, to complain with good spirits, and to demonstrate, with much wit, that he was extremely dull. But I dare say you have too much genuine vivacity, as well as good taste, to enter much into the bastard sort of alacrity—the intoxicated bustle that rages in empty heads and full pockets, by Royal proclamation. I should not object if the *cui bono?* could be answered. But in the present desperate size of power and depopulation of spirit, so much and so expensive pains seem little better than a curious folly. If a man's brains must be blown out, why need he gild his pocket pistol, much less purchase a great gun—unless it be a *Scotch canonade*, which, it must be confessed, will do the business, *con amore*, for England or Ireland?

'Yours ever,

'H. BOYD.'

I continued farming at Bradfield, and also reading and writing with much attention, as about this time I had formed the intention of delivering lectures on agriculture, and had prepared several. The original hint came from Mr. Wedderburn,[1] who persuaded me to persevere in this plan; but the lectures never took place. I was highly honoured by the commendation and partiality of a friend, Dr. Watson,[2] the celebrated Professor at Cambridge, afterwards Bishop of Llandaff, who wrote thus: 'We owe to the agricultural societies, and to the patriotic exertions of one deserving citizen (Arthur Young, Esq.), the present flourishing condition of our husbandry' ('Chemical Mag.' vol. 4).

I find from an application of my friend, Arbuthnot, that the Bishop of Chester was at this time collecting materials for a work on population by the Rev. Mr. Howlett,[3] and had desired Arbuthnot to apply to me for assistance. I was myself meditating such a work,

---

[1] Alex. Wedderburn, Earl of Rosslyn, Baron Loughborough. In 1778 Attorney-General; in 1793 succeeded Lord Thurlow to the Chancellorship. Died 1805.

[2] Richard Watson, a celebrated prelate. In 1796 he published an answer to Paine's *Age of Reason*. He was left an estate worth 24,000*l.* by a Mr. Luther, an entire stranger to him, author of many theological works and memoirs of himself. Died 1816.

[3] Died in 1804. There is a notice of this writer in Watts' *Bibliotheca Britannica*.

but complied with the request, and transmitted the collections I had made to the Bishop, who wrote me a most obliging letter.

'Your facts are clear and decisive, and the conclusions you draw from them, unanswerable. The only difficulty I am apprehensive of is that as his work is now pretty far advanced, and is already larger than I could wish he will not be able to take in the whole of your papers, especially as I observe that he has in some part of his pamphlet fallen into the same train of reasoning as yourself. If, therefore, you would allow him to take only your two general tables of baptism before and after the Revolution, and the two more recent periods of thirty years each, which is the very method he has himself adopted, subjoining such of your observations as are the most important and are not in some measure anticipated by him, he will be most exceedingly obliged to you, and will, I am sure, be very ready to acknowledge in proper terms the sense he has of your goodness to him.'

I had also a sad letter from my friend Arbuthnot on his return from France, but it was written in so melancholy a strain on his own situation and that of his wife and family, that it has often made my heart ache to read it. By Lord Loughborough's interest he got an appointment in Ireland under the Linen Board,[1] which carried him to that country, where he

---

[1] Irish Linen Board, established 1711; the Board abolished 1828. We do not learn upon what business Mr. Arbuthnot had gone to France.

lived but a few years. I lost in him by far the most agreeable friend I was ever connected with.

At this time I was much engaged in making a variety of experiments in expelling gaseous fluids from specimens of soils, the results of which were afterwards published in 'The Annals of Agriculture.' As I met with some difficulties I wrote to Dr. Priestley, stating them, and begging information. He very liberally and politely answered all my enquiries, encouraging me to proceed with my trials, and I received several interesting letters from him.

'Birmingham: Dec. 12, 1781.

'Dear Sir,—If I had any remarks or hints respecting the subject of your experiments, I should certainly with much pleasure have communicated them long ago. I meant, indeed, to have made a few more experiments on the growth of plants in the course of the last summer, but the weather was so bad, and the sun shone so little, that I dropped the scheme. All I can do, therefore, in return for your *facts*, is to mention one that I have lately observed. I readily convert *pure water* into *permanent air*, by first combining it with quicklime, and then exposing it to a strong heat. The weight of the air is equal to the weight of water, and no part of the water is turned into *steam* in the process. During the whole of it, a glass velum, interposed between the retort and the recipient for the air, remains quite cool and dry. The air I procure in this manner is in part *fixed air*, but the bulk of it is such as a candle would hardly burn in it, but is such as I should imagine would be the best for plants, which would purify it and render it fit for respiration. And as this kind of air would be yielded in great abundance by volcanoes, from calcareous matter in the earth; such was perhaps the original atmosphere of this earth, which according to the Mosaick account (which you must allow me to respect) had plants before there were any land animals.

'This letter I fear is hardly worth sending you; your objects and mine are so very different, though now and then coinciding; but mine have seldom any practical uses, at least no immediate ones, whereas yours are highly and immediately beneficial. Wishing you the greatest success, and wishing you and all philosophers joy of the near prospect of peace,

'I am, yours sincerely,

'J. PRIESTLEY.'

This year's memoranda: 'Wrote "Emigration," an ode.'

In the autumn of this year I spent a month at Lowestoft, where the sea air and bathing agreed so well with me that I do not recollect in my life ever having spent a month with so continued a flow of high spirits, which received no slight addition by the society of a very handsome and most agreeable girl, whose name I have forgotten.[1]

In a letter from Dr. Burney (of this year) he rallied

[1] That Arthur Young's society was equally agreeable to the other sex Fanny Burney tells us. In the gossipy, ecstatic journal of her girlhood she writes: 'Last night, whilst Hetty, Susey, and myself were at tea, that lively, charming, spirited Mr. Young entered the room. Oh, how glad we were to see him!'

me with much wit on my culture of the earth instead of the Muses. This friend of mine had a happy talent of rendering his letters lively and agreeable, indeed they were a picture of the man, for I never met with any person who had more decided talents for conversation, eminently seasoned with wit and humour, and these talents were so at command that he could exert them at will. He was remarkable for some sprightly story or witty *bon mot* just when he quitted a company, which seemed as much as to say, ' There now, I have given you a dose which you may work upon in my absence.' His society was greatly sought after by all classes, from the first nobility to the mere *homme de lettres*. He dressed expensively, always kept his carriage, and yet died worth about 15,000*l*., leaving a most capital library of curious books. His second wife was my wife's sister, the handsome widow of a Mr. Allen, of Lynn, who in a short life in commerce made above 40,000*l*., leaving her a handsome fortune and her two daughters equally provided for.

This year I had a controversy in the 'Bury St. Edmunds News' with Capel Lofft, Esq.,[1] on the proposal which originated with the Earl of Bristol,[2] for building a 74-gun ship and presenting it to the public. I wrote

---

[1] A Suffolk squire, ardent Whig, and of considerable literary attainments. At his expense was published Bloomfield's *Farmer's Boy*.

[2] Frederick Hervey, Episcopal Earl of Bristol. The *Annual Register* for 1803 has the following: 'His love of art and science was only surpassed by love of his country and generosity to the unfortunate of every country. He was a great traveller, and there is not a country of Europe in which the distressed have not obtained his succour. He was among the leaders of Irish patriots during the American War, and a member of the Convention of Volunteer Delegates in 1782. He was on this

a paper in favour of this scheme, which so pleased Lord Bristol that he complimented me on my eloquent, spirited language, and he caused a numerous edition of it to be printed and given away. Lofft attacked the scheme as unconstitutional, I retorted, and a paper war ensued which lasted for some time, and was afterwards published. The Earl of Shelburne, at that time Minister, wrote several letters to Lord Bristol in which he appeared highly gratified by this plan. Capel Lofft at the conclusion of our controversy wrote to me a very polite letter, expressing his satisfaction that our names should be united in the same publication. These papers were read with much avidity, and established the Bury paper in which they were written, to the great emolument of the proprietor.

Prince Potemkin, the Russian Prime Minister, sent this year to England three young men consigned to the care of M. Smirnove, chaplain to the Russian Embassy, who requested that I would fix them in my immediate vicinity, in order that I might pay some attention to their progress and acquisitions. This I readily did, and took every means to have them well instructed in the English mode of cultivating land.[1]

1782.—This year Mrs. Cousmaker, sister to my mother, died in her house at Bradfield. She was a

---

occasion escorted from Derry to Dublin by volunteer cavalry, receiving military honours at every town. He died at Albano, Rome, surrounded by artists whose talents his judgment had directed and whose wants his liberality had supplied.'

[1] By an irony of fate, Arthur Young, who had found farm after farm in his own hands a disaster, was now by general acceptance the first European authority on agriculture.

maiden lady who never would marry, though she had several advantageous offers. She left me her house and two farms, and a long annuity in the funds of 150*l.* a year, which expired about fifteen years afterwards. She had 300*l.* per annum of three annuities, the whole of which had once been left to me, but being much offended with my wife she gave half of it to another person. She also left me her carriage and horses. She was a very religious character; the bequest in her will by which she left the farms to me was not expressed exactly according to her mind, and she therefore altered it with her own hand after executing the will. This vitiated the legacy, on consulting Lord Loughborough, and he had doubts upon the question; but upon taking the opinion of several great lawyers, they declared the legacy null, and that the estates lapsed to the heir of law. This was John Cousmaker, Esq., of Hackney, who very generously declared that he would not take advantage of the error, and desired that Joshua Sharpe, a celebrated solicitor, might draw up a deed, by which he might make good the intention, which was accordingly done. Such an instance of uncommon liberality deserves to be recorded for the credit of mankind.

This year the Episcopal Earl of Bristol lived at Ickworth both summer and winter, and having very early called upon me after coming to the title and estate, a great intimacy took place between us; and Lord B. desired me to dine with him every Thursday, which I did through the whole year. Mr. Symonds, Professor of Modern History at Cambridge, Sir John

Cullum,[1] author of the 'History of Hawstead,' a very learned antiquary, and the Rev. George Ashby, Rector of Barrow,[2] another antiquary, and a man of universal knowledge, who for many years wrote a multitude of papers in the 'Gentleman's Magazine,' being constantly of the party. It was a trait in this nobleman's character, which deserved something more than admiration, to select men distinguished for knowledge and ability as his companions.

Lord Bristol was one of the most extraordinary men I ever met with. He was a perfect original—dressed in classical adorning; he had lived much abroad, spoke all modern languages fluently, and had an uncommon vein of pleasantry and wit, which he greatly exerted, and without reserve, when in the company of a few select friends. When abroad, and for many years afterwards, he lived in a manner that was not very episcopal. He had been so long absent from Ireland that the Primate wrote him three letters of remonstrance, and the answer he sent him was to do up and send in three blue peas in a blue bladder. The old proverb symptomatic of contempt, 'Oh! that is but three blue peas,' &c., is well known. The Bishop removing, he could not be forced back, and remained where he was. In my life I never passed more agreeable days than these weekly dinners at Ickworth. The conversation was equally instructive and agreeable. This eccentric man built in Ireland a large and very

[1] *The History and Antiquities of Hawstead and Hardwicke, in Suffolk.* The second edition appeared in 1813, with notes by Sir T. Gery-Cullum.

[2] Author of many antiquarian treatises.

expensive round house, on a plan as singular as himself; and, what was more extraordinary, a repetition of it at Ickworth. The shell of the body was finished and covered in; the wings scarcely begun, and nothing done towards completing the centre. Above 40,000*l*. was expended, and it would require much more than forty more to finish it on the original plan, after which it would be nearly uninhabitable. Lady Bristol used to call it a stupendous monument of folly; but the most extraordinary circumstance in relation to it was, that he began it while he disliked the spot, from the wetness of the soil, and would often tell me that he should never be such a fool as to build in so wet a situation. It was then generally imagined that as he must inherit Rushbrooke he would wait till that period, and if he built at all, would do it there. It was begun and carried on till the time of his death without his ever having seen it; and he often declared in letters that he never would set his foot in England till it was finished and furnished with all the *vertu* that he had collected in Italy. He never did set his foot in England again, for the shell of this fantastic building, and that of its still more extraordinary possessor, were finished at the same time, and my Lord left the whole, as if by design, a burthen to his son and successor, with whom he had been on the worst terms, and from whom he gave away by will the very furniture of the old habitable house at Ickworth. At the Thursday dinners I, of course, met all who were visitors to the family, among whom Lord B.'s uncle, General Hervey, was sometimes present. This was another uncommon character in some respects, but had not half the originality of his brother. He, too, was a most determined infidel, but had so far an expectation, not only of a future state, but also a kind of instinctive belief of the possibility of rewards and punishments, that acting happily for others, poor man, if not for himself, this half-faced belief made him one of the most charitable men living. His morning rides were generally amongst the poor of the neighbouring parishes, amongst whom he distributed clothing, food, and bedding, with money to take them out of difficulties, in a spirit of liberality rarely equalled, and gave away during a long course of years more in charity than thousands who had ten times his fortune. This instance may excite a reflection upon the weakness of judging a man's religion only by his works; for surely it would be a strange absurdity to take the measure of piety in the heart by any circumstance of the conduct which would be emulated or surpassed by an infidel. But what is charity when the right motive is wanting?

In my library [1] is a complete edition of Rousseau's works, given me by the Earl of Bristol.

About this time my friend, the Rev. Mr. Valpy,[2] who had for some time been Usher at the Grammar School of Bury St. Edmunds, was elected master of that at Reading, and a correspondence commenced which lasted many years. He was a most learned, ingenious and agreeable man, in so much that I greatly regretted

[1] Sold by auction in December 1896.
[2] Richard Valpy, D.D., 1754–1836, distinguished scholar, voluminous writer on educational works, and author of the famous Greek and Latin grammars.

his departure, feeling most sensibly the loss of his society. I have been occasionally connected with him since, and shall always hold him in great estimation for his learning, his talents, and sincerity of friendship. My son was under his tuition for some years. In the following letter my brother describes the state of this nation, which he thinks miserably bad :—

'Eton College: Oct. 31, 1782.

'Dear Arthur,—I wrote to you three days ago, and yesterday I received yours, complaining that I write no politicks. If you can, I cannot think of them with any degree of patience. We are a ruined people, tearing ourselves to pieces, everyone thinking of his party and himself, and no one caring for the publick, and that is the truth whatever you may hear or read. There is not a blockhead in England, who can only read and write and some who can only sign their names, of whom I could give you instances, who does not think himself qualified to new model the constitution. All true regard for liberty, and law, and a free government is gone, and there seems to be a general resolution not to be governed at all, which must end in despotism. We have no Ministry, nor do I see how we can have any. The whole summer has been spent in enlisting recruits against the winter. The friends of the old Ministry give out that Lord North has the decisive votes, which I think may be true. He was very lately unengaged, and, I am glad to hear, has declared positively against all innovations. For I am sure there is neither honesty, nor knowledge, nor abilities in this generation, to be trusted with altering our constitution. There are but two modes of governing—by power, or by influence. I desire to be governed by influence, but not that the influence may be so great as to be equivalent to power. I think that the Bill,[1] taking away the votes of the Revenue officers, will have great effect if ever executed, and am against proceeding further till I see the consequences of that Bill. I would annihilate the enormous plates in the Exchequer, but that would not much affect the influence of the Crown. As to increasing the Navy— what do you mean? Can you possibly increase your Navy without increasing the number of your seamen? And can you increase them without increasing your trade? You have already more ships than you can man. When your silly Suffolk scheme of building a ship was first mentioned to Lord Keppel, he said: If they could find him seamen he should be obliged to them, for he had ten more ships ready if he had seamen to put into them. We have got into one of those stupid wars which the Tories have always clamoured for, a naval war with France, without any land war in which our men might die in German ditches; we pay no subsidies to German princes for defending themselves, and you see how it has succeeded. The French having no diversion of their wealth to a land war are superior at sea, as any man of common sense might have foreseen. If your Suffolk gentry would take care

[1] This Bill to disable Revenue officers from voting in Parliamentary elections was introduced April 16, 1782, and read a third time on the 25th; read a third time in the House of Lords by 34 Contents to 18 Non-contents. *See* Hansard.

of their own duty and suppress the smuggling on their coast, it would be well. The Parliament will supply Government with money, levied equally on the subject, to build ships as they are wanted; and Government is by common law armed with power to avail itself of every seaman in the country; and that is the only just and equitable way of providing a Navy.

'I shall be in town next month, and will call on our Aunt Ingoldsby. I am sorry to hear that my mother's memory fails so fast; it frightens me out of my wits every time I forget anything.

'Yours very affectionately,

'J. YOUNG.'

CHAPTER VI

FIRST GLIMPSE OF FRANCE, 1783-1785

Birth of Bobbin—Ice baths—'The Annals of Agriculture'—A group of friends—Lazowski—First glimpse of France—Death of my mother—The Bishop of Derry—Fishing parties—Rainham.

On May 5 of this year my dear Bobbin was born.[1] I passed the year at Bradfield, and was much in the society of many neighbouring gentlemen. At this time I was a desperate bather, going into the water every morning at four o'clock each winter, and with or without the obstruction of a thick coat of ice, having often to break it before I could bathe. All my friends much condemned the practice, and assured me that I should kill myself, but it became so habitual that their prophecies were vain. As soon as I was out of bed I continued my favourite practice, walking about two hundred yards to a bath I had constructed, and plunging in, notwithstanding the inclemency of the weather.

I had this year a severe fever, which occasioned several of my friends, with all the acrimony that a departure from the usual modes of life occasions,

---

[1] 'My lovely Bobbin'—christened Martha Ann—the adored child whose loss at the age of fourteen was the great sorrow of Arthur Young's life. The pet name of 'Bobbin' originated in that of 'Robin,' which the child gave herself but could not pronounce.

strongly to dissuade me from persisting in my scheme. I myself was firmly persuaded that it was not, as they declared, the cause of my illness, and therefore when I was perfectly recovered resumed the practice, which I continued for many years; and I once at Petworth, at Lord Egremont's, went into the bath at four in the morning, when the thermometer was below zero. Upon coming out, walked into the shrubbery, and rolled myself in the snow as an experiment to see the effect on my body; it had none, except that of increasing strength and activity, and was not at all disagreeable.

In January commenced one of the greatest speculations in my life—the publication of 'The Annals of Agriculture.' I had long meditated such a work, and corresponded upon it with Mr. Whyman Baker, of Ireland, who had promised communications. The plan which first suggested itself was peculiar, and to the exclusion of all private profit—with a constant publication of the printing and publishing accounts—but the booksellers applied to, rejected the idea, and the work appeared monthly, with very indifferent success, for about a twelvemonth. The correspondence being highly respectable, and no papers inserted without the name and place of abode of the writer, it rose gradually to the support of itself, and after a time enabled me to insert a great number of plates. It would have proved a very profitable publication but for the many numbers which were obliged to be reprinted. Printing only 500 afterwards occasioned reprinting another 500, still a third 500. This created so large an expense that it swallowed up everything that wore the resemblance of profit, and many years afterwards I continued reprinting various numbers for the sole object of completing sets; this formed a back current; which carried away what would have been profit. It may be added that many of those papers written by myself, forming perhaps a third or fourth of the whole work, may be reckoned among my most valuable productions, and have received the sanction of approbation, by being translated into several foreign languages. It is an anecdote which cannot be generally known, that two very able letters, which came under the name of Robinson, the King's shepherd at Windsor, were really the production of his Majesty's own pen, describing what he had long been intimately acquainted with, the husbandry of Mr. Ducket. The King took in two sets of the work, one of which he regularly sent to that farmer; and in the interview which I had with his Majesty upon the terrace of Windsor, the first word the King said to me was: 'Mr. Y., I consider myself as more obliged to you than to any other man in my dominions,' and the Queen told me that they never travelled without my 'Annals' in the carriage. Lord Fife informed me that he himself always had the 'Annals' sent him the moment they were published, but still he always found that the King was beforehand with him, for upon the first of the month, while the number was unopened upon his table, riding out and meeting his Majesty, he at once spoke to him on a paper of his own (Lord Fife's) in that number, showing that he had read the whole before it had met the eye of the author.

Among the letters I received this year the following may be particularly noted :—

From Lord Bristol, Bishop of Derry
'Londonderry: April 23, 1783.

'A thousand thanks to you, my dear friend, for your recollection of me at so many miles' distance, and for your summary Gazette of the present miscellaneous state of our neighbours, but no thanks at all to you for wishing me back to the foggy, fenny atmosphere of Ickworth, in preference to the exhilarating and invigorating air, or rather ether, of the Downhill. When you are *vapid*, if ever those *pétillant* spirits of yours are so, come and imbibe some fixed or unfixed air at the Downhill, where a tree is no longer a *rarity*, since above 200,000 have this winter been planted in the glens round my house; come and enjoy the rapidity and the success with which I have converted sixty acres of moor, by the medium of two hundred spades, into a *green* carpet, sprinkled with white clover. Am I not an adept in national dialect? Come and enjoy some mountain converted into arable, and grouse metamorphosed without a miracle, into men; come and teach a willing disciple and an affectionate friend how to finish a work he is barely able to begin.

'In all my leases to the tenants of the See, I have providently, and with a long forecast, made a reservation to myself of all the bog and mountain lands deemed unprofitable. Well, these I am enabled by statute to grant in trust for myself during sixty-one years. Now is the moment to execute this great purpose; the *reserved* acres amount to several thousands, and upon one mountain only I have received proposals for building 200 cabbins (cabins); the limestone is at the bottom of the hill, and the turf at the top. What gold may not this chemistry produce, and who do you think would himself submit to vegetate at Ickworth whilst he can direct such a laboratory at the Downhill?

'Can Ashby crawl—*Quantum mutatus ab illo*? I shall next expect to hear of Arthur's creeping. Mure I knew always to be a prince in his ideas; I am glad to hear he is able to be so in his works. Cullum can dignify any subject, and interest his reader in the most insignificant, so I conclude we all read even his Hawstead Antiquities with pleasure and instruction. But what is Symonds[1] about? not six yards round I hope like Falstaff—*Ipse quid agis, quae circumvolitas agilis thyma?*[2] Pray ramble once more to Ireland either by the proxy of a letter or in person. You will ever be welcome to your affectionate friend,

'BRISTOL.'

This year Arthur Young, an American prisoner, wrote to me asking charity; it deserves to be mentioned that in a book called 'England's Black Tribunal'[3] there is a list of emigrants to America in the seventeenth century, at the head of whom stands the name of Arthur

---

[1] Dr. J. Symonds, Professor of Modern History at Cambridge, was LL.D., and wrote a book, *Hints and Observations on Scripture*.

[2] The Bishop misquotes from memory. The quotation is from Horace, *Ep.* Bk. I. iii. 21; *agis* should be *audes*.

[3] Published 1703, giving an account of the trial of Charles I., of Montrose, &c.

FIRST GLIMPSE OF FRANCE 115

Young. The following letters are from James Barry,[1] the celebrated painter. This was a very singular character. I sat to him for the portrait which he inserted in his famous painting for the decoration of the Society's room.[2] I met him often at Dr. Burney's, and always found him to abound with original observations, which marked a character peculiarly his own. He always seemed to me to be proud of his poverty.

'Adelphi: April 1783.

'Dear Sir,—I am very much obliged to you for your kind letter, and hope your goodness will make every allowance for my not having answered it sooner, but of all things I hate writing at any time, more particularly at present, when I had resolved to allow myself some days' Sabbath, to the utter exclusion of all manner of labour, even of that which was most agreeable to me. I shall be sincerely obliged to you for your corrected copy of my account of the pictures,[3] and the freer and the more extensive your strictures are the more thankful I shall be; whatever is for use shall be adopted, and I will further promise you that whatever may not be to the purpose shall be thrown aside with as little reluctance as if I had written it myself. I expect to find you on a wrong scent in what you call *my violence*, which you may think *has been carried too far*, and I shall have a pleasure in setting you right as

[1] Died in great poverty, 1808, and was buried in St. Paul's Cathedral.
[2] The Society of Arts, Adelphi.
[3] This apparently refers to Barry's report of the Royal Academy.

to that matter the first time we meet. You will find nothing has arisen from resentment, nothing from a desire of retaliating, nothing from paltry, interested views; such motives, though I might be inclined to make allowance for them in others, I should reprobate in myself. It appeared to me a bounden duty to point out for the common good whatever I could discover of those quicksands, shoals, and rocks that obstruct and endanger our *viaggiatori* in the *belle arti*, and I am confident that the arts and the reputation of the country will receive essential service, whenever this chart (of which I have made but a rude sketch) shall be perfected by some man of more information and better abilities (though perhaps not of more love for truth, for the public and for science) and of penetration, energy, vivacity and perspicuity, to treat this matter as it deserves.

'Though I don't wish to hurry you, yet I hope your copy will come soon; I accept your terms, or rather I insist upon them, but do not content yourself with what you may have written in the margin, in which, upon this occasion, I am sorry to believe you must be straitened for want of room; however, you can stick papers between the leaves, and in charity spare not the rod, as it may save the child. I have on all hands got more praise than I well know what to do with, and something else may now be more profitable to me.

'In what you say of yourself I feel for the country— the loss is theirs, not yours. God Almighty has so ordered matters in this world that it is praiseworthy and honourable when genius and abilities will struggle to exert themselves for the service of others; it was for this end they were given, and with the consciousness of these honest and dutiful endeavours such men must be contented, and, indeed, ought to be happy, as no more can depend upon themselves. Others are to be accountable, and to receive glory or infamy for what is done on their part in the assistance or the obstruction they may have flung in the way. Farewell!

'Yours most affectionately,
'J. BARRY.'

'Adelphi: July 1783.

'Dear Sir,—I am delighted with your account of Ireland, 'tis wise, candid, bold, exceedingly humane, and just what the nature of the case required. I have long been sick at heart of the timid, trimming, mistakingly prudent, and palliating conduct of those writers who have been hitherto quacking and dabbling with the sores and miseries of that country, and was without the least hope of ever seeing this matter undertaken by any man of such sufficient courage, philanthropy, or charity (which are indeed but different points of view of the same virtue), as might obtain for us a fair, open and entire exposition of this unexampled and very melancholy case. Judge, then, what a pleasure I am receiving in the perusal of your book. You have, I find, probed the evil to the bottom, and left me without a wish. The men of Ireland are surely much indebted to you, and will, I trust, one day acknowledge it, but for the present you must have patience and ought to bear with them, as the illiberality or meanness you may justly complain of may fairly be ascribed to an unhappy combination of circumstances, owing principally to the tyrannical monopolising disposition and rascally interference of your own forefathers, who had with the most abominable and diabolical policy employed their whole skill and power utterly to erase from the minds of Irishmen all those noble and generous feelings which were incompatible with a servile and enslaved condition, and which ultimately estranged them from the exercise of even the ordinary vulgar virtues.

'In situations where men are divided into large bodies of tyrants and slaves, little good is to be expected. Their vices may differ, but they are all equally remote from virtue, truth, justice, gratitude, the love of excellence, or any other of those qualities which constitute the real dignity of human nature. Those who are attached to no country or description of men, but for the ends and furtherance of humanity, by equal justice and happiness, will with me rejoice and give Almighty God thanks for the dissolution of whatever has hitherto obstructed the growth and spreading of virtue, and for that just sense of the human dignity which is now diffusing itself so extensively in Ireland, and gives fair prospect of a plentiful harvest (in due season) of those other virtues which, though but thinly scattered in England, are at present, I fear, in vain to be sought for anywhere else.

'Yours most affectionately,
'JAMES BARRY.'

At this period commenced a most agreeable acquaintance with a French gentleman who came to Bury, and I must dilate a little on the origin of his journey. The Duke of Liancourt[1] was Colonel of a French regiment, the quarters of which were at Pont à Mousson, in Lorraine, to which he went every year, according to the regulations of the French army. At that place he accidentally met Monsieur de Lazowski,[2] son of a Pole, who came to Lorraine with King Stanislas. The Duke was so struck with his manner and conversation that he resolved to cultivate his acquaintance. About that time he was in want of a tutor for his two sons—not for the common purposes of education, but to travel with them. He accordingly engaged Lazowski to make the tour of France with these lads, the Count de la Rochefoucault and the Count Alexander de la Rochefoucault. The Duke thought it an important part of education to become well acquainted with their own country. During two years they travelled over the greatest part of the

---

[1] The friend of Louis XVI., who summoned courage to announce the fall of the Bastille. 'It is a revolt?' said the King. 'Sire,' replied the Duke, 'it is a revolution.' This amiable and well-intentioned man leaned towards a constitutional monarchy; finding this hopeless, he emigrated, returning after exile to Liancourt (Seine and Oise), ending his days among a community he had raised morally and materially. Died 1827.

[2] His brother must not be wholly judged from Madame Roland's portrait, penned in prison. The 'Queen of the Gironde' no more than her fellow-partisans was free from political animus. It is true that Lazowski threw himself into the very heart of *Sans-culottisme*, and that his funeral oration (1792) was pronounced by Robespierre. His alleged share in the September massacres requires stronger evidence than that of his bitterest enemies at bay.

kingdom on horseback. The Duke was so well pleased with the conduct of Lazowski on this journey that, having determined to send his sons to England in order to acquire the language of that country, and, generally, in compliance with the Anglomania which then reigned in France, he continued Lazowski in his situation and sent them all three to England. Among other objects in France, Lazowski had given some attention to agriculture, particularly in its connection with political economy. On his arrival in London he made enquiry who could most probably give him information relative to agriculture, manufactures, commerce and other national objects. Among others I was named to him by some person who was so partial in his representations that he at once determined to fix at Bury for a short time, which he understood was the nearest town to my country residence. He and the two young men went to the Angel Inn, from thence hired convenient apartments, and enquired where I resided. At that time I was absent, and Mr. Symonds, understanding that two young men of fashion from France were at Bury, introduced himself and showed them various civilities, and when I returned brought them over to Bradfield. From that time a friendship between me and Lazowski commenced, and lasted till the death of the latter. He was about forty years of age, and in every respect a most agreeable companion. He soon made rapid progress in the English language, which he spoke not only with fluency, but often with extreme wittiness. There was not in his mind any strong predominant cast; but the grace and facility of his manner, with suavity of temper, made him a great favourite, and being also highly elegant and refined, he often produced impressions which were not easily effaced. From his general conversation in mixed society it was not readily concluded that he could or would attend with great industry and perseverance to objects of importance. But this would have been erroneous, for he exerted the greatest industry in making himself a master of all those circumstances which mark the basis of national prosperity, and he formed in his own mind a very correct comparison of the resources both of Britain and France. He often expressed to me much surprise at what he thought on this subject in England, and declared that the ignorance of the French relative to their great rival was most profound. The Duke of Liancourt was highly gratified by his correspondence, and after he had resided some time, first at Bury and afterwards with Mr. Symonds, he was directed to take the young men a tour through England and Scotland, which he did. The Duke himself came over on a visit to Symonds while his sons and their tutor were in the house. Soon after his arrival in England, hearing that there were such carriages at Bury as were called buggies, and desiring to make use of all sorts, he ordered one to be hired to convey him and Lazowski to Bradfield. On its coming to the door, Lazowski perceiving that, though it was drawn by one horse only, it ran upon the quarter,[1] he would have persuaded

[1] 'That part of a horse's foot between the toe and heel, being the side of the coffin.'—*Farrier's Dict.*

the Duke not to attempt driving, as it would be 20 to 1 that he would overthrow it; but the Duke, full of presumption, held such prudential advice in contempt, and, whipping away, had not gone half a mile in a cross road before he overturned the carriage, and in the fall dislocated his shoulder. The Duke was conveyed to Symonds. Lazowski instantly rode off to inform me of the accident, and the Duke expressed no more desire to drive carriages he had never seen. Lazowski's connection with the Duke was not put an end to when the education of his sons was finished; he was so useful that he continued his salary and an apartment in the Hôtel de la Rochefoucauld, Paris, and I often admired the independent spirit with which he lived in the family. A dinner did not often pass without an argument between him and the Duke, which was carried on with a great deal of heat on both sides. On such occasions Lazowski never gave up the shadow of an opinion, and being gifted with more natural fluency than the Duke, he had usually the better of the argument. This was equally to the credit of both. His employment was chiefly drawing up memorials upon political subjects for the Duke's information, who was a vain man, and, without doubt, figured in conversation by this subsidiary assistance. His vanity appeared in one circumstance in which he attempted much more than he could perform. While he was in the bath, or dressing by his *valet de chambre*, he had three secretaries, to whom he pretended to dictate at the same time. One of them told Lazowski that it was scarcely credible how they were fatigued by his incessant blunders. Yet in France, perhaps, this very attempt gave a sort of reputation. It was suspected that he merely attempted this in imitation of Cæsar, who did the same thing, but in a very different manner, it is presumed, from the D. de Liancourt. With a view similar to that of retaining Lazowski, he gave an apartment to Jarré, an officer who had long been in the Russian service, and afterwards became famous for burning the suburbs of Courtray. He was well known in England as General Jarré, and placed at the head of the Military Asylum at Wycombe. While I was in France, M. Jarré published an octavo volume under the title of 'Crédit National,' a whimsical work, in which the arguments were very ill supported. Lazowski always showed me great friendliness, and I returned it with great constancy and truth. Among all the men I met with in France, attached to the higher classes or constituting them, all were infidels, and poor Lazowski of the number. He never lost himself so completely as when he entered into an argument upon the truth of Christianity with the Bishop of Llandaff, for, though civilly done, the Bishop ground him to powder. The latter, of course, thought him nothing but a frothy Frenchman, like most of his countrymen, with Voltaire in his head and the devil in his heart, all of whom would have talked the same language had they had the same opportunity. Before Lazowski and his pupils had learnt English, Symonds took them to Cambridge, and introduced them to the Bishop, who, understanding that the young men were of high rank in France, and knowing that he spoke French himself with difficulty, put on his canonicals to receive his foreign guests, and, entering the room with a most stately air, addressed them all in Latin, hinting to Symonds the propriety, as Latin was the language of that learned University, and, therefore, in using it he was classically right. The Frenchmen, of course, replied with plenty of bows and grimaces to every learned sentence rolled out in most majestic tone from the Bishop's mouth, but giving no other answer. The Bishop was at last compelled to address them in his broken French: 'Latin, gentlemen, is our language here, but perhaps you had rather I should speak in bad French than not use that language at all!' and then relaxing his episcopal dignity, he conversed with them at ease and quieted their ruffled spirits.

1784.—This year I took a journey with my son for farming intelligence into Essex and Kent, &c., and, being at Dover, we went over to Calais just to enable us to say that we had been in France. But I had another motive, which was to see M. Mouron, and the capital improvements that gentleman had made near Calais. We lived three or four days at Dessein's celebrated inn. M. Mouron not only showed me his great farm, but explained to me every circumstance of the improvements, which I printed in the 'Annals.' Some years before the Empress Catherine had sent over seven or eight young men to learn practical agriculture, two or three of whom were fixed with my friend Arbuthnot, and others in different parts of the Kingdom. They were under the superintendence of the Rev. Mr. Sambosky, who wrote to me at Bradfield earnestly requesting that I would go to London and examine all the young men, that he might take or send them to St. Petersburg. This I accordingly did, and examined them very closely, except one, who refused to answer any questions from a conviction of his absolute ignorance. I gave a certificate of the others' examination, and I asked Sambosky what would become of the obstinate fool who would not answer. He replied that without doubt he would be sent to Siberia for life, but I never heard whether this happened. One of them, by much the ablest, remained in England, and became in time Chaplain to the Russian Embassy, in which situation he is at the present time, and held in general esteem. The intended establishment of an Imperial farm never took place, and after at least an expenditure of 10,000*l.*, the men on their arrival were turned loose, some to starve, some driven into the army, and others retained by Russian noblemen. In this wretched and ridiculous manner did the whole scheme end, which, under a proper arrangement, might have been attended with very important effects. Prince Potemkin, one of the first noblemen in the Russian Empire, must have been animated with truly liberal and enlarged ideas, or he would not now have sent three young men to learn practical agriculture. It gave me the greatest pleasure to be able to promote their enquiries during a part of their residence here.

1785.—This year I wrote a note in the 'Annals' relative to a great work I had long been engaged in, which it may not be here amiss to insert, viz.: to collect, under regular heads, all the well-ascertained facts that are scattered through books of agriculture, and, *inter alia*, in other works, with those to be deduced from the common practice of various countries; to interweave experiments made purposely to ascertain the doubtful points; and to combine the whole into regular elements of the Science is the great desideratum at present. It is a work more proper for an Academy on a Royal foundation than for any individual. But as no such Academy is to be looked for, and as all private societies pay their attention to desultory objects, as often to those already ascertained as to points in which we want information the most, I undertook the work myself more than ten years ago.[1]

I had this year the misfortune to lose my mother, to whom I was most tenderly attached, and with the greatest reason, as her kindness and affection for me had never failed during the course of her whole life. She had been educated in the most religious manner by her father, Mr. de Cousmaker, of whom mention has already been made as a character eminently pious, but it was not till the loss of my sister, Mrs. Tomlinson, that deep affliction recalled in her heart those sentiments of religion which had been

[1] This project developed into one much more formidable than the writer at this period conceived, namely, that monumental history—or, rather, encyclopædia—of agriculture never destined to see the light. For three-quarters of a century the ten folio volumes of manuscript garnished the library of Bradfield Hall, perhaps once in twenty years to be taken down by some curious guest. What was to have been Arthur Young's crowning achievement and legacy to future ages is, fortunately, not wholly lost to posterity. The ten volumes are now housed in the MS. department of the British Museum.

BRADFIELD HALL AS IN ARTHUR YOUNG'S TIME.

so assiduously cultivated in her youth. She was always extremely fond of me, and ever eager to do what could contribute to my satisfaction, both as to worldly views, but especially as to my eternal interests.

The tranquil bosom of my good mother's hermitage —my native Bradfield—once more opened its arms to receive us, little more than to come to close the eye and receive the last signs of that beloved parent. Blessed spirit!—may my hitherto restless days finish as thine did, who didst meet death with the tranquillity of a healthy life, and mightst have said with as much justice as an Addison, ' See with what peace a Christian can die.'

Upon her death this patch of landed property [1] devolved to me by a previous agreement with my elder brother, and by my mother's will, written at his desire with his own hand. But that agreement before it terminated cost me a mortgage of 1,200*l.* The transaction does my brother's memory too much honour not to mention it. He was entitled to 2,000*l.*, but knowing the smallness of the property, and humanely considering that I had a family unprovided for, that he had an ample income and no family at all, he generously demanded and took no more than 1,200*l.* Whether such things happen among relations or strangers, they should be mentioned for the credit of the human heart.

My correspondence this year was, upon the whole, interesting, as a few of the letters will show. From the

[1] Bradfield Hall was sold on the death of Arthur Young's last descendant, the late Arthur Young, Esq., in 1896.

Earl of Bristol, a panegyric on agriculture; another from the same, an animated defence of the Presbyterians.

'Downhill, Coleraine: Jan. 15, 1785.

'My dear Arthur,—I am mortified, and should really be ashamed to see your entertaining letter so long unanswered, but that the multiplicity, as well as variety of my occupations, bereave me sometimes of the most pleasing ones; from sunrise to long after sunset I am not a moment idle, either in mind or person, and I can venture to assure you that agriculture, being the basis of all public and private virtues, as it banishes laziness, fortifies the body, leads to fair and honest procreation, provides sustenance and multiplies the tenderest and most endearing ties in nature, has no little share both of my time and attention. Let one hundred and fifty men daily employed verify my assertion; let the rocks which disappear and the grass which succeeds to them corroborate that evidence. But, then, what have I to do with the English plough? Neither our soil, nor our climate, nor our labourers are the same; we are poor and you are rich; when industry has approximated a little of our wealth to yours perhaps we may be tempted to adopt your luxury in agriculture, unless before that you shall have discovered your errors and so saved us the trouble of retracting what we have not had time to adopt.

'As to my Presbyterians, I am glad you are modest enough not to censure those, whom you are honest enough to confess you do not know; all the harm which I find in them is that they love the rights of mankind, and if in pursuing them for themselves they refuse to participate with their fellow citizens, I would join in your execrations, and set them a better example than hitherto they have received from our church. Adieu! let me hear from you sometimes when you have nothing better to do, and tell Symonds, with my affectionate compliments, that I have recovered my lost map of the Pontine marshes, and will send it by the first opportunity. If you ever see the learned and good-humoured Rector (Reverend George Ashby) don't let him forget

'Your affectionate friend,
'BRISTOL.'

'Downhill, Coleraine : March 9, 1785.

'Dear Arthur,—I have but just received yours of the 19th, and though I do not think my letters worth paying for, yet since you do, and I have a leisure half hour, have at you. And in this duel of our pens, who would expect a Bishop of the Established Church to be an advocate for the anti-Episcopal Schismatics, called Presbyterians, whilst a man whose religion lies in his plough and his garden, that is, with the Goddess of the one and with the God of the other, to be so zealous an opponent? My defence rests principally on this point, that they have as good a right to differ from me as my ancestors from our joint ancestors, or the Church established above twelve hundred years before.

'As to their political principles, I think them, from

their system of parity, and from their practice in most parts of Europe, infinitely more favourable to political liberty than ours.

'Witness Germany and Switzerland and the short reign of *Old Nol*.

'You say, "But their political principles never became powerfully active without involving their country in a civil war." And are there not two words to that bargain, and does not the *pot* call the *kettle*, &c. &c.?[1] You might as well object the same to all good citizens when oppressed by bad ones; you may as well object the same to the first Brutus and to the second; you may as well object it to Luther and Melanchthon. Did the Presbyterians ask anything unreasonable when they desired to have *their* nonsense tolerated as well as other nonsense? for if it be nonsense 'tis paying *it* too great a compliment, and ourselves too bad a one, to persecute it; and if it be good sense, surely, for one's own sake, as well as that of our neighbours, it deserves a better reception than persecution.

'When I see Switzerland and Germany pacified for above 150 years, after throat-cutting for 140, by the single means of a reciprocal toleration, and by the Pacta Conventa of 1648,[2] which allowed them to share those loaves and fishes alternately monopolised by each party, I must confess, if I were Frederick the First of Oceana, or of Atlantis, I should not hesitate to begin my reign with that system with which most

---

[1] Proverb, 'The pot calls the kettle black.'—*Bailey's Dict.*
[2] The Peace of Westphalia.

sovereigns are compelled to close theirs! The rights of humanity, dear Arthur, the rights of humanity form a great article in my creed, and that religion, or sect of religion, which can teach otherwise may come from below, but surely did not descend from above.

'Believe me, our whirlwind is not past, perhaps 'tis only just beginning; yet three hundred labourers with their spades fill my mind's eye with as pleasing and as satisfactory ideas as the whole Coleraine Battalion with their muskets before my door. If in this whirlwind *I* can direct the storm, so much the better for humanity, but not for the lank-haired Divinity, nor the frizzle-topped Divinity, nor the hocus-pocus Divinity.

'I love agriculture because it makes good citizens, good husbands, good fathers, good children; because it does not leave a man time to plunder his neighbour, and because by its plenty it bereaves him of the temptation; and I hate an aristocratical Government because it plunders these honest fellows; because it is idle; it is insolent; it values itself on the merits of it, and because, like an overbearing torrent, the farther it is removed from its fountain head, and the less it partakes of its original purity, the more desolation it carries with it; and because, like a stinking, stagnated pool, it inflicts those very disorders which it was the chief merit of its spring and fountain head to heal and remove.

'Adieu.

'Ever affectionately,

'BRISTOL.'

My brother, the Rev. Dr. Young, Fellow of Eton College, in this letter informs me that the King reads my 'Annals' and is much pleased with them, and highly approves of my arguments to show that we are far enough from being in a ruined state.

'Eton College: May 1, 1785.

'Dear Arthur,—I have two of your letters to answer; the latter directed to Worcester, why, I know not, for I never intended to be there till the beginning of next month. I see no reason for your being at the expense you allude to for the public, and think you ought to be indemnified; you cannot afford these journeys to London, and so I would plainly tell the Ministers.

'Yesterday se'nnight as I returned from the chase the King spoke to me of you in very handsome terms; I find that he reads your publications.

'He commended particularly your recent periodical work as being very useful, and was much pleased with your argument to prove that we are not a ruined people, but have great resources. I told him that you had been sent for by Mr. Rose,[1] which he did know.

'You wrote to me some time ago that you were of the same opinion with Lord Sheffield, but now you write that the commercial part of their measure[2] is very good, but the political part is very bad. How do you reconcile this, for Lord S. is against the commercial part?

[1] George Rose, President of the Board of Trade. Died 1818.
[2] This measure is referred to on page 137.

'I wish you would explain this, for I am against both parts, though, I confess, no judge.

'You ask whether I continue my new trade of hunting. If you think it is a profitable one you are much mistaken; so far indeed it is, that I hope to take this year twenty pounds out of my apothecary's bill; I have not been for some winters so well as I have been since I took to hunting, and I hope to continue the trade next year. I was yesterday seven hours and a half on horseback, and rode certainly fifty-five miles, besides fifteen more home from Henley in a post-chaise, which is pretty well at fifty-seven years old.

'I have two very fine horses; the King, who is generally but moderately mounted, will tell you the two best in the hunt.

'Why would you not call on me when you were in town?

'Adieu, dear Arthur.

'Yours affectionately,

'JOHN YOUNG.'

From Dr. Valpy, who corrected a poem I sent him, and, to my surprise, approves of my poetry:—

'My dear Friend,—I beg your pardon again and again for keeping your poem so long. Unhappily I had mislaid it, and chance only recovered it. There runs a vein of fancy through your poetry which stamps a high character upon it, and would your genius but stoop to the minutiæ of correctness would raise you to an exalted rank in that line. Whether you will approve my alterations or not I cannot tell, but it would be difficult to point out more inaccuracies in the poem. You obliged me much by your introductory number. I had sent for one before, with a view to lend it to my friends and to engage them to become purchasers of the work. It is very correctly written, except that sometimes you use *shook* as a participle.

'Everybody here is Pitt mad. Addresses upon addresses crowd the avenue to St. James's. It has even been proposed to offer Mr. Pitt a seat in Parliament for this town if Mr. Neville can be engaged to put up for the county. Our county meeting was no bad an epitome of the House of Commons. We had some excellent speeches. I had occasion to be at the Oxfordshire meeting—a most shabby wrangle and scene of illiberal confusion. I admire Mr. Pitt—and do not like Fox; but ought not a dissolution to have taken place, or the people have instructed their representatives rather than suffer the House of Commons to be so degraded? What are your sentiments on this unhappy dissension? Sorry, very sorry I am that you would not come down to Reading. I am certain you must have met with an opportunity. It was my intention last Christmas to have paid you a visit, but I had some friends with me. Next Christmas, however, I mean to see Suffolk, if possible. Cullum is still here.

'The present state of my school is this : six-and-thirty boarders and three parlour boarders, besides day scholars. I have two ushers. I sometimes hear of your brother, but I have not met with him. I am told he has a mortal aversion to everything that comes from Oxford.

'*March* 18.—I hope your family and the materfamilias are in a prosperous way. Pray give my best respects to Mrs. Young, and remember me to the young ladies and my old scholar. Something I have heard of another child. One of the greatest luxuries that I sigh for in life is that you lived near me. But inconveniences of absence do not seem likely to be prevented by your endeavour to come after me. Let me, however, hear from you as often as you can.

'Adieu.

'R. VALPY.'

I find by memoranda that I was busied in the imagination of new fish-ponds,[1] taking lively interest in and examining how much of the low meadow at Bradfield could be laid under water. What led me to this folly is not easy to conceive, because I could have afforded to attempt the making of an ocean as much as of a pond; but how often is the register of a life the register of human folly?

I was (this year) elected an honorary member of the Royal Society of Agriculture of Paris.[2] About this time I went on a farming journey to the Bakewells,[3] in Leicestershire; it was a very instructive journey and

---

[1] Arthur Young's fishing parties are described in Fanny Burney's *Camilla*.

[2] Founded 1785.

[3] Robert Bakewell, died 1795, a celebrated grazier. It was wittily remarked that 'his animals were too dear for anyone to buy, and too fat for anyone to eat.'

in which I gained a great deal of valuable information. I also spent several days about this time with Lord Townshend[1] at Rainham and his uncommonly agreeable young wife, equally elegant and beautiful. During my visit I had an ample opportunity of admiring the noble picture of Belisarius by Salvator Rosa, a performance which can never be too highly commended. With the agreeableness of this noble family, and especially of Lady Townshend, I rendered my visit extremely pleasing.

The noble Lord, to whose liberal attention I owe much information, came to his estate in so high a degree of cultivation, owing to the unrivalled exertions of his grandfather, that little was left for him to perform; a life of great activity and service, had the situation of his property been different, would not have allowed a minute's attention. These notes will, however, show that Lord Townshend has not been idle at Rainham.

On my arrival there I was anxious to view that part of the estate chiefly near the house, which was improved by a man who quitted all the power and lustre of a Court for the amusements of agriculture.

Charles, Lord Viscount Townshend, who was Ambassador Extraordinary to the States General in 1709, a Lord of the Regency on the death of Queen Anne,

---

[1] 'Turnip Townshend,' ancestor of the Lord Townshend here named, was celebrated in the famous lines—

> 'Why of two brothers, rich and restless, one
> Ploughs, burns, manures, and toils from sun to sun;
> The other slights for women, sports, and wines,
> All Townshend's turnips and all Grosvenor's mines.'
> *Pope's 6th translation of Horace.*

Knight of the Garter, Lord Lieutenant of Ireland, twice Secretary of State, and Lord President of the Council, resigned the seals in May 1730, and, as he died in 1738, it is probable that this period of eight years was that of his improvements round Rainham.

The Irish propositions [1] which were at this time under the consideration of Government meeting with many unforeseen difficulties, I had a letter from Mr. Rose requesting information relative to the comparative circumstances of the two kingdoms, and Mr. Pitt thought the information so much to the purpose that he desired Mr. Rose to write to me requesting my attendance in town. I accordingly went, and gave Mr. Pitt the information he wished, at the same time answering an abundance of collateral enquiries, for which I received a formal letter of thanks. My correspondence with Mr. Rose recurred several times after these interviews. In his third letter he requested to be informed of the amount of a labourer's consumption of taxed commodities, in order to ascertain what excises and other taxes such consumption supports. 'I conceive,' he wrote, 'that the articles consumed by that description of people are leather, candles, soap, beer, probably some spirits, and perhaps a small quantity of starch. I wish also very much to know what their chief diet is, and the price of the articles in the different parts of the country.' [2]

---

[1] This seems to refer to Mr. Pitt's resolutions upon the commercial intercourse between England and Ireland. The debate thereon began February 22, 1785. *See* Hansard.

[2] How different would be the list of a labouring man's 'necessaries' in these days!

CHAPTER VII

FIRST FRENCH JOURNEY, 1786–1787

Death of my brother—Anecdotes of his character—Dr. Burney on farming — Greenwich *versus* Eton — Blenheim — Correspondence with Dr. Priestley—County toasts—French projects—First French journey.

THIS year my brother died. He was in the habit of hunting with the King, and having heard of a very fine hunter to be sold in Herefordshire, he sent his servant to purchase him. It was the end of the season, but the King appointing one day more for the sport, Dr. Young determined to try his new horse, and he went in company with another gentleman to the field. His friend observed to him that his horse tripped in an odd manner, to which Dr. Y. replied: 'It is the last day of hunting, and I shall see how he performs.' 'Take care,' said the other, 'that it is not the last day of your life.' He persisted in the trial, and was for a time much pleased with his horse in several leaps; in taking another it struck its own legs against an obstruction, threw his rider, whose neck was instantly broken. He was taken up dead and carried home. Thus died my nearest relative, who was a man of very peculiar talents and of most singular originality of character. He had a great deal of eccentric wit, and was extremely beloved by many intimate friends, amongst whom were several of the Townshends, Cornwallises, and the Duke of Grafton, with whom he was on the most intimate terms, and was a great favourite of the Duchess. Cornwallis, Archbishop of Canterbury, valued him so much for his rectitude of conduct in this that he determined to promote him to the best preferment that should fall in his gift, and I have several letters from him repeating this intention. Thus ended a life that promised so many advantages, for he was high in favour with the King, who was pleased not only frequently to converse with him, but to ask his opinion respecting many sermons which were at that time published. Thus high in expectation of further promotion, to lose his life in so unexpected and sudden a manner was indeed singularly awful and unfortunate. It was a dreadful blow also to all my son's hopes, for as he was educating at Eton for the Church, my brother, who had his turn as Fellow of Eton and Prebendary of Worcester in about seventy pieces of preferment, and had passed all by that came to give away, stood high in the lists purposely with a view of promoting Arthur.[1] There was in Dr. Young a steady rectitude of principle, an absolute abhorrence of every mean and unworthy action, great natural parts, and as he had been Captain (I think), or very near it, of Eton School, he went to King's at Cambridge a capital scholar.

The following anecdote relative to my brother I

[1] Arthur Young's only son, born 1769.

copy from a letter to my wife, written by my old friend Professor Symonds :—

'I assure you, Madam, that I was really at a loss to conjecture whether you were in earnest or not when you desired an answer to your letter; but in case you were in earnest (which I can now hardly think, since the question might be answered better in conversation), you must be surprised and offended by my neglect; but I defy you to have been more surprised than you will be at my charging your husband with this letter. I concealed from him the purport of it, but judged it necessary to inform him that there was not the shadow of an intrigue between us.

'So far the prologue; now for the anecdote, which is just as interesting as thousands are which are daily propagated. It was about two years before the divorce of the Duchess of Grafton that her Grace and Lord March played at "brag" for two or three hours one evening at Euston; the others—viz. the Duke and Mr. Vary and Jack Young—looked over without playing at all. Lord M. had been very forward in "bragging," but threw up his cards afterwards when he had three knaves, whether he had a presentiment that the Duchess had three aces or whether he had artfully seen her hand. This cowardice struck Jack Young so sensibly that he fixed his eyes very sternly on Lord M., and addressed him thus: "Why! March, thou art the most dunghill Scots' peer that I ever met with." His Lordship instantly arose from his chair, filled with indignation, and whilst he was wavering whether he should use a poker or some other instrument, the Duke said to him: "I find, Lord March, that my friend Jack Young treats you as he constantly treats my wife and me." This prudent and good-natured interference disarmed Lord M., and they all passed the evening pleasantly. You may depend upon the truth of this story, as I had it from Mr. Vary.

'I remain, dear Madam
'Yours, &c. &c.,
'J. SYMONDS.'

The next anecdote was considered at the time by all who heard it to redound to the credit of my brother. In one of his visits to Euston he arrived unexpectedly and late in the afternoon, and immediately went to the room always appropriated to him to dress for dinner, and thence proceeded directly into the dining-room, when, to his astonishment, he perceived sitting at the head of the table the notorious Nancy Parsons instead of the Duchess. He instantly drew back, at the same moment extending his arms to mark his astonishment. The Duke went up to him with a conciliatory air, took his arm and said: 'Come, come, Jack, these things are always done in a hurry without consideration. I had no time to make alterations or inform you. I will explain afterwards.' But he only answered with a shake of his head, and, shrugging up his huge shoulders, retired, mounted his horse, and reached Bradfield the same night, a distance of nearly fifteen miles.

It should be remembered at this time the Duke was Prime Minister and the Doctor looking up to him for further preferment. By this he lost a bishopric.

I was at Bradfield, and received an express [1] from Dr. Roberts, Provost of Eton, to inform me of the accident, which called me thither at once. I resided there some time on account of my brother's affairs, dining every day with the Provost and Fellows. On the same account I was obliged to go to Worcester, where he was a Prebendary and Rector of St. John's in that city. Dr. Y. died without a will, as he had often told me he would do. When all his affairs were settled I returned to Bradfield. So sudden and dreadful an accident affected me deeply; there is something in such deaths that strikes every feeling of the soul. In the midst of the rapid movements of that animated amusement, in one moment to be hurried into another world without one thought of preparation has something tremendously formidable in it; yet every one is liable to deaths equally sudden, and the suggestion ought to be universal : 'Prepare to meet thy God.' The misery is that thousands sitting in their chairs and with ample time for preparation are apt to think of any subject rather than this most important of all.

Arthur Young to his Wife.

[No date, but evidently written at this period.]

'As I should be sorry to keep from you anything that must give you pleasure in your welfare of your children, I shall report a conversation with Dr. Langford, the under-master, who my brother got the Prebendary of Worcester for by speaking to Lord Sidney.

---

[1] Express, *n.*, a messenger sent on a special errand.—*Webster.*

'On his calling on me I lamented the loss—in which he joined warmly—spoke highly of my brother as his friend. I said that my bosom had all the feelings of affection for him, but that the loss to my poor boy was nothing short of ruin. He had no friend left. "No," replied he, "don't say that, for give me leave to say that, feeling as I do the obligations I have been under to Dr. Young, I must be allowed to call myself his friend. If I succeed in life I will be a friend to him, and I hope his progress in his learning will permit me to be so." He said more to the same purpose, and as he is a rising man in a situation that gives him power to act according to his feelings, I hope he will remember it. But the account Mr. Heath gives me is by no means satisfactory, and sorry I am to say that Arthur seems determined to do little for himself. He is now at a crisis, and sinks or swims. I gave Mr. Heath three guineas that he might encourage him with a crown now and then (as from himself) when he did well, but don't write of that to him, and desired him to write me when he was negligent. My brother's affairs turn out very badly; bills to the amount of 360*l*. now lie unpaid before me here, besides Worcester, and I can see no more than 260*l*. to pay it. I hear a bad account of the Rectory at Worcester, but suspend all judgment till the whole is before me.

'A. Y.'

Two honours were this year added to my name, by being elected into the Patriotic Society of Milan and that of the Geographical Society of Florence. I had also a visit from a Polish nobleman, Count Kalaskowski, who spent some time with me at Bradfield. The letters I received this year were numerous, and many of them very interesting. From the number I have selected the following:—

From Dr. Burney, on reading my 'Annals' and a character of Handel. This was after he had been at Bradfield.

'August 1, 1786.

'What have I without an inch of land to do with farming? Is it the subject or manner of treating it, or both that fascinated me, when you first were so kind, my dear friend, as to send me some of your "Annals of Agriculture"? I was in the midst of my winter's hurricane and immersed in other pursuits, but now, having conversed with some of your correspondents, seen your farm, and rubbed up my old rusticity, all my love for country matters returns, and I sincerely wish myself a villager. You seem to have worked yourself up to a true pitch of patriotism, and I think, besides the instructions the essays convey, that your knowledge on the subject, and animated reasoning, and admonitions, must have a national effect. Your book fastened on me so much on the road that I hardly looked on anything else. Mr. Symonds' essays on "Italian Husbandry"[1] are extremely curious, and furnish a species of information totally different from what can be acquired from the perusal of any other author. Many of the communications in the three first volumes, of which I have almost read every word,

[1] Published in the *Annals*.

seem to me instructive, amusing, and masterly. My countryman, Mr. Harris, of Hanwood, in Shropshire (the birthplace of my father and grandfather), seems a notable planter. As editor and chief of the *Agricola* family, I think you merit the thanks of every Englishman, not only who loves his country, but who loves his *belly*, for if your discoveries, improvements, and instructions are followed, we may certainly always find upon our own island *de quoi manger*.

'Now I would not have you, my dear Arthur, put contempt upon my praises, as coming from a Londoner, whom you may regard as a mere Cock-neigh immersed in the vanities, follies, and dissipation of the Capital, for then I'd have you to know that I reckon myself a countryman born and bred as much as yourself. I never was within the smell of sweet London till I was eighteen, and then, you know, I lived during nine of the best years of my life in Norfolk among the best farmers in Europe. Indeed, if I were ten or a dozen years younger than I am, I believe I should take your white house and all the land about it you could spare, and enter myself for your scholar, and run for the give and take plate; you know that I have been *giving* lessons all my life; it is now high time I should take some. As to London, if it were not for a few friends whom I sincerely love, and for its vicinity to several branches of my family, I would take half a crown never to see its sights or hear its sounds again.

'My friend, honest Arthur, who is a very ingenious, good-natured lad, will deliver to you a copy of my account of the "Commemoration of Handel;" it is not so good a one as I wish to send, though the best in my possession. I beg when you have nothing better to do that you will read it without too strong prejudices against Old Handel; for though he is called a Goth by fine travelled gentlemen, accustomed to more modern music and to posthumous refinements, yet candour and true knowledge must allow that he was the greatest man of his time, and that he had a force and majesty that suited our national character, and when you look at the list of his works you will allow that his resources were wonderful. His own performance on the organ was perhaps more superior than that of any inhabitant of this country, even than his compositions. Upon the whole, though I am far from wishing to put an extinguisher upon every other candidate for musical fame, yet it would be the height of injustice not to allow that this country was much obliged to his genius and talent, and that the late performances of his productions do honour to the cultivation of musick in this kingdom, as well as to our national gratitude.

'I beg you will present my affectionate compliments to Mrs. Young, and best thanks for the hospitality and kindness with which she treated us at Bradfield; and pray give our hearty love to the gentle, sweet, and amiable Miss Bessy.

'And believe me to be, with very sincere regard,
'Your affectionate
'CHARLES BURNEY.'

From John Symonds, Esq., on the examination of the boys at Greenwich School for speaking Latin.

Gold medal &c. given to master and boys. [A curious letter.]

'St. Edmund's Hill: December 1786.

'My dearest Friend,—I returned hither yesterday, and shall go to Euston on Thursday to pass five or six days there. The Bishop of Peterborough will return with me, but whether on Wednesday or Thursday se'nnight I know not, but I will send you a line soon after I get there, and I hope you will keep yourself free from engagements those two days. You may possibly have seen or heard of a remarkable circumstance that does equal honour to the Society of Arts and to Greenwich School.

'The Society decreed a gold medal to that schoolmaster who should teach his boys to speak the best Latin. This was claimed last week by the schoolmaster of Greenwich.[1] Sir William Fordyce and my friend Professor Martin were appointed Examiners. More, the Secretary, requested Bishop Watson to attend, who excused himself, as he was obliged shortly to leave London. Five boys attended with their master. The Examiners had prepared a great number of questions such as boys may be supposed to understand. These were put in Latin and answered in Latin without hesitation. The boys were then ordered to withdraw into a private room together, and to make an original composition in Latin without the help of a dictionary. This they all performed in half an hour. Then the Examiners asked numberless questions in English, which were answered immediately in Latin. The gold

[1] Dr. Egan, Royal Park Academy.

medal was given to the schoolmaster, and five silver ones of equal value to the five boys, who were pretty much upon an equality, and what is surprising is that not one of the five had learned Latin longer than two years and a half, and the eldest of them was not above thirteen years. You may be certain that this is true, as I saw it in a letter from Martin to his brother-in-law, the Vice-Chancellor, and he concludes it by saying "that they all spoke Latin with fluency, propriety, and elegance." Were I possessed but of a small portion of the fire with which you are animated, I should cry out with a generous indignation, "Blush, ye proud seminaries of Eton and Westminster," &c. &c. &c.

'My compliments *aux Polonais*.

'I am now set down in earnest to renew acquaintance with my Italian *agricoltori*.

'Ever affectionately,
'JOHN SYMONDS.'

In a Westerly Tour I made this year, amongst numerous other places I visited Blenheim, and made the following memorandum :—

'Viewed the pleasure ground at Blenheim, the enclosed part of which consists of 200 acres, with the water near 300. It can scarcely be too much admired; the whole environ of the water is fine, various in its feature, with the character of magnificence everywhere impressed. The cascade scenery, viewed independently of the new improvements, is extremely pleasing, and indeed wants nothing but a deeper and more umbrageous shade for an accompaniment. The new walks, caves, fountains, and statues do not, however, seem entirely calculated to add to the beauty of the scenery. The most splendid view is from the walk leading from the cascade to the house. There are two points nearly similar, where are benches; the water fills the bottom of the vale in the style of a very noble river; few, indeed, in the kingdom exceed it. We may conjecture that if Brown, in the exultation of his heart, really said that the Thames would never pardon his superb imitation for exceeding the original, it was the view from one of these benches that inspired the sentiment. The proud waves that roll at your feet; the declivity steep enough to make the water and every contiguous scene more interesting to the eye; the opposite shore, a hill spread with wood that hangs with forest boldness to the water; the whole is formed to make an impression on the mind. No ill-judged decoration weakens by dividing the effect; no intruding objects hurt the simplicity of the scene. I know not any artificial scene that is finer. The concluding one where the water expands is great, but I think inferior to this. But to return——

[*Here the narrative breaks off.*]

It appears this year[1] that I was engaged in a pursuit entirely new to me, that of making many new and pneumatic experiments on expelling gas from soils, manures, and various other substances, in order to

[1] The writer's memory is at fault here. His correspondence with Dr. Priestley is dated 1783. The letters, however, are given here, as otherwise they would not be intelligible.

ascertain whether there was any connection between the quantity and species of such gas (from *Geist*, German for ghost, spirit. Authority, B. of Llandaff, *see* Newman's ' Trans. of Boerhave's Chemistry ') and the fertility of the soils from which my specimens were selected. It seems that I prosecuted this enquiry with diligence; and as it was my commencement in chemistry, I corresponded upon the subject with Dr. Priestley, and went to Cambridge for the conversation of Mr. Milner, then Professor of Chemistry in that University. The result of my experiments was very remarkable, for I decided, after a very careful deduction from the result of all my trials, that there existed a very intimate, and almost unbroken, connection between the fertility of land and the gas to be expelled from it. This was an entirely new discovery belonging to me only, and it has been quoted by many celebrated chemists in a manner which showed that they considered me as the origin of it. I sent a detail of my trials to the Royal Society, through the hands of Mr. Magellan,[1] as my paper contained some eudiometrical experiments made with the eudiometer invented by that philosopher. Mentioning to a friend what I had done, ' You have been very foolish,' observed the friend, ' for depend upon it your paper will never get into the "Philosophical Transactions." ' Expressing my surprise, I demanded the reason. ' Why, know you not,' he replied, ' that there is a most inveterate hostility between Sir J. Banks and Magellan,

[1] Mr. Magellan. This gentleman, often mentioned in A. Y.'s correspondence as descendant of the great Portuguese discoverer, seems to have attained some proficiency—even eminence—in science.

from a violent quarrel, and Sir J. is not a man to permit anything to be printed that comes through hands offensive to him, especially as the paper is to the credit of Magellan's instrument?' The event proved the truth of this prediction, but this did not prevent my labours being duly appreciated by those who were the most competent judges. In the pursuit of these trials I gradually established and furnished a laboratory, sufficient for my own enquiries, at about 150*l*. expense.

From Dr. Priestley

'Birmingham : Jan. 27, 1783.

' Dear Sir,—There is no person I should serve with more pleasure than you, because there is no person whose pursuits are more eminently useful to the world. You alone have certainly done more to promote agriculture, and especially to render it reputable, in this country than all that have gone before you. But the little I might do to aid your investigations will be reduced to a small matter indeed by my distance from you.

' All that I should be able to do with water would be to expel by heat all the air it contains, and then examine, by nitrous air, how much phlogiston that air contains, but it is very possible that the fitness of water for irrigating meadows may depend upon something besides the phlogiston it contains. Experiment alone can determine these things. I never heard before of the inference, you say, has been drawn from my doctrine with respect to the use of light in vegetation.

I know of no use that light is of to the *soil*. The whole effect is on the *living plant*, enabling it to convert the impure air it meets with in water or in the atmosphere into pure air. When that end is effected that water is of no further use to it. Plants will not thrive unless both their leaves and roots be exposed to air in some degrees impure. This I have fully ascertained, but I am afraid that the doctrine is not capable of much practical application.

'I know of no method of conveying phlogiston to the roots of plants but as combined with water, and this seems to be done in the best way by a mixture of putrid matter. Water will not imbibe much inflammable air. I find volatile alkali to contain much phlogiston. It is indeed almost another modification of the same thing.

'Since my last, I have hit upon various methods of converting water into permanent air. It is sufficient to give it something more than a boiling heat. If I only put an ounce of water into a porous earthen retort, I get a hundred ounce measures of air from it, and when I have, in this manner, got near an ounce weight of air from the same retort, it has not weighed one grain less than it did.

'I shall be glad to hear the result of your experiments, and am truly sorry that I can do so little for you.
'J. PRIESTLEY.'

'Birmingham: March 31, 1783.

'Dear Sir,—I received from Mr. More [1] two bottles of water, one marked X, which Mr. Boswell informed

[1] Secretary to the Society of Arts.

him was from the spring mentioned in his "Treatise on Watering Meadows," and another without any mark from a spring arising in a bed of sand, and I examined them immediately. I found the former to contain air much purer than that of the atmosphere; but the latter air was much worse, that is, phlogisticated; a candle could hardly have burned in it. This last I should think to be the better spring for the watering of meadows, or perhaps it might have been better corked; for on the 19th, though I put the corks in again immediately, but without any cement, I found the air in both very pure, more so than the purest before, and hardly to be distinguished, and they were so this day when I examined them again. They should be examined on the spot. The air in the spring from the sand was much warmer than that in my pump water, or than that of water in general. But water exposed to the open air soon loses the phlogiston it contains.

'Perhaps much of the effect of water on meadows is that, at this time of the year, it comes out of the earth considerably warmer than the roots of the grass. What think you of this?

'I expect to set out for London this day three weeks, and shall stay there about a fortnight. I should be glad to meet you there, when we shall find an hour's conversation better than all our correspondence. Wishing you success in all your laudable pursuits.

'I am, dear Sir,

'Yours &c. &c.

'J. PRIESTLEY.'

At Chadacre, six miles from Bury, resided John Plampin, Esq.[1] who had three daughters, all, at this time, unmarried and at home. I was intimately acquainted with them. Two of these ladies were much distinguished by their beauty, and reigned as toasts throughout the county: Sophia married afterwards to the Rev. Mr. Macklin, and Betsy married in 1794 to Orbell Ray Oakes, Esq. of Bury. I introduced my friend Lazowski to these ladies, and he was much at Chadacre, admiring not a little the youngest of them. They persuaded their father to give a ball, at which the Duke of Liancourt, his two sons, Lazowski and myself were present, and the evening passed with uncommon hilarity till the rising sun sent us home. Mr. Symonds afterwards gave a weekly ball when the Frenchmen were with him, and these parties were uncommonly agreeable.

Early in the spring of 1787 I received a letter from a friend at Paris, Mons. Lazowski (who had resided two years at Bury, much to my amusement and satisfaction, with the two sons of the Duke of Liancourt), to inform me that he was going with the Count de la Rochefoucault to the Pyrenees, and proposed my being of the party.[2]

'Liancourt: April 9, 1787.

'Dear Sir,—I was at Liancourt when I heard from you the last time, so that I was very uneasy upon the bill which you had drawn upon M. de Vergennes, who could not be informed by me about it, but very happily

[1] An old Suffolk family. Captain Plampin, mentioned in the French travels, is noticed in the new *Dictionary of National Biography*.
[2] M. Lazowski's broken English is given as we find it.

my letter to him went at a proper time, and it has been paid. Nothing wants now but to have turnips, as your English wit whispers it. But we have another matter to settle together, if you are not now incumbered. I told you by the last that it could be, but I would travel this summer. The case is that the Count is, for the sake of his health, obliged to go to Bagnères-de-Luchon, in the Pyrénées, to drink those waters; he asked from me to be his companion, and his relations seemed to be glad of it. I did therefore comply with his demand, and we are going about the middle of May, which is the time just of your coming over to France. Now will you come with us? Such proposition is not a foolish one. We will pass by a part of France in going, and come back by another part, so that you will see almost the two-thirds of this kingdom. You will learn the French; with us everything will be explained to you; in short, I will be with you, and that is enough, I hope. That part by which you will pass through is not an uninteresting one. Look upon a map. You will pass through the Limousin and Toulouse in going, and in coming back by Bordeaux, &c.; the Pyrénées are very worth to be seen, and, besides, if nothing very extraordinary prevents it, we intend to go to Barcelona in Spain, in order to see the Catalogne,[1] the finest province after that travel. I must not tell you that I shall be another Arthur here for you, not that I presume to say that you will find in me an Encyclopædia living as I did in you, but your friend, and therefore to your commands in Paris and everywhere.

[1] Catalonia.

Our manner of travelling is very convenient to you also; we go with our own horses, you will have one, my servants will be yours, nothing therefore shall be too much expensive. Have you your horse? Is it possible to come over with him at a proper time? If not, do write to me a word, and the Count and I will do our utmost to get one cheap enough, between fifteen and twenty pounds. If you cannot be ready here for the 15th of May, we will expect five or six days, but you see that it is impossible to expect more, since the Count must drink the waters; in two words, you seemed to wish to see this kingdom, never you will have such an opportunity; if I am obliged to stay at Bagnères, nothing will prevent you to make some excursions in the environs, and you will speak French very well. The whole depends of your family business. If you cannot now, then you will wait till September, and we will be at Paris; but you must give greatest of attention to it, and as soon as your mind will be fixed upon anything pray do write to me. What devil are you doing about the notables? (*sic*) I suppose you know my mind about the whole by my letter.[1] M. de Calonne is exiled, so is M. Necker. What will be the result I do not know, but the notables have missed the way, and they know nothing of the matter; but public business must give way to what I make a proposal to you, it is question of nothing else but to travel together a thousand miles, without more expense but that you would spend anywhere, &c. &c.

[1] It has been found impossible to include this letter from want of space.

so you may go to the devil if you don't speak well of me and my prospect. My best compliments to M. Symonds &c. &c. chiefly Lady Gage and Sir Thomas.

'Yours for ever,

'LY.

'Do not forget to write and to speak about your horse, whether you will bring yours, or if we must get one for you.'

This was touching a string tremulous to vibrate. I had so long wished for an opportunity to examine France. In the survey of agriculture which I had taken in England and Ireland, of about 7,000 miles, I had calculated, from facts, the rent produce and resources of those Kingdoms, and I had often reflected on the importance of knowing the real situation of France; the effect of Government; the state of the farmers, of the poor—the state and extent of their manufactures with a hundred other enquiries certainly of political importance; yet strange as it may seem not to be found in any French book written from actual observation, all that I was before able to learn having been composed in some great city without travelling beyond the walls. I should accept a very unsatisfactory work upon sheep, written by Mons. Cartier, employed and paid by Government. I had but little time given me to consider of the proposal, but I wrote to learn if they travelled post, because I previously determined in that case not to go. And, further, I requested to know if I were to travel at any other expense than that of myself and horse. The answer was that they travelled with their own horses, and did not propose making more than twenty or twenty-five miles a day; that my expense would be merely what I stated, and mostly in a cheap part of the kingdom. This most agreeable plan I instantaneously acceded to, and soon set out for France on horseback. At Dover, being detained, I copy the following note on that expedition :—

'*Tuesday, May* 15, 1787, *Dover.*—Had the packet sailed this morn as I expected I should not have scaled, as I never did before, Shakespeare's Cliff. By the way it is by no means so formidable as I expected from it. I think the look down from its perpendicular position very striking, and when I reflected how much more it must be from the summit, the reflection, perhaps, injured the principal effect (*sic*). This is a proof that we ought never, when a powerful impression is wished, to advance to the principal point gradually. It should come upon us at once; nor should I have seen Mr. Harris's drill plough,[1] which I liked much better from seeing it than from the print. But I principally should have wanted time to run over my accounts, to review the debts and credits of several loose memoranda, and find from the result that I had not acted imprudently or unguardedly in omitting the necessary preparations to such a journey. My dear child, my lovely Bobbin, I left in perfect health, the rest of my family well and provided for in every respect as they themselves had chalked out, the 'Annals' lodged in the hands of a man on whose friendship and abilities I could entirely confide. Revolving these circumstances

[1] A sort of plough for sowing grain in drills.

in my mind gave me pleasure, so that I could hardly regret in the evening the day which in the morning I had pronounced lost. At night I went into a bye boat [1] and had a villainous passage of fourteen hours. Nine hours rolling at anchor had so fatigued my mare that I thought it necessary for her to rest one day, but next morning I left Calais.

'*November* 8.—Wait at Desseins three days for a wind, Dover, London, Bradfield, and have more pleasure in giving my little girl a French doll than in viewing Versailles.' [2]

The journey to France cost me 118*l*. 15*s*. 2*d*. Things bought, 20*l*. 17*s*.; books, 8*l*. 16*s*. 6*d*.

This year I had a long visit at Bradfield from M. Bukaty, nephew to the Polish Ambassador, a heavy, dull man with a Tartar countenance. His intention was to learn agriculture, but he made a poor progress. My correspondence this year contained much variety, and I have reperused many of the letters with much pleasure. In the number were the following :—

From Sir J. Sinclair [3] on clothing for sheep, which he sent and desired me to buy. I did so, and the rest of the flock took them I suppose for beasts of prey, and fled

---

[1] A chance or passing boat.

[2] As Arthur Young's letters, with trifling excisions, are incorporated into the famous travels, I do not give them here. His anxiety about Bobbin is ever apparent. 'Give Bobbin a kiss for me. God send her well,' he writes to his eldest daughter Mary; and, in another letter, 'Remember me to your mother, and tell Bobbin I never forget her.' 'The Robin,' or Bobbin, was now five years old.

[3] Statist, political and agricultural writer; born 1754, died 1835. Sat in Parliament for several constituencies, and took an active part in political and scientific movements; was also a voluminous writer.

in all directions, till the clothed sheep jumping hedges and ditches soon derobed themselves.

'Whitehall: April 11, 1787.

'Sir,—I went yesterday to Knightsbridge, and have ordered the canvas for covering the sheep, which will be ready next week, and I shall be glad to know how it can be best forwarded.

'My idea is to put the coverings on immediately after the sheep are shorn, when I imagine it would be comfortable instead of distressing to the animal. That the experiment may have full justice done I send you three covers of oil skin, three of pretty strong unoiled canvas, and two done over with Lord Dundonald's tar. If lambs are apt to die of cold, would it not be of use to them?

'I am, Sir, your obedient servant,
'JOHN SINCLAIR.'

From Mr. Symonds, an account of his tour in the West &c., of the King and Queen's visit to Whitbread's Brew House; duties to the Crown, 52,000*l.* per annum for the brewery alone.

'Sunning Hill: July 12, 1787.

'My dear Sir,—I wrote to you from Cornwall, and hope you received the letter which was directed to Creil. I am returning from a tour through Devonshire, where I visited Mount Edgecombe, Dartmouth, Teignmouth, Torbay, Dawlish and Exmouth. At Exeter I passed ten days with my old friend the Bishop, Dr. Ross, and however I may have lost my time in other things I certainly was not deficient in my religious duties, for during the ten days I attended divine service nineteen times, taking in his Lordship's private chapel and the cathedral.

'After visiting most of the fine seats in Somersetshire &c. including Lord Radnor's famous triangular house, I came to Salisbury, where I met several old acquaintances, and among the rest Mr. Windham, who published Doddington's Diary, and who permitted me to look over the vast collection of Doddington's private correspondence, and to copy what I pleased.

'From Salisbury I came hither, having made nearly a thousand miles in my gig, without suffering the least inconvenience, either from weather or accident. Could I do better than to end, as it were, my tour with a visit to the "Monarch's and the Muses' Seats"?

'The only public news that you can now think of abroad is whether we are to have peace or war; but I have heard here from very good authority that Thurlow, Lord Stafford, and Mr. Pitt are for peace, and that 'tis thought the latter will resign if things take a different turn.

'Whitbread expended not less than 15,000*l.* in entertaining the King and Queen at his brewery. They left off working it three days before—new clothes—the floor carpeted, and three or four sets of china made on purpose at Worcester after the most beautiful models of Sèvres, that the Royal Family might be entertained separately, though in the same rooms. The King asked Whitbread what he paid for duties to the Crown, and his Majesty was not a little surprised to hear that he

M

paid 52,000*l.* for the Brewery alone. You will say all that is kind for me to the Count and Lazowski. Madame de Polignac[1] &c., together with the French Ambassador, have been at the Terrace, where they were received by the King and Queen. At Bath the French ladies broke the standing rules by all going to the ball much too late, and on foot, which is not common, and one danced in coloured gloves.

'You and I shall agree about the Liancourt Plough as well as most other things. The Duke's ideas of farming resemble those of Mons. Baron, whose self-conceit is exceeded only by his ignorance, and who must inevitably starve, if he had to gain his bread by farming, and practised for himself.

'Adieu. Ever faithfully yours,

'J. SYMONDS.'

[1] The Prince and Princess de Polignac, after receiving countless honours, privileges, and substantial favours from Louis XVI. and the Queen, were among the first to desert them. The present head of this ancient house married a daughter of Mr. Singer, inventor of the sewing-machine.

CHAPTER VIII

TRAVEL AND INTERNATIONAL FRIENDSHIPS, 1788-89-90

The Wool Bill—Sheridan's speech—Count Berchtold—Experiments—
Second French journey—Potato-fed sheep—Cost of housekeeping—
Chicory—Burnt in effigy—Correspondence—Third French journey
—With Italian agriculturists—Bishop Watson and Mr. Luther—
Correspondence—Literary work—Illness—The state of France.

EARLY in the spring I was deputed by the wool growers of Suffolk to support a petition against the Wool Bill [1] which at that time made much noise in the agricultural world; and in which I united with Sir Joseph Banks,[2] who was deputed by the county of Lincoln for the same purpose. I was most strenuous in the cause. By this Bill the growers of wool were laid under most insufferable restraints by its patrons the manufacturers, under the false pretence which had upon so many occasions been listened to by the Legislature, that immense quantities of wool were smuggled to France; on the gross fallacy of which they made good use, in taking those measures which answered their only design, that of sinking the price.

[1] A Bill prohibiting the exportation of wool passed the House of Commons, May 15, 1788.
[2] President of the Royal Society, and supporter of the cause of agriculture and science; died 1810.

I applied to many of the leading members of both Houses of Parliament, but to very little effect. Those who deputed me were very desirous that I should see Mr. Fox on the subject; and Sir Peter Burrell, who was also greatly hostile to the Bill, and acted at that time as Lord Great Chamberlain of England at the trial of Mr. Hastings, recommended me to take an opportunity of the managers for the Commons, waiting at that trial to desire to speak with Mr. Fox in the manager's box; and with this view gave me a pass ticket for the whole trial, by means of which I could be at the bar ready to serve such an opportunity when it offered. These tickets were sold at twenty guineas each; and this afforded me many opportunities of much entertainment. I accordingly saw Mr. Fox, and found him by no means inclined to patronise any opposition to the Bill. All that could be done was to make him a master of certain important facts of which he was ignorant, and which did seem to have some little weight with him. It may here be observed that as I was walking one day in Fleet Street with my pass ticket and a 20*l.* note in my pocket book, I was hustled unskilfully by a knot of rascals, who picked the book out of my pocket, but I missing it instantly, luckily observed it on the pavement near my foot, and seized on it immediately, and the rascals went off at once. By means of this ticket I was present when Mr. Sheridan made the speech that rendered his eloquence so celebrated.[1] I was examined at the Bar of the Houses of

[1] 'Then came the Oude case, that lasted no less than twenty-one days, and ended by a speech from Sheridan on which great labour and

Lords and Commons, and published two pamphlets on the subject of the Wool Bill.

But notwithstanding all the opposition that was made to the measure, after moderating some of the most hostile clauses the Bill passed; but the manufacturers experienced so determined and vigorous an opposition that they would hardly engage again in any similar attack upon the landed interest. In the course of this business I experienced a strange instance of roguery in an Ipswich attorney named Kirby. This man was appointed secretary and receiver of the Suffolk subscriptions for supporting the expense of opposing the Bill. He paid the reckoning twice at the 'Crown and Anchor' when a few persons dined there; and after that, under various pretences, when money was to be paid; and on a moderate computation put more than 100*l.* into his own pocket. I was unwilling to believe it, but upon his death a few years after it was found that he was one of the greatest knaves the devil ever created.

My deputation by the county of Suffolk to represent it, in opposing the Bill at the bar of the two Houses of Parliament, in the same manner as Sir Joseph Banks, a highly eminent character for influence and affluence, was deputed by the county of Lincoln, did me much honour, and shows that a prophet may sometimes be esteemed, even in his own country. The reader who is desirous of becoming acquainted with this

pains had been bestowed. This speech had been looked forward to as rivalling the great Begum speech of the same orator' (Knight). Is not A. Y. here thinking of the great Begum speech of an earlier session?

portion of the history of wool in England may consult my Question of Wool—my speech that might have been spoken—my Reasons against the Bill, and various other papers by myself, inserted in the 'Annals.'

The opposition certainly would have been successful if Mr. Pitt had not found what so many ministers have experienced before—that the trading interest at large is a hundred times more active than the landed interest; for very few counties exerted themselves on this occasion. Had half of them acted like Suffolk the Bill would have been inevitably lost, and had I not been a resident in Suffolk that county would have slept with the rest. It may not be amiss to observe that a pamphlet was published, entitled a 'Letter to Arthur Young, Esq., on the Wool Bill, by Thomas Day,[1] Esq.,' from which the following is an extract:—

'If we are delivered from the present danger, I know no one who has so great a claim to the public gratitude as yourself. As soon as the storm began to gather, your active eye remarked the curling of the waters and the blackening of the horizon, while all our other Palinuruses were quietly slumbering around. Distinguished, therefore, as you long have been for literary talents, you have now added a nobler wreath, and a sublimer praise to all you merited before.' Mr. Day in this letter calls my opposition to the Bill 'A noble stand in defence of the common liberties.'

---

[1] The author of *Sandford and Merton* died 1789 from the kick of a colt, which he had refused to have broken in on account of the cruelty usually involved in the process.

'*April* 22.—I was examined on the Wool Bill in the House of Commons. It was a most hard-fought battle between the manufacturers and the landed interest; the Bill laid heavy shackles on every movement of wool near the sea coast, and was opposed with great resolution, both by Sir Joseph Banks and myself.

'We opposed it both in the Commons and the Lords, both being examined at the Bar of the two Houses; the manufacturers on this occasion were so hotly opposed that Sir Joseph thought they would be quiet in future. I was of a different opinion, being convinced that they never would omit any opportunity of imposing their shackle on that insensible, torpid, and stupid body "the landlords of Britain."'

About this time Count Leopold Berchtold [1] visited me at Bradfield. But part of the time which he spent in Suffolk (I being absent) was at the 'Angel' at Bury, where he lived an extraordinary life of retirement and economy. He daily went out, and employed the whole day in writing and reading. Such temperance has scarcely been known. He drank neither wine nor beer, and would dine upon a potato or an egg.

He told the landlord of that inn that he could not live in the manner of other travellers, but that he might charge what he pleased for his apartments. He was a most extraordinary personage. His father had a considerable estate in Bohemia, and one reason for

[1] Died 1809. One of the most active members of the Royal Humane Society; fell a victim to his devotion in attending the sick and wounded Austrian soldiers on the field of Wagram.

the son's travelling over a great part of the world was the extreme disgust he took at the measures of the Emperor Joseph II., which were oppressive and ruinous to the nobility &c., constantly changing his ill-formed political schemes. He had lived in the principal countries of Europe long enough to become a master of their languages, in every one of which he printed a work which he conceived might be useful to the inhabitants. When at Bradfield he was working hard to learn Arabic, as he proposed passing from England to Morocco, thence to Egypt and Arabia. This journey afterwards he executed, and returned home to Bohemia through the greatest part of the Turkish Empire; and, after escaping a thousand dangers, as he was going to Vienna was murdered by banditti.

He was very tall and graceful in his person, of a handsome, expressive countenance, and as elegant as if he had passed his whole life in a Court. Though invested with the Order of St. Stephano by the Grand Duke of Tuscany, Leopold, he never wore it in England, as his father being alive made it necessary for him to live economically. His conversation was intelligent and pleasing, his knowledge almost universal. He travelled much on foot; and once through France or Germany—I forget which—when he was beset by three or four robbers; but he assumed so much firmness in his manner, with so resolute and determined an air, and with so threatening an attitude of defence, that, after a pause, the robbers retired, thinking it best to let him alone. He had a sabre or some other weapon, and said that they might have had the worst of it if they had made the attack, as he had before been set on in the same way more than once.

His first business in every country was to study unremittingly till he had perfectly learnt the language, as without this he considered men and women but as cows and sheep. He then applied himself with singular assiduity to understand those branches of human industry or political economy for which the country was most celebrated, and for this purpose applied to those who were most able to satisfy his inquiries. He was introduced to me by Anthony Souga, the Imperial Consul at London, who gave him the highest possible character. When he had registered these inquiries and printed a book in the language, he left the country for some other.

The grand object of Ct. B.'s investigations and inquiries seemed to be not so much the good of the countries he visited, as to possess himself of a great mass of that sort of knowledge which might be most useful in adding to the welfare and happiness of the inhabitants of that estate to which he was born, and which was a very extensive property. He spent some time with me in Suffolk gleaning agricultural information, intending to apply it to the farmers and peasants of his paternal estate and of his own favourite Bohemia, from which he often lamented that he was driven by the folly and tyranny of Joseph II. It was with great concern that I heard of his very unfortunate and untimely death about ten years after leaving England. He was about thirty-six years of age when in Suffolk, was possessed of various and uncommon powers, built mentally and bodily on a great scale, talked English like a native, walked like a giant, and was of all the multitude of foreigners who frequented my house the most persevering and the most intelligent.

This year I made some experiments on the distemper in wheat called the smut, which were amongst the most satisfactory and decisive that I ever found, and in which I corrected some errors of Mr. de Tillet,[1] and proved, too clearly to be doubted, the proximate cause and prevention of that disease.

It is almost intolerable, after experiments so decisive, that so many men, through ignorance of what I had done, should for a long time have been bewildering themselves upon the same subject, and continuing to do so to the present day, publishing, too, the greatest errors. These experiments are inserted in the 'Annals.'

This year I set out on my second journey to France in the month of July. I made this alone, my cloak-bag behind me; and I did not travel thus an[2] hundred miles before my mare fell blind. I have heard and read much of the pleasure of travelling; how it may be with posting—*avant-couriers* preparing apartments and repasts—I know not. Let those who enjoy such comfort pity me, who made 3,700 miles on a blind mare! and brought her (humanity would not allow me to sell her) safe back to Bradfield. I claim but one merit—that of practising in the midst of all this folly the severest economy in travelling.

In the winter Mr. Macro took a seat in my postchaise on a farming tour across Essex and into

[1] See vol. x. of the *Annals of Agriculture*.   [2] *Sic*.

Sussex, where we spent a day or two with Lord Sheffield.

In this tour I learned that General Murray had 4,000 South Down sheep, and that he fed them with potatoes. This was sufficient. To come into the country on the search for sheep and potato intelligence, and not to see such a man, would not be to make a very wise figure when we returned home. But I had not the honour to be known to the General. No matter; 4,000 sheep fed on potatoes were an object before which form must give way. I wrote a card, stating our pursuit, and wishes to have it gratified, desiring leave to view his flock. Those who know the General's liberality and passion for agriculture will not want to be told what the answer was. We spent five days in his house, and found it the residence of hospitality and good sense.

Mrs. Murray had resided nine years in the island of Majorca, being the daughter of the English consul. She gave me many particulars relating to that island, and, among others, that the climate was by far the finest she had ever experienced. She never was for a single hour either too hot or too cold, nor ever saw a fog; but the people were unpleasant, ignorant and bigoted.

I was always very regular in keeping accounts, but do not often mention them in this detail; I may, however, just observe that I seemed to have been no bad economist, as the total expense of house, garden, stable, servants, and keeping a postchaise with not a little company, cost in four months 97*l*. 2*s*. 3*d*., or at the rate of 291*l.* 6*s.* 9*d.* per annum; how it was done I forget. If such an expense be compared with the present times [1] it will show the enormous difference, arising principally from the desperate increase of taxation, which has crippled so many classes of the kingdom; but I had a large farm in my hands. On being at London, some time after, I went to Esher and spent a day with Mr. Ducket, examining his farm with great attention; he dined with me at the 'Tun,' and I had a very interesting conversation with him to a late hour, upon all the points of his husbandry.

In this year I first introduced the cultivation of Cichorium Intybus [2] at Bradfield, and registered it in the 'Annals of Agriculture;' it was at first upon a small scale, but sufficient to convince me of the vast importance of the plant. I brought the seed from Lyons in France, and gradually extended the culture till I had above one hundred acres of it; the utter stupidity of the farming world was never more apparent than in their neglect of this plant, so repeatedly recommended in the 'Annals.' The Duke of Bedford kept ten large sheep per acre on a field of it.

The following letters were among others received this year:—

From B. H. Latrobe, Esq., on my being burnt in effigy at Norwich by the manufacturers (*in re* Wool Bill), a very lively letter.

---

[1] Written about 1816.
[2] Wild chicory or succory, used by the French as a winter salad, and in the adulteration of coffee.

'Stamp Office, Somerset Place: May 22, 1788.

'Dear Sir,—We have been waiting for your arrival in town *patiently* for the week past, and I am afraid we must now make up our minds to wait *patiently* a great deal longer, as the passing of the Wool Bill has not been able to bring you to town. By the word *We* I mean my brother, our friend the lord of slaves,[1] myself, and I dare say it includes fifty other people whom I have not the honour of knowing. We have been three days past laying our heads together to find out some method of *doing you honour in effigy* in order to make up to you in some measure the disgrace you have undergone (as is creditably reported about town) of being burnt in effigy by the wool manufacturers at Bury. My brother is for procuring your effigy, and after having crowned it with a wreath composed of turnip roots, cabbage leaves, potato-apples, wheat-ears, oats, straws, &c., and tied with a band of wool, thinks it ought to be placed upon its pedestal (being the volume of Virgil's "Georgics") to be worshipped by the real patriots; Mr. Huthhausen thinks a plain ribbon a sufficient honour for a man whose ideas can admit of the belief of slavery in Silesia; and, as for myself, I am of opinion that a man whose life has been devoted without fee or reward to the service of the public has so great a reward arising from the consciousness of having done good, and so just a claim to honour, that I shall not trouble my head about methods to *increase it*. But I must beg your pardon for this

[1] Refers (see below) to a work by Baron Huthhausen on the servitude of the Silesian peasantry.

lady-like chat, though your having been burnt in effigy is enough to make any pen run wild. . . . I could wish that a favour I have to beg of you were not inconvenient.'

[The writer requests that some remarks of his own on the book named above may be inserted in the 'Annals.']

From Edmund Burke, Esq., on an application I made to him relative to the Wool Bill. [*Unfortunately no copy can be found of this letter.*]

Sir Joseph Banks gives me joy of being burned in effigy at Norwich (Bury?) on account of my opposition to the Wool Bill :—

'Soho Square: May 13, 1788.

'Dear Sir,—With this you will receive the "Instructions given to the Council against the Wool Bill." [1]

'I have corrected the whole, but I fear you will find it miserably deficient in point of composition, but as I am not ambitious on that head I mean to be satisfied if I am intelligible.

'I give you joy sincerely at having arrived at the glory of being burned in effigy; nothing is so conclusive a proof of your possessing the best of the argument. No one was ever burned if he was wrong—the business in that case is to expose his blunders—but when argument is precluded firebrands are ready substitutes.

'Believe me, dear Sir,

'Yours faithfully,

'J. BANKS.'

[1] For this article see *Annals of Agriculture*, vol. ix. p. 479.

1789.—I had yet work to do in France; the survey of that kingdom was not completed in the journeys of the two preceding years. I did not hesitate therefore, but as soon as business at home would permit me to be absent I set out on my third expedition, June 2, and went to Paris in the diligence. As the carrying specimens of remarkable soils and of manufactures, wool, &c. was so inconvenient, I made this journey in a chaise. Through the kindness of the Duchess d'Estissac (de Rochefoucauld) I was most agreeably received at the Hôtel de la Rochefoucauld, and as the States General were assembling I went thither to the Duke's apartment, where I met many persons of note, such as the Duke of Orleans, the Abbé Sieyès, Rabaut St. Étienne,[1] &c. and was present at an interesting debate in the National Assembly. I spent some time at Paris, which I quitted on my third journey on June 28. I felt much regret on taking leave of my excellent friend Monsieur Lazowski, whose anxiety for the fate of his country[2] made me respect his character as much as I had reason to love it for the thousand attentions I was in the daily habit of receiving from him. My kind protectress the Duchess d'Estissac had the goodness to make me promise that I would again return to her hospitable hotel when I had finished the journey.

At Toulon I sold my horse and chaise, as I had been informed that I could not thus travel with safety in Italy. I embarked at Toulon to save one or two stages,

---

[1] Son of a Protestant pastor of Nîmes, member of the Constituent Assembly; guillotined 1784. See *Letters of Helen Maria Williams*.

[2] His country by adoption; Lazowski was a Pole.

which gave me an opportunity of viewing the fine harbours of that port. On leaving Nice I went by a *vetturino* to Turin, and was fortunate in making the acquaintance of some of the gentlemen that accompanied me. At that capital I was introduced to various lovers of the plough, and received much valuable information. From this place I went to Milan, where through the kind attentions of the Abate¹ Amorette, a true lover of agriculture and a friend of its professors, I was introduced to a variety of persons who afforded me much intelligence and accompanied me to the seat of the Count di Castiglioni, sixteen miles north of the city, with whom I passed sufficient time to give me an opportunity of remarking the country life of an Italian nobleman of high consideration.

From Milan I went to Lodi through one of the finest scenes of irrigation in the world. At the latter place I assisted in the whole operation of making a Lodesan, called Parmesan cheese in England, and thereby learnt a few circumstances in that manufacture, which I afterwards applied with success in making cheese in Suffolk. At Lodi I attended the opera, where the Archduke and Archduchess with the most splendid company were present, and it gave me particular pleasure to find such a house so filled in a little town quite dependent on cows, butter and cheese.

At Bergamo I was electrified by the fine eyes of an Italian fair, and just as I was making a nearer approach, impeded in it by the sudden appearance of her husband.

At Verona I viewed its celebrated amphitheatre

¹ Abbot.

and gained some agricultural intelligence, then on to Vicenza and Padua, where I stayed some days, having introductions to several professors, then by the canal to Venice, where I employed several days in viewing that singular place and numberless curiosities to be found in it. It fully answered my expectations.

At Bologna I was so fortunate as to meet Mr. Taylor, of Bifrons, in Kent, with his very agreeable family. By him I was introduced to such of the nobility of the place as had a taste for farming, which, with some excursions in the vicinity, enabled me to understand the agriculture of the district.

Thence I travelled to Florence, where my time was divided between agriculture and the Tribuna, that is, between Farmers and Venuses.

I was here introduced to many celebrated characters and to others able to give me valuable agricultural information. At home we had a very pleasant party, and abroad our eyes were feasted with all that Art or Science could produce.

Quitting Turin [on the return journey] I joined company with Mr. Grundy, a considerable merchant, from Birmingham. We crossed over Mont Cenis on our route to Lyons.[1]

During the winter of this year I met Dr. Watson several times at my friend Symonds', and shall here copy a private note I made on that celebrated character.

I was well acquainted with him for some years before he was made a Bishop as well as long after.

---

[1] 'January 30, 1790. To Bradfield, and here terminate, I hope, my travels.'—*Travels in France*, Bohn's Library.

Nor is it strange that I should be assiduous in cultivating a connection with a man of such extraordinary powers, who had a most peculiar felicity in bringing all the stores of a richly furnished mind to bear as occasion required in conversation. His memory was wonderfully retentive, and he had the art of speaking upon subjects with which he was not well acquainted without betraying any ignorance. He had a clear, logical head, great promptness of application, and the utmost fluency of expression, but sometimes with an affectation of enunciation in a delicate manner which did not at all become the native sturdiness of his disposition. He had a mathematical calculating head, which enabled him readily to apply scientific researches to the ordinary purposes of life. His style was always uncommonly perspicuous. The King once said to him, 'I know not how it is, my Lord, but when I read any of your publications I am never for one moment at a loss for your meaning, whereas in reading the works of other very able men their want of clearness often makes me doubtful.' 'Sir,' replied the Bishop, 'we are very assiduous at Cambridge to study Euclid and Locke.' Almost from being made a Bishop he became a disgusted man, because he never could procure a translation, and it was supposed that the Queen was influenced against him by Bishop Porteus, who had not so high an opinion of him as many others. He was once speaking to Porteus in praise of Locke's 'Reasonableness of Christianity,' and said in the course of conversation, 'I presume, my Lord, you are of the same opinion.' But Porteus, who had not been able to get in a word for some time, with a firmness not perhaps common with him when conversing with such a man as Watson, said, 'Indeed, my Lord, I am quite of a different opinion'—then left the room abruptly.

Watson disapproved of his daughter learning Latin, but was very assiduous to procure her translations of the Classics. Upon coming to the University, or not long after, he found himself very deficient in Classical learning, and applied to recover lost time with indefatigable attention. He was tutor to Mr. Luther, of Essex, at Cambridge, and was useful to him in the great contested election for that county. Soon after, Luther, as was supposed from motives of economy, went to France, and, in his absence, some malignant reports were spread to his disadvantage. Watson saw the great importance of trampling upon them immediately; not trusting to any correspondence, he went to Paris, and represented to him the necessity of instantly returning and showing himself in every company that was possible. Luther felt the propriety of the advice, and directly returned with the Doctor, whose conduct upon this and many other occasions made such an impression on his mind that he left him a good estate in the very heart of the Earl of Egremont's at Petworth, so that part of it joined not only the park, but the garden. To purchase this estate was a very great object to Lord E., and the Bishop, not liking to ask too high a price in the years' purchase for the land, made a valuation of a great quantity of young timber on what would be the future value of the trees, and by this means contrived to have a very great price for the estate. It was too great an object to Lord E. to be refused; but the Bishop did not escape without censure.

Count Leopold Berchtold published this year his 'Hints to Patriotic Travellers,' which in a very handsome manner he dedicated to me. My correspondence was somewhat numerous. I could give a long list, but shall only mention the following:—

From Count Bukaty, Polish Ambassador, invitation from the King of Poland.[1]

'Holles Street: May 27, 1789.

'Sir,—I acquit myself of my old debt of gratitude which I owe you in returning my sincere thanks for all the kindness which my nephew has experienced from you and your family during his residence at Bradfield Hall. I left him in Poland to spread your name and superior merit, which is already so well known and justly admired all over Europe. Your well-deserved fame reaching his Majesty the King of Poland, and his brother, the Prince Primate, makes them wish to see you once in that country, whose natural riches consisting in agriculture might be essentially improved by your transcendent knowledge therein. It was already their intention to establish there a Society of Agriculture, had it not been for the present political circumstances, which necessarily take up all their time and attention. I would be exceed-

---

[1] This letter is interesting as written by the last representative of that unhappy country in England. We read in Knight's *History of England*, vol. v., that, on the reassembling of Parliament after the partition of Poland no allusion whatever was made in the House of Commons to that event. The final partition treaty was signed in 1795 by Russia, Prussia, and Austria.

ingly happy, Sir, when you will be present in Town in order to have some conversation with you on the subject. In the meantime, I take the liberty to ask your favour in informing me where I could get the machine for separating corn from chaff, whereof the drawing was brought to Poland by my nephew?

'I have the honour to be, with the greatest respect,
'Sir, your most obedient, &c.,
'F. BUKATY,
'Envoy Extraordinary of Poland.'

From Dr. Burney

'Chelsea College: Oct. 20, 1789.

'My dear Friend,—I have begged a corner of this sheet from your daughter Bessy to congratulate you on your safe arrival on Classic ground after the perils and dangers of Gothic ground. How insipid will the history of the present times in this last country render all other history! And what weight will it not give to what has been long called the history of Fabulous times! The Poissardes are but the Amazons of the present day, and the leaders at the attack of the Bastille the Hercules and Theseus. The fetching the King, Queen, and Royal Family from Versailles, and the total demolition of the ancient government of the Kingdom, have no type in history or fable, ancient or modern. The nobles and clergy indiscriminately stripped of their honours and property, not to give it to others of the same rank and class, but to the mob, who are helping themselves to whatever they like, and destroying whom and what is not honoured with their approbation in a more successful and effectual way than our Wat Tyler or Jack Straw ever intended, and which would have astonished even J. J. Rousseau had he been living, in spite of his ideas of an *égalité de condition*. But whether a totally levelling scheme can be rendered permanent in a great Empire or no, time, not experience, can show. I used to think *la loi des plus forts* only existed among savages, and that in Society there were tall minds as well as tall bodies, but none such have as yet appeared in France. But let us talk of Italy, where I found no want of tall minds, even in these degenerate days. I am glad you seem to like the farming of the Milanese. I was particularly struck with it all through Lombardy, and think you will find even among the peasantry shrewdness, industry, and ingenuity. In all the great cities I found philosophers, mathematicians, and scholars, as well as musicians; these last, indeed, make more *noise* in the world, and, being travellers, spread their own fame into remote countries, while the drone and scientific part of a nation are seldom heard of out of the walls of their colleges or towns till after their decease. Indeed, almost all those I knew personally nineteen years ago in Italy are now no more! Padre Boccaria at Turin, Padre Boscovich at Milan, and Padre Sacchi. This last, I believe, is still living. But Count Firmian is dead, to whom I and every English traveller was much obliged by his hospitality and kindness. You probably owe the same obligation to his successor, with whose name even I am unacquainted. If you go to Padua you will probably stop at Verona, where there are always men of learning and science. But you must not judge of the present state of musick in any part of Italy unless you remain there during the Carnival. At other times (except at the great fairs) the principal theatres are shut, and the others supplied with such riff-raff as our Sadler's Wells during summer. If Guadagni had been living, you would have him at Padua, and if I had not engaged him to the Pantheon, Pachierotti, whom we expect here in a few days. Pray go to the church of Sant' Antonio on a festival; there Tartini used to lead and Guadagni sing. If Padre Valetti is living, the Maestro di Capella, pray present my compliments to him and enquire after the sequel of his Treatise. I have as yet only seen the first part. I likewise beg to be remembered to Signor Marsili, the Professor of Botany, and Padre Columbo, the Professor of Mathematics: the first was some time in England and speaks our language; the second was the great friend of Tartini, and left in possession of all his manuscript papers. Enquire what is become of them, and try to get intelligence of the disposal of Padre Martini's papers, books, and sequel of his 'History of Musick' at Bologna. Enquire likewise when you meet with intelligent musical people what are the defects of the newest and best of the great Italian theatres. No plan is, I believe, as yet adopted for rebuilding ours. Le Texier has a model made with many conveniences and more magnificence than our former theatre could boast, but whether it will be adopted, or whether it is to be wished that a Frenchman should ever have the management of an Italian opera, I know not. However partial he or his countrymen may seem to German and Italian musick, I know by long observation that they are totally ignorant of, and enemies to, *good singing*, without which what are the two or three acts of an opera but intermezzi or act tunes to the ballets? I perceive, however, that, amidst all the horrors of Paris, they suffer Italian operas to be performed in Italian and by Italians, which were never allowed before, except at Versailles; but these are only burlettas; serious operas so performed might have some effect on the national taste in singing. But les Dames des Halles, their excellencies *Mesdames les Poissardes*, furnish them with "other fish to fry" at present; so I shall say no more of France, but that I pity most sincerely every honest man who has the misfortune to be resident in that distracted kingdom.

'God bless you, my dear Sir, and give you health and spirits to enjoy your rational and useful enquiries.
'CHARLES BURNEY.'

[The following extracts from Arthur Young's letters home, and letter to his darling Bobbin, then aged five, are worth giving. With very slight excisions all letters to his daughter Mary are incorporated in the 'French Travels.']

'*Lyons, Dec.* 28, 1789.—Symonds says Arthur has set off very well at Cambridge, which I am very glad to hear. God send him understanding enough to know the value of these four years there, which are either lost absolutely or applied to the amelioration of all his life after. French and Italian or German after four years at Cambridge may qualify it for anything.'

From another letter to the same :—

'I found here your Mother's two letters, of which I can hardly make head or tail; according to custom they are so cross written and so crammed and topsy-turvy, that, like the oracles of old, they may be made to speak whatever is in the reader's head, alley croaker (*sic*) or "Paradise Lost" are all one.'

From a third letter, dated Florence, November 18, 1789 :—

'I received here a letter from you, and two from your Mother; yours is dated October 17, one of hers the 30th, the other no date, and not a word of Bobbin in it. What a way of writing, and this to a man 1,400 miles from home. I am greatly concerned for Mr. Arbuthnot, though his silence made him dead to us from the time he went to Ireland. I never knew a family which was the centre of every mild and agreeable virtue so shattered into nothing by a man's failure. I have long and often regretted that period. . . . I took 100*l*. with me, and it lasts exactly six months, buying books included. . . . Good night. Thank God, Bobbin is well; give her a kiss.'

To his youngest Daughter, Martha (Bobbin)
'Moulins: August 7, 1789.

'My dear Bobbin,—I fully expected to have heard from Mary here, and to have known how my dear little girl does, but I was much disappointed and found no letter from England.

'I think it high time to enquire of you how you pass your time—what you do—how Mr. Mag (the pony) does, and the four kittens; I hope you have taken care of them and remembered your Papa wants cats. Do the flowers grow well in your garden? Are you a better gardener than you used to be? The Marq. de Guerchy's little girls have a little house on a little hill, and on one side a little flower garden, and on the other side a little kitchen garden, which they manage themselves and keep very clean from weeds—Bobbin would like much to see it.

'I have passed through perils and dangers, for a part of the country is infested by 800 plunderers in arms, yet have burnt in only one district near Mâcon twelve chateaus; but I am now passed the worst and hope to escape at last with whole bones. I have a passport, and am carried to the Bourgeois guard at all the towns.

'Pray, my little girl, take care, and keep clear from weeds the row of grass I sowed in the round garden, on right hand about ten yards long, but don't take up anything like grass. And if the two willows which I brought last year 1,000 miles from France are alive yet, give them some water; one is by the hole, and the other by Arthur's garden—I made little mounds around them. You do not know, my little Bobbin, how much I long to have a walk with you at Bradfield. It is a sad thing I have no letter here; I shall have none till Clermont. I desire a particular account of my farm to be sent here.

'I have been ill from heat and fatigue, and had a

sore throat, but by care and an antiseptic diet I am now, thank God, quite well.

'What do you think of the French at such a moment as this with a free press? yet in this capital of a great province there is not (publickly) one newspaper to be seen; at a coffee house, where twenty tables for company, not one. What blessed ignorance. The Paris m—— have done the whole, and are the only enlightened part of the K——.

'Adieu, my dear B.

'I am, yours affectionately,

'A. Y.'

[In a note A. Y. writes :]

'I found Madame la Comtesse de Guerchy a very pleasant, agreeable woman, and among other trifles which occurred at their house was an expedition into the kitchen to teach me to make an omelette, the operation attending which occasioned no little merriment both in the kitchen and parlour. I succeeded pretty well.'[1]

1790.—All this summer I was employed in preparing my [French] Travels for the press. In October I had a violent fever, which brought me to the brink of the grave. I made a minute of that illness in the following words : 'From almost the bed of death, it pleased the Divine Goodness to raise me up, and I remember it was in perfect hardness of heart and free from all true or grateful feelings. I was in a state of

[1] The passage occurs in the small memorandum-book from which I have occasionally quoted particulars o yearly expenses, &c.

blindness and insensibility, on which I reflect with horror and amazement.'[1]

I cannot speak of the ingratitude of my heart to God at this period but in the strongest terms, as it amounted to a degree of insensibility quite unaccountable. I fear that not one thought of God ever occurred to me at that time, and I doubt whether [it was so], while one evening I had resumed the habit of prayer, that is, of those formal prayers which an unconverted person may repeat without any real devotion; and yet during my delirium the physician afterwards told me that I one day broke forth into one of the most eloquent and sublime prayers he ever heard, to his utter astonishment.

During my recovery I wrote that melancholy review of my past life, which is printed in the 'Annals.'

[1] Vol. xv. 1791, *My Own Memoirs*.

CHAPTER IX

PATRIOTIC PROPOSALS—1791-92

Illness—Correspondence with Washington—The King's gift of a ram—
Anecdotes—Revising MSS.—Patriotic proposals—Death of the Earl
of Orford—Agricultural schemes—Correspondence.

THE year opened with a continuation of that severe illness which had confined me for some months. The following notes are from a journal I kept at that time:—

This year my daughter Elizabeth married the Rev. Samuel Hoole, son of the celebrated John Hoole, translator of Tasso and Ariosto. He is a very sensible, moral man of strict integrity, and always behaved to my daughter with much tenderness.

This same year my correspondence [1] opened with General Washington. Having been applied to to procure some implements for his husbandry, I wrote to him offering to procure any article in that line which he might have occasion for, and accordingly afterwards sent him many, amongst others the plan of a barn, which he executed, and is represented by a plate in the 'Annals of Agriculture.'

[1] These letters were sold by Sotheby, Wilkinson & Co., London, December 1896.

This year his Majesty had the goodness to make me a present of a Spanish Merino ram, a portrait of which I inserted in the 'Annals.'

How many millions of men are there that would smile if I were to mention the Sovereign of a great Empire giving a ram to a farmer as an event that merited the attention of mankind! The world is full of those who consider military glory as the proper object of the ambition of monarchs; who measure regal merit by the millions that are slaughtered; by the public robbery and plunder that are dignified by the titles of dignity and conquest, and who look down on every exertion of peace and tranquillity as unbecoming those who aim at the epithet *great*, and unworthy the aim of men that are born the masters of the globe.

My ideas are cast in a very different mould, and I believe the period is advancing with accelerated pace that shall exhibit characters in a light totally new, and shall rather brand than exalt the virtues hitherto admired; that shall place in full blaze of meridian lustre actions lost on the mass of mankind; that shall pay more homage to the memory of a Prince that gave a ram to a farmer than for wielding the sceptre obeyed alike on the Ganges and on the Thames.

I shall presume to offer but one other general observation. When we see his Majesty practising husbandry with that warmth that marks a favourite pursuit, and taking such steps to diffuse a foreign breed of sheep well calculated to improve those of his kingdoms; when we see the Royal pursuits take such a direction, we may safely conclude that the public measures which, in certain instances, have been so hostile to the agriculture of this country, have nothing in common with the opinions of our gracious Sovereign; such measures are the work of men, who never felt for husbandry; who never practised it; who never loved it; it is not such men that give rams to farmers.

October 21.—A letter to-day from General Washington—Gracious! from the representative of the Majesty of America, all written with his own hand. Also one from the Marquis de la Fayette desiring my assistance to get him a bailiff that understands English ornamental gardening; for both he gives fifty louis[1] a year—this is a French idea to unite what never was united, and, when gained, reward it with wages little better than a common labourer.

October 24.—Dined yesterday at Sir Thomas Gage's to meet the Miss Fergus's and Dr. and Mrs. Onslow. This Dr. was the youngest son of the late General Onslow, brother of my godfather, the Speaker, in whose family my dear mother was for many years upon the most intimate footing of private friendship.

When a boy I was frequently at his house, and well remember having this Arthur, a child, on my knee. Mrs. Onslow mentioned how much she had heard Mr. Boswell talk of my works. I fancy Boswell, from some things I heard of him, and it seems confirmed by various passages in his 'Life of Johnson,' has a sort of rage for knowing all sorts of public men, good, bad, and indifferent, all one if a man renders himself known he likes to be acquainted with him. Mrs. Onslow reported

---

[1] Louis d'or at this time worth 24 francs.—*Littré.*

to me the following conversation which took place at the Prince's table :—

The Prince of Wales, with a large company dining with him, said, 'The three greatest coxcombs in England are in this room. Here is my friend Hanger,[1] the Duke of Queensberry must come in for the second;' he made a pause, enough for the company to stare for the third, and added, 'for the third, it is certainly myself.'

When Sir W. Courtenay asked Lord Bute for a peerage, he carried his pedigree with him. Lord Bute examined and pretended to be a good judge of those things. He told Mr. Symonds that nothing could be clearer or more unquestionable than his descent lineally from Louis le Gros of France, the relationship with the House of Bourbon which occasions the mourning of a day in the Court of France for the death of a Courtenay.[2] Lord Bute told him his demand of a barony was too modest, and that he should be a Viscount, which he was accordingly.

October 26.—In preparing my Travels [in France] for the press, I experience strongly the importance of an author's having composed so much more than he means to print as to be able to strike out largely.

My agreement with Richardson was to have six shillings a volume for all sold of one guinea quarto volumes, but when Rackham's compositor came to cast

---

[1] The well-known Colonel George Hanger, afterwards fourth Lord Coleraine. 'He served in the Army during the American War, and was afterwards a distinguished character in high society. Wrote his *Life, Adventures, and Opinions.*'—*Annual Register*, 1824.

[2] See on this subject Gibbon's *Rome*, vol. xi. ch. lxi.

off the MS. he found enough for two large quarto volumes, since which discovery I had to strike out just half of what I had written; and the advantage will be very great to the work. I read the books as they are wanted for the press again and again, reducing the quantity every time till I get it tolerably to my mind, but yet not to the amount of half. The work is certainly improved by this means, and I am strongly of opinion if nine-tenths of other writers were to do the same thing their performances would be so much the better; for one reads very few quartos that would not be improved by reducing to octavo volumes.

November 23.—I was five days last week at the Duke of Grafton's, Admiral, Mrs., and two Miss Pigots were there—she [Mrs. P.] is sister to the Duchess, the Admiral is a very worthy man—Mr. Stonehewer there also, and old Vary. I spent two days in taking the level of the Duke's river for four miles, in order to see how much land he might water, and the improvement his estate is capable of is very great indeed. The character of this Duke is original; he is uncommonly sensible, there is no stuff in him; he is cold, silent, reserved, and even at times sullen, and he is removed from all that ease and suavity which render people agreeable; yet there is such a solid understanding, and so much learning and knowledge on certain topics, that one must value him in spite of our feelings.

Very little of the conversation interesting enough to be worth recording. I was also at a new club which

Ruggles[1] has instituted at Melford, which might have been an agreeable thing had there been half a dozen only.

The following are [among] the letters preserved this year:—

From Dr. Burney, congratulations, pleasant anecdotes, and an account of a large auction of books, &c. :—

'Chelsea College : Jan. 7, 1791.

'My dear Arthur,—The precipice on which you have so long been scrambling for life seems to be more dangerous than any one of those which I had to encounter from Sarzana to Genoa or Genoa to Final. In the first of these scrambles during three days and three nights on a mule without bridle (except that of Jack Ketch) or saddle, I had a torrent called the Magra roaring in my ears at a perpendicular distance of eight hundred or a thousand feet, and, in the second, the Mediterranean, during a storm which no vessel could weather. In the darkest night I ever *saw*, with the artificial lights of our lanterns extinguished by the violence of the wind, at every twenty or thirty yards the *pedino* (a man on foot to guide the mule) cried out, " Alla montagna! alla montagna, Signore!" which was an admonition to alight and crawl on all fours over broken roads on the ridge of a precipice.

'Now let *me* play the *pedino's* part to your worship, and admonish you to be very careful how you travel in the perilous way to health which you have still to pass, after your escape from the great precipice ; for

---

[1] Th. Ruggles, author of a *History of the Poor*, reprinted afterwards from the *Annals of Agriculture*. Many passages were omitted, in accordance with the wishes of Pitt.—*Lowndes*.

which escape, as an Italian would say, "*io me ne congratulo non meno con me medesimo che con voi.*"

'But besides congratulating you on your amendment, I have for some time wished to tell you that in the Paitoni catalogue of Italian books now selling by auction at Robson's room, there are many on Natural History and Agriculture. Now as you have dipped into Italian literature and farming, it struck me on seeing the catalogue that there may be several works that you would wish to purchase, particularly as the Italian books of Science have hitherto sold at this auction for almost nothing. I purchased nearly fifty volumes of poetry and miscellanies, and my bill did not amount to five pounds. The books are in exceeding good condition, and most of them such as have never appeared before in the Osburn, Payne, or Robson catalogues. I am inclined to think that this sale will enrich future catalogues in our country for many years to come. Indeed I was so tired of eternally meeting with the same book over and over again that I had no longer patience to read them.

'If you see any you wish I will get them purchased, but as neither your Bibliomania nor mine has ever raged to such a degree as to wish to buy in at any price, it will be necessary to say that we mean not to vie with those who being more curious in *books* than *authors* procure them at any price to look at and not to read. A rich acquaintance of mine, and a customer of old Tom Payne, has often bought books in languages of which he knew not a single word, merely because they were beautifully bound or very scarce.'

From another letter :—

'I have not time nor space to lengthen my letter, or I should tell you of a long conversation I had last Sunday at Lady Lucan's blue-stocking conversazione with Lord Macartney about you. He has just come from Ireland and wanted to know whether you were recovered—whether you come to London this winter, as he wished to communicate some memorandums he made in perusing your "Irish Tour" while he was in Ireland. He is a charming man, to my mind.

'Poor Fanny[1] has been very ill indeed, and we have been in expectation of her coming to nurse, but she will risk the dying at her Majesty's feet to show her zeal before she can be spared, I suppose.

'I have had the great Haydn here, and think him as *good* a creature as *great* Musician. As to operas, the Pantheon advertises to open as a theatre; it is the most elegant in Europe, Pacchierotti says, but it has great enemies. The Haymarket folks have not yet obtained a licence, at which they affect surprise, though they were told so before their building was a foot high. Old Mingotti is come over with her scholar Madame Lobo, the intended first woman of the Haymarket. It will be a busy and memorable season in the history of tweedle-dum and tweedle-dee quarrels.

'Adieu!
'Believe me,
'Yours very affectionately,
'CHARLES BURNEY.'

[1] Dr. Burney's daughter, Madame d'Arblay.

'Chelsea College: Sept. 21, 1791.

'My dear Friend,—I am quite ashamed of not answering your kind and hearty letter of invitation sooner. But a listless and irresolute disposition has made my mind for some time past as flimsy as a dishclout, and I must *confess* that I have invariably " left undone those things which I *ought* to have done "— "for there was no health in me," indeed, not enough to enable me "to do many things which I *ought not* to have done." Original sin and depravity just enabled me to *read* when I should have *written*, and to lie in bed when I should have got up, &c. I wished to commit other *guess* crimes than those, to have rambled over a great part of the kingdom and revelled with distant friends. But prudence, in the shape of rheumatism, and in many other hideous shapes, prevented me. Yet, in spite of all these admonitions, I had a month's mind to accept of your hospitable offer. But we have guests at our apartments now, my two aged sisters, and, when they depart, winter will begin to show his sour face and chain me to my chimney corner till after Christmas, when I shall be unfettered, merely to be dragged into the hurry and din of London, which are every year more and more insupportable. I have long ceased to like the country, except in long days and fine weather, and, in winter, prefer London with all its horrors and fatigues to rural amusements. Indeed, autumn with all its golden glow and variegated charms for landscape painters is to me a constant *memento mori*, with its withered leaves tumbling about my ears; and all my most severe attacks of rheumatism have been during the equinoctial winds and rains; so that I am afraid of trusting myself far from home at this season of the year, as one can be sick and cross nowhere so *comfortably* as at home.

'Having scribbled my apology, I must now hasten to congratulate you and Mrs. Young on the marriage of our dear and worthy girl Bessy.[1] The match, indeed, is not splendid for either in point of circumstances; but they are quite as likely to scramble happily through life, with good hearts and wishes limited to their means, as the richest peers and peeresses in the land, who generally outlive their income, be it what it will, and have mortifications incident to pride and disappointed ambition which little folk know nothing about. They (I mean our young couple) have my hearty benediction and good wishes. A man without family attachments is an awkward and insulated being, but a woman without a mate is still more insignificant and helpless; and, having become adventurers in the matrimonial lottery, I sincerely hope they will gain a prize in the fortuitous distribution of such happiness as reasonable mortals have a right to expect.

'I dare not venture on French politics. What a marvellous period in the history of that nation! I think the clergy and many worthy people of the lower class of nobility have been cruelly used, and that the mob is at present too powerful and insolent. Too much has been promised them, and nothing short of an agrarian law will satisfy them. The word tax, *taille*,

---

[1] Arthur Young's daughter Elizabeth, the first wife of Rev. Samuel Hoole.

impost, are carefully avoided in the National Chart. But they must be levied under some denomination or other, and, I fancy, " contribution " will be as detestable a term in France, ere long, as "free-gift" was in England during the last century. I wish the worthy people of France may enjoy the rational liberty which seems now in their power, but I question whether the inhabitants of that kingdom in general will deserve the ample liberty which is offered them, or know how to use it. I think them so fickle and frivolous that I should not be surprised if in a few years they were as tired of their new Government as the English at the death of Oliver Cromwell. In the meantime what has happened in America and France will shake every sovereignty upon earth. The French Guards laying down their arms when ordered to fire on the mob will make mobs formidable things in every country, for whenever a similar defection happens a revolution must be the consequence.

'I am sorry not to be able to give your friend, Mr. Capel Lofft, an account of any Lyre in modern times having been in use that has been constructed, strung, and tuned on the principles of the antients. Innumerable volumes have been written on their division of the scale and genera. Kircher, indeed, calls a Vielle a hurdy-gurdy, Lyra mendicorum. And a Viol da Gamba, with additional strings and new tuning, was in the last century called a Lyra-Viol. Mace,[1] Playford,[2] Simpson,[3] I believe, and others describe this

[1] Th. Mace, author of *Music's Monument*.
[2] T. Playford, author of *Music's Delight, &c.*, 1668, 1676.
[3] C. Simpson, author of *The Division Viol*, 1687.

instrument. But though many modern instruments have had the honour of being called Lyres, yet none of them resemble the antient in their form or in the manner of playing them. The Mandoline is the only modern instrument played with anything like a plectrum. Vicenzio Galileo, the father of Galileo, in his tract, "Della Musica antica e moderna," published at Florence 1602, speaks much of the similarity of the antient Lyre and Cythara, but gives more proof from antient authors of their *difference* than *identity*. He tells us, however, that "the modern Harp, which is nothing but the antient Cythara with many strings, was brought into Italy from Ireland." Now the Irish harp is a single instrument of few strings, partly brass and partly steel, and of such small compass as to admit no bass, being confined to mere melody. Carolan, the celebrated modern Irish Bard, played only the treble part of tunes. And it seems to me as if this simple instrument resembled the antient Lyre and Cythara more than any other modern instrument with which I am acquainted. Pray tell Mr. Lofft that I have examined Bonanni's description of all the musical instruments that are known, with engravings of them all, but found nothing satisfactory about a modern Lyre. This book was published at Rome 1722. I have likewise looked into Ceruti's new edition with corrections, 1776, without success.

'I am, my dear friend,
'Yours affectionately,
'CHARLES BURNEY.'

From Dr. John Symonds on the political state of the country—an account of a conference between Mr. Pitt and the Duke of Grafton :—

'Bates' Hotel, Adelphi: April 19, 1791.

'My dear Young,—Hope you will not expect to hear me talking on Agriculture; of that you will have a sufficient taste from seeing the wonderful knowledge exhibited by all the House of Commons in the Corn Bill. You will look for something on politics, though the newspapers themselves sufficiently show the straits to which Mr. Pitt is driven; for his majority is such as will ruin any Minister if a war be unpopular; and had the American war been so at first, it is not probable that Lord North would have dared to pursue it, though he was so strongly supported in Parliament.

'The truth is, some of Mr. Pitt's bosom friends absolutely refuse to vote with him on this occasion. Among these are Wilberforce and Banks. The Duke of Grafton desired his son-in-law, Mr. Smith, to tell Mr. Pitt he wished to have some conversation with him; Mr. Pitt very politely came and staid half-an-hour, and the Duke used every argument he could think of to convince him, both of the impolicy and injustice of the war, "that the augmentation of taxes coming upon the neck of the cessed ones, and malt tax, which made a great noise, would occasion universal discontent, if not worse effects; that we ought to lay no stress upon the promises of a Turkish Ministry and advantages in the Turkey trade, which must chiefly accrue to France from her situation, and other causes;

that what we could do in the Baltic was merely to burn a few villages and distress individuals, as the Russian fleet would lie securely among rocks, that Russia appeared to act with moderation in desiring to retain Ockzakow only; and that to plunge this nation into a vast expense, merely to serve the King of Prussia's views, when we could obtain no benefit from it, would expose the Ministry to very great censure, more especially as we entered into it as volunteers, not being obliged to it by the terms of the Treaty." Other things which his Grace said I omit, as every argument has been used in the House of Commons. The conference ended as conferences of this sort generally do—each of them kept to his opinion.

'You observe probably in the papers, that on Baker's motion, Pole Carew moved the previous question and contended "that the interests of all are closely connected even in respect to things not stipulated by treaty." This judicious doctrine was first advanced by the Chancellor, and Mr. Pitt defended in his speech on Baker's motion. According to this doctrine, there is no difference between defensive and offensive treaties; all the writer's *de jure gentium* should be burnt, and, indeed, most of the European treaties also; and it is certain that under such circumstances England ought never to make an alliance on the Continent unless a Continental war were actually broken out; otherwise she could not foresee the consequences to which she would be exposed.

'Charles Fox said in his speech on Baker's motion "that Mr. Pitt dared not to enter into the war, and that he kept a majority together at present by his assurance that there would not be one."

'This is, perhaps, the case; but however it may be, it is certain that Faukner, Clerk of the Council, is sent to Berlin, and most persons think with a view of showing the King of Prussia the impossibility of persuading this country to enter into a Russian war. Had Mr. Pitt felt the pulse of the Parliament and people before he delivered the King's message, he would have saved his credit, though he might have been blamed; but he has now run into the horns of a dilemma, as the logicians call it. If he prosecute the war, he will infallibly be ex-Minister, and bad consequences are to be apprehended in a country oppressed by taxes and heated by political pamphlets; if he give it up, he will lose all his influence in the eyes of Europe, and teach foreign Courts that no confidence is to be placed in an English Minister. His friends lament very much this last circumstance.

'Adieu!

'JOHN SYMONDS.'

A circumstance in the exploits of my public career which made, perhaps, a more general impression than any other event of my life, was the proposal in 1792 for arming the property of the Kingdom in a sort of horse militia. My first suggestion of this idea was in May (of that year). Should any have claimed it, or should any hereafter form such a claim, it ought in truth and strict candour to be absolutely rejected. The proposal was more formally made in August of the same year in the 'Annals,' vol. xviii. p. 495, under the title of French events.[1] In the end of 1792 and the beginning of 1793 these papers were collected and much enlarged in a pamphlet entitled, 'The Example of France,' &c. which ran speedily through four numerous editions, and excited a very general attention. The author was publicly thanked in resolutions of associated assemblies, and my great plea of a horse militia produced almost immediately three volunteer corps of cavalry, which multiplied rapidly through the Kingdom. It is not known that any persons or any bodies of men ever laid claim to a priority in this idea; accordingly my health was the first toast given for being the origin of those corps, which, when assembled, had this opportunity of publicly declaring their opinion. The scheme took with astonishing celerity, and became the parent of a measure of a very different complexion, which was putting arms into the hands of thousands without property, and upon whose allegiance and constitutional principle but little reliance could be placed. Government received demands for arms to the amount of above 700,000 men. The Ministers were alarmed, and saw too late the consequence of their own blindness and incapacity. They refused their consent, in many cases without properly discriminating between men with and without property, and felt themselves in so awkward a position that it is no wonder their conduct continued void of any steady adherence to the principle of the original proposition.

[1] See the *Travels in France*, Bohn's Library, p. 335 *et seq.*, for the views therein set forth.

Had my plan not only been adopted but carried into execution, strictly upon the principles I had explained, we might from that moment to the present have had a horse militia, absolutely under the command of Government, numbering from 100,000 to 200,000 men, which might, by progressive improvements, have been matured into a force efficient for every purpose. It is very seldom that so private an individual can by a happy thought become the origin of a system which, had my principles been steadily adhered to, would have been attended with inconceivable benefit, and none of those evils, real or imaginary, afterwards attributed to volunteers in general.

The pamphlet rendered the author exceedingly popular among all the friends of government and order, and as unpopular among the whole race of reformers and Jacobins. I was not content with the mere theoretical idea, but in my own person put it into practice, and enrolled myself in the ranks of a corps raised at my recommendation, in the vicinity of Bury [St. Edmunds], and commanded by the present Marquis of Cornwallis, then Lord Broome, having with this intention learnt the sword exercise at London of a sergeant, who was eminently skilled in it. My example was followed by gentlemen of fortune, several of whom were also in the ranks and refused to be officers. This was a part of the plan of particular importance, for had gentlemen accepted only the situation of officers, the spirit of entering the corps among yeomen, farmers &c. would have been much cooler; but when they saw their landlords, and men of high consideration in the neighbourhood, in the same situation, their vanity was flattered, and they enrolled themselves with great readiness, and the great object of property of such importance in case of revolutionary disturbance was thus secured.

Some years afterwards, being at the Duke of Bedford's at Woburn, I sat at dinner by a gentleman of great property, captain of a troop of yeomanry, who told me that whenever his troop met he always drank my health after the King's, for being the undisputed origin of all the yeomanry corps in the kingdom, possibly arising from extracts from my writings on the subject having been much circulated in the newspapers.

This year my valuable and very sincere friend, the Earl of Orford, died. The public papers that have announced the death of this noble lord have recorded the ancestry from which he was descended, the heirs of his honours, and the inheritors of his wealth, and have dwelt upon the titles that are extinct or devolved, together with all the posts and employments that are vacant. To me be the melancholy duty of noting what is of much more moment than the descent of a peerage or the transfer of an estate—the loss of an animated improver; of one who gave importance to cultivation by a thorough knowledge of political economy, and bent all his endeavours towards making mankind happy by seconding the pursuits of the farmer and the enquiries of the experimentalist. I leave the lieutenancy of a county, the rangership of a park, and the honours of the bedchamber to those in whose eyes such baubles are respectable. I would rather dwell on the merit of the first importer of Southdown sheep into Norfolk; on the merit of sending to the most distant regions for breeds of animals, represented as useful, not indeed always with success, but never without liberality in the motive; on the patron and friend of the common farmer, not the lord of a little circle of tenants, but the general and diffusive encourager of every species of agricultural improvement. Nor did he associate with the useful men because he was not qualified for the company of higher classes, for his mind was fraught with a great extent of knowledge; it was decorated by no trivial stores of classical learning, which exercised and set off the powers of a brilliant imagination, and thus qualified, alike for a Court or an Academy of Science, he felt no degradation in attending to THE PLOUGH. By the death of this noble personage the 'Annals' have lost a valuable correspondent, and their editor a warm friend. Notwithstanding the immense list of Peers, seven or eight only have become correspondents in this work. The insects of a drawing-room, the patrons of faro, the luminaries of Newmarket, are spared; while the hand of death deprives the farmer of a friend, Norfolk of a protector, and England of a real patriot.

Lord Loughborough was the Judge at the Summer Assizes this year at Bury, and I being on the Grand Jury, he sent a note to inform me that he was alone at his lodgings, and desired me to come and chat with him. This I did, of course, and in our conversation he mentioned that there was an estate of 4,400 acres of land in Yorkshire on the moors, in the vicinity of Paitley

Bridge, to be sold for 4,000*l*., that it was chiefly freehold, and enclosed with a ring fence, also that there was a neat shooting-box on it built by the Duke of Devonshire, who hired the grouse. I assured his Lordship that he must be mistaken, for it was impossible that such a tract of land under several circumstances which he named could be on sale for half an hour without being purchased. He answered that nobody would buy it, as the land was all moor or peat, and covered with ling, but that some neighbouring farmers gave, he believed, 100*l*. per annum for the whole as a walk for mountain sheep. I told him that it seemed so extraordinary to me that I would go immediately to view it. He said the proper persons to apply to to view it were Sir Cecil Wray, Dr. Kilvington, and another gentleman. I accordingly went immediately to Yorkshire, and, taking up my quarters at Paitley Bridge, enquired till I found a person who knew the whole estate perfectly well, and engaged him early the next morning in order to make the tour of the whole property. It appeared to me to be wonderfully improvable, and that very considerable tracts to the amount of some hundred acres were palpably capable of irrigation and improvement, evidently applicable from the case of a small watercourse for conducting the water to an old smelting mill, but long neglected. This course had overflowed and converted the ling, over about fifteen acres, to grass. I asked my conductor what this grass would let for with a small cottage and stable for cows; he said, 'Certainly fifteen shillings an acre.' It was sufficiently evident that improvements might be wrought at a very small expense, and that building was remarkably cheap, from every material except timber being found on the spot, and lime at a small distance. There was a small farm in cultivation to produce oats, and the appearance not unfavourable. As I knew that a land surveyor well acquainted with all this country resided at Leeds, I determined to go thither to bring him over to view, and give his opinion as to the value of the property. This I did, brought him over in a postchaise, and rode with him over the principal part of the estate. His opinion confirmed my own, nor must I forget to mention that this estate was to be purchased without money as it was offered on its own security in mortgage.

In the enclosure of this immense waste, called forest, there were two allotments purchased by the proprietors, one of 1,638 acres, and another of 1,113, in all 2,751 acres, which were a copyhold tenure, at a small fine certain. In addition to which they hired, at the same time, on a long lease, 1,614 acres more, being an allotment to the King, at a rent of 50*l.* in money, and 50*l.* to be laid out on improvements. The whole, situated half-way between Knaresboro' and Skipton, I found walled in; three farm-houses built, with barns and offices of various sorts, and lands annexed, and partly subdivided, to the amount of about 400 acres; the remaining 4,000 in one vast waste. These farms produced the rent of 44*l.* 5*s.* The game was let at 30*l.* with the use of a handsome shooting-box, sufficient for the residence of a small family. Peat dug from the bogs produced from 6*l.* to 8*l.* a year; and the great

P

waste was let at 100*l.* a year, which, for 4,000 acres, is at the rate of sixpence per acre. The annual rental was therefore about 181*l.* per annum. From these circumstances it appeared clear to me that the purchase could not well be an unfavourable speculation. 2,750 acres (throwing the leasehold entirely out of the question) for 4,400*l.* is exactly 32*l.* an acre fee simple for land that paid a mere trifle in poor rates and land tax,¹ and tithe free; it did not seem therefore to be necessary that the produce should amount to three shillings, for if the rent was reckoned only at one shilling it was but thirty-two years' purchase. I determined, therefore, to make it, and concluded the transaction as soon as possible.

My plan was, to let my farm in Suffolk, of about 300 acres, and transfer the capital, with some additions, to the gradual improvement of this large tract; and, in doing this, I should have begun with one farm on the Southern extremity, near the turnpike road, of three or four hundred acres, let separately for 20*l.* a year, but all a waste, and, in addition to this, have run a watering canal from one of the streams, till from 100 to 200 acres were below the level, walling such tract in. Thus prepared, I found myself at last in a situation to realise the speculations I had so long been busy in—when a new scene of a very different kind opened upon me—but of that hereafter.

The following are the letters of this year reserved. From J. Symonds, Esq., an account of the Duke of Grafton's illness:—

¹ All the public charges on 4,000 acres amounted only to 14*l.*

'Euston: Jan. 30, 1792.

'So you tell me that I know not how to stay at home! but this is a visit of pure friendship, for the duke likes very well to chat with me, though he is so nervous as hardly to bear with strangers. Yesterday Lord Clermont, who is very intimate with him, came hither, but he was too much for the duke, and had he not gone away this morning, the duchess would have hinted it gently to him. What would you do with such nerves?

'Last night, intead of reading a sermon or charge, I read to the whole company (by the duke's desire) your essays on the police of corn and capital employed in the French husbandry, with which he had been so pleased. Lord Clermont, who has lived much in France, and though a man of pleasure, had inquired much into the state of that country, was not more delighted than surprised with them. "Well, then," said the duke, "as you like them so much and intend to buy the book, recommend it as much as possible to your friends in the great world." This he engaged to do. His Lordship gave a pressing invitation for you and I to pass two or three days with him; he fixed upon the month of May, which will suit me, and, I hope, you.

'As an inducement I was to tell you that he has marled four hundred and fifty acres with a hundred and twenty loads an acre—this is an object.

'J Symonds.'

J. W. Coke, Esq., M.P., proposing some laws for the benefit of the poor in their present distress:—

'Holkham: Oct. 23, 1792.

'Dear Sir,—I have no better motive to urge for addressing myself to you upon the subject of this letter than that I know of no man so well qualified as yourself to give me the information I stand in need of, should my plan be thought practicable and useful by you, otherwise I should take shame to myself to intrude for a moment on your time, which I esteem so precious, as it is always most usefully employed in the most laudable pursuits.

'Having turned my thoughts much of late to the most probable causes of the discontent among the lower classes of people in this country, I find that the high price of provisions, especially of bread, has been invariably the motive assigned by them whenever they have assembled in a tumultuous manner. And this is not surprising, as the existence of a poor man's family must depend upon that last-mentioned necessary article, most truly his staff of life. It is surely, then, the interest, as well as the duty, of the landed proprietors to endeavour by every means that can be devised that the poor may never suffer in this respect. Now, it has occurred to me that perhaps a Bill might be framed to fix an assize on flour according to the average price of wheat.

'That millers should be obliged to grind for all persons at a certain sum per bushel instead of toll; persons being at liberty to inspect their corn whilst grinding, and that allowance should be made to millers for any alleged deficiency in grinding. All complaints to be heard in a summary way before a Justice of the Peace, and the complaint to be made within six days. The average price of wheat to be taken from the nearest market at the discretion of the Justice. Penal clauses should also be enacted against millers adulterating wheat and mixing water with the meal to increase its weight.

'These loose hints I submit to your superior judgment and better information; but, from my own observation, I do suspect the poor suffer greatly from the shameful practices and combinations of the millers, which I should be proud to check by bringing a Bill into Parliament as one of the representatives of the great arable county, should you approve the idea and would have the goodness to lend me your assistance in framing the Bill.

'I must also mention another cruel grievance to the poor, that there is no legal restraint on shopkeepers in villages respecting their weights and measures.

'Could no means be devised to protect the buyer from the artifices of the seller without injury to the latter in their honest gains? Why might not magistrates have the power of punishing for short weights and measures, complaint to be made within six days?

'I remain, dear Sir.
'Yours very sincerely,
'J. W. COKE.'

From Dr. Burney on my 'Travels' and his own engagements :—

'Chelsea College: July 17, 1792.

'My dear Friend,—Your very kind and hearty invitation to Bradfield came at a time when I was utterly unable to answer it. I was just emerged from the sick room into daily hurry and business, for which I was but little fit, and am still detained here by an unusual number of engagements for this time of year, the end of which I am not able to see. If my *patients* had walked off as early as I wished them, or if, like other *doctors*, I could have them put to their long home by a dash of my pen, I really believe I should not have been able to resist the lure you threw out; but now, if I am able to travel, or fit for any house but my own, I have two positive engagements on my hands of long standing: the first to Mickleham, to my daughter, Phillips, where I promised, as soon as I could pronounce myself a convalescent, to go and complete my cure; the other is to Crewe Hall, in Cheshire, whither I have been going more than twice seven years; and at which place I was so sure of arriving last August, that my correspondents, at my request, addressed their letters to me there. This year the claims upon me and Fanny have been so powerfully renewed by Mrs. Crewe that nothing but increased indisposition can resist them. She has promised to carry us down by slow journeys, and, if it should be necessary for me to go to Buxton for my confounded rheumatism (which, though less painful, still deprives me of all use of my left paw), she will even accompany me thither. My poor wife is also in sad health, and we are neither of us fit for anything but to *con ailments* with those who are as old and infirm as ourselves. But we send you a splinter[1] from us, before we were quite broke up and unfit for service. It is not sufficient to improve your fire of a wet day, but may perhaps be of some little use in the way of kindling.

'I thank you heartily for your very interesting book of "Travels." It is in public perusal of an evening, and has fastened on us. The parts of France which you have traversed were to me almost unknown. I never saw the Loire or the Garonne. No one can accuse you of drowsiness, like old Homer and such folks; you are always awake, and keep your readers so. We are now in the midst of that most astonishing of all events, the French Revolution, and like your narrative extremely. Though an enemy to the old tyranny, you neither reason about the rights of man like Wat Tyler or even Tom Payne. You saw coming on all the evils which anarchy has occasioned. You have long seen the futility of theory without practice among French agriculturists, and the political philosophers who think themselves wiser than the experiences of all antiquity, and not content with anything already done, must needs set about inventing an entire new government, and you see what a fine mess they have made of it.

'Yours ever,
'CHARLES BURNEY.'

[1] His daughter Sarah, the writer of several ingenious and interesting works.—A. Y.

From Miss Burney, afterwards Mdme. d'Arblay, writing on some traits of my character, &c.:—

'Chelsea College: July 17, 1792.

'Nay, if you talk of your difficulties in fabricating an epistle to me, please to consider how much greater are mine in attempting to answer it. You! a country farmer, the acknowledged head of " the *only art worth cultivating*," as you tell us,—the contemner of every other pursuit, the scorner of all old customs, the defier of all musty authorities, the derider of all fogrum superiors,—in one word a Jacobin. You afraid? and of whom? a Chelsea pensioner? One who, maimed in the royal service, ignobly forbears, spurning royal reparation? One who, though flying a court, degenerately refrains from hating or even reviling kings, queens, and princesses? One who presumes to wish as well to manufactures for her outside, as to agriculture for her inside? One who has the ignorance to reverence commerce, and who cannot think of a single objection to the Wool Bill? One, in short, and to say all that is abominable at once, one who in theory is an aristocrat, and in practice a *ci-devant* courtier?

'And shall a creature of this description, the willing advocate of every opinion, every feeling you excommunicate from "your business and bosom," *dare* to write to *you*? Impossible!

'Whether I shall come and see you all or not is another matter. If I can I will.

'P.S. Will Honeycomb says if you would know anything of a lady's meaning (always providing she has any) when she writes to you, look at her postscript. Now pray, dear sir, how came you ever to imagine what you are pleased to blazon to the world with all the confidence of self-belief, that you think farming the only thing worth manly attention? You, who, if taste rather than circumstance had been your guide, might have found wreaths and flowers almost any way you had turned, as fragrant as those of Ceres.'

My reply:—

'You, "the willing advocate of every feeling I excommunicate from my bosom," knew you had thrown so bitter a potion into your letter that you could not (kind creature!) help a little sweetening in the postscript; but must there in your sweets be some alloy? Could you not conclude without falling foul of poor Ceres?

'Your letter, or rather your profession of faith, is one of the worst political creeds I remember to have read; you see no merit but beneath a diadem. In government a professed aristocrat, in political economy a monopolist, who commends manufactures, not as a market for the farmer, but for the much nobler purpose of contributing to adorn your *outside*; and who can attain not one better idea of the immortal plough than that of giving some sustenance to your *inside*. But, by the way, is not that inside of yours an equivoque? Do you mean your real or your metaphorical inside, your ribs or your feelings? If you allude to your brains, they are by your own account a *wool*-gathering. Do you mean your heart, and that the philosophical contemplation of so pure an engine as the plough is the sustenance of your best emotions? How will that agree with the panegyrist of a court and the satirist of a farm? Or is it that this inside of yours is a mere bread and cheese cupboard, which, certes, the plough can furnish? Or is it a magic lanthorn full of gay delusions, lighted by tallow from the belly of a sheep? Till you have settled these doubts, I know not which you prefer, manufactures for improving your complection, or agriculture for farming your heart. Nor must you wonder at such questions arising while you use terms that leave one in doubt whether you mean your head or your tail. I know something of the one; the other is a metaphor. Though there is high treason against the plough in almost every line of your letter, yet the words *If I can I will* are not in the spirit that contains the Eleusinian mysteries; they bring balm to my wounded feelings.'

CHAPTER X

THE BOARD OF AGRICULTURE, 1793

The Board of Agriculture—Secretaryship—Residence in London—Twenty-five dinners a month—The King's bull—The Marquis de Castries—'The Example of France'—Encomiums thereof—Correspondence.

THE most remarkable event of this year was the establishment of the Board of Agriculture.[1] I found that Mr. Pitt had determined that I should be secretary, and Mr. Le Blanc, of Caversham, informed me that this new board was established with a view of rewarding me for my 'Example of France.' In a conversation with Lord Loughborough on the attendance required, he remarked, ' You may do what suits yourself best, I conceive, for we all consider ourselves so much obliged to you that you cannot be rewarded in a manner too agreeably.' If the appointment of secretary be considered, as it has been by many, a reward for what I had effected, it was not a magnificent one; the salary, 400*l*. per annum, would have been desirable had it left me more time in Suffolk, but when I found a very strict attendance attached to it, with no house to assemble in

[1] By Act of Parliament, 1793.

except Sir John Sinclair's, and in a room common to the clerks and all comers, I was much disposed to throw it up and go back in disgust to my farm; but the advice of others and the apprehension of family reproaches kept me to the annoyance of a situation not ameliorated till Sir John was turned out of the Presidentship by Mr. Pitt, and the Board procured a house for itself.

My letter to Mr. Pitt, asking for the secretaryship of the new Board of Agriculture :—

'Bradfield Hall : May 20, 1793.

'Sir,—I am informed by Lord Sheffield and Sir John Sinclair that the establishment of a Board of Agriculture is determined.

'It has been the employment of the last thirty years of my life to make myself as much a master of the practice and the political encouragement of agriculture as my talents would allow. I have examined every part of the kingdom, and have farming correspondents in all the counties.

'It is impossible I should know what is your intention in relation to the office of the secretary; but the same wisdom that established the Board will, without doubt, give such an appointment to that office as may fill it in a manner the best adapted to the business.

'Should I be happy enough to appear in your eyes qualified for such a post, and you would have the goodness to name me to it, it might lessen the anxieties of a life that has been passed in the service of the national agriculture ; and I should feel with unvarying gratitude the obligation of the favour.

'I have the honour to be, sir, with the greatest respect,

'Your most humble and obedient servant,

'ARTHUR YOUNG.'

My reply to George Rose, Esq., on his communicating to me Mr. Pitt's approbation of my appointment :—

'Bradfield Hall: May 30, 1793.

'Sir,—It is with pleasure that I acknowledge the receipt of your letter, as it shows that, whatever may be the result of the present business, my exertions have met with the approbation of Government, whose public-spirited and laudable views I have long been solicitous to second.

'The salary you mention is, I confess, less than I imagined would be assigned to the office, but its being adequate or not depends entirely on the circumstances of attendance, duty, residence, &c. If these be arranged on a footing any way liberal, the sum is equal to my desires; and I shall in that case accept the office with pleasure. If, on the contrary, these points be so fixed as to overturn my present pursuits in life, they would render a larger salary less valuable to me than the sum you mention.

'From the nature of the Board, intended to consist, as I understand, of members of the two Houses, with the objects in view, I take it for granted that the points above mentioned may, without the least impediment to the business, be easily arranged.

'Trusting in this entirely to Mr. Pitt and yourself, I beg your good offices that, if I should have improperly expressed my meaning, you will do me the justice to rely on the integrity of my views, and not imagine me eager in making a bargain for profit with a great and liberal benefactor.

'I have the honour to remain &c.
'ARTHUR YOUNG.'

What a change in the destination of a man's life! Instead of becoming the solitary lord of four thousand acres, in the keen atmosphere of lofty rocks, and mountain torrents, with a little creation rising gradually around me, making the black desert smile with cultivation, and grouse give way to industrious population, active and energetic, though remote and tranquil, and, every instant of my existence, making *two blades of grass to grow* where not one was found before—behold me at a desk in the smoke, the fog, the din of Whitehall. 'Society has charms'—true; and so has solitude to a mind employed. But the die is cast, and my steps may still be said, metaphorically, to be in the furrow. My pleasures are of another sort; I see daily a noble activity of zeal in the service of the national husbandry in the President—of that happy effort of royal patriotism, commendable and exemplary; and I see in so many great and distinguished characters such a disinterested attention to the public good, and such liberality of spirit in promoting it, that the view is cheering, whether in a capital or a desert.

The two situations were incompatible with each

other. I therefore advertised the estate for sale; and nothing proves to me how very ill understood waste lands are in this kingdom than the advertisement being repeated near a twelvemonth before I could sell it with much less profit than I had reason to expect. So large a contiguous tract, in many respects so eligible for improvement, I thought would have been a favourite object with numbers; as to the ignorance of those who *viewed* and *rejected* it, I can only pity them.

The attention I received from individuals was, however, very flattering, for I find, by an old memorandum book, that I dined out from twenty-five to thirty days in the month, and had, in that time, forty invitations from people of the highest rank and consequence. Here I copy a memorandum made at the time: August 21, 'I feel an advancement of a certain kind since the publication of my Travels, well calculated to add agreeably to a new sphere in life by means of this new Board; but how it will turn out is not easy to conjecture, and my "Example of France: a Warning to Great Britain"[1] is applauded in a manner of which I had not the slightest conception. The Ministry commend it most highly, and express themselves in [a way] truly gratifying to my feelings. The last time I was in town, the Chancellor dwelt on the idea of how much they were all obliged to me, and treated me as a man that *must* be gratified when I was explaining my wish to reside but little in London. And Rose's

[1] This recantation of Arthur Young's former democratic utterances was published in June 1793.

report from Mr. Pitt was equal; his own expression was that I had beat all rivalship and produced the most useful work printed on the occasion, &c. Thus I come with all the advantages I could wish—and I could see in every eye and hear from every tongue of numbers to whom Sir John Banks introduced me on the Terrace at Windsor that I was considered as one to whom the nation was obliged. The King spoke to me, but not so graciously as some years before; and this brought to my mind a visit which Mr. Majendie and his brother, the Canon of Windsor, paid me at Bradfield, when the latter asked me in a very significant manner whether I had not said something against the King's bull, as it was commonly reported that I had fallen foul of his Majesty's dairy; so I suppose the man who showed me the cattle reported to the King every word I had said of them, and possibly with additions. Who is it that says one should be careful in a court not to offend even a dog? However, Sir J. Sinclair reported to me some days afterwards that his Majesty had expressed to him great satisfaction at my appointment to the secretaryship of the Board.

About this time I met Sir John Macpherson, from Bengal, but now from Italy. He came by the Rhine; had a conversation with the King of Prussia on my 'Travels,' which his Majesty was reading, and commended greatly. He saw also the Marshal de Castries,[1] who was likewise reading them, and praised me in the highest terms. Sir John Macpherson told him that he

---

[1] Marquis de Castries and Maréchal of France. Joined the *émigrés* on the Revolution, and served in Condé's army.

had found my accounts of Lombardy so uncommonly just and accurate that he intended seeing the author as soon as he arrived in England. 'Tell him, then,' said the marshal, 'that I did not know France till I read his admirable work, which astonishes me for its truth, and extent and justness of observation;' and the next day he wrote to him pointing out an error of mine in the passage relating to his opening the French West Indies to foreign navigation. No man can speak in higher terms of a book than Sir John does of this. He says it is the best that ever was published. It is something whimsical that the ladies should tell me it is as entertaining as a romance, and that statesmen should praise it for its information. Faith! I had need be flattered to be kept in good humour—losing my time doing nothing in London in August.

September 9.—Dined at Pinherring's, the American ambassador; he is a gentleman-like man; but for his company, though this was a great entertainment, there was such a motley group as would be difficult to find; they were so indelicate as to call for a war with England.

I preserved the following among letters of this year:—

From the Countess of Bristol

'January 4, 1793.

'Dear Sir,—In spite of a bad cold, which makes me very heavy and ill qualified to write to *un homme d'esprit*, I must say a word or two in answer to your letter, and also assure you that the one you enclosed for Lord Bristol was forwarded by the same post to his agent in town.

'Do I recollect reading your "Travels"? Yes, certainly, and the great pleasure and instruction I received from them; but the approbation, I assure you, came from a better quarter, or I should not have presumed on its being worth your acceptance. However that may be, I am much pleased with the effect, and fairly confess that I did wish to set your pen a-going, because you had *experience* and *facts* to write upon, and that I knew your warm colouring would suit the picture—in short, I saw you were a convert. I wished you to make others, and if I have been the least instrumental by awakening the spark in you, I shall feel that I am not wholly useless to the community where providence has placed me. I think everybody with talents is called upon, particularly at this time, to use them for the good of their once happy country, and I know of no one better qualified than yourself to employ your eloquence usefully.

'The pamphlet you mention, of *an earnest address to farmers*, was brought to me amongst others, and I immediately said it was yours—but pray rescue it from its mangled state and print it again as it was written. I flatter myself that you intend to send me the "Example of France: A Warning to Britain," for which, I assure you, I am very impatient.

'I write from Lord Abercorn's, and wish I could hear anything, but upon every subject there is at this moment an awful pause. It is hoped that the Alien Bill may be passed to-morrow, it is so much wanted, and that the wretched state of the French armies and their dissentions at home may make it unnecessary for us to declare war. Three Prussian officers of rank have been arrested for treasonable correspondence with Dumouriez, which, they say, is to explain the Duke of Brunswick's retreat; and now it is supposed that Custine's army cannot escape him.

'I saw two gentlemen who were in Paris a fortnight ago, and who told me that the treasury would hold out very little longer, that bread was scarce, commerce destroyed, and the people either in fury or despair, the whole town affording a melancholy scene of poverty, distrust and disorder—houses shut up, public buildings destroyed, churches turned into warehouses, &c. &c.

'For want of better materials I send you a print which I think is not a bad one, considering the double part Mr. Fox has acted. I thank you for enquiring after my daughters. Lady Erne is not yet returned from Hampshire, Lady Elizabeth is with the Duchess of Devonshire at Florence, and Lady Louisa is here, and desires her compliments.

'I am, sincerely yours,
'E. BRISTOL.'

From the same

'Bruton Street: March 20, 1793.

'Dear Sir,—I have just seen in the *True Briton* of this morning that the thanks of the association at the "Crown and Anchor" were voted to you for your last publication, which, I assure you, gives me great pleasure; at the same time it reminds me that I have too long deferred mine, but which I now beg you will accept. I like it very much, and think it is admirably well written, and calculated to inform the ignorant and deluded of their real danger. I should have told you so long ago, but waited to hear the opinions of those from which I thought you would receive more satisfaction; and I can now assure you that your pamphlet is much liked by Lord Orford and several others of good judgment. And I think you may, without flattery, consider yourself as one of the means which has rescued this glorious country from the destruction which was preparing for it.

'There are great events impending just now. I pray God to direct them for our good.

'I am, dear sir,

'Your sincere humble servant,

'E. BRISTOL.'

From Lord Bristol (Bishop of Derry), objections to my proposal for selling all lambs at Harrington Fair.

'Ratisbon: Jan. 17, 1793.

'My dear Arthur,—Why will you make me a request with which I cannot in prudence comply? And why must I say *No* to a man whom I wish only to answer with *Yes*? You are as great a quack in farming as I once was in politics, and therefore, knowing the force of the term, I must be on my guard against you.

'*No* reform, dear Arthur, at this time of day. Ipswich has an old prescriptive right to our lambs—we have sold them well at that market; buyers are accustomed to it; have their connections there of every kind; may very possibly not come to Horningheath for many years. Let the buyers advertise that they wish to change the market, and I, though a great heretic against most establishments, will be none against them. Adieu! magnanimous Arthur. Reserve your prowess for a greater object than distressing poor Ipswich by bereaving it of its ancient patrimony.

'We have a sheep fair here, too, at Ratisbon, but of old horned rams, and not of young Suffolk lambs.

'Yours cordially,
'BRISTOL.'

From Thomas Law, Esq., who resided long in Bengal, on the application of the Corn Laws.

'Weymouth Street: Jan. 5, 1793.

'Sir,—I have fortunately obtained the perusal of your "Travels," and the sentiments conveyed therein so totally coincide with my observations of eighteen years upon the extensive continent of Asia, that, upon your arrival in town, I shall be happy to convey to you any information in my power respecting the agriculture of Bengal, Behar, and Benares.

'When a member of a grain committee during a drought, I pursued your system, which coincides with that of Adam Smith, viz.: All our object was to prevent impediments to the free transport of corn, being convinced that it would be removed from an abundant province to one which was less productive, and, like water, find its level, and that the interest of merchants would convey it from cheap places to dear ones, and thus promote the general good. I could impart to you many fatal instances of the intervention of powers by fixing the price and by forcing corn to market.

'I can show you the thanks of a resident who presided in the capital of an extensive district threatened with a famine, and who wrote to me asking my opinion upon the following propositions: First, " Shall I raise subscriptions to supply the poor with rice at this crisis?" *Answer*, " You will thereby not only encourage a concourse to your city of persons whose expectations will be deceived, as their numbers will exceed the amount of your gratuities, and you will thereby destroy many; but you will enhance the price in the city." Secondly, " Shall I compel the granaries to be opened, and fix a moderate price?" *Answer*, " By no means. You will thereby deter the merchants from bringing grain to market, and will thereby starve your inhabitants. Your power can only extend to a certain limit, and within that the merchant will not enter. If supplies are coming to you, those who have grain for sale will have advice of it, and hurry their grain to market; but if you compel them, you will stop all imports by such forcible interference. Have you calculated at what price the merchant buys at a distance, at what expense he brings it, &c.? In short, you have the choice of the alternative—whether for a day or two you will submit to want, and then be relieved by the exertions of those who always hasten to a good market; or whether you will gain popularity for a day or two by a compulsory expenditure of the quantity within your grasp, and then fall a martyr to an exasperated starving people." He adopted the first, and thanked me in the strongest terms.

'About that time, when Government intended to purchase grain to supply certain places, I protested against it, because those places would entirely rely upon Government management; for no merchant would convey to places where Government by a sudden import might overflow the market—if London were to be supplied with every want by a contract or monopoly, the effect is easily foreseen.

'In respect to a fixed land tax, I can show you some very satisfactory papers upon the subject; as I had to contend against some very able advocates for periodical equalisation, and at length have obtained a fixed land tax for ever. In Asia we have metayers, as in France; we have surveyors of the crop. In short, to a gentleman of your philosophic and agricultural turn I may prove a welcome referee. To the many pertinent questions you will put, you will, no doubt, find many deficient replies, for I am conscious of having omitted much. Unluckily I had never seen your able productions, and had too often to find the truth by the experience of error.

'Many serious evils may be prevented if a person of your influence could have conveyed to Asia your sentiments upon *taxation, the corn, trade*, &c., for the perusal of the several servants entrusted with the charge of vast districts with numerous industrious subjects. If Necker committed such palpable mistakes after so much experience, must not young men in the company's service be subject to fatal errors where the instruction of books is not always to be attained, or the advice of the well-informed, as in Europe?

'I remain, with respect, sir,
'Your most obedient humble servant,
'THOMAS LAW.'

From the Right Hon. Edmund Burke, highly praising the 'Example of France':—

'Mr. Burke thanks Mr. Young for his most able, useful and reasonable pamphlet. He has not seen anything written in this controversy which stands better bottomed upon practical principle, or is more likely to produce an effect on the popular mind. It is, indeed, incomparably well done. We are all very much obliged to Mr. Young, and think the Committee ought to circulate his book.

'Duke Street, St. James's: March 5, 1793.'

From Dr. Burney, on my 'Example of France,' &c.:—

'Chelsea College: May 12, 1793.

'My dear Friend,—I cannot let Mrs. Young return without sending you my best thanks for the second edition of your excellent pamphlet. Indeed, if I were singular in approbation of it, you might think me a cleverer fellow than I shall seem among the crowd of your admirers. What is a single name in a list fifty yards long? And if I were to tell you what numbers of first-rate judges have spoke well of your performance, I should want more room than Mr. Sheridan's friends at Glasgow. I shall only just specify those who would be at the head of a complete list, if I had time to make one: Mr. Burke, Lord Orford, who, on my asking him if he had seen your pamphlet, pointed to it, " There it is; I read nothing else ; " Mrs. Montagu the same; a large party of bluestockings at Lady Hesketh's all agreed that your book and Hannah More's " Chip "[1] were the best on the subject. When I made Mrs. Crewe read the first edition, she wrote me word that she had perused it with great attention, and that she found it contained stubborn facts, to each of which she should say with the grave-digger, " Answer me that and unyoke." Last week, in a note she sent me from Hampstead, she says : " Mr. Arthur Young's pamphlet makes a great noise, and, I think, I never knew any book take more; it is reprinted, you know, with additions." In the communication of the latter information she got the start of me; the second edition could not have been out three days but you are meditating a third. I like your additions to the second much, particularly what concerns the reform of Parliament.

'I wish you could overhaul Grey's speech as well as Charles Fox's on that subject, and in an appendix expose the weakness and inconsistence of both. Only observe how both confess that there *was* danger to our constitution " from opinions favourable to the principles and measures of France," after so stubbornly and pertinaciously denying in Parliament the existence of any such danger ; challenging Government to prove it,

[1] *Village Politics*, by Will Chip, 1793; price 2*d*.

and saying that "the Proclamation, call of Parliament, Alien and Traitorous Correspondence Bills, were mere Ministerial juggles" to increase influence, diminish liberty, and encourage excess of loyalty. "But," says Mr. G. "that *danger* must now be much lessened, as all approbation of those principles, or imitation of that example, is now improbable, totally discredited, and removed from all political speculation and practice." What, then, is all the defence of France and Frenchmen by the Opposition? And why is every measure condemned in Parliament that tends to put an end to their anarchy and ambition? Why is war against them so censured? Why is it always called the war of kings and despots? Why is the Minister so importuned to make peace with regicides and assassins, determined to force, if possible, every nation upon earth to adopt their measures? Mr. Grey repeats in his speech, "All dread of the example is completely removed, and that none could suppose him, or any other party in this country, favourable to that example." What is this but open falsehood? Mr. Fox allows that "there *was* a party whose wild theories certainly aimed at an impracticable perfection, that could only have been pursued by means subversive of every part of our constitution." Yet there never was any danger! Mr. G. says, in express terms, "that his motion extended to an alteration in the present government of the country." But he had no specific plan ready of his own, or that he chose to father. But as all the petitions he and Mr. Sheridan brought in for a reform *demanded* nothing less than universal suffrage, and as these gentlemen either drew up or approved the contents of these petitions, we may easily judge what was the general plan of our Jacobins, if they could have had the tinkering of the constitution.

'Grey seems to me a silly fellow, with a greater wish than abilities to do mischief. Charles Fox's speech is more a panegyric on the constitution than on his friend's motion. When every man is left to himself to reform an old constitution or make a new one, no two will be found of a mind on the subject. Sherry's speech was nothing to the purpose. There was no attempt of the phalanx which I so much dreaded, as the doubling our *tiers état*. Thank God, their great gun has flashed in the pan! The mountain has laboured in vain. You know I hope that the gang in Parliament, like Egalité's creatures in the "Convention," is called the *Mountain*. And it has been called by a punster of the party *Mount Sigh-on*. I fear the war will be long and bloody; and how it will end who can tell? Nothing but a vigorous prosecution of the war can save the whole civilised globe from destruction. After disdaining in the House the principles which they had suggested and encouraged out of it, I should not wonder if the Scotch and English petitioners for reform on the basis of *universal suffrage* should mob and *September* their friends the demagogues whenever they can catch them. I don't love mischief, but I do cordially wish something of that kind were to happen.

'Adieu.

'Ever yours sincerely,

'CHARLES BURNEY.'

From Dr. Symonds, high encomiums of my 'Example,' &c.

'Prince of Wales Coffee House: April 8, 1793.

'Traveller Coxe[1] desired me to tell you how charmed he was with your pamphlet; nay, he had begun to write five or six lines to you, but thought afterwards it was taking too great a liberty. One thing, however, he wishes you to expunge in your next edition, viz.: a reflection on Sunday schools as not being founded on truth. You must not be surprised at this, for he is a zealous patron of them, and has explained the Catechism in print for that purpose. Wherever I go I hear your "Example of France" spoken of in the highest terms as to the matter.

'Everyone agrees that no political writer whatever has set the representation of property in so clear and just a light. Bishop Douglas, who has written many good pamphlets, and is therefore the best judge, makes no scruple to declare frequently that you deserve from Government a most ample reward; but we both wish, as well as others, for your sake, that the second edition may be printed more correctly.

'You should come to town and be presented, or, at least, take an opportunity to walk on the Terrace at Windsor, where you would not fail of being marked out. Bishop Watson's appendix has rendered him *rectus in curia*. A few days ago he was at Court, talking with Lord Dartmouth, who mentioned the word philosophy, which the King overhearing, came

---

[1] William Coxe, 1747-1828, author of *Travels into Poland, Russia, Sweden, and Denmark*, &c. &c.

to the bishop, and said, 'I have read the best sort of philosophy, my lord, in your sermon and appendix, which has wonderfully pleased me." The bishop, of course, made his bow, and then the King went on, "You write so concisely and so forcibly, that everyone must be convinced by your arguments;" on which the bishop replied, "I like, Sir, to step forward in a moment of danger." The King rejoined, "You have shown a good spirit, and it could not be done in a better manner." Should the last volume of "Clarendon's Letters" come in your way, I would advise you to read the famous one from Sir John Colepeper to Secretary Nicholas; which is always esteemed as a wonderful instance of political sagacity, as it foretold that the Restoration would be accomplished by Monk! But I think there is another part of this letter which shows equal sagacity, viz.: his desiring that Charles would not send over any foreign troops into England, as this measure would not fail of uniting the English against him; whereas, if they were left to themselves, he would always have a strong party, and must sooner or later be restored. I am fully convinced of the truth of this reasoning; and of what use is history unless it be considered as a school for modern politicians?

'Why did you not let me know whether your second edition had gone to the press or not? Before I left Cambridge I saw a gentleman who told me that Sir William Scott had mentioned in a letter to one of his friends there that it was by far the most convincing and best pamphlet that had been published.

'All I could wish is that you had not stigmatised

all reformers with the name of enemies to the state; or, at least, you intimated it. I was always myself an enemy to reform in Parliament, and continue to be so; yet I know some warm advocates for it, who mean as well to the benefit of this country as you can possibly do.

'Dr. Hardy and Sir Henry Moncrief (a Scotch clergyman) are come to solicit a Bill for the enlarging of the stipends of the Scotch clergy. They do not apprehend much difficulty in carrying it through the Houses, though the addition must be supplied out of the tithes in the hands of lay proprietors. Hardy is Professor of Ecclesiastical History at Edinburgh—a most sensible man, with great liberality of mind. Sir Henry is a polished man, and likewise a man of business. I hope to see them both at St. Edmund's Hill, and you must meet them. You should get Hardy's pamphlet, the "Patriot," published in Scotland on the present emergency; there are in it many excellent things.

'You seem in your letter to be still apprehensive of some plots and insurrections.

'Plot! Plots! was the catch-word in King Charles II.'s time. Sir H. Moncrief and Dr. Hardy laughed at Dundas's account of the political riots in Scotland. They absolutely denied the existence of them —considered them as political; and when you read Hardy's pamphlet, you will see that he would not have failed setting them forth if they had deserved any consideration.

'Adieu! I should not have come to London had it not been on account of my ecclesiastical foundling.

'JOHN SYMONDS.'

From Dr. Symonds

'September 1, 1793.

' My dear Sir,— I do not wonder that you smiled at the affected secrecy of Macpherson concerning the Censomento. The book to which he alludes cannot be the " Bilancio dello stato," &c., which was written to please Count Firmian. I knew well the gentleman who wrote it and gave it to me, as I often met him at dinner at the count's.

' Sometimes he was too decisive. One day he said at the count's table that the Bresciano contained 800,000 inhabitants now. As Count F. knew that I had just come from Brescia, and had not lost my time there, he asked me what number there was; on which I told him that there were 376,000 according to a census taken a few years before. The count smiled, and looked very attentively on Carpani (for that was the author's name), who never liked me so well after that day, nor had Count Firmian so high an opinion of him. You possibly may not know the history of Sir John Macpherson. He offered the Duke of Grafton, when he was at the head of the Treasury, a vast collection of jewels, by order of the Nabob of Arcot, which the duke absolutely refused, and Bradshaw, his secretary, also. Sir John, thinking that the nabob would not believe that he had offered the present, published for his own vindication the answers of the duke and Bradshaw, for which he was turned out of the company's service, as he was pursuing an interest then opposite to its interests.

' Scotch influence not long after restored him. You

will find the letters in Lind's appendix to the defence of Lord Pigot. You are now, of course, so much of a politician as not to be surprised (shall I say disgusted?) at Macpherson's conduct. The opinion of the King of Prussia as to your book I value not a straw; but that of the Marshal de Castries certainly carries with it great weight.

'He is one of the few who adhered to Necker from gratitude, when the latter was turned out of his post about ten years ago; and I heard a very good character of the maréchal when I was last in France. St. Paul, as you and the duke are pleased to call him, is finished, and the preface is on the stocks.[1]

'Why do you wish Clarke had commented on the Epistle to the Romans? Locke and Taylor have done it admirably; and easy as you may think the Gospels are, they have been rendered much more so by Clarke.

'What do you mean by saying that the Gospels want no explanation? St. John is extremely difficult in some parts, notwithstanding Clarke's paraphrase; and I think, with Markland, that he is as yet very far from being perfectly understood. Adieu!

'I remain,
'Ever your sincere friend,
'JOHN SYMONDS.'

[1] Evidently an allusion to some work of the writer.

CHAPTER XI

THE SECRETARYSHIP, 1794-95-96

The Secretaryship and its drawbacks—Social compensations—Illness and death of Elizabeth Hoole—Letters of Jeremy Bentham and others—A visit to Burke—Home travels—Enclosures.

THE Board of Agriculture, meeting in February, arranged the President's plan for the attendance of their officers. By these laws all the officers of the Board were bound to attend, with no other exception than the months of August, September and October, with one month at Christmas and three weeks at Easter. These laws, ready cut and dried when the Board met, were adopted with no other alterations than such as the President himself had made in them, previously to their being presented at the meeting. Lord Hawke had examined the rules and orders of many societies, and found that in all letters communications were addressed to the Secretaries, and answers given by them. Sir John Sinclair struck this out, and directed all such communications to be to the President (himself), and for him also to sign all letters. This at once converted the Secretary into nothing more than a first clerk. I saw not at first the tendency of the alterations; but I soon felt their effect. All letters

R

were dictated by the Secretary and written in a book; this book was altered and corrected at the will of the President, and such alterations made as in respect of agriculture were absurd enough; the whole done in such a manner as not to be very pleasing.

In addition to this, Sir John Sinclair gave the Board the use of his house, which ensured another circumstance hostile to my feelings. There was only one room for transacting the business, by the Secretary, under-Secretary, two clerks, to which Sir J. after added the constant attendance of an attorney, for assisting in the business of a general Enclosing Act, about which the President busied himself some years in vain. As I was determined to pass all the vacations at my farm in Suffolk, six journeys of myself and servants became necessary, and caused a considerable expense. I also was compelled to hire lodgings at the expense of two or two guineas and a half per week, and when I experienced the full career [1] of all these circumstances, I deliberated repeatedly and carefully with myself, whether it would not be cheaper to me to throw up the employment. Long after, upon review of the whole, I was amazed that I had not done it, more especially as my plan for settling on the moors in Yorkshire was offered to my choice. I was infinitely disgusted with the inconsiderate manner in which Sir John Sinclair appointed the persons who drew up the original reports, men being employed who scarcely knew the right end of a plough; and the President one day desired I would accompany him with one

[1] Career, general course of action or procedure.—*Webster*.

of these men, a half-pay officer out of employment, to call on Lord Moira to request his assistance in the Leicestershire Report, when this person told his Lordship that he was out of employment and should like a summer's excursion. To do him justice, he did not know anything of the matter. Still, however, he was appointed, and amused himself with his excursion to Leicester. But the most curious circumstance of effrontery was, that the greater number of the reporters were appointed, and actually travelled upon the business before the first meeting of the Board took place, under the most preposterous of all ideas—that of surveying the whole Kingdom and printing the Reports in a single year; by which manœuvre Sir John thought he should establish a great reputation for himself. Consequently by his sole authority, who could not possibly know whether the members of the Board would approve or not such a plan. I was a capital idiot not to absent myself sufficiently to bring the matter to a question, and leave them to turn me out if they pleased. Mr. Pitt would probably have interfered and effected the object I wanted, and, if not, would have provided for me in a better way. However, I made use of the opportunities that offered to frequent the company of those that were agreeable to me; for a part of the time was pretty regularly passed at the conversaziones of Mrs. Matthew Montagu and the Countess of Bristol, where I met an assemblage of persons remarkable for every characteristic of the *bas-bleu* mixed with great numbers of the highest rank. [I was] also at many similar parties upon a smaller scale at Mr. Charles Coles', the intimate friend of Soame Jenyns, and to whom he left the property of his works. The *petits soupers* at Mrs. Matthew Montagu's, and to which she asked a selection of eight or nine persons, were very pleasant, the conversations interesting, and this select number more agreeable than I ever found full rooms. On my first coming to town in the spring of 1794, I enquired of several members of the Board whether there was not a farmers' club in London, and was surprised that there never had been any institution of the kind. I determined to endeavour at establishing one, and spoke to the Duke of Bedford and the Earls of Egremont and Winchilsea, who much approved the idea, and applying also to a few more, I directed cards to be sent them from the Thatched House Tavern,[1] in order to establish a club. This meeting was fully attended, and a book being called for, the club was instituted, and several rules entered, and the meetings appointed once a fortnight during the sittings of Parliament. This club became very fashionable,. and applications to be elected were very numerous, from the members of both Houses of Parliament; and it subsists to this day, but has for some time been very ill attended. This was occasioned by too free an election of all who offered. While the club was limited to fifty members it was well attended, but afterwards such numbers were received, and with so much facility, as greatly to injure the establishment. I have one remark to make upon clubs; the life and soul of them is limitation to a selected few, and to

[1] This appears to have been the place lately known as the Thatched House Club, St. James's Street, Piccadilly.

blackball the great mass of applicants, selecting merely such as will form a very valuable addition to the society, which probably may not amount to more than one in twenty. The annual subscription was two guineas : one to the house, one to form a fund at the disposition of the club. The latter gradually accumulated till it amounted to 700*l.* or 800*l.* Both Sir John Sinclair and I were strenuous that this might be applied to some useful purpose, and with difficulty we got an appropriation of fifty guineas as a reward for the best plough that could be produced ; but the money assigned to advertisements being much too small, the offer was unknown, and no plough produced.

A member once proposed that the 800*l.* might be given to charitable institutions; but this was negatived in an instant, and the sum is still left (1812) unemployed in the funds.

While the club flourished the members who most generally attended were the Dukes of Bedford, Buccleugh, Montrose, the Earls of Egremont, Winchester and Darnley, the Lords of Wentworth, Somerville, de Dunstanville, Sheffield, &c. &c.

I often dined at Charles Coles', where I met repeatedly Jacob Bryant,[1] Mrs. Montagu, Mrs. York, Mrs. Garrick, Hannah More, Mrs. Orde and Soame Jenyns. The conversation at these parties on the publications of the day, anecdotes of the time, with the conduct of many of the great men of the age, was usually very interesting. Alas ! alas ! how few of these persons

---

[1] 1715-1804. Author of numerous works on speculative history, in one of which he denied the existence of Troy.

are now left. I was very eager in listening to every word that fell from Hannah More, though not nearly so much so as I should have been many years after.

I had an incessant round of dinners and many evening parties, and generally with people of the highest rank and consequence, but I was not pleased, being discontented with my employment, and disgusted with the frivolous business of the Board, which seemed to me engaged in nothing that could possibly produce the least credit with the public. After five months' residence at London, I went to the Duke of Bedford's at Woburn on my way to Bradfield, spending some days very agreeably in company that could not fail of being interesting.

This year my second daughter Elizabeth, who, as I have mentioned before, was married to the Rev. John Hoole, died of consumption. She was of a most amiable, gentle temper, and in a resigned frame of mind, which gave me much satisfaction. The last visit I paid her at Abinger, in Surrey, she was very weak, yet not suspected to be so near her end. But at the last parting with me, she did it in so feeling and affectionate a manner as seemed to imply that she thought she should see me no more. It made me, for a time, extremely melancholy, which was shaken off with great difficulty. I took a tour into Hampshire, where I passed several days with Mr. Poulett at Sombourne, taking an account of the agriculture of that district, the result of which examination was printed as an appendix to the original Hampshire Report.

On the meeting of the Board in 1793, Sir John

Sinclair had particularly requested me to draw up a Report for the County of Suffolk, to effect which I took several journeys into different parts of the county at some expense, and formed the Report which was printed in 1794. I never executed any work more commended in Suffolk than this. I had no remuneration.

Letters received this year :—

From Jeremy Bentham, Esq., enquiries into the landed property of Great Britain and into the rental and value of houses :—

'Hendon, Middlesex: Sept. 1794.

'Dear Sir,—Permit my ignorance to draw upon your science on an occasion that happens just now to be a very material one to me. I have a sort of floating recollection of a calculation, so circumstanced, either in point of authority or argument, as to carry weight with it, in which the total value of the landed property in this country (Scotland, I believe, included) was reckoned at a thousand millions, and that of the movable property at either a thousand millions or twelve hundred millions. Public debt did not come, I think, at least, it ought not to come, into the account; it being only so much owned by one part of the proprietors of the two thousand or the two thousand two hundred millions to another.

' Upon searching your book on France, which was the source from whence I thought I had taken the idea, I can find no calculation of the value of the movable property, nor even of the immovable in an explicit form ; on the contrary, in the instance of the immovable, I find suppositions with which any such estimate appears to be incompatible. The land tax at four shillings, I find, you suppose, were it to be equal all over the country, would be equivalent to as much as three shillings, on which supposition the rental (the tax of four shillings producing no more than two thousand millions) would amount to no more than 13,000,000*l.*, nor consequently the value, at so many years' purchase, say twenty-eight, to more than three hundred and sixty-four millions; or at thirty, to three hundred and ninety millions; to which, in order to complete the calculation of the landed property of Great Britain, that of Scotland would have to be added.

'The population of the three kingdoms you reckon in two places at eleven millions; but in another place at fifteen. Is the latter a slip of the pen? or, in the two former places, was only two kingdoms (England and Scotland) in your view, though three are mentioned? A circumstance that seems to favour the latter supposition is, that the population of Ireland is well known (if I do not much misrecollect) from recent and authentic sources to be a little more than four millions; and as Scotland turns out to contain a million and a half, this would leave nine and a half millions for England, which, I should suppose, would quadrate in round numbers with Mr. Howlett's calculations, to which we refer; a book which, from forgetfulness, I have never made myself master of, and to which, being in the country, I have no speedy means of recurring.

'Now what I wish for is as follows: (1) a calculation (or, I should rather say, the result) of the value of the landed property of Great Britain reckoned at [so many] years' purchase, two prices—a peace price and a war price—could they be respectively of sufficient permanence to be ascertained, would be of use.

'(2) A calculation of the value of the personal, *i.e.* immovable property of Great Britain.

'(3) The amount of the population of Great Britain.

'What I am a petitioner for is the benefit of your judgment and authority upon the three several subjects; by reference, if there be any other person's calculation that you are satisfied with; otherwise from your own notes; and, in either case, a word or two just to indicate the sources from which they are taken would be an additional help and satisfaction.

'The occasion of the trouble I am attempting to give you I expressly forbear mentioning; not only for want of space and time, but more particularly that it may be impossible, and might, upon occasion, be known to be impossible, that the response of the Oracle should have received any bias from the consideration of the purpose for which it was consulted.

'I am, dear sir, with never failing esteem and regard,

'Yours ever,
'JEREMY BENTHAM.'

'Q.I.P.: Sept. 30, 1794.

'Dear Sir,—A thousand thanks for your kind letter —sorry you should fancy you have been bathing[1] for health—hope it was not true—only idleness—we can't afford to have you otherwise than well.

[1] Probably an allusion to A. Y.'s habit of air baths.

'Must prefer [1] you once more, "Rental of England twenty-four millions." Good! but houses, such as those in town, and others that have a separate rent, are included? I suppose not; since for them you would have given a separate and different price in number of years' purchase.

'In one of your tours you guess this article at five millions. Do you abide by that guess? I think the number must have increased since then considerably; that was, I believe, about twenty years ago. London and the environs must since then have increased, I should think, at least a quarter of a million. How many years' purchase would you reckon houses at, upon an average, old and young together? Shall we say sixteen? I should think, at the outside.

'I am, dear Sir,
'Your much obliged,
'JEREMY BENTHAM.
'A. Young, Esq.'

The two following letters are from Mrs. Hoole, Dr. Burney's favourite, Miss Bessy, to her father:—

To Arthur Young, Esq.

'Sidmouth: Feb. 22, 1794.

'Dear Sir,—We came hither from Lynn near three weeks since, as Mr. Hoole informed you. We are in very warm and comfortable lodgings, and the woman of the house is very attentive and obliging. The air of this place is very mild and very moist, but they tell

[1] Prefer, to set forth, propose.—*Webster*.

us the healthiest of any upon the coast. Mr. Hoole has been on to Exmouth, which, upon the whole, he does not like so well. We do not find that Devonshire is cheaper the further you go, but the contrary, at least on the coast.

'With regard to myself, I do not find I am any better for this journey, indeed I have had more fever and cough since I came here than ever I had. I am at present better, but I know that is owing to a very strict regimen which I have lately taken to. The weather has been very unfavourable, for though it has not been cold we have had almost constantly either rain or wind. We have been absent from home near nine weeks, and Mr. H. must very soon return to his curacy; he will either take me with him or leave me here, and we wish very much to know what you advise, considering *all circumstances*.

'This place is certainly warmer than Surrey, but we have heard here, as at Lynn, that it sometimes proves unfavourable in consumptive cases. I do not think Abinger at all in fault; I have been well or *better* there than anywhere. But I am not unwilling to be left here, if it should still be thought advisable. Will you have the goodness to write as soon as you can, as we shall not determine till we hear? Mr. Hoole has had but one letter from you about a month ago. This I mention lest you should have sent any which may have miscarried.

'Believe me, dear Sir,
    'Your affectionate Daughter,
        'ELIZABETH HOOLE.

'Perhaps you may like to know something of the price of provisions: Meat $4\frac{1}{2}d.$ per lb.; poultry is reasonable; chickens from 2s. to 2s. 6d. a couple; milk 2d. a quart; butter 10d. per lb.'

Postscript from Mr. Hoole

'I fear this journey will be of no avail. I do not think our dear Bessy is in any immediate danger, but I much fear this cruel disease is gradually preying on her strength.

'S. H.'

'Sidmouth: March 18, 1794.

'My dear Sir,—I was very sorry to find from your letter that what I had written had made you uneasy; I am certain you think me worse than I am; indeed it is very foolish to write my symptoms to my friends, as they give way perhaps, or some of them, in a short time, as is my case. I am now quite free from pain, and can sleep on one side as well as the other; I think the last blister was of use. I have been twice in the warm bath since Mr. Hoole went. My cough must have its course.

'I had a very kind letter from Agnes yesterday; she offers, if she can get permission, to come and stay with me until Mr. Hoole returns, and adds, if she cannot, Mrs. Forbes says she is at liberty, and would willingly come; but I would not bring them down upon any account, as I am more comfortably settled than anybody would suppose, and I am sure Mr. Hoole will be back in a short time.

'Sidmouth is certainly very mild; we have had no

cold winds, but this clear weather suits me better than that warm moist weather we had in February. But I cannot walk by the seaside; there is always wind, and it seems colder than anywhere else.

'I would not blame Mrs. F. in the least; I might have been the same or worse anywhere; if anything in the air disagreed with me, it was the moisture. We have no post from hence, either Monday or Tuesday. I wrote to Mr. Hoole last Sunday, or would have answered yours sooner. The quickness, or rather rapidity, with which our letters arrive from town, seems surprising—a letter put in one night we have the next. It is not the custom indeed to deliver them at night, as the post comes in so late as nine, but if you send they will give you them. At Lynn, which is about the same distance from town, they deliver them at six in the evening, but we have here a cross-post to send for them nine miles.

'I beg you will not think me worse than I am, and believe me,
  'Your affectionate Daughter,
    'ELIZABETH HOOLE.'

From J. Symonds, Esq.

'Cambridge: March 27, 1795.

'My dear Sir,—I am to thank you for two letters, which should not have lain unanswered if a retirement like mine would have furnished me with any materials. However, I must take notice of your way of arguing. You say "the people in France *are* starved, and assignats *are* destroyed," with significant dashes. You told me just the same in 1793 and 1794, and venture it once more. Assuredly you seem to reason like the old wizard Tiresias in Horace, " Quicquid dicam aut erit aut non." Whether your predictions be verified or not, you assume, like Tiresias, to speak the truth.

'I always thought with you, that Mr. Pitt would receive no real benefit from his new friends; but I have heard the Duke of Grafton say that he would not have entered on the war if he had not been able to detach some from the Opposition. If this be so, there is great reason to lament that he could detach them.

'We have received here the Bishop of Llandaff's speech on the Duke of Bedford's motion, published by Debrett. It amazed me to find that the Bishop of Durham ventured to speak after him. A gentleman who heard them both says that Watson's was rich, clouted cream, and Barrington's thin, meagre, blue skim milk, frothed up with an egg, but with so weak a froth that it rose only to fall instantly. We are told that after Æschines was banished, in consequence of Demosthenes' speech *de coronâ*, one of Æschines' friends carried to him in his banishment a copy of Demosthenes' speech; on which the former said, " But what if you had heard it ? "

'Two fellows of this college, who heard Watson, bear the same ample testimony to the excellent manner in which he delivered it.

'You tell me "that our situation is prosperous beyond all example;" I should think so too if it were unnecessary to multiply loans. The complaints of the dearness of the necessaries of life seem to pervade the whole island, and I fear they must still be dearer. If we be forced to persist in this war (and how are we to get out of it, it is difficult to see) the middle class of the people, of which you and I form a part, must be driven down to the lower. They hold it is a principle not to tax the lower, but to tax luxuries, so that the middle class will be forced to abandon everything but necessaries, and then the upper class must pay all. This, to use your words, "*must render us prosperous beyond all example.*" I rather accede to Charles Coles' declaration in his last letter to me: "Alas! our glory is gone to decay." A day or two ago I was looking into the famous pamphlet of my old friend, Israel Mauduit,[1] on the German war, in which I stumbled on the following sentence, very applicable to our entering into this *just* war to save the Dutch : "Is Britain to make itself the general knight errant of Europe, to rescue oppressed States, and exhaust itself in order to save men in spite of themselves, who will not do anything towards their own deliverance?" Adieu!

'Yours sincerely,
'J. SYMONDS.'

1796.—In the spring of this year I waited on Mr. Pitt, by his appointment, in order to answer some enquiries of his relative to the propriety of any regulations by Parliament of the price of labour.

I answered all his enquiries, and could not but admire the wonderful quickness of his apprehension of

---

[1] Israel Mauduit, son of a Dissenting minister; at first the same, afterwards merchant; published *Considerations on the German War*, 1760, &c. &c. See *Chalmers' Biog. Dict.*

all those collateral difficulties which I started, and of which he seemed in a moment to comprehend the full extent. I found him hostile to the idea.

March.—Among various dinners [was] at Mr. Burke's and at Mrs. Barrington's parties. In May dinners at Duke of Bedford's, Duke of Buccleugh's, and Mr. Jenkinson and Lady Louisa's; her manner is not the most agreeable, [but] she has ease and elegance. I have long known her at Ickworth.

May 1.—For some time past the following advertisement has appeared in many of the London papers: 'Speedily will be published a letter from the Right Hon. Edmund Burke to Arthur Young, Esq., Secretary to the Board of Agriculture, on some projects talked of in Parliament, for regulating the price of labour.' The appearance of this advertisement induced Sir John Sinclair to write to Mr. Burke to propose to him that he should undertake to draw up for the Board the chapter of a general Report which was intended to treat on the subject of labour and provisions.

The question in the House of Commons was decided before the publication could appear, and it was supposed that Mr. Burke had, in consequence, abandoned the intention of publishing his ideas. But Sir John, not having received any answer, or, at least, any that was satisfactory to him, requested me to take his chariot and go to Gregory's, in order that I might discover whether that celebrated character continued his intention of throwing his thoughts upon paper.

I reached Mr. Burke's before breakfast, and had every reason to be pleased with my reception.

'Why, Mr. Young, it is many years since I saw you, and, to the best of my recollection, you have not suffered the smallest change; you look as young as you did sixteen years ago. You must be very strong; you have no belly; your form shows lightness; you have an elastic mind.'

I wished to myself that I could have returned anything like the compliment, but I was shocked to see him so broken, so low, and with such expressions of melancholy. I almost thought that I was come to see the greatest genius of the age in ruin.

And I had every reason to think, from all that passed on this visit, that the powers of his mind had suffered considerably.

He introduced me to his brother, Mr. W. Burke, to Mrs. B., and to the Count de la Tour du Pin, an emigrant philosopher and naturalist.

After breakfast he took me a sauntering walk for five hours over his farm, and to a cottage where a scrap of land had been stolen from the waste. I was glad to find his farm in good order, and doubly so to hear him remark that it was his only amusement, except the attention which he paid to a school in the vicinity for sixty children of noble emigrants. His conversation was remarkably desultory, a broken mixture of agricultural observations, French madness, price of provisions, the death of his son, the absurdity of regulating labour, the mischief of our Poor-laws, and the difficulty of cottagers keeping cows. An argumentative discussion of any opinion seemed to distress him, and I, therefore, avoided it. And his discourse was so scattered and interrupted by varying ideas, that I could bring away but few of his remarks that were clearly defined.

Speaking on public affairs he said that he never looked at a newspaper; 'but if anything happens to occur which they think will please me, I am told of it.' I observed there was strength of mind in this resolution. 'Oh, no!' he replied, 'it is mere weakness of mind.' It appeared evident that he would not publish upon the subject which brought me to Gregory's; but he declared himself to be absolutely inimical to any regulation whatever by law; that all such interference was not only unnecessary but would be mischievous. He observed that the supposed scarcity was extremely ill understood, and that the consumption of the people was a clear proof of it; this, in his neighbourhood, was not lessened in the material articles of bread, meat, and beer, which he learnt by a very careful examination of many bakers, butchers, and excisemen; nor had the poor been distressed further than what resulted immediately from that improvidence which was occasioned by the Poor-laws.

Mr. Burke had not read Lord Sheffield's Memoirs of Gibbon. On my observing that Mr. Gibbon declares himself of the same opinion with him on the French Revolution, he said that Gibbon was an old friend of his, and he knew well that before he (Mr. G.) died, that he heartily repented of the anti-religious part of his work for contributing to free mankind from all restraint on their vices and profligacy, and thereby aiding so much the spirit which produced the horrors that blackened the most detestable of all revolutions.

Upon my mentioning Monsieur de Mounier and Lally Tollendal, he exclaimed, '*I wish they were both hanged!*'

He seemed to bear hard upon the Duke de Liancourt, and to allude indistinctly to some report of my having opened an hospitable door to that nobleman, and having received a bad return. I defended the duke, and had not the conversation been interrupted I should have discovered what he meant by the remark. The same observation has met my ear on other occasions, but was never explained.

Mrs. Crewe arrived just before dinner, and though she exerted herself with that brilliancy of imagination which renders her conversation so interesting, it was not sufficient to raise the drooping spirits of Mr. Burke; it hurt me to see the languid manner in which he lounged rather than sat at table, his dress entirely neglected, and his manner quite dejected; yet he tried once or twice to rally, and once even to pun. Mrs. Crewe, observing that Thelwel was to stand for Norwich, said it would be horrid for Mr. Wyndham to be turned out by such a man. 'Aye,' he replied, 'that would not *tell well.*'

She laughed at him in the style of condemning a bad pun. Somebody said it was a fair one, he said *it was neither very bad nor good.*

He gave more attention to her account of Charles Fox than to any other part of her conversation. She spoke slightingly of him, and gave us some account of his life at Mrs. Armstead's. She says he lives very little in the world, or in any general society, for years past; that his pleasure is to be at the head of a little society of ten or twelve toad eaters, and seems to contract his mind to such a situation.

The conversation would have become more interesting had not Mrs. Crewe been so full of a plan for Ladies' Subscriptions for the Emigrants, and consulting him so much on the means of securing the money from the fangs of the Bishop of St. Pol de Léon, whose part, however, Mr. Burke took steadily. This business was so discussed as to preclude much other conversation. Mr. Burke has been at Gregory's twenty-nine years; and I was pleased to remark that he lived on the same moderate plan of life which I witnessed here five-and-twenty years ago.

Mem. 'To search for that visit.'[1]

My visit on the whole was interesting. I am glad once more to have seen and conversed with the man who I hold to possess the greatest and most brilliant parts of any person of the age in which he lived. Whose conversation has often fascinated me; whose eloquence has charmed; whose writings have delighted and instructed the world; and whose name will without question descend to the latest posterity. But to behold so great a genius so depressed with melancholy, stooping with infirmity of body, feeling the anguish of a lacerated mind, and sinking to the grave under accumulated misery; to see all this in a character I venerate, and

[1] No note is to be found among papers concerning this visit.

apparently without resource or comfort, wounded every feeling of my soul, and I left him the next day almost as low-spirited as himself.

In May the Duke of Buccleugh carried me to see Mr. Secretary Dundas's farm at Wimbledon, where I was to give my opinion of the mode of draining it. I found his people throwing money away like fools. They know nothing of the matter. This duke is another determined farmer, and seems to like conversing on no other subject.

This year I undertook a journey through the western counties, through Devon into Cornwall, returning by Somersetshire, and published the register of it in the 'Annals of Agriculture.' I happened to be at Exeter at the time of the quarter sessions, and dined with thirty magistrates, Mr. Leigh, clerk of the House of Commons, being chairman. I did not know him personally, and joined more warmly in a conversation on the Enclosure Bill,[1] than I should have done had I known that I was speaking to a person so much interested against it. Mr. Leigh was very decided in his opposition to the measure, asserting that there was no protection for property in any other mode of proceeding, which had been so long the established custom. I very eagerly refuted this observation till some

[1] Enclosure Bill. 'At the Revolution of 1688 more than half the kingdom was believed to consist of moorland, forest, and fen, and vast commons and wastes covered the greater part of England north of the Humber. But the numerous Enclosure Bills which began with the reign of George II., and especially marked that of his successor, changed the whole face of the country. Ten thousand square miles of untilled land have been [? had been] added, under their operation, to the area of cultivation.'—Green's *History of the English People.*

gentleman present spoke to Mr. Leigh, alluding to his official character. This was one proof of what I had often heard, that the officers of the two Houses of Parliament were of all others the most determined opposers of that measure. The reason is obvious; they have very considerable fees on the passing of every private Act,[1] and the clerks of the House have a further benefit which might not be compensated in any equivalent that might be given them; because they solicit many of the bills. Still, as there is so plain a precedent which has existed for many years in the case of the Speaker of the House, who has 6,000*l.* per annum instead of all fees, it seems no difficult matter to give an equal equivalent to the clerks for all their profits, including what they might make as solicitors.

[1] Abolished (saving the rights of the then holders of office) in 1812. 52 Geo. III. c. xi.

CHAPTER XII

ILLNESS AND DEATH OF BOBBIN, 1797

Illness of Bobbin—Letters of Bobbin and her father's replies—Dress minutes at the opera—Hoping against hope—Bobbin's death—Seeking for consolation—Retrospection—Beginning of diary—Correspondence.

THIS year, so fatal to every worldly hope, which overturned every prospect I had in life, and changed me almost as much as a new creation, opened in the common manner by my going to London to attend the meeting of the Board [of Agriculture]. I brought my dear angelic child[1] with me, who went to school in January, in good health but never in good spirits, for she abhorred school. Oh! what infatuation ever to send her to one. In the country she had health, spirits, and strength, as if there were not enough with what she might have learned at home, instead of going to that region of constraint and death, Camden House.

The rules for health are detestable, no air but in a measured, formal walk, and all running and quick motion prohibited. Preposterous! She slept with a girl who could hear only with one ear, and so ever laid on one side; and my dear child could do no otherwise

[1] Now fourteen years old.

afterwards without pain; because the vile beds are so small that they must both lie the same way. The school discipline of all sorts, the food, &c. &c., all contributed. She never had a bellyful at breakfast. Detestable this at the expense of 80*l.* a year. Oh! how I regret ever putting her there, or to any other, for they are all theatres of knavery, illiberality, and infamy.[1] Upon her being ill in March I took her to my lodgings in Jermyn Street, where Dr. Turton attended her till April 12, when I carried her to Bradfield. He certainly mistook her case entirely, not believing in a consumption, and by physic brought her so low that she declined hourly; he stuffed her with medicine at a time when sending her at once to Bristol or even to Bradfield she went little more than skin and bone, with prescriptions for more physicking under a stupid fellow at Bury, who purged her till she was a spectre. On June 13 she went to Smiths' (Bradfield neighbours), and there complained 'that such a young girl as I who came for air and exercise should be *thus crammed with physic.*' Poor thing! her instinct told her it was wrong, but she submitted.

From Bobbin to her Father

'My dear Papa,—I received your letter this morning. Thank you for it. My strength is much the same as

---

[1] This passage has been crossed out with a pencil, but is given as showing the *régime* of young ladies' schools a hundred years ago. In another note occurs the sentence, 'Brought my dear little girl from Camden House to London.' Presumably Camden Town is meant, at that time being less than suburban.

BOBBIN' (MARTHA YOUNG).

From a miniature by Plymer.

ILLNESS AND DEATH OF BOBBIN

when I saw you; my appetite is getting better a good deal. Mr. Smith saw me yesterday, and said it was a running pulse, but that he thought me better. I think if anything I am better than when I saw you. Thank you for the wine, which I have not yet received, but suppose it is at Bury. As for the bad news, I am tired of it. I want, and should very much like, a nice writing-box to hold pens, ink, paper, all my letters, &c., in short everything exact; this is just the thing for a birthday present. As for sweet things, I do not wish for them particularly; any little thing that you think wholesome I should be glad of. The weather [is] as yet so bad that I cannot stir out. Remember me to the party, and thank Mr. Kedington for waking me at six o'clock on the Monday morning.

'Believe me, dear Papa,
'Your dutiful Daughter,
'M. YOUNG.'

His Reply

'My dear Bobbin,—I am much obliged to you for the description you gave me of your health, but I beg you will repeat it directly, and do not forget appetite, pulse, sleep, pains, swelled legs, fever, exercise on change of weather, thirst, &c., for I am extremely anxious to know how you go on. I have looked at a great many writing-boxes, but find none yet under 1*l.* 5*s.* and 1*l.* 11*s.* 6*d.*, but I hear there are good ones to be had at 15*s.* The moment I can find one I will buy and send it packed full of seals, or something else.

'Politics are melancholy, for the fleet is satisfied,

the army is not, and the same spirit [there] would be dreadful. To-day, it is said, the Duke of York has declared the intention of raising the pay of Infantry, which is wise, but it may not be done to satisfy them, and in a moment they might be masters of the Tower, Bank, Parliament, &c.; however, let us hope that measures will be taken to prepare for the worst. The French will make no peace with us, but bring all their force to the coast and ruin us, if they can, by invasion expense.

'I cannot read half your mother's letter; but enough to see that she is very angry, for I know not what. I am not paid, and have nothing to send.

'Dear Bobbin,
'Yours affectionately,
'A. Y.'

Bobbin to her Father

'My dear Papa,—I received your letter this morning, for which I thank you. My appetite is a great deal better, pulse rather too quick, sleep *very well*, no pains, no swelled legs, no fever. We have had Sunday, Monday, and yesterday fine, and only those since you went. I walked in the Stone Walk. Pray send my writing-box as soon as you can, and, as you see by this, I want writing paper to write to you and Griffiths; I hope you will put some into it. I think one under a guinea will not be of any use to me. I saw Mr. and Mrs. O. Oakes[1] in Bury yesterday, they have made

---

[1] The county belle, Betsey Plampin, married some years before to Mr. Orbell Oakes.

but a short stay in town. I am much obliged to you for the wine and porter, which I have received safe. Remember me to the party, write soon, and believe me, dear papa,

'Your dutiful Daughter,
'M. YOUNG.

'*N.B.*—By the time Mr. Kedington comes his strawberries will be ripe; ask him if he would give me a few if I send for them. Pray remember a patent lock, so it will be a guinea besides that.'

Reply

'I was very glad to receive my dear Bobbin's letter, for it gives the best account I have yet received of your health. As you wish a guinea box you shall have one, though I can very ill afford it at present. As to your mother's ideas of my being paid, nothing can be said to it, if she knows better than I do. Her intelligence that I have sold the Exchequer annuity is like all the rest; if it is of longer duration than I supposed, so much the better for those who have bought it of me, and the worse for me.

'Lady Hawkesbury, Lady Hervey and Lady Erne[1] have given the Macklins and me some opera tickets several times—last night for the benefit of the sailors' widows and orphans, under Lord Jarvis; but sailors are not in fashion; the pit was not more than two-

---

[1] Lady Mary Hervey, the beautiful daughter of the Earl of Bristol, Bishop of Derry. Her portrait, by Gainsborough, was on show at Agnew's in 1896.

thirds full. They go out of town on Sunday or Monday. The weather has been very hot. Yesterday I could scarcely get from the Board home, for coaches and crowds along all the streets near St. James's, &c. The King is low-spirited at the thought of parting from his daughter. The Duchy of Wurtemburg is in the very jaws of France, and the prospect not favourable. Every person that comes from France asserts the same, that their whole force will be brought against this country. I have been sent for, and had an interview with a cabinet minister on arming the landed interest; but I fear nothing will be done effectually, though they seemed determined that *something* shall. Don't mention this out of the family. I will put paper in your box, changing the lock will take some time, but you shall have it, I hope, on Monday. Continue to write me. Tell your M. [mother] I have no money; therefore, why worry me? She might as well ask blood from a post.

'Dear Bobbin,

'Yours affectionately,

'A. Y.'

From Bobbin to her Father

'My dear Papa,—I received your letter this morning and am extremely obliged to you for your attention about the writing-box, but if it be not purchased, I have seen one at Rackham's which suits me exactly in every respect, therefore, if you will send a patent lock, I can have it put on. The price of Rackham's is a guinea, but if you have bought it I shall like it as well.

ILLNESS AND DEATH OF BOBBIN

My chief complaints are weakness, and a very bad cough, nothing else that I mind. I dare say you were entertained at the opera.

'I have just got six of the most beautiful little rabbits you ever saw, they skip about so prettily, you can't think, and I shall have some more in a few weeks. Having had so much physic I am right down tired of it. I take it still twice a day; my appetite is better. What can you mind politics so for? I don't think about them. Well, good bye, and believe me, dear papa,

'Your dutiful Daughter,
'M. YOUNG.

'Saturday.'

His Reply

'Monday.

'My dear Bobbin,—I received your letter this morning, and am sorry it did not come in time to stop my buying this box, which is twenty-five shillings besides carriage; but I hope you will like it; the lock is good and not common. I cannot afford a patent one, which is fifteen shillings alone.

'I am sorry to hear you have a bad cough and are weak. God send this fine weather may make you well soon. Continue to let me know how you do, particularly your cough. You do not say if you are upon the whole better, nor whether you have got on horseback yet, which I must have you do, at all events, or you will not get well at all. Be more particular—what physic do you take?

'You are right not to trouble yourself about

politics. Mr. and Mrs. M. went out of town this morning.

'The Directory of France has ordered all my works on Agriculture to be translated in twenty volumes, and their friends here would guillotine the author. The "Travels" sell greatly there in French, the third edition coming.

'Adieu.

'Yours affectionately.

'I have just time to send this [writing-box]. I intended it by coach, but as I am sure the seals would be ground all to powder, I think it best by waggon, which will explain the reason of your not having it so soon as I hoped and promised, and I think you would be vexed to have your collection spoiled. It goes by Bury waggon. Your pincushion box won't come in it.'

Note from A. Y. to Bonnet (*Farm Bailiff*)

'Miss Patty is to ride out in the chaise or whisky, or on double horse, whenever Bonnet is not obliged to be absent from the farm. If he is at market when the days are long and Miss Patty rises early, she can have a ride before breakfast.

'Bonnet to pay Miss Patty a shilling a week.'

To Bobbin from her Father

'My dear Bobbin,—I know your understanding, and therefore shall not write to you, young as you are, as a child. Mrs. Oakes writes me from Smith that Dr. T.

ordered you physic which you have not taken, at the same time that he does not at all like your case. Now this is a very serious business for your health, and consequently it makes me very uneasy. You are extremely weak by your own account, and steel is to strengthen. I gave it with my own hand to my father for a year, and with great effect; why you should doubt the efficacy of anything prescribed by so great a physician is more than I can understand; as to ill tastes, it is beneath common sense to listen to anything of the sort.

'But, my dear Bobbin, you ought to bring some circumstances to your recollection; the expense I have been at is more than I can afford, and I am now paying your school the same as if present. It is surely incumbent on you to consider, that when a father is doing everything upon earth for your good, yet you ought from feelings of gratitude and generosity to do all you can for yourself. I ask nothing but what another would positively insist on, and would order violent means of securing obedience; I, on the contrary, rely on your own feelings and your good sense, and so relying, I do beg that you will take everything ordered without murmur or hesitation, for I assure you it is with astonishment I hear that you have omitted this some time. Call your understanding to your aid, and ask yourself what you can think must be my surprise at hearing that while all around you are anxious for your health, that you alone will be careless of it. It is a much worse thing than ill health, for I had rather hear you were worse in body than that you had a malady in your heart or head. Think seriously of such conduct, and I am confident it will cease, for I know your disposition, and that makes me the more surprised, for knowing your good temper so well as I do it is perfectly astonishing. I am sure I shall hear, and it will be with great pleasure, that you are acting worthy of yourself; and having so much patience in your illness, you will show it in this, as in so many other things. (The first cheap lobsters I shall send you three by mail, the weather being hot.) I think you are not strong enough to ride a dicky alone. Surely double-horse would be better, but if you have tried you must be able to judge. Pray continue to write me constantly, for you must know how anxious I am to hear exactly your case.

'God bless you, my dear girl. I talk of your physician and your physic, but God forbid you trusted to either without asking His blessing regularly. You tell me that you always say your prayers; you cannot deceive God, and I hope you have a reliance on His blessing, which you cannot have if you do not ask it, and gain the habit of asking it.'

From Bobbin to her Father

'My dear Papa,—I received your letter yesterday. Thank you for your advice; I had taken the *steel* and *draughts* long before I received it, besides which I take some more stuff [1] . . . . and ask him [the doctor] like-

---

[1] Some medical questions the child wishes put to her London doctor are here omitted.

wise how long the steel, &c., must be taken before you feel any effect from it, for one might take physic for ever without receiving any benefit. Let not my giving you my opinion make you think that I do not take mine regularly; I assure you I do. My dear papa, how can you imagine that I should ever neglect my prayers? No! believe me, I know my duty too well for that. I believe *once*, the last time I was at the cottage, when I was too weak to say them out of bed, I then said them when Betty brought the asses' milk. One morning I fell asleep and forgot them; I thought of it at night, and told her to remind me of them, which she did—this she can tell you. I thank you for some fine cod and lobsters, which came very fresh and good.

'I am much the same as when I wrote last, my cough very troublesome still. I called on Mrs. Belgrave, she was gone to town. Adieu, my dear papa. Believe me

'Your dutiful and affectionate Daughter,

'M. YOUNG.'

His Reply

'Saturday.

'My dearest Bobbin,—The moment your letter came I went to Dr. Turton, but he was, as I feared he would be, out. However, I shall call on him this evening and send you his answer by to-morrow night's mail, if he is not gone to Kent, which I hope he will not be. If so, I cannot see him till Tuesday, as I shall be Sunday and Monday at the Duke of Bedford's. . . . I am of opinion you should leave off steel till you have my answer. . . . It is to give you strength. . . . You are a very good girl for having taken it, and equally for saying your prayers. Always preserve the habit of doing so. God protect and bless you!

'Two 64's and fifteen merchantmen have left the mutineers under a heavy fine, and it is expected the rest will do the same very soon, and then Admiral Parker and Co. will swing. Great expectations of a peace. Tell Mary, St. Paul's would come to B. as soon as Dr. T., but her thought was a good one.

'Write me again soon.

'Yours very affectionately,

'A. Y.'

To Bobbin from her Father

'Jermyn Street: Friday.

'My dear Bobbin,—As I desired you to write to me twice a week I expected a letter yesterday, but hope when I go by and by to the [Board] that I shall find one from you, for I am very anxious to hear how you do, and what Dr. Turton has ordered Smith to do for you. I had a very disagreeable journey to town, and did not sleep a minute, but, thank God, did not take cold; went to bed next night at nine o'clock and recovered the fatigue. The Macklins and Kedington were in a good deal of rain. They have been at two plays; I go to none. K. lives with us, and I am to charge him what he costs. They will go somewhere every night. I order everything just as usual before I go to the Board, and though I am to pay no more than my common expenses when alone, yet, as I necessarily live much better, I think it but fair to be quite economical, and we have a great deal of pleasant laugh at my pinching them, and not permitting their being extravagant. I allow no scrap of a supper which they make a rout about, for they come hungry as hounds from the play, and drink porter when they can get it; the wine I lock up, and have been twice in bed when they return. If you saw them devour at breakfast you would laugh; K., who is to be with the Oakes' when they come (we have hired Merlin's for them), threatens that he will give us nothing but potatoes.

'The news you see. It is said that there will be mutinies in the army as soon as the camps are formed; if so, and no immense army of property to awe them, the very worst of consequences may be expected. Ireland is in a dreadful state of alarm and apprehension—in a word, everything wears a threatening appearance, and nothing but the greatest wisdom and prudence can save us.

'I hope you have got rid of your lameness, and use your legs much more than you did when I was with you. Pray, my dear Bobbin, exert yourself, and take much air and exercise on the Stone Walk, which will do in all weathers except rain. I have not seen anybody yet except Lord Egremont.

'Tell Arthur to write to the Lewes bookseller that the Board buys two hundred copies and finds the plates, that is the copper, so that it must be to him not a hazardous speculation. Adieu, my dear girl.

'Yours affectionately,
'A. Y.'

Bobbin's Reply

'My dear Papa,—I received your letter this morning. I am sorry you had not a pleasant journey. Every day since you went we have had nothing but rain all day (most part of the night) long, so I have not been able to stir out, only in the chaise. I am much the same as when I saw you, but hope that when we have fine weather I shall get better. My leg *is* a great deal better. Mr. Smith advises porter, the beer is so new. . . . If you like to send a quarter cask my mother will pay the carriage; she has no opinion of Bury porter. If you send it by the Diss waggon let me know when it comes; if you don't like this, order Bonnet to get me some at Bury. What terrible news you write me in your letter. I really have nothing more to tell you; write soon, and believe me

'Your dutiful Daughter,
'M. YOUNG.

'N.B.—Papa, you said you would send me some red wine, as there is none drank here; he speaks very much against my drinking so much water without red wine in it, because my ankles swell so much.'

The following were memoranda noted at the time :—

The 11th of June I went to the Duke of Bedford's sheep-shearing, and got back (to London) on the 16th. The next day I had a letter that terrified me so much that on the 19th I set off for Suffolk, and went directly to Troston Hall (the seat of Capel Lofft, Esq.), where the dear dear child had been carried some days before for change of air. Good God! what a situation I found her in, worse than I had conceived possible in so short a time, so helpless and immovable as to be carried from a chair to her bed, evidently in one of those cruel consumptive cases which flatter by some favourable symptoms, yet with fatal ones that almost deprive hope.

Good Heaven! what have I to look forward to if I lose my child? For her own sake I know not what to hope; the world is so full of wickedness and misery, and she must be so innocent and free from crimes, that her lot hereafter, I hope and have confidence in the mercies of God, will be blessed. Ought I then, but from selfishness, to wish her here? Yet a fond father's feelings will be predominant. Oh, save her, save her, is my prayer to God Almighty!

Dr. Wollaston, the eminent physician at Bury, has been consulted; he gives little hopes, but advises a milk and vegetable diet, and said that sea air and a humid mild climate would be good. I next wrote to Dr. Thornton, who recommended an egg and meat diet; and Mr. Martyn, in a letter, desired me to try the inhaling of ether; in fact, all has been done that the urgency of the case required, but, alas! she is past the assistance of all human power. After remaining a week at Troston I wrote into Lincolnshire for a house at Boston, with a view to be near the sea, in case she should be able to support a short voyage; and the air of that low place is reckoned preferable to the keen air of Bradfield. We travelled with slow and short journeys on July 5 to Bradon—still more exhausted; on the 6th to Wisbeach—no alteration yet from the change of air; on the 7th only to Long Sutton—worse, greatly fatigued, and a very bad night. Oh! the lacerated feelings of my wounded heart! To see the child of my tenderest affection in such a state! growing hourly weaker and more emaciated, during the last week being even unable to stand. It is beyond my power to describe what is struggling within me! My sorrow has softened me and wrings my very heart strings! How hard does it appear submissively to bow to that text—'He that loveth son or daughter more than Me is not worthy of Me.' I have but one consolation, which prevents my utter depression and despair. I trust in the goodness of her Almighty Creator and in the merits of her blessed Redeemer, that They will, in the mercy of omnipotence, pardon what slight offences she may have been guilty of, and receive her into that heavenly mansion which I humbly hope her innocence may expect. I pray fervently for Their mercy, and only wish that I was worthy of being heard. May my future life be such as to make an hereafter the great view, aim, and end of my remaining life! The 8th we reached Spalding, too much fatigued to go on, thinking that an air so different from what she had left might have given some ease. Vain hope! No effort of the kind appears. The 11th we arrived at Boston, and she bore the journey well. Alas! it was her final stage in this world!

The next day she was still worse, but even now gave one of those traits which displayed her delicacy,

ILLNESS AND DEATH OF BOBBIN

for upon finding that her mother was detaining Dr. Wilson with questions, she reminded her of it by saying, 'Mamma, you forget there are other ladies wanting the doctor.' On the 13th the crisis of her sufferings was approaching; she whispered to me as I sat by her bedside, 'I hope you pray for me.' At about eleven o'clock she asked her sister Mary to read a prayer as usual, and attended with apparent fervour, putting her hands together in the attitude of devotion.

My poor dear child breathed her last at twelve minutes past one o'clock on Friday morning, the 14th. I was on my knees at her bedside in great agony of mind. She looked at me and said, '*Pray for me.*' I assured her that I did. She replied, '*Do it now, papa,*' on which I poured forth aloud ejaculations to the Almighty, that He would have compassion and heal the affliction of my child. She clasped her hands together in the attitude of praying, and when I had done said, 'Amen'—her last words.

Thank God of His infinite mercy she expired without a groan, or her face being the least agitated; her inspirations were gradually changed from being very distressing, till they became lost in gentleness, and at the last she went off like a bird.

Thus fled one of the sweetest tempers and, for her years, one of the best understandings that I ever met with. She was a companion for mature years, for there was in her none of the childish stuff of most girls. And there fled the first hope of my life, the child on whom I wished to rest in the affliction of my age, should I reach such a period. But the Almighty's will be done, and may I turn the event to the benefit of my soul, and in such a manner as to trust through the mediation of my Redeemer to become worthy to join her in a better world. Her disposition was most affectionate, gentle, and humane; to her inferiors, full of humility, and always ready to perform acts of beneficence, thus attaching the poor by her charity, whilst she was equally courted by those above her for that fascination of manners possessing the attraction of the loadstone. Her countenance in health beamed with animation, and her dimpled cheeks smiled with the beauty of a Hebe. Dear interesting creature! Endowed, too, with a sensibility that shrunk from the gaze, her appearance in society produced [*here the sentence breaks off*].

What a scene have I described for a fond father to witness!

On the 15th the Rev. S. Partridge and his wife came to give us what comfort they could, and took us in a most kind and friendly manner to their house. I determined that her remains should be carried to Bradfield, having a warm hope of being animated to a more fervent devotion by the idea of her ashes being deposited in our own village church. To the departed spirit it is less than nothing—to me it may do good, and I have need of working out my salvation with fear and trembling. I feel that a wretched and depressed state of mind leads me to more Christian thoughts and more favourable to religious impressions than prosperity, or ease, or happiness, as it is called, and therefore hope I am justified in doing it; and if my family think the same, they also will derive benefit.

After a day passed in deep sorrow, Mr. Partridge read one of his sermons on the intermediate state of departed souls, and which I afterwards found was one of Jortin's.[1] From many passages of Scripture it was made clear that they are conscious, and if good in this life, happy.

On Monday, the 17th, I arrived at Bradfield, where every object is full of the dear deceased.

On going into the library the window looks into the little garden in which I have so many times seen her happy. O gracious and merciful God! pardon me for allowing any earthly object thus to engross my feelings and overpower my whole soul! But what were they not on seeing and weeping over the roses, variegated sage, and other plants she had set there and cultivated with her dear hands. But every room, every spot is full of her, and it sinks my very heart to see them. Tuesday evening, the 18th, her remains arrived, and at midnight her brother read the service over her in a most impressive manner. I buried her in my pew, fixing the coffin so that when I kneel it will be between her head and her dear heart. This I did as a means of preserving the grief I feel, and hope to feel while breath is in my body. It turns all my views to an hereafter, and fills my mind with earnest wishes, that when the great Author of my existence may please to take me I may join my child in a better world.

O merciful Saviour, that took on Thee our nature and feelings, grant me Thy Holy Spirit to confirm and

---

[1] John Jortin, D.D., born 1696, died 1770. His numerous theological and historical works have been frequently reprinted.

strengthen these sentiments; to repent of all my sins and errors, and enable me for the rest of my days to look steadily towards that better world where, I trust, the innocence of my child, united with her piety, have given her a place. Sure, sure, I shall pray with a more fervent and sincere devotion over the remains of her whom I so much wish, when it pleases Heaven, that I may join. This was my motive.

The 19th I went into a little chamber which I had neatly fitted up about three years ago. My dear child had decorated it with some drawings and placed her books on the shelves, and left it in that order and regularity which followed all her actions. I burst into tears while viewing it, and felt such a depression at my heart that I thought I should have sunk on the floor. It shall never be altered, but everything continued as she left it.

20*th*.—Again looked at her garden, and a new one she had marked out and planted under a weeping willow. No day arrives but some new object is presented to move all the springs of affection and regret; and what day can pass in which these melancholy feelings will not predominate? In the meantime I read the Scriptures, and Jortin and other sermons, with an attention I never paid before; and may God of His mercy confirm this disposition, and enable me thus to turn this heavy misfortune to the benefit of my soul. Dispositions which company, travelling, and other pursuits would have tended to banish, I wish to cherish; a melancholy has produced in me a more earnest desire to be reconciled to God than any other event of my life, and proves that of all the medicines of the soul, sorrow is perhaps the most powerful.

Business, pleasure, and the world, tend only to stifle this seriousness of thought, and to prevent the mind from looking into itself and examining the foundation of all its future hopes. For these three days I have continued perusing no books but the New Testament and sermons, of which I have read many.

21*st*.—Hoed part of my dear child's garden under the window, and carried her bonnet and cap to her chamber. They produced many tears, for I yet continue weak as a babe. Read the whole Gospel of St. John, two sermons of Tillotson on the state of the blessed, and two of Dr. Horne's on the purification of the mind by troubles and the government of the thoughts. I had before in this week read all the Epistles, the Hebrews, and the Acts of the Apostles, and also Bryant's 'Authenticity of the Scriptures.' Such studies are my only consolation. I give full attention, and hope for the blessing of God's Holy Spirit, that I may not let it be vain, or ever suffer the world to wipe out this taste for the things that concern another world. I attempt the regulation of my thoughts, and to contemplate the goodness and mercy of the Deity; but my misery for the irreparable loss I have suffered yet weighs me down.

22*nd*.—Hoed the rest of her garden. Symonds and Carter spent the day at the Hall. I wish they had not come together, I wanted conversation with them separately on the question I had read a good deal of, the sleep of the soul after death till the resurrection.

Symonds will not admit that we can draw any satisfactory conclusion for or against it, but Carter allows Dr. Jortin's reasoning in his sermon on that subject. In the evening I read what Dr. H. More [1] says upon the subject, who is strenuously against it. A state of insensibility is a dreadful idea, and I find consolation in the conviction that my dear girl is now happy.

23rd.—Sunday; passed it, I hope, like a Christian. At church sitting over the remains of my child! Oh! what a train of feelings absorbed my soul. In the evening read St. Luke's Gospel and took a most heart-sinking melancholy walk. I cannot yet bring my mind to sufficient tranquillity to throw into one little memoir these and other particulars.

Examined the willows she planted on the island. Oh! that they were thriving oaks that promised a longer duration, but they may last as long as anybody that will care for the planter. Continue to read Scripture, and some of Secker's [2] and Ogden's [3] sermons, and again began 'Bryant on Christianity.' I pray to God with all the fervency I feel to give me the grace of His Holy Spirit, that I may turn this loss to the benefit of my soul. Dr. Jortin, in his seventeenth sermon, most truly says, 'It is adversity which seizes upon the future as prosperity dwells upon the present.

---

[1] Henry More, D.D., born 1614, died 1687. In 1640 published *Psycho-Zoia; or, the Life of the Soul.* His philosophical and theological works have been reprinted.

[2] Th. Secker, Archbishop of Canterbury, born 1693, died 1768.

[3] Samuel Ogden, D.D., born 1716, died 1778.

On the 25th I read Littleton's [1] 'Conversion and Apostleship of St. Paul.' I had brought down from London a new political pamphlet of Howlett's on a subject that was once interesting, but I can attend to nothing except inquiries which in some degree connect with that habit of mind which flows from my recent loss.

Mrs. —— called to persuade me into company for regaining cheerfulness. Alas! it will come, I fear, much too soon, and what is it good for? Sorrow is the best physician to heal a soul that has been too careless in its duty to God.

Will the world, and pleasure, and society contribute like grief to secure me a probability of joining in another world the spirit of her I mourn?

26th.—I read part of Dr. Clarke's [2] 'Demonstration of the Being and Attributes of God,' as much as I could understand without too intense an application, and then part of 'Butler's Analogy.' Prayed to the Almighty in the middle of the day. The morning is the proper time, but when we are tired and sleepy, the evening I think an improper period to offer either thanksgiving or petitions to the Divine goodness.

Why, oh! why must we have misfortune and sorrow to make us sensible of our duty to our heavenly Father and our Saviour and Redeemer? How difficult to instil a right attention into young people.

[1] Adam Littleton, D.D., born 1627, died 1674.
[2] Samuel Clarke, D.D., born 1675, died 1729. The piece alluded to was the first Boyle Lecture. Of his works Dr. Johnson remarked, 'I should recommend Dr. Clarke's works were he orthodox.'

I am, however, thankful that my dear child was naturally serious and, I believe, well disposed in this respect; with what joy I now read the following passage in a letter I received from her while she was ill at Bradfield before I came down: 'My dear papa, how can you imagine that I should ever neglect my prayers? No! believe me, I know my duty too well for that.'

What now would be the idea of any improvement or accomplishment compared with the least trait like this?

27*th*.—Called for a few minutes on some neighbours. They all want me to dine with them, but such society to a mind diseased yields no food for reflection, and is, therefore, not fit for me. I could associate with nobody with comfort, but those whose religious acquirements could tend to strengthen my present habits.

I continue to read Butler, also two sermons by Conybeare [1] on angels; looked at the miniature which my wife has of the dear girl, a most striking likeness by Plymer;[2] wept over it with feelings easier imagined than described. I will have a copy of it; 'twill serve, at least, as a melancholy remembrance, and, I hope, recall my mind should it ever wander from the lamented original.

28*th*.—Finished Butler's 'Analogy.' It does not quite answer the idea I had formed of him, though a

[1] John Conybeare, D.D., born 1691, died 1755. 'A great champion of revelation.'

[2] Plymer; in Redgrave's *Dictionary of Artists* written 'Plimer.' Two brothers therein mentioned, Andrew and Nathaniel, both miniature painters and exhibitors at the R.A.; born 1763, died 1837; born 1767, died 1822.

powerful work; but he demands a second perusal, but does not even then promise to be perfectly clear. Read also Mr. Locke's 'Reasonableness of Christianity,' which is a luminous convincing work, and must have done great good. Watered dear Bobbin's garden and read over her letters. She had, for her early years, a most uncommon understanding and a penetration into character wonderful for the age of fourteen. On reviewing her last illness I am filled with nothing but the most poignant regret and self-condemnation for putting so much reliance in the medical tribe, for she had the personal attendance or correspondence of five physicians and none agreed. I did for the best and spared nothing, but had she been a pauper in a village she would, I verily think, have been alive and hearty. Such are the blessings of money; it has cost me 100*l.* to destroy my child, for I do not think one shilling was bestowed which did not in one way or other do mischief.

Whilst I was in much anxiety about my child's health I bought Mr. Wilberforce on Christianity.[1] I read it coldly at first, but advanced with more attention. It brought me to a better sense of my dangerous state; but I was much involved in hesitation and doubt, and was very far from understanding the doctrinal part of the book. This was well, for it induced me to read it again and again, and it made so much impression upon me that I scarcely knew how

[1] *Practical View of the Prevailing System of Professed Christians in the Higher and Middle Ranks in this Country, Contrasted with Real Christianity.* Published 1797, and frequently reprinted.

to lay it aside. It excited a very insufficient degree of repentance, and a still more insufficient view of my interest in the Great Physician of souls.

It is rather singular that a trifling circumstance at this time first brought me acquainted with Mr. Wilberforce, whose book I had been again perusing for the fourth time with increased pleasure, and to whom I had more than once thought of writing for his opinion on the intermediate state and original sin. On arriving at Boston, what was my surprise on receiving a letter from him relative to Parkinson's subscription to some book on agriculture, and apologising for the application to a stranger. I seized the pen with eagerness to reply, writing largely about his own book, praising it greatly, and telling him of my wish to apply to him. Should this (I thought) be productive of a connection that might confirm my pious resolution, I might, perhaps, be justified in attributing it to the interposition of God.

I hope that the thought is not presumptuous. Is it the spirit of my sweet girl that is thus friendly to me? How pleasing an idea!

July 29.—Having excused myself from dining out with the Balgraves, a note from her this morning. But it will not do. Company and the world will only draw off my mind from those religious contemplations and that course of reading which is favourable to prayer, repentance, and reformation. I wish not to lessen my grief or banish my feelings of that sorrow which turns my heart at present to seek God. I dread it will come but too soon; and were it not for this apprehension I should go on my journey to Lincolnshire for the Board directly, but I wish to confirm these feelings and earnestly pray for the Divine grace to preserve them to the extirpation from my heart of love for the world or any of its follies.

[*Note added by A. Y. in* 1817.]

Throughout many of the succeeding notes, several expressions occur not all consistent with true evangelical religion; but I would not afterwards alter them, because I wished to ascertain, on the re-perusal of these papers, what was at the moment of my affliction the state of my mind and of my faith; and when I consider what were the books which I read and admired, I cannot be surprised at any such remarks falling from my pen.

I have often reflected on the great mercy and goodness of God in not permitting my religious opinions to be permanently injured by some of the works which it will be found I so eagerly perused at a period when I could not have one moment's conversation with any truly pious character. Two circumstances probably contributed to this effect: first, the incessant attention which I gave to reading the New Testament; and secondly, my ardent study of Mr. Wilberforce's 'Practical Christianity,' though without thoroughly understanding it.

The solitary life I condemned myself to, or, to speak with more propriety, which alone I relished, while reading sixteen or seventeen hours a day, and in which I consequently rather devoured books than read them, was, I think, very advantageous, and possibly more so in the final result than if my authors had been more truly sound.

I have since perused many works which, had they fallen into my hands at that time, would probably have made me quit my retirement and rush into the society of men who would have conducted me, in my then state of mind, to the utmost lengths of enthusiasm.

The writers I consulted were well calculated to lay a certain solidity of foundation in the great leading truths of Christianity, which formed a basis whereon it was easy afterwards to raise a more evangelical edifice.

In all this business I cannot but admire the goodness of the Almighty in protecting me from many evils to which I might easily have been led by my troubled feelings.

[*Diary continued.*]

Read Dr. Isaac Barrow's sermon on submission to the Divine will. He seems a powerful writer, but his language is debased by expressions void of all dignity. Read a good deal in Barrow on the pre-existence of human souls. Very singular; the texts on which he builds support him very faintly, yet there is a degree of probability in the system consonant to reason.

30*th.*—Prayed to God over the remains of my dear child, and the circumstance fills my mind with that melancholy that is not unsuitable to religious feelings. I do not wonder at the custom of the primitive Christians praying at the tombs of the departed, it is an obvious and natural prejudice.

Finished Barrow, and wrote to my friend Mr. Cole

to desire he would apply to his neighbour, the learned Bryant, to know his opinion of that question. Began Dr. More on the ' Immortality of the Soul.' Capel Lofft spent the day with us ; his conversation is ready on any subject, and mine led to serious ones, which he seems to like. We had much that was metaphysical on the soul (pre-existence), a future state, &c. He is of opinion that heaven is not so very different from our ideas of what this world might be, as are commonly entertained ; and rightly observes, that if death, evil, anxiety, and disease, with corporeal passions, were banished, this earth would be a heaven ; and that the knowledge of one another hereafter is not at all inconsistent with our Saviour's expression, *'in My Father's house are many mansions.'*

31*st.*—Read Littleton's sermon on the necessity of well husbanding our time. It is excellent, he has thoughts and modes of expanding his observations that are beyond the common run. Laid aside Dr. More on the 'Immortality of the Soul;' he gets so high in the region of fancy, and is so full of jargon and supposition, under the formula of demonstrations, that I am disgusted with his farrago ; and [there is] so much on witches, apparitions, &c., as to be mere rubbish.

Read Sherlock's sixth sermon on the ' Immortality of the Soul,' which is an admirable one. I see plainly from what I feel upon occasion of the severe, dreadfully severe misfortune that I have met with, that under great afflictions there can be no real consolation but in religion. I have mused and meditated much on what philosophy, as it is called, could afford in such an exigency, but the amount would be no more than the employment of the mind, and preventing its dwelling without interruption on the loss sustained, the comfort to be drawn from it would be weak and vain; but the Gospel offers considerations which bear immediately on the source of the evil; affords matter of consolation in the certainty of another life, and in those promises which meet the yearnings of the distempered soul; diffuses a calm and quiet resignation to the Divine will, under the pleasing hope of seeing those again in the next world whom we have loved tenderly in this. To me it seems that when this wish is founded on a virtuous object here as that of a parent and a child, the very hope is an argument in its favour, because it is perfectly consistent with infinite benevolence to grant it—and the desire must be universal in every human mind.

August 1.—Read about half of Sherlock on 'Immortality,' but my patience was then quite exhausted; the verbiage is such that it sickens one, though I approve the doctrine entirely and agree with him in everything. What a loss! that excellent books for matter should be so written, or rather spun into such endless circumlocutions that time is wasted for want of compression. Read three or four sermons of Littleton —clear, lucid, and impressive.

At night a Dane came, recommended by Sir J. Sinclair. Unfortunate to all my feelings. I refuse dining with all my friends, and to be tormented with a trifler who can speak neither French nor English.

My mind is in a state that cannot bear interruption. I love to mope alone, and reflect on my misery.

August 2.—Began Scott's [1] 'Christian Life,' but Smythies having sent me the sixth volume of Bishop Newton's [2] works, containing a dissertation on the 'Intermediate State,' I read it with equal eagerness and satisfaction. It exceeds on that subject all I have yet met with. He is of opinion, in which all agree, that good spirits will know each other; and probably, from the parable of Lazarus, have some knowledge of what passes on earth. But that is of little consequence in comparison with the most consoling and comfortable idea contained in the first opinion. And what a call is it to strive with earnestness and ardour to arrive at a situation that will recompense us in so great a degree for every evil and sorrow we can meet with in this world. Can I then hope, by dedicating the rest of my life here to God, to join my dear child hereafter, my mother, my other daughter, and my sister; and should it so please the Almighty in His mercy, my father and brother? Of the females I can have little doubt, or rather none. I know too little of the lives of the others to venture to pronounce. Read also Bishop Newton's dissertation on the Resurrection, general judgment, and final state of man. They are all excellent, and I rather devoured than read them. These books I must buy to read again with more attention.

3rd.—The Dane is gone, and therefore I am left to

---

[1] Th. Scott—the friend of Cowper—born 1747, died 1821, chaplain to the Lock Hospital.

[2] Th. Newton, born 1704, died 1782; edited *Paradise Lost*.

my favourite contemplations. Newton's dissertations are consoling, for they leave me no doubts about that hideous doctrine, the sleep of the soul, which, however it might have been suited for the dead, is dreadful to those they leave behind. For the rest of my life to know that my dear child is in a state of conscious existence, and consequently happy, is the first of comforts; but to feel the enlivening warmth and light of the sun, thinking that she felt nothing, but slept in the cold grave, would have almost sunk me into it. No! she lives, and as there is reason to believe, the departed spirits have some knowledge of what passes here. What a call is it to conduct myself so as to give no pain to her! Let me imagine myself for ever seen by the spirits of my mother and my child. Let me have a keen feeling of the pain any unworthy action or impure thought would give to them, and of the pleasure they would reap from seeing the reverse; that I was so living as gave them a hope of my joining them hereafter. Let me, if possible, entertain this persuasion till I am convinced of it. I cannot have the thought without being the better man. Oh! guard me against relapsing into evil negligence, the two certain fruits of pleasure and prosperity.

What are the friendships of the world! What consolation, what comfort!

When most wanted it is sure to fail. One has business, another pleasure; one, a family, another a husband, all have something to render them broken reeds to such as are in want; and whether the boon be comfort or money, they prove the same to the touchstone. Who have been my friends? Symonds and Carter are good men, but I have seen them [of late] only once. Who must I name but Ogden, Sherlock, Jortin, Bishop Newton, Butler, Locke, and Clarke? These have told me how to make a friend not like to fail in the time of need, my God and my Saviour. May I strengthen and confirm that friendship and turn it to be a habit of my life! And thou, most gentle spirit of my departed child, if it is allowed thee to look down on earth, be my guardian angel and lead me to everlasting life, to join thee to part no more!

4th.—Read three of Bishop Sherlock's sermons and one of Dr. Clarke's, also some passages in his 'Demonstration of the Truth of Revealed Religion.'

5th.—Read a very good sermon of Bishop Sherlock on Redemption, the third in fourth volume. Bishop Butler on human ignorance, excellent. This subject, in the books I have yet read, has not been sufficiently treated, it might be made to refute all the infidels, and draw mankind to a more religious life.

My dear girl's books are come, her unfinished work, her letters, &c. Melancholy employment to unpack and arrange them in her room. If any difference I think of her with more, rather than with less regret; yet I hope and trust, not without resignation to the Almighty will of the great and good Being whose providence has deprived me of her. I think I feel that this deep regret, this calm sorrow will last my life, and that no events can happen that will ever banish her from my mind. Ranby called and I conversed with him about her till tears would, had I continued it, stopped my speaking. I hate and pity those who avoid talking to the afflicted upon the subject which causes their affliction, it argues a little trifling mind in one party or the other.

Read Bishop Sherlock's 'Dissertation respecting the Sense of the Ancients on the Fall of Man,' which seems to me (who am, however, no judge) a very clear and satisfactory work. He appears to have a singular talent in reconciling seeming difficulties in knotty texts of Scripture, and opens every subject with great clearness and an acute spirit of discrimination.

I suppose there must be some commonplace book of divinity, but I know not whose; a collection of luminous passages from such an immensity of writings as there are on this most important of all subjects would be very useful; yet every man should make his own, selecting such topics and observations as come home to his own case and bosom.

Were I not going now a most uninteresting journey, I would do this for myself. This tour hangs on my mind; nothing would suit my feelings so well as to stay here in my present melancholy gloom, reading divinity, and endeavouring so steadily to fix my mind on eternity and the hope of joining my dear child, as to work a change in my habits, my life, my conversation, and pursuits; and to do all that human frailty will permit to reconcile myself to the Almighty. These thoughts, however, I shall try to preserve in spite of a journey. I will take the New Testament and Wilberforce with me, and read a portion every day, and spend the Sundays in a manner I have never done yet in travelling.

August 7.—To Ely. Called for a moment on Carter, who thinks so highly of Bishop Newton that he intends to buy his works.

At Ely quite alone, and no resource but in my own melancholy ideas. My first thought was to send to a Mr. Hall, who has hired Tattersall's farm, or Mr. Metcalfe, a minor canon, who has written in the 'Annals of Agriculture'—but I rejected the scheme and kept to solitude. As soon as I finished dinner I began Mr. Wilberforce for the fourth time, reading with renewed attention. I hear many objections to him, of his being a Presbyterian engrafted on a Methodist, but it is arrant nonsense. My mind goes with him in every word. View the Minster and Trinity chapel, and venerate the piety of former ages that raised such noble edifices in honour of God the Almighty giver and governor of all things. I once thought such buildings the efforts of superstition, perhaps folly! How different are my present sentiments! for what can be more rational than to raise temples of a character that shall impress some idea, however weak, of the sublimity of that infinite Being who made and pervades all that exists, except His own great creative self!

8th.—Rise at five, write to my friends Dr. Valpy and C. Cole. To Peterborough. Much time for reflection, and it is singular that even while I am depressed with deep melancholy at the loss I have sustained, yet unholy ideas and imaginations will intrude. Is this the devil and his powers of darkness which buffet and beset us? Is not depravity and sin so inherent in our natures that we are ever liable to these wanderings which so disgrace our nature at better moments? But the conclusion, whatever it be owing to, is clear, that the government of the thoughts is an essential part of our duty, as Johnson has well explained in an admirable 'Rambler.' Such thoughts, unresisted, seize and take possession of the mind, and they cannot do that without leading to action and all the guilt that may follow. Repel the first germinating principle of the idea, and the difficulty is not great; but indulge the pleasing dream and the heart is vitiated, for the imagination is impure.

[*The remainder of the diary, in the same strain, is much too long for insertion. Here are a few closing sentences.*]

September 2 [in Yorkshire].—To what is it that I shall return? My child no more! To what at London? Solitary in my lodgings, where am I to send for her whose cheerfulness gilded every scene, and little pleasing ways lent such a charm to render her presence such a comfort to me? All gone—gone for ever! Of that description of feelings what remains? A blank!—a desert! . . . Cried over the hair of my sweet departed Bobbin! Never more in this world to see thee again!

October 15.—I have torn my heart to pieces with looking at my dear child's hair! Melancholy remains, but how precious when their owner is no more! I am to see her no more in this world. Gone for ever!

London, November 13.—This day se'nnight I came to town with Mrs. Y. and Mary. I knew it would be a very uncomfortable plan; but to do as I would be done by made it proper.

November 26.—I have been a week at Petworth, an interesting, splendid, gay and cheerful week, and, as too often the case, a vain, frivolous, and impious one. Sir John Sinclair would have me on the Sunday go to Goodwood. Never a serious word, never a soul to church from that house to thank God for the numerous blessings showered down upon it, and the means of good which 60,000*l*. a year confers. Yet Lord Egremont does all that could be wished as far as humanity, charity, and doing moral benefits can—but no religion. In the chapel, no worship, no hats off but my own—dreadful example to a great family and to his children and to 2,500 people in the town. I talked to Arthur, and strongly recommended to him to attend constantly and to keep himself clear from such a want of piety. He disapproves of it much; and I pray to God that yet he may not be corrupted by such evil examples, but imbibe a dislike to such want of gratitude. I watched for opportunities of serious remark, but none of effect offered except one observation on Lady Webster's infidelity in religion, when I threw in a word or two. The very virtues of such people do mischief by recommending their irreligious example.

The following letters are selected from those received this year:—

From Dr. Burney

'Chelsea College: March 16, 1797.

'My dear Sir,—You have applied to a very incompetent person for political consolation in addressing me, an old notorious alarmist who has long seen evils approaching even worse than those which have already arrived. I wish anything had happened to convince me that my mental eyes had been as short-sighted as those in my head. But, alas! things are going on everywhere from bad to worse. My foolish countrymen, nay, worse, the wicked and incurable democrats who inhabit the same island, so far from being cured by the savage cruelties and universal misery brought about in France by the Revolution and the treatment of other countries which she has conquered and even fraternised with, still long for a revolution here, without even wishing to avert any of the evils which have happened elsewhere, from the diabolical character and principles of her inhabitants! I have seen that a wish to break the Bank has long been formed, and I even have been advised to get all the cash I could for my notes if I had any; and the person who advised this measure, who had never been at the Bank before in his life, and was forced to inquire his way thither, had been bullying the harassed clerks to give him cash for a forty-pound note, for no other purpose than to lock it up. Seven millions of guineas were issued for notes in one week! Of this sum 300,000l., it is said, were for notes presented by the English Santerre. A banker from Norwich had collected notes to the amount of 400,000l., with which he came post to London in the same seraphic hope of breaking the Bank; but unluckily for his benevolent plan, the further issuing of cash had been stopped the night before his arrival. The favourite Jacobin plan at present is to make this nation and all Europe believe that we are really in a state of bankruptcy, and that the notes now in circulation will be soon of as little value as French assignats, reporting every day that they are at a very considerable discount, which God forbid should ever happen. For my own part, I would starve myself to death sooner than buy, even food, by the parting with a bank note for a farthing less value than it has hitherto had. But the poor Duke of Bedford, Mr. Cooke, the dissenting manufacturers, &c., are so distressed for want of cash to pay their workmen, that they are *obliged* to dismiss them. And this, to be sure, is not done with an intention of throwing all the blame upon Government and making furious rebels of all the persons discharged. Everything is seen and represented in the blackest colours—the French always right and the Administration wrong. For if opposition should ever be obliged to allow the present ministry to be right, why change it? And down they must pull every person and thing above them, even if, like Samson, they are crushed in the ruins, which I have not the least doubt will be the case if ever the revolution they seem so determined to bring about should happen.

'The ballot has fallen upon me to furnish a man and a horse to the Provisional Cavalry,[1] which has occasioned me much trouble and vexation. The expense, had it been double, I would have paid with alacrity, for the defence of everything dear to honest men, during such

[1] Alluding to the movement suggested by A. Y., and ultimately carried out, of forming regiments of volunteer cavalry, in view of the menacing attitude of France.

a war and with such enemies; but the business of recruiting, clothing, accoutring, &c., is so new to men of peace, that they know not how to go to work. Three substitutes that I had engaged have disappointed me, and the horse I have purchased I am not sure will pass muster. Had Government levied a tax of five or ten guineas upon each horse that was kept for pleasure, either in or out of harness, and done the business of raising a certain number of cavalry themselves, it would have been better done, and ladies and superannuated gentlemen (like my worship) would have escaped infinite plague and vexation.

'I am exceedingly sorry that your dear and charming little daughter is not well.

'I am, with sincere regard,
'My dear Sir,
'Your affectionate Friend,
'CHARLES BURNEY.'

From Edmund Burke, Esq., alluding to the projects in Parliament before named for regulating the price of labour.

'Bath: May 23, 1797.

'Dear Sir,—I am on the point of leaving Bath, having no further hope of benefit from these waters; and as soon as I get home (if I should live to get home) should I find the papers transmitted me by your Board I shall send them faithfully to you; though, to say the truth, I do not think them of very great importance.

'My constant opinion was, and is, that all matters relative to labour ought to be left to the conversations of the parties. That the great danger is in Government intermeddling too much. What I should have taken the liberty of addressing to you, had I possessed strength to go through it, would be to illustrate or enforce that principle.

'I am extremely sorry that any one in the House of Commons should be found so ignorant and unadvised as to wish to revive the senseless, barbarous, and, in fact, wicked regulations made against free trade in matters of provision which the good sense of late Parliaments had removed. I am the more concerned at the measure, as I was myself the person who moved the repeal of the absurd code of statutes against the most useful of all trades, under the invidious names of forestalling and regrating. But, however, I console myself on this point by considering that it is not the only breach by which barbarism is entering upon us. It is, indeed, but a poor consolation, and one taken merely from the balance of misfortunes.

'You have titles enough of your own to pass your name to posterity, and I am pleased that you have got spirit enough to hope that there will be such a thing as a civilised posterity to attend to things of this kind.

'I have the honour to be,
 'With very high respect and esteem,
  'Your most obedient, humble servant,
   'EDMUND BURKE.'

Mr. Burke died July 7 [*note by A. Y.*].

From John Symonds, Esq., on public affairs, very gloomy, with much condemnation of Mr. Pitt.

'St. Edmund's Hill: June 8, 1797.

'At the time, my dear sir, that I received your letter I was travelling over Italy, in order to figure in your "Annals of Agriculture;" but the state of that country has been so much *bouleversé*, that my head has been turned in reflecting upon it, as is most probably the case with the greater part of its inhabitants.

'You ask me what plan I could propose to save the country. Arm, undoubtedly, as you say; but how to do it most effectually I pretend not to determine. You justly reprobate volunteering infantry.

'Charles Cole tells me you have something in the press upon this subject. To fill the army or navy with defenders or volunteers, is the way to pave the way to our ruin. But I should begin with proposing a scheme which would probably be heard with disdain, and which has been rejected by the King: recall Lord Camden; appoint Lord Moira, Lord Lieutenant, with full powers to emancipate the Roman Catholics. He is much respected in Ireland as well as in England, for the opinion formed of him from his civil and military knowledge and moral character. I have heard Lord Bishop Douglas, who is no mean estimator of mankind, often say, that he wished he could see Lord Moira one of the Secretaries of State.

'Were the Catholics satisfied, Ireland might bid defiance to the French, and, perhaps, some regular infantry might thence be sent to England, which, the Duke of Grafton said lately in the House of Lords, was much wanted here. But it is in vain to speak or write about Ireland.

'We govern there by a faction—the Beresfords, Fitzgibbons, and Fosters—whose emoluments, including their relations and dependents, fall not short of 100,000*l.* per annum; some think much more. Now the Polignacs under the old government had not more than 50,000*l.* per annum, including a bishopric. This the Duchess of Liancourt one day made out to me upon paper, yet she was willing enough to exaggerate the profits of that family; especially as the old duchess just before had been cast in a lawsuit with one of them.

'Your idea of applying to Bonaparte pleases me much. He would probably do more towards effecting a peace than a hundred Malmesburys and St. Helens. It will be curious to see what terms Pitt will propose. There seems to be no doubt but that the French will insist on having all the places taken from them; and probably a restitution of twelve or fourteen ships of the line, and perhaps a sum of money by way of *indemnification,* for this word was always in the mouth of our Premier. After this, an ample recompense to the Dutch and Spaniards, whose interests the French will consider as their own. A fine peace indeed, after so many absurd and haughty declarations of our ministry! A peace there must be or an insurrection, if considerable taxes be proposed to continue the war. Not that these would be of any avail; for were the French merely to line their coasts from Ostend to Calais with troops, and do nothing else, their point would be carried. At the very time that a separate peace was made by the Emperor with the French, Mr. Pitt, in the House of Commons, called him "our great and good ally." It was but two days after that the news came of his defection, which every thinking man naturally expected.

'Mr. P. seems determined to do dirty jobs to the last; whilst our enemies are almost at our gates, the subscribers to the loyalty loan must forsooth be rewarded because many of them are his Parliamentary friends. Should you hear your knight open himself on this subject, remind him that a million or a million and a half are wanted to pay the arrears of the Civil List; that professors, whose stipends are fixed by Acts of Parliament, are in danger of losing the profits of a couple of years from an abominable clause in Burke's Bill. Remind him of a remarkable circumstance in Sully's memoirs. When Henry IV. was in great distress for money it was proposed to him to decline paying any stipends to the professors in the University of Paris. "No," said he, with an honest indignation, "I will never consent to that; retrench the expense of my table instead of touching their emoluments." Such an answer, and such conduct in conformity to it, reflected peculiar honour on a prince who had never been trained up in the study of polite letters.

'Carnot[1] cannot be too much commended for ordering your agricultural works to be translated and published. It was giving his countrymen a mass of knowledge, founded on experiment not to be procured in their own writers. He showed very good sense in sacrificing party prejudices. Would Pitt have acted thus in his situation?

'I have not read Wilberforce's "Practical View of Christianity," nor am I indeed much solicitous about it, for my faith is not built upon establishments but on the New Testament, which I have considered with as much attention as most of our divines. W. is a strict Calvinist, and is therefore orthodox, for he is supported by our Articles of Religion. I who think that the Articles on this head are not founded on Scripture, am a heretic, as I take you to be also. It is very observable that the young theologians of Geneva are at this day instructed much more in Ostervald's[2] Catechism than in Calvin's books. The death of that worthy man and excellent master of Italian, Isola, is an exceedingly great loss to me, for he has managed all my little concerns at Cambridge for twenty years. He can have left nothing for his family but his good example. So respected was he by every one, that when a long illness and his wife's death prevented him from making his usual earnings, and he was unavoidably loaded with heavy debts, they not only raised for him 180*l.* by private

[1] Carnot, the 'organiser of victory,' grandfather of the late lamented President of the French Republic. Almost alone of the Senate, Carnot refused to sanction the *coup d'état* of Napoleon, 1799.

[2] J. F. Ostervald, Swiss Protestant divine, born 1683, died 1747. All his works have been translated into English.

subscriptions in the Colleges, but in the following year the University gave him 100*l*. out of the public chest. I shall be very careful in recommending his successor, for Isola always told me that most of the Italians in England were rascals, and he therefore had no communication with them when they came to Cambridge. I allowed him twenty guineas a year, as few learn Italian. The profits from teaching it are hardly sufficient to maintain one who has a family; for parents in general are so foolish as not to require of their sons the learning of that language, though their intention is to send them into Italy.

'Adieu! You will repent provoking me to write.

'J. SYMONDS.'

From Jeremy Bentham, Esq., on the poor, &c.

'Queen Square, Westminster: Sept. 8, 1797.

'Dear Sir,—It was but the other day that I became master of a complete series of your "Annals of Agriculture;" accept my confession and record my penitence. Having on my return from my long peregrination on the Continent lent to a friend—who had lent to another friend, whom we neither of us could recollect—the twenty-five or thirty numbers which I had taken in before that period, I postponed from time to time the completion of the series in hopes of recovering the commencement of it. When at last shame and necessity got the better of procrastination, what a treasure of information burst upon me. No—so long as power without —— and without —— shall have left an annual guinea in my pocket (blanks are better here than words) not a number of the "Annals" shall ever be wanting to my shelves. Hold —don't take me for a Jacobin now, nor even for a croaker. What I allude to is not any *common* burden, such as you land-owners and land-holders grunt under, but my own ten thousand pound tax—my privilegium —a thing as new to English language as it is to English practice—sole and peculiar fruit of the very particular notice with which I have been honoured by ——.

'This waits upon you with a proof of a blank pauper population table, framed for the purpose of collecting an account of them in as many parishes as I can. Knowing so well your zeal for all zeal-worthy objects, and mindful of your often experienced kindness, I cannot on this occasion harbour a doubt of your assistance. Is it worth while to give the table the indiscriminate circulation of your "Annals"? At any rate your editorial Majesty will, I hope, be pleased graciously to grant unto me your royal letters, *patent* or *close*, or both, addressed to *all*, and if need be, *singular*, your loving subjects my fellow correspondents; charging and exhorting them, each in his parish—and as many other parishes as may be—to fill my tables and send in their contributions.

'Along with the table you will find a MS. paper, exhibiting the importance of the information I am thus labouring to collect; you will print it or suppress it as you think best. I also send in MS. a table of cases calling for relief; a general map of *pauper land* with all the *roads* to it. Few, if any, of the projects I have seen but what have appeared (the arch-project not excepted) to bear an exclusive—at least a predilective—reference to some of these cases, overlooking or slighting the rest. I send it in the state in which I propose printing it for my own book; but, in the meantime, if it be worthy the honour of a place in the " Annals," it is altogether at your service. This preparatory insertion will turn to the advantage of the work itself, if any of your correspondents (not forgetting their editor) would have the goodness to contribute their remarks to the emendation of it. You will not easily conceive—few heads, at least, but yours are qualified to conceive—the labour it has cost me to bring the two tables to this state. As to the work at large, it will occupy two independent, though connected volumes. Pauper systems compared; pauper management improved—the last the romance, the Utopia, to which I had once occasion to allude. Romance? How could it be anything *less*? I mean to an author's partial eye. In proportion as a thing is excellent, when established, is it anything but *romance*, and theory, and speculation, till the touch of the *seal* or the *sceptre* has converted it into practice. Distress, at least, distress, the very life and soul of romance, cannot be denied to mine; for in this short and close-packed specimen already you behold it in all its shapes. Magnanimous president! accomplished secretary! ye, too, have your romance. Heaven send you a happy catastrophe and a *fettered land* "a happy deliverance." Patience! patience! ye too, before you are comforted, must bear to be tormented.

'Apropos of presidents. The high priest of Ceres, having divined or not divined my recent occupations, has been pleased to send me a mandate in form, summoning me to devote myself to this branch of his goddess's service, that the fruit of my labours may be consecrated in her temple at Whitehall; so that whatever other requisites may fail me, I shall be in no want of auspices.

'I fear you will say to yourself that the Observations [1] I have sent you are a sad farrago, but your miscellany, how superior soever to others in subject-matter and contents, has this in common with them, that half-formed ideas, so they have but matter in them, are not prohibited from presenting themselves. It is part of the character of your correspondents to have more of *substance* about them than of *form*; and of the many recommendations which join in drawing so much good company to your *conversazione*, one, nor that the least, is the convenience of being admitted to it in boots. Mine (you will say) have hobnails in them; for, somehow or other, the very idea of the person to whom I am addressing myself has insensibly betrayed me into that sort of playful confidence—that *épanchement*, as I think the French call it—which I have always felt in his company.

'Believe me, with the most serious respect,
'Ever yours,
'JEREMY BENTHAM.'

---

[1] These 'Observations,' above referred to, are inserted in vol. xxix *Annals of Agriculture*.

CHAPTER XIII

DIARY AND CORRESPONDENCE, 1798, 1799, 1800

Assessed taxes—Society—Mr. Pitt and the Board of Agriculture—A foolish joke—Dinners to poor children—Interview with the King—Royal farming—Correspondence—Bradfield—Incidents of home travel—Portrait of a great lady—Correspondence.

January 9, 1798.—At Petworth. This is the way in which I keep a journal; had I the abilities of Johnson it might be an excuse, but I am as idle as he without the talents that enabled him to think to good purpose.

London has passed away till the vacation without much to note, yet always something; for I met many at Mrs. M. Montagu's parties twice a week, whose conversation was interesting. Very few dinners, for the town was empty. Attended divine service at Mr. Cecil's chapel, and ought to have made memoranda.

The breakfast at Wilberforce's with Mr. Serjeant, Hawkins, Brown, Thornton, &c., all members in committee on the assessed taxes.[1] Miss Griffiths, the friend and mother of my ever dear Bobbin at school, coming to

---

[1] Assessed taxes. On December 4, 1797, Mr. Pitt introduced a Bill for trebling the amount of assessed taxes. This was again debated in the House of Commons in January 1798, and finally passed. See Hansard's *Parliamentary History*.

board with Mrs. Y.; these and many more articles all passed over, and, above all, the reflections which thronged in my mind on the conclusion of that year which deprived me of my child and turned my heart so imperfectly to God Almighty. Without that event how should I have been able to bear the stroke of the taxes, my share of which will I fear be 100*l.*

Had I been out of debt it would have been comparatively light, but I am seized about some bills which yet remain, and which, if I pay,[1] I shall not be able to pay those taxes. I have advertised my cottage and eighty acres of land to let, but no chance of getting such a rent as I know I ought to have to make letting answer.

I have been here with Lord Egremont above a fortnight. A good deal of rabble, but some better. Lord Spencer, Lord Althorp, Lord Dungarvan, Lord Milton, Lord Stair, Sir John Shelley, Mr. James Feiryman, &c. I shall stay the whole vacation.

February 14.—Another great gap, in which time I was four days with the Duke of Bedford at Woburn, with a strange party, for all in all I think the most strange I have been in for many years. Trevis, the pseudo-Venetian Jew, who came long ago to England, has run through a great fortune, reduced from 200,000*l.* to 1,200*l.* a year, having shined with most satanic light in the annals of gallantry; Lady Stanhope, Lady Cadogan, and a hundred more. Strong

---

[1] In a memorandum-book of the preceding year occur the following entries: 'Receipts, 901*l.*; debts, Dec. 31, 986*l.*' Debts seem to have been a burden throughout A. Y.'s long life.

parts, wits, originality (name evidently omitted here) and at seventy-one sings wonderfully; Lord Lauderdale, who is a very pleasant, easy, cheerful companion with knowledge, and so more capable of doing mischief; Lord Maynard, Johns the parson, Bob Lee, Bligh, &c. The duke has much good sense and clearness of head.

On my return to town, Lord Carrington applied to me to get a drainer for Mr. Pitt at Holwood. I told him none to be had but from a distance, and at a considerable expense; that perhaps it was an easy job, and if so his own people could do it if the drains were marked out for them, and I would go and look when nobody there. Next day he came again from Pitt with thanks, and desiring me to go when he was there.

I went, and examined the land. A hill wet from springs, the cure obvious. So I am to do it for him. He and Lord Auckland and Lord Carrington walked round the place with me, and then returned to a cold dinner, where we debated the Board of Agriculture, and Pitt seemed pleased with my idea of Government hiring the Bishop of Llandaff's house for the Board, and so getting rid of the difficulty of not being able to quit Sir J. Sinclair's without sixteen members agreeing in the affirmative, a stupid statute they made.

By the first reports of the Board, and a multitude of other expenses equally useless, Sir John ran the Board so much in debt that it became a question of great difficulty how they should be enabled to carry on any business at all. Through a spirit of liberality in many individuals, a subscription was set on foot, and ten guineas apiece by members and honorary members, which kept them for some time on their legs. The revenue of the Board went entirely to printers, above eighty reports in quarto, with broad margins, having been given away to any who would accept them; and they were in general so miserably executed, that they brought the institution into contempt.

While Sir John Sinclair was engaged in this pursuit he thought of nothing but the establishment of his own character, and imagined that his indefatigable exertions, misplaced as they were, gave him a claim to the attention of Government, and, it is said, induced him to ask a peerage. But Mr. Pitt not acceding to the proposition, he next desired to be a Privy Councillor. When this second gentle request failed, he set hard to work to form a party of his own in the House of Commons in opposition to Government, which by degrees completely estranged Mr. Pitt from him; and he was, by the votes of the official members, turned out of the chair. Lord Carrington taking me to Holwood, we walked about the place for some time before Mr. Pitt came down. When he arrived, ordering a luncheon, he said he had desired Lord C. to bring me, that he might understand what members of the Board of Agriculture were proper to fill the chair.

I named Lord Egremont. 'He has been applied to,' rejoined Mr. Pitt, 'and declined it.' I then mentioned Lord Winchilsea; the same answer was eturned. I named one or two more, but the minister seemed not to relish their appointment. I next said Lord Somerville, who was famous for the attention he had paid to some branches of husbandry. Mr. Pitt's reply was, 'He is not quite the thing, but I doubt we must have him,' and the conversation concluded with an apparent determination that Lord S. should be the man. He was accordingly elected; and I, the same day, received the orders of the Board instantly to look out for a house (because Sir John S. being turned out would no longer volunteer his), which I accordingly did, and fixed upon one in Sackville Street, into which the Board immediately moved their property, and appointed the secretary to reside in the house, with an allowance of one hundred guineas a year for paying the porter, keeping a maid in the house in summer, and finding coals and candles.

April 8.—A long gap, in which much has happened. The election, and Sir J. Sinclair deposed. The world gives its all to politics, but it was not caused solely by that motive; his management of the 3,000*l.* a year was next to throwing it away, and gradually created much disgust; had his industry been under the direction of a better judgment he would have been an admirable president. I have hired a house for him and myself in Sackville Street. Crag, the clerk, wants an apartment, and I have befriended him with Lord Somerville, the new president, much against my own convenience, for the house is not large enough; but, do as we would be done by, must be a rule far more obeyed by me in future than formerly, and it is more a convenience to him than an evil to me. It would be easy for me to prevent it, and time has been that I should have taken that part; but God send me the power to follow better dictates. I have been twice more at Holwood. I have written a new pamphlet, a 'Letter to Wilberforce.' I have worked hard at my Lincoln report, and the election, with the business public and private concerning it, has been on the whole such a worry, that I long for a week or two of privacy and quiet, to render my mind more tranquil; it seems as if my whole life is to be lost in a bustle. I am now going to Petworth, and within the week to Bradfield; there I hope to make a momentary retreat, and have time for recollection. I do not suffer anything to distract me on a Sunday, or I should be lost in this hurry, and everything serious driven from my mind. I have anxiety also about my new habitation on another account, which is the doubt whether they will furnish it for me; if they should not, it will be a most heavy burthen of at least 200*l.*, and an unjust one, elected as I am annually.

Last Sunday se'nnight a new scene of sorrow and vexation. Arthur sent me a foolish letter of his written to Lloyd from Dover, by way of a stupid joke, describing an ideal conversation with some of O'Connor's jurymen,[1] to frighten Lloyd, who sent it to Lofft, and he to Walker, to Erskine, &c. It was read in court at Maidstone, and Lord Egremont told me it had an immense effect, exciting universal indignation.

The Attorney-General pledged himself to punish it. The Jacobin papers kindly assigned it to *Arthur Young*, so all believed it to be me. I had a letter contradicting sent to four papers, and have been in

---

[1] A. O'Connor, concerned with others in an address to the Directory France; tried for treason at Maidstone, 1798; found not guilty. See *Annual Register*, 1798.

incessant worry ever since, writing for explanation, employing Gotobed and Garrow, and seeing Lord Egremont often on it. I sent an express to the Attorney-General, with a letter to him, and another to O'Connor's counsel. All agree Lofft to be a base villain, pretending so much friendship for all the family, and keeping the letter ten days in spite of Lloyd demanding it, and never asking any explanation or naming it to Mrs. Y., Mary, or A. I have fretted about this affair and worried myself terribly, and with reasons, for it will be the utter ruin of my son. Possibly a fine of 500*l.* and two years' imprisonment if he is not able to prove it to be a jest. To avoid being punished as a rascal, he must prove himself the greatest fool in Christendom, which he certainly is, for the letter was unquestionably a humbug.

June 23rd.—I have had a roasting three weeks languishing for the country; but, however, not discontented, and bringing my mind with some success to submit cheerfully to everything I meet with. Arthur has been in Kent and procured nine or ten affidavits of the jurymen; those who refuse he never set eyes on till he made the application, so he has cleared himself to me, but whether it will do for the Attorney-General is another question. It is a sad business, and will be very expensive, when I can ill afford it.

I have been four days at Woburn with Lord Somerville—a very great meeting. The duke desired me to preside at the lower end of the table; he told me to keep Stone from it.

I have been thrice at Holwood and conversed with

Mr. Pitt every time, but it is only on farming. No wonder. Reading Baxter's 'Serious Call to a Holy Life,' which I have done with great pleasure, and have begun it a second time. I think it an admirable performance. Charity and a universal intention to please God in everything are recommended with great ability.

I have forgotten to add a word about my new habitation. It is an admirable house, and Mrs. Young's only apprehension was the plan of Cragg, the first clerk, having apartments in it; but when it came to be debated, Lord Carrington procured it entirely to me, with an allowance of 90*l.* a year for a porter, maid, coals, &c. Upon the whole it is an arrangement which is equal in all to 100*l.* a year to me, and in comfort, saving me the trouble of thrice a year seeking lodgings, as good as a hundred more.

I am thankful to God for it, and may He give me His grace not to apply to ill uses the favour of His providence.

July 14*th!!!*—This day twelvemonth it pleased God to take to Himself my ever dear and beloved child. In the evening at the Hall, my wife and self, children, and Miss Griffith joined in prayer.

[The remainder of the diary, chiefly detailing morbid religious introspection, is not of sufficient interest to include.]

Notes from Memorandum-book

March.—A dinner for fifteen poor children, 11*s.* 10*d.*[1]
Another dinner for thirty-seven children, 16*s.* 6*d.*

[1] These dinners to poor children were given in memory of Bobbin.

Another dinner for forty-seven children, 1*l*. 6*s*. 6*d*.

April.—This month seven dinners to about forty-eight children each time.

May.—Four dinners to about forty-eight children each time.

This year I sold the copyright of my 'Travels' for 250 guineas.

April 1799.—In London. I am alone, therefore at peace. I rise at four or five o'clock and go to bed at nine to ten P.M.

I have no pleasures, and wish for none, saving that comfort which religion gives me; and the sooner I make it my only pleasure the wiser I shall be. I go to no amusements, and read some Scripture every day; never lay aside my good books but for business. I have dined out but little, and wish for no more than I have. I get into habits of reading and writing, and don't like to quit them; privacy, and silence, and retirement suit me, and I am content. New servants, all; and the cook, a two-handed Yahoo, and cannot boil a potato. No matter, I am passed being troubled at such things, but I like old servants, and can't bear this change.

May 4 of 'this year I went to the opera with Mrs. Oakes;[1] and that amusement which had for so many years been my delight, I met so coldly as to be almost asleep through much of the performance. What a change had taken place in my mind! This was the last public diversion at which I have been present.

I thank the Father of mercies that I have yet

[1] *Née* Betsy Plampin.

retained my attention to religion, that I have read few books but those of devotion, that I live very retired without any regret, that I rise at four or five o'clock, and never omit my private devotions, morn and eve, and but rarely family prayer. Thank the Almighty goodness I have almost weaned myself from the world.

June 4.—The King's birthday. I have been in Kensington Gardens to see the King review 8,000 volunteers of London and Westminster. These corps owe their origin I may, without presumption, say to me, and I should in a former part of my life have been full of mortification and envy at the gay and brilliant situation of others, whilst I was a humble spectator lost in the crowd, 'the mob' as I should once have called them; but, thank God, I had no such ideas, and am more free from sin of such thoughts than I am from that of entering this note of it. My mind was much occupied in thinking of such multitudes of people of all ranks, all ages, from infancy to decrepitude, gay, lively, and running at the tilt of pleasure, followed by more splendid scenes of courts, balls, dinners and all, all to be in a few years in their graves, their souls in their eternal doom, thoughtless as they may now be.

I work myself as often as I can, and as much as I can, into meditations on the utter vanity of all such scenes and thence to the inanity.

July 1.—Wrote Mrs. Oakes an account of my visits to the King's farm. I got Sir J. Banks to ask his leave to see his farm. He gave it readily, and said he would order Frost, his bailiff, to show me everything completely. I wrote, but my letter came, by mistake of the post, after I was there myself; and as Frost knew the King would like to see me, he went when likely to meet him on his return from a review. The Queen, Prince of Wales, the Princesses, &c., were in two sociables, and the King on horseback, with his train of lords, aides-de-camp, &c. He inquired who I was, and called me to him; rode up to the Queen, &c., and introduced me. The Queen said it was long since I was at Windsor, &c., not recollecting me at first; they passed on, and then the King rode with me over his farm for two and a half hours, talking farming, asking questions without number, and waiting for answers, and reasoning upon points he differed in. Explained his system of crops, his reasons, with many observations; enquired about the Board, the publications of it, the 'Annals,' and asked if I continued to work on my 'Elements,' which I have been many years about; recommended me to compress the sense of quotations in short paragraphs, '*as there are many, Mr. Young, who catch the sense of a short paragraph, that lose the meaning of a long one*;' said the work would be highly useful. Those who read the two letters of R. R. in the last ' Annals,' written by his Majesty, will see how clearly he expresses himself. He enquired about my farm, grasses, sheep, &c.; he has himself only 160 lambs from 800 ewes. His strong land farm is in admirable order, and the crops all clean and fine. He was very desirous that I should see all, and ordered Frost to carry me to two or three other things next morning. I found fault with his hogs. He said I must not find fault with a present to him; the Queen was so kind as to give them from Germany, and while the intention was pleasing, we must not examine the object too critically. '*The value of the intention,* Mr. Young, is greater than a better breed.' He told me he learned the principles of his farming from my books, and found them very just. Quoted particularly the 'Rural Economy:' Cattle give manure, and manure corn. '*Well understood now, sir, but not so well before you wrote.*' When I said anything that struck him he turned about to tell it to the nobles that followed. He is the politest of men, keeps his hat off till every one is covered. An officer with a lady in a whisky drew in his horse as he saw the King crossing the road, taking his hat off. The King rode up to him, uncovered, and conversed a little, and afterwards said, 'I think it is Captain Thorp, of such a regiment.' What a memory!

Enquired much about the Duke of Bedford's party at Woburn, &c. &c. I forgot three-fourths. He was in high spirits, and looks remarkably well.

My son this year married Miss Jane Berry, daughter of Edward Berry, Esq. The connection arose from her being at school with my dear Bobbin at Campden House, and afterwards visiting us at Bradfield.

Selected letters from those received this year:—

From Count Rumford on lime-kilns and cement for fire-places, &c.

'Brompton Row: Jan. 8, 1799.

'Dear Sir,—On my return to town last evening from Broadlands I found your letter. I beg you will present my best compliments to Lord Egremont and assure his lordship that it would give me very great pleasure to visit Petworth and see the various improvements he has, and is, introducing into the neighbourhood; but my stay in England will be but short, and, as I have more to do in the meantime than it will be possible for me to execute without being very industrious, I must devote all my time to those occupations in which I am engaged.

'I wish it were in my power to give you any satisfactory information respecting lime-kilns, but I have not yet had leisure to complete the experiments I had projected, and which are necessary in order to enable me to form decided opinions on that subject. The kiln I had constructed at Munich not being well built, and being forced with too intense a fire before the masonry was properly dried, cracked, and burst open from top to bottom, so that no just conclusions can be drawn from the imperfect experiments that were made with it.

'With regard to the best materials for withstanding the action of intense fire, I believe common fire-bricks, as they are called, to be one of the best. I am just now employing them in the construction of open chimney fire-places, and they seem to answer perfectly well. In laying them I have a cement of clay and brick dust instead of common mortar.

'One of the best kinds of cement for resisting the action of fire I ever met with was composed of equal parts of brick dust, quick lime, and iron filings, mixed up with blood. It unites itself firmly to metals as to bricks and stones of all kinds, and even the most intense fire seems to have very little effect on it. It may even be made to join metals to stones, or even wood to metals. Our soap boilers in Bavaria use it to join the wooden tops of their boilers to their copper bottoms, which it does in so effectual a manner that they are very seldom found to leak. It was from them I learnt the secret of the composition of this most useful cement. I have no doubt but it would be found to answer very well for plastering the backs and covings of open chimney fire-places. I wish you would make a trial. If it should be found to answer it would be a most important discovery, for in that case bricks would certainly be as good, or even better, than fire-stones for constructing fire-places.

'I am, dear Sir, with unfeigned regard and esteem,
  'Yours most faithfully,
    'RUMFORD.'

From the Duke of Grafton

'Piccadilly: 1799.

'Dear Sir,—I had but just time to cast an eye on Mr. Wilberforce's letter last night, and seeing that the references are so many to texts of Scripture, I must desire you to leave it with me till I can have a good hour's leisure to give it that consideration which everything from him must deserve.

'I wish Mr. Wilberforce[1] and myself were agreed upon all points as we are on the (I fear) hopeless

[1] Referring to a long letter from the great Wilberforce on 'Original Sin.'

attempts to abolish totally the slave trade. Depend upon it that no one who knows that gentleman so little honours him more than myself; nor do I impute any opinions or dogmas to him which I have not learnt from his writings. I believe him to be an upright, sincerely pious and beneficent character, treading a road that leads to future happiness, even should he be under great but involuntary errors. Will he say the same of any one of those whom he improperly calls Socinians? For, though they honour the memory of Socinus, they do not follow his faith; far from it, for they acknowledge no masters on matters of religion but Christ and His Apostles.

'Yours very faithfully,
'GRAFTON.'

From Dr. Burney [1]

'Dover: Sept. 11, 1799.

'My dear Sir,—Your letter [arrived] at Quarley after I had left my friend Mr. Cox, and was returned to Chelsea preparing for a journey into Kent. I have been here and hereabouts near three weeks in the thick of all the military bustle of this county. My headquarters are at my friend Mr. Crewe's house in this town, the best it affords, and is taken for three months. Mr. Crewe, being colonel of the Second Royal Cheshire Militia, is quartered at Hythe, but comes over frequently, Mrs. and Miss Crewe being stationed here. The Duke of Portland and Lady Mary

[1] The *Letters of Maria Josepha Holroyd* give an amusing account of the events here described.

Bentinck came hither on a visit last Thursday, and remained inmates with us till yesterday morning. Being within eight or nine miles of the camp on Barham Downs and seven of Walmer Castle, we have been there several times, have dined twice at Sir Charles Grey's, the commander-in-chief at the camp, and twice at Walmer Castle with Mr. Pitt, Mr. Dundas, and Lady Jane Dundas, who does the honours, and is a most amiable, sweet, and charming woman. Mr. Ryder and Lady Susan have a small house just by the castle, and Mr. Canning is lodged within its walls. The Duke of York was there for several days before he embarked for Holland. WE, that is Mrs. and Miss Crewe, with Lady Mary Bentinck, went in one coach, and the Duke of Portland, with your humble servant, in another, at five o'clock on Sunday morning to see the third embarkation launched. The wind was furiously adverse, but it was done with wonderful dexterity, quickness, and cheerfulness, without accident. The Duke of York and Mr. Dundas were on the beach, the ladies were all in tears; the soldiers in high *spirits*, and all fun and jollity. We afterwards went to Walmer Castle to breakfast, and as the Duke of York was not to embark till the evening, Mr. Pitt invited Mrs. Crewe and her party to stay and take an early scrambling dinner. This was accepted, and we remained in the castle while the cannon on its ramparts were fired on his Royal Highness entering the launch in sight of a fleet of at least two hundred sail of ships, by which he was saluted; and we saw the flash of every gun, and heard the report which was brought to us by the raging east wind, *forte, fortissimo*. It was a glorious sight! God prosper the expedition, and grant that those brave men who are gone so cheerfully to fight our battles and those of all Europe, may come home with honour and whole bones. The Duke of Portland's youngest son, Lord Charles Bentinck, sailed with the Duke of York, and young Crewe sails to-day with the last embarkation, being lieut.-colonel commandant of the Ninth Regiment of Infantry. The hymn to the Emperor and Souvarow's [1] march have been sung and played to all these great folks with good effect and applause. Lady Susan Ryder and Miss Crewe sing it admirably, and I join in the chorus. I have obliged all the ladies mentioned above, including Lady Grey, with copies of these compositions; they are all musicians, and are the personages in the world most deserving of such a favour, and where the granting of it will be of most use.

'I congratulate you on the great events of this wonderful campaign, not forgetting the acquisition of the Dutch fleet, which, I am glad to find, is ordered to England. The Duke of Portland received a letter yesterday before he left Dover from his son, who is with Marshal Souvarow (pronounced Souvaroff), of the battle of Novi, confirming all that the French have told us of the death of their General Joubert, of Moreau's being unhorsed, and all his staff killed, wounded, or prisoners. It has cost the Allies 5,000 men. However,

---

[1] On November 4, 1794, Souvarow took Warsaw, when 8,000 soldiers and 12,000 men, women, and children were massacred in cold blood. See *L'histoire générale de Lavisse et Rambaud*, vol. viii. p. 358. It is to be hoped that Dr. Burney was in ignorance of this.

it seems to put an end to all other fighting and resistance by Jacobin armies of Italy.

'I intend returning in about ten days, but have a visit of a few days to make on the road to Sir William and Lady Fawcett, at Eltham.

'God bless you.

'My dear Sir,

'CHARLES BURNEY.'

1800. *Bradfield.*—I never come to this place without reaping all the pleasure which any place can give me now. It is beautiful and healthy, and is endeared to me by so many recollections, melancholy ones now, alas! that I feel more here than anywhere else. Here have I lived from my infancy, here my dear mother breathed her last, here was all I knew of a sister, and the church contains the remains of my father, mother, and ever beloved child! Here, under my window, her little garden—the shrubs and flowers she planted—the willow on the island, her room, her books, her papers. There have I prayed to the Almighty that I might join her in the next world. All that locality can give an interest to in this world is here—sweet Bradfield, to use an epithet of my dear mother fifty years ago at Bath!—the scene also of many and great sins; and of none perhaps greater than the black ingratitude of never thanking God with fervency for the blessing of such a spot till misery turned my heart to Him, and oh! how cold my thanksgivings compared with what I ought to feel!

To me it has, however, often been a source of foolish

uneasiness. I have reflected on the increasing taxes and burthens on land and houses in this kingdom as the inevitable cause of ruin to all little estates; they are gone or fast going in this country, and what hope can I have that this should remain in the posterity of so poor a person as I am?

I have preserved it by a life of industry and singular success, or it had gone long ago. But such thoughts are wicked. All is in the hands of the great Preserver and Disposer of all earthly as well as all other existence.

How few years are passed since I should have pushed on eagerly to Woburn! This time twelvemonth I dined with the duke on the Sunday. The party not very numerous, but chiefly of rank; the entertainment more splendid than usual there. He expects me to-day, but I have more pleasure in resting, going twice to church and eating a morsel of cold lamb at a very humble inn, than partaking of gaiety and dissipation at a great table which might as well be spread for a company of heathens as English lords and men of fashion.

In my way from Royston to Baldock, passing a village I saw a couple of cottages which seemed very miserable. Alighted therefore and entered one. The woman said she was very unhappy. I enquired why? Her daughter was now dead in the house. How old? Thirty-eight. Married to a glazier in London. She had been down with her mother some time for health in a decline, and died two days ago. 'I hope she died a good Christian.' 'I hope so,' replied the woman, who seemed to feel very little. And it is the blessing of God that they do not—they cannot afford to grieve like their betters. It was odd that I should happen to stop and enter a cottage with a corpse in it, but nothing interesting followed. God forbid it should be for want of my sifting and enquiring more—but nothing led to it. The husband was expected soon, and the woman has a son, a miller, who keeps her, a cow, and she had a good pig feeding at the door. She was, however, thankful for the trifle I gave her.

My adventures increase and have a strange similitude. Passing through Millbrook, near Lord Ossory's, some cottages, with corn in their gardens, on the slopes of a narrow sandy vale, caught my eye, but speedily passing it was a second thought to stop the horse and walk down to them. There are thirteen of them, and all inhabited by owners. A hemp weaver, who lives in the first I entered, gave me an account of them all, and amongst the rest he named Underwood's, who had a large family, and was sadly poor. I went to it. Poor indeed! the cottage almost tumbling down, the wind blowing through it on every side. On a bed, which was hardly good enough for a hog, was the woman very ill and moaning; she had been lately brought to bed, and her infant was dead in a cradle by the bedside. What a spectacle! She had four children living; one, a little girl, was at home, and putting together a few embers on the hearth. My heart sank within me at the sight of so much misery, and so dark, cold, tattered and wretched a room. Merciful God, to take the little child to Himself, rather than leave it existing in such a place. What a sight! I entered another cottage, which was lately built, neat and cheerful, the Widow Scarboro's; she earns something by washing, but her smoky chimney most uncomfortable. No wonder, with the old broad high fire-place. In the depth of winter the door must be open. I told her how to cure it, but I wished to give her a Rumford grate and see it fixed. Impossible! and her evils are nothing to poor Underwood's.

But how strange yesterday to find a dead woman in a house, and to-day a dead child, and in such an accidental manner, as it seems, to enter just these houses. No chance; the more I see, the more I reflect, the more I am convinced that the providence of the Almighty directs everything, but in a manner utterly incomprehensible to us; and it is the more incomprehensible from our paying so very little attention to it. If every one was to be careful to observe all such apparently accidental events, they would have reason to acknowledge the hand of Omnipotence. In three days how has what the world calls chance conducted my steps!

These poor people know not by what tenure they hold their land; they say they once belonged to the duke, but that the duke has swopped them away to my lord (Lord Ossory). How little do the great know what they swop and what they receive! What would be a blessing poured into their hands if they knew how to use it. What a field is here! How very trifling the repairs to render these poor families warm and comfortable! Above their gardens on one side there is a waste fern tract now enclosed, from which small additions might be given them, yet would enable them to live from their ground at least much better than at present. What have not great and rich people to answer, for not examining into the situation of their poor neighbours?

To Woburn Abbey. Here is wealth and grandeur and worldly greatness; but I am sick of it as soon as I enter these splendid walls. I had rather be amongst the cottagers at Millbrook had I but the means of aiding them. I will see Lord Ossory, and try to do something for them.

In these farming tours [1] of mine, vain ideas will too often rise in my mind on the importance of my labour to the public good; and were the improvement of agriculture alone to be considered, I believe little doubt could be entertained. But what is the tendency of all these improvements except to add to the wealth and prosperity of a country that is already under a most heavy responsibility to the Almighty for innumerable temporal blessings; repaid with the black ingratitude of irreligion, and a general contempt of everything serious or sacred. Carriers' waggons and stage coaches are passing here every hour in open defiance of the laws

---

[1] Note by A. Y. at close of year's diary: 'In the summer, in consequence of much conversation with Lord Carrington on the importance of enclosures, I proposed to him that I should take a tour expressly for the purpose of ascertaining what the effect had really been in practice. He approved of the idea, and desired me to execute it; and, in regard to the expense, I told him that if he would allow 100*l.*, I would expend it in travelling, and report to him the country travelled and the enclosures examined, and then he might extend or not the undertaking at his pleasure. He approved the plan, and I accordingly employed twenty weeks on the journey.'

of God and man; and the Sabbath is the sure day of labour for all travelling gentlemen. What horses are they that rest, that can by any means be made to work? Our fields are made to smile with cultivation for the profits of men thankless to Heaven. Can such a country continue to be thus blessed? I fear and dread some terrible reverse, and have the only hope that the prayers of religious men, Methodists as they are called, may be heard, and avert the misfortunes we deserve. It damps all vanity of public good attending such attempts as mine, to think of the use that is made of great wealth. Affliction and poverty may do something in bringing nations, like individuals, to their senses; but to increase the wealth that adds to our irreligion and ingratitude, is of a very poor importance indeed, and too questionable to permit one vain thought to be fairly founded.

July 7.—Breakfasting at Huntingdon from Kimbolton, after spending just a week with the duke and duchess. It has been so pleasant and agreeable that I am unhinged on quitting them. The duchess pleases me as much or more than any woman I have met these many years. Her character in every worldly respect is most amiable. There is a native ease, simplicity, and *naïveté* of character in her which delights me; and when I consider the life of the Duchess of Gordon, her mother, the great patroness of every dissipation, I am amazed at this secluded young duchess, who never goes to London, loves a retired life, and is quite contented on a fortune very moderate for the rank of her husband. She gave me her whole history, from going one summer for some weeks to drink goat's whey on the mountains many miles beyond Gordon Castle, and running up and down the hills bare-footed, driving down the goats and milking them ; and being delighted with the place and the life, though no human being within many miles except the family and an old woman of the solitary house. This was the case of all the girls ; she never went to school, and laid in a fine stock of health, and with it a sweetness of temper and simplicity of character which, joined with an excellent understanding, contributed so much to form her as she is at present, calculated to be a blessing to her husband. She loves him, and behaves with a most exemplary and unexampled patience and mildness under his connection with Mrs. ——. I like her greatly,[1] and wish I could add that she was religious. She goes to church often, she says, and brings her four lovely children up to attend it ; but I see she has no sense or feeling of real religion, which I spoke of repeatedly, and earnestly recommended. The next time they come to Culford they both promised to come and see me, and will do it I have no doubt. The spectacle in this age of seeing a very plain table, a plain unaffected way of living, and everything about them modest and moderate in scale, very little company, and never at London, yet all cheerfulness and content, even under the above circumstance, speaks a good heart and an amiable temper, as much

[1] In the *Annals of Agriculture*, vol. xxxv. p. 432, occurs the following: 'If a farming traveller comes to Kimbolton, and forgets its mistress, may his sheep rot and crops blight! A young duchess, ever in the country, loving it, and free from a wish for London—a character that, if I was to give my pen scope, it would run wild on such a subject.'

as such can be good with the Almighty coming in for so poor a share of its attentions. I do and will pray to God that He will give her His grace to change in this respect, and then she will be a pattern for her sex.

July 7.—To Huntingdon, St. Ives, and Holywell, at the Reverend Mr. Hutchinson's, who was long at Kimbolton, and had livings given to him by the late duke; [has] four stout, well-looking, unmarried daughters, that have been marriageable some years. A common spectacle, and everywhere from the same cause: the fornication of men with the abandoned of the sex robs thousands of such virtuous and good girls of husbands. The more I reflect, the more I see the reason of God's wrath and denunciations against this vice in Scripture, however natural it is, and however powerful the temptation. The more the temptation the more the wickedness to throw so many into it, by depriving those of husbands to whom God has given the right, but of which the vice of man deprives them. Every man would have his wife, and every woman her husband, were it not for whores and whoremongers. Christianity is in everything consistent with reason, morals, and the religion of nature.

At St. Ives [met] a drunken beast, a doctor of divinity, is intoxicated every day; drunk about the streets; introduced himself to me, and breathed like a puncheon of rum in my face.

Sunday, 20th : Downham.—I have had a busy week and gained a great variety of good intelligence; but what is it all but vanity and vexation of spirit if examined with view of a superior nature! However, it is my undoubted duty to do my best, and I must approve upon the whole of exerting as much industry for the Board as ever I did upon my own account. My employment is not only lawful, but useful; God grant me to render it as much so to the poor as circumstances will permit. In this week I have been at Wing's at Thorney Abbey. A party of ladies [here], Mrs. Ansel of Ormsby in Lincolnshire and two daughters. They attacked me, but with politeness, on my rabbit article in the Lincoln report. I found from their conversation on Wilberforce and H. More that they are good Christians, so they might say anything; but we parted very good friends. At March: Reverend Mr. Jobson and a vulgar steward, a prating but a useful fellow, Wandby, dined with me.

At Downham: Lemon, Dashwood, and a poor fen man Talbot. I have gone on well for the object of my journey; would that I went on as well in the great journey to the next world! At church twice; Mr. Dashwood in his sermon spoke very properly on a topic which I have often thought should be inveighed upon vigorously: the great indecency of people sitting when they should kneel, which is now everywhere so common; but in the afternoon a better congregation and no sermon! For a clergyman to have an audience collected ready to hear him and yet quit the church without preaching, how very lukewarm he must be in care of souls who can bring himself without violence to such a conduct! Is this the way with Methodists as they are called? God forbid! With a church thus filled as that of England is, who can wonder at Sectaries increasing? All is poor work when men are not in earnest—when they are not as animated and eager in their sacred calling as others are in their business and shops. A parson should always think: what would St. Paul do on this occasion?

Sunday, August 3.—Dined last Tuesday with the Grand Jury at Cambridge, and in the afternoon Lord Hardwicke took me with him to Wimpole. On the Thursday, a great public day, seventy-three at dinner, turtle, venison, and everything that could be. A Lord Lieutenant's gala which has not been these four years. Lady Cotton, Sir Wm. Rowley's sister, there all the week, and a Miss Coburn. Lady Margaret Fordyce has uncommon talents, and reading and languages, French, Italian and German, but I mistake if she is not a bit of a fury when she has a mind. I don't like her countenance. Lady H. pleases me better. Lord H. is very clever, has very good parts and a clear head, a man of business. I was pleased to find that he went twice to church, and read a long prayer at night to all the family, taken from the Liturgy. I shall be here a week, and have idled none of it away, but beat the country well for enclosures. I have not, however, broken my resolution of passing Sunday alone without being [misled], for even in such a family I had a farming expedition to the next parish, and conversation is never religious—I hope I shall do it no more.

Night.—Lord Hardwicke had all the family together, and read a long prayer taken from the Liturgy, from almost every part of it. I am glad to find a great Lord who is not ashamed of praying to God. May there be many such!

4th.—I left Wimpole, and the 9th came to Bradfield after a journey of eight weeks, thanks to the Almighty, in health and safety. There passed a week, staying two Sundays. Mrs. Y. in great health, and when that is the case in too much irritation—God forgive her—life is a scene of worrying, time trifled with, a book never looked in, quarrels and irritation never subsiding. My daughter and daughter-in-law reading cart loads of novels. While at Bradfield I received from Sir J. Banks, confidentially, many enquiries about the means of encouraging the culture of hemp; they are therefore apprehensive of a war with Russia. At the time of the Russian armament I was consulted on the same subject by Lord Liverpool, but they do nothing except on the spur of the moment, and then never effectually. Heaven avert more wars, those scourges of humanity! This first week of my second journey [1] I have laboured very hard in my enquiries, and travelled many miles on bad roads, not finishing the day till six in the evening, and then dining and having much writing. Such a life I should earnestly wish to avoid if I had a home tolerably comfortable, but mine is so far from that description in almost every respect that I submit the better to being ever in harness. It is the will of God, and my duty is to submit with cheerfulness.

October 6th : Hounslow.—Found near twenty letters at the post-office, and, among the rest, two from Parker of Ripon, attorney to Sir Cecil Wray, Kilvington, and

[1] Full accounts of these tours are given in the *Annals of Agriculture.*

Allanson, to inform he had orders to hold me to bail on my bond to them on buying Knaresboro' Forest, as Abbey of Northampton has not paid one shilling rent or interest. This is a fine affair; it is true there is land security for the 4,000*l*. of double the value, but who am I to get to bail me? I fear this is the hand of God working against me, and that He means me chastisement. The Lord's will be done! I shall pray earnestly to be spared, but if it is His will, be it done, and may He grant me resignation, patience, and submission to His correction. It comes heavy at the moment, for I was much injured at Enfield by coffee out of copper, as I suppose, with a violent purging colic and vomiting, and left by it in a state of great debility of body; this stroke of fresh anxiety cuts therefore. May God be appeased and spare me the affliction.

Last Sunday I read much in Hale's 'Contemplations: Moral and Divine,' in which the Providence of God is treated more to my mind than in any other book I have read. I have derived on various occasions, as well as the present, much consolation from that most excellent work, which I now earnestly recommend to my children, and hope if they should ever read these words, they will think of their father and follow his advice to make that great lawyer's book their constant companion.

On the close of this century it may not be improper to look back through the period of my own recollections in order to reflect on some eminent names that may be mentioned as forming the principal constellation of talents which have distinguished the period; and the more readily because I have had the honour of conversing with most of them, and being well known to several. In minuting such a list I may name the following, viz.: Burke, Pitt, Fox, Johnson, Reynolds, Barry, Burney, Miss Burney, H. More, Wilberforce, Soame.

The following are the selection of this year's letters :—

From Jeremy Bentham, Esq., queries sent from the Treasury to the Board of Agriculture

'Queen's Square Place, Westminster ; June 14, 1800.

'Dear Sir,—Underneath is a question, which I have just been calling in Sackville Street to beg the favour of your answer to, for my *own* information. It is in contemplation to make the purport of it the subject of a reference to the Board of Agriculture from the Treasury. The occasion seemed to be of a nature particularly favourable to the enabling the public to avail itself of the services of the Board, and may perhaps have the effect of placing the utility of that Institution in a new and additional point of view; while the dignity of its members, and the manner in which it is composed, will give such a title to public confidence, in respect of the grand point of superiority to all personal considerations, as would in vain be looked for in any other quarter capable of being applied to for such a purpose. In this light I have just been mentioning the matter to Mr. Nepean, who entered so thoroughly into it as to say he would himself propose it to the Treasury to make such reference.

'On enquiring I had the mortification of learning that the Board had adjourned to some day in November: but would there be no such thing as the calling an extra meeting, if not to the Board at large, of a Committee for the purpose of receiving a reference from such a quarter, and making a Report? If not, possibly the opinion of the Secretary might be accepted of as the only obtainable succedaneum to the opinion of the Board; for where else could any other equally competent opinion be obtained? But howsoever the matter may stand with regard to the Board and Mr. Secretary, I hope Mr. Young will not refuse an old correspondent the favour of an answer for his own guidance, and that as speedy as possible; for it is for this answer that I wait to enable me to fill up a blank with figures, the propriety of which is what is proposed as above to be made the subject of reference to the Board. If you are unable to guess my reason for interfering in the business, so much the better, but if you *have* your conjectures, all I can do is to beg (which I do with the utmost sincerity) that you would forbear letting them find their way, directly or indirectly, to any person to whose lot it may fall to concur in making the Report. It was at Mr. Nepean's express recommendation that I called in Sackville Street for the purpose of conversing with you in person: but, if your absence be not fatal to the business, I shall be much better pleased with the opportunity of transacting it in this manner without any other communication than what will show itself in black and white. I am not *sure* but the Report from the Board might be waited for without much inconvenience till their regular time of reassembling: but till Mr. Young's answer is obtained, or is known to be unobtainable, everything is at a stand. And a business in which the public has an interest of no inconsiderable magnitude, and for the conclusion of which all parties are impatient, sleeps, and, in short, if it does not come at farthest before this week is at an end, the hopes entertained of an answer from a quarter thus respectable must be deserted. But these matters are so perfectly A.B.C. to Mr. Young that I am sanguine enough to hope, if not for a definitive solution, at least for an answer with an approximation, and announcing a definitive solution in a few days, by return of post.

'I am, dear Sir, with all respect,
'Your faithful humble servant,
'JEREMY BENTHAM.

'Now for my question—A sum having been allotted in March, 1793, for the maintenance of a certain number of persons, of the lowest rank of life, in provisions, clothing, bedding, washing, firing, and lighting, how much, if anything, per cent. ought to be the additional allowance made at present in consideration of the intervening rise of prices? The calculation to be grounded not on the prices of a particularly bad year (such as the present), but on the probable average of a future term—say of twelve years.

'P.S.—Relative to the "Annals"—I have got a titbit for your "Dragon" (the name Dr. Hawksworth used to give his magazine), some facts which to me are as new as they are interesting, relative to the effect of the rise of prices on the wages of the self-maintaining labourers in agriculture, and the mode of provision for the burthensome. The author, a very intelligent and respectable clergyman, Mr. North, Rector of Ashdon in Essex. They are contained in two or three letters :[1] the moral of them appears to lean to two practical results, both of them I believe as alien to your notions as to mine, viz. rating wages and restricting the size of farms. At the same time what they indicate is certainly a disease, the mischief of which, however, would, I am inclined to think, be much exceeded by that of the least mischievous of the above two remedies. But if capable of an answer, they are, at the same time, highly deserving of one; and this not only on account of the facts themselves, but on account of the good sense as well as candour with which they are delivered.

'J. B.'

From J. Symonds, Esq., to the Speaker of the House of Commons, &c.

'Euston: November 30, 1800.

' My dear Sir,—I came hither on Friday and shall go home next Saturday. I hear there are three pamphlets lately published that command much attention— Lord Sheffield's,[2] Sir Thomas Sturton's, and " Candid Enquiries," etc. When does your Board intend to enter the lists? The Duke says it has shown him

---

[1] These letters are inserted in the *Annals of Agriculture*, vol. xxxv. p. 459.

[2] Lord Sheffield published *Remarks on the Deficiency of Grain* 1799–1800, and *Observations on the Exportation of Wool from Great Britain to Ireland*, 1800.

great politeness by the attention it has paid to a proposal of his. If you have not got "Islington on Forestalling," &c. you should buy it, for several statutes, absurd as they are, you will find set forth clearly and methodically—I should not properly say clearly (but this is no fault of the editor), for we do not know what statutes may be said to be declaratory of the common law, or not. Did you not rejoice with me that Sheridan animadverted on those judges who had thundered their anathemas against forestallers, &c.? I am persuaded that some of the riots owed their origin to the intemperate language so extra-judicially used. I was sorry to see the turn which affairs took upon the Report of the Committee. Had Pitt been silent about the Jacobins, and had your friend Wilberforce abstained from abusing Grey's connections and Sir Francis Burdett's speech, there would probably have been a great unanimity. The more Wilberforce endeavoured to exculpate himself, the deeper he seemed to plunge. He was well advised by Sir F. B., who seldom harangues with any propriety, "to think more, and speak less."

'When I mentioned agricultural books I ought not to have appeared insensible to the pleasure I received from perusing the greater part of Burke's pamphlet, very lately published by Dr. Lawrence. You, I find, make there a distinguished figure in the foreground. Do you approve of what Burke says about the distilleries?

'A few minutes before I came hither on Friday a very melancholy event took place. Winterton, the

Groom of the Chambers, had been seen walking by the side of the river near the mill, not far from the house, and was never heard of afterwards till his body was found in the river. The Coroner is expected to-day, and he will probably instruct the jury to bring in their verdict, "lunacy," as some of the servants had observed in him marks of insanity a few days preceding.

'If you can spare five minutes from the service you pay to the Board and to the public, favour me with a few lines. You live now more with politicians than with farmers.

'What will be the result of our breaking with the Emperor of Russia, whose conduct Mr. Pitt truly calls "strange versatility and caprice"?

'Tell me a good deal, for the Duke has no regular correspondent in Town now that Stonehewer is here.

'I was with you at Bradfield when Buonaparte's first offers for a peace were published.

'You said you thought the Ministry would pay attention to them, and do you think that, upon the whole, we can make as good a peace as them, the French having been almost driven out of Italy?

'Adieu.

'Yours sincerely,

'J. SYMONDS.'

CHAPTER XIV

DIARY CONTINUED, 1801–1803

Public affairs and prophecy—The divining rod—The appropriation of waste lands—The word 'meanness' defined—South's sermons—Projected theological compendia—Correspondence—Journalising to 'my friend'—Anecdote of Dean Milner and Pitt—Death of the Duke of Bedford—Napoleon and Protestantism.

March 20.—It is in vain to complain of gaps; if I had but attention enough to write only two lines every day I should have hope of going on. I have been thinking more seriously of the Journal, and of converting it to use as a memento of the progress I make in the only business worth real attention—my salvation through the merits of the Blessed Saviour. For this purpose I must fix on some hour of the day to be regular at it, and, if I hold my resolution, it shall be immediately after my prayers in the morning, being always up at 4 A.M. and sometimes at 3 A.M. I am then sure to be uninterrupted; positively I will begin to-morrow morning.

21st.—Dined yesterday with Lord Somerville. I did not like the day. Duke of Montrose, Duke of Athol, and Lord Rossmore sent excuses, but the Marquis of Abercorn, Lord Dalkeith, Lord Villiers, Lord Barrington, Mr. McDougal, Mr. Baird, and two Scotch members were there, the last but one a hard-headed, sensible man.

Much conversation, particularly farming. This morning Sir A. St. John Mildmay called to have my opinion of a Bill he is now bringing into Parliament to enable the clergy to give leases of their tithes beyond the term of their lives. The Archbishop has not negatived it, but such a Bill can no more pass than the abolition of tithes; it is open to such frauds that perhaps it ought not to pass.

My chief misfortune in having little society with well-disposed minds: I know few except Wilberforce and Cecil; the latter I rarely see, and W. is so full of business that I might nearly as well be unknown to him. I will urge him to form a Society to meet once a week for conversation merely on religion.

22nd, Sunday.—To be eager and alert in rising at 4 A.M. for all my secular employments and sluggish on the Lord's Day, when, if I rise, it must be to His worship, seemed long ago a snare of Satan, which, blessed be God, I have resisted. I was yesterday at the Society for Bettering the Condition of the Poor, the Bishop of Durham in the chair; it is an excellent institution, and may call down the blessing of God—may that Being grant them his grace to do good from right motives! With the Duke of Bedford on the Smithfield Society, and the whole day full of business, which, on the Sabbath, I banish as much as I can from my mind. In the evening my son and daughter only at home, and therefore I got an hour's religious conversation with them on the times and the Prophecies.

I have been too negligent of improving such opportunities, but the tremendous moment in which we live, so lately having seen the country without King, without minister, with a famine, and seven wars! If it be not a moment to call people to a serious recollection, nothing can ever do it.

So near the expiration of the 1,260 years of Daniel and St. John; the Turkish Empire on the point of destruction; a strange and unthought-of establishment in Egypt, a country that is to have much to do in the return of the Jews—ourselves in India, they may have some unknown relation to that phial to be poured out on the Euphrates to make way for the Kings of the East—altogether combine strangely to give suspicion that we are on the eve of some great events which are to usher in the final consummation of all things, and consequently the fall of the ten Kings of Europe. The times are truly awful, and demand such piety and resignation as no other period of modern history even approached to.

23rd.—At the Lock yesterday. Scott is now my favourite preacher, and I have heard him ever since I came to Town with great pleasure and attention in spite of a very bad manner. His matter is most excellent. Received the Sacrament.

24th.—Called yesterday on Mr. and Mrs. Montagu in their great house. It is said he has just lost a coal pit that was worth 6,000*l.* or 7,000*l.* a year; I had a card for her Monday parties, and not having been, I apologised. I must now and then go after Easter. But all company of the sort is flat to me. I have just made up the annual account for 1800, and the loss upon the year is 22*l*.; this meeting a tax on paper which will cost 48*l*. a year is alarming. I had entertained many vain hopes that the work after so many years' continuance would have stood its ground, but I know not what to think. Now I must print only six instead of seven sheets, and try so for another year. If I lose then, I must give up the work, much as it will hurt me. The 'Agricultural and Commercial Magazine' and the 'Farmers' Magazine,' which approach more to the nature of newspapers, and which have contained hardly one paper of real importance, have been selling well; such is the world, its judgment and discernment!

28*th*.—Yesterday the Board proceeded to Hyde Park in a body to see the experiments of Captain Hoar on the *Virgula divina*. He, many years ago, saw Lady Milbank's surprising faculty of discovering springs, and trying, found that he had it himself. He is recommended to the Board by Mr. Lascelles, member for Yorkshire.

I found from the conductor of the waterworks at the reservoir then at work, that the twig in Mr. Hoar's hand when he crossed them turned up in a surprising manner. He seemed, in the opinion of Sir Joseph Banks, to fail once, but in the four trials I watched, and in which I know he could not be acquainted with the direction of the pipes, he succeeded completely. Next Tuesday another trial.

To-morrow will be published in the 'Annals' the first parts of my essay on applying waste lands to the better support of the poor. I prepared it some time ago for the Board, as it was collected in my last summer's journey; I read it to a committee—Lord Carrington, Sir C. Willoughby and Mr. Millington—who condemned it, and, after waiting a month, Lord C. told me I might do what I pleased with it for myself, but not print it as a work for the Board; so I altered the expressions which referred to the body, and sent it to the 'Annals.' I prayed earnestly to God on and since the journey for His blessing on my endeavours to serve the poor, and to influence the minds of people to accept it; but for the wisest reasons certainly He has thought proper not to do this, and for the same reasons probably it will be printed without effect. I think it, however, my duty to Him to do all I possibly can. Such events and circumstances I am well persuaded are entirely in His Divine management, and that we are mere instruments in His hands. Whether I print or not is a matter wholly unimportant, but the use made of it is in the hands of the Almighty alone. I am well persuaded that this is the only possible means of saving the nation from the ruin fast coming on by the misery of the poor and the alarming ruin of rates. God's will be done!

29*th*.—Yesterday at the Farmers' Club. I have little relish of these meetings, unless given to farming conversation, and this was nothing but wrangling about the disposition of money. Sunday before Easter.— Company and talk, eating and wine; sitting up late are ill preparations for the Sabbath.

31*st*.—The Duke of Bedford and Lord Winchilsea at the Club; filled up vacancies and settled the premiums. The Board greatly attended yesterday, and adjourned for the holidays.

Captain Hoar is turned over to Lord Egremont, of whom the Bishop of Durham said that he possessed of all the men almost that he ever knew the clearest head and most penetrating understanding. I asked Lord Carrington to employ Arthur while I am absent; he said it was mean to make him a clerk—but everything is wrong that is proposed to this man, even the things which, let alone, he would propose himself.

Honest industry in a lawful employment cannot be mean, especially in an employment that he likes. This is one of the world's prejudices, and rotten like all the rest.

April 4.—At Bradfield. The pleasure of coming into the country from such a place as London is great and pure. The freshness and sweetness of the air, the quiet and stillness, the sunshine unclouded by smoke, the singing of the birds, the verdure of the fields, the budding out of vegetation, altogether is charming.

I have only an old woman who keeps the house in our absence, and never was so attended before; but no matter—I am quiet, peaceful, and living economically, and shall, I hope, be very well contented. Divine service was worse done than anything; Sharpe, who is past everything, preaches and reads worse than any human being; this is lamentable. That point is the glory of London; one can find churches where our attention is commanded by instruction.

I never saw the wheat look better, thanks to God! My farm is the source of disquiet as well as pleasure—such bailiffs as I must keep execute everything badly, except just what they have always been used to; and with great expenses there are always many things sadly neglected. With such absences as I am forced to, this must be the case.

I have read Barrow's sermons chiefly since I came down. That on Good Friday excellent, on Whit Sunday capital, and on the prophecies of the Messiah such as would convince an infidel, were not infidelity true hardness of heart.

5th.—At the Sacrament, none but Green and his wife, and the clerk and his wife. How much have the clergy to answer for! Reading Barrow and South's sermons, 'The Image of God in the Creation,' which is full of wit. Barrow is a most powerful writer, he pours out a torrent of matter, a stream of mind, as Johnson said of Burke; an amazing flow of conception and of expression, forcible and varied; a rich command of language, and such fertility that one of his sermons would make ten modern ones.

The life I am getting into here of walking and reading is such a contrast to that at London as to be a most pleasant change and recreation to my soul and body.

From January 20th I had been so loaded with business of the requisitions from the Committees of Lords and Commons, and reading 360 essays, that I was employed every day from morn to dinner. I rose at 4 A.M. regularly, sometimes sooner, even at 3 A.M., and neglected my 'Elements'[1] entirely on this account. All was for the Board, and not free from anxiety. Here I shall have a fortnight's refreshment and relaxation,

[1] *The Elements of Agriculture.*

thanks to the Almighty for it, and that He blesses me with health to enjoy it.

7th.—Yesterday at 2 o'clock I walked to Bury, for I have neither horse nor chaise to go in or on. Dined with my friend[1] alone. I had much talk, and tried hard to impress her with good religious notions, but I fear in vain; she will not be converted but by misfortune and misery, her easy prosperous situation will prevent it. I can only pray for her.

I have made an experiment in living here not unimportant. I drink no wine or beer, only a pint or one-third of a bottle of cider at dinner. I care not what I eat, I have only one maid and no helps, and could thus live for a trifle in a cottage. In such times such trials may have their use beyond the Christian propriety of self-denial; but my collection of good books are a great comfort, which, if deprived of, I should miss terribly. I rise at 4 A.M., walk up to my neck in the garden pond, pray, and then read till breakfast; read, walk, and farm till dinner, and so on till it is dark, and no moment hangs heavily on my hands. I reproach myself with indolence for not going among the cottagers, but they come to me numerously, and having descriptive lists I know enough to do more than I am able, but I ought to go to their houses and examine their state well.

I have been reading Watson's Collection,[2] and am forming a table of striking passages, and think to have

---

[1] Mrs. Oakes, *née* Betsy Plampin.
[2] *A Collection of Theological Tracts*, by the Bishop of Llandaff, 6 vols.

them copied for arranging with the many I have already written, and may print it some time or other under some such title as this : *A course of reading on the origin, truth, and doctrines of the Christian Religion.* I know of no book of evidences that includes all ; by taking the most impressive passages on each subject from many books, and disposing them in a lucid form, I think I could produce a very useful work without presuming to compose any part of it myself. May the Lord afford me His Spirit should I go on with the design, but with my employment it would be a business requiring much time !

9th.—Dined with Mr. and Mrs. Balgrave. Balgrave is a good-tempered Suffolk parson, neglects the duty of his church, idle, indolent, drinks his bottle of port and reads his newspaper, but what is called a respectable character, no vices, nor any imprudent follies.

10*th.*—Symonds dined with me and took a bed. The Duke of Brunswick marching into Hanover will, he says, be a keen revenge.

When he married our King's sister, Lord Bute (who told the whole to S. while travelling with him in Italy) promised him the government of Hanover as soon as it should be vacant, with the King's knowledge. The Marquis of Granby conveyed the assurance. When the vacancy happened the Prince of Mecklenburg was talked of. Lord Granby wrote to Lord Bute to remonstrate, who went to the King and Queen, and urged the real necessity of adhering to the promise. All in vain, the Queen prevailed, and her brother, not two degrees better than ——, was appointed. The Duke of Brunswick never forgave it, and when invited to England rejected the idea with anger. Symonds saw him at Venice and noted the asperity of some of his expressions.

11th.—Reading Sherlock's sermons. In those on the truth of Christianity, and a defence of the mysteries of it, I know none equal; excellent indeed and clear, persuasive, and convincing; but I have some doubts on the vitality of his faith. In the third discourse of the second volume he says: 'Here is a plain proof of what the work of the Spirit is. It brings proofs to the reason of man, but does not bring the reason of man to the proofs.' I conceive just the contrary, the proofs themselves are clear, full, and abounding with what ought to produce universal conviction, but men, for want of the Spirit, turn their back, neglect, or despise them.

It is the business of the Spirit to take away the heart of stone, and then the proofs are manifest: the heart and reason of man are really brought to the proofs.

12th, Sunday.—The ground white with snow, and the wind cutting. I am up every morn at 4 A.M., and walk to the garden pond; habits will do anything. I do not mind it at all, and sometimes stand in the wind till dry; it is, however, sharp work.

A nonsensical letter from Lord Carrington requiring me to go to the Treasury for the 800*l.* for the Essays, which is entirely the treasurer's business. He is as unfeeling as a log; this is a return for my being at work from 4 A.M. in the morning for ten weeks. I should once have been full of indignation and abhorrence; thank God, I am more calm. I shall go on Friday instead of the Monday following. But I wish he had let me alone. I am vexed, but the world is full of nothing but great miseries or teasing vexations, the more the better; they wean us from it effectually.

I have been here ten days and have not visited one poor family. My heart reproaches me. I have given as much as I apprehended I could afford, but that is laziness. The cold winds and sleet have kept me too much in the house. It is easier to give than to be active in doing good. I have four days more. Oh, let me be stirring in doing good! Indolence is inexcusable. If I thought I had but a little time to live, with what energy would all this be done! And how soon may I be trembling on a death bed! Have mercy on me, O God, and give me grace to serve Thee with activity and vigour. Read the whole book of Job. I can read, think, speculate, write, and meditate, but in doing good am negligent and slothful. I have had a passing fit of melancholy from looking at my ever dear daughter's picture, which I carry with me everywhere, and never think of her but to bless God for having in some measure (how imperfectly!) brought me to Himself. Age coming on apace; the world fading faster still; horrible threatenings in the aspect of public affairs; small hope of any comfort underived from religion. How black and dreary would all my prospects be were it not for the consolation I draw from a most lively and never varying faith in the truth of Christianity, in the *full assurance* of immortality ! What would be my situation without this only balm of my existence? Domestic comfort a blank; my friends dropping into the grave, and the infirmities of age in near prospect.

Gratitude and thanksgiving to my blessed Saviour for affording me grace to believe; and with it all the comfort that remains for me in this world. My child! My child! Oh, may we meet in heaven!

13*th*.—The poor people of the neighbouring villages crowd here to my great distress. I give all something, and wish I could give more; but I dread falling into the dark impropriety of giving too much, of making what would seem and be a parade of charity or generosity with other people's money, which is somewhat the case with a man who gives while he has debts unprovided for. I truly know not what rightly to do in this case. The evil just described is great, and ought to be avoided, but at the same time what ought I to think of myself who have been always ready to spend and run in debt for forty years together; and then should take up so strictly as to do nothing for miserably poor people in such times as these? Surely on such an occasion we should be exerting every power to relieve them!

20*th*.—Friday to London. Saturday, Farmers' Club. An argument with Lord Egremont, &c., on land for the poor; everybody is against it. What infatuation!

21*st*.—Last night at Mrs. Montagu's conversazione. I had some [talk] with the Bishop of Durham, who agrees with me on the poor; with Lady Harcourt, who wants restrictions on farmers; with Lord Somers, who told stories of supernatural movements of furniture in Norfolk.[1] I left it very early though invited for all March and April. This is the first of my going.

London very disagreeable to me, and has made me compare in my mind my present situation with a large income, and that of living in a cottage in the country upon 100*l.* a year, without trouble or anxiety or business, except to make my peace with God. I liked my time alone with my old woman [servant] at Bradfield much better than here. I had nobody to wrangle and quarrel with me.

May 4.—Yesterday I was at church in the morning with Mrs. O. Oakes at the Lock, and heard Scott, and in the evening at the Surrey Chapel to hear Rowland Hill. Neither of them pleased, though she admits Scott's matter was excellent. She was most struck with the extreme fervency of Mr. Wilberforce's devotion, who, sitting in the reading desk for the convenience of hearing better, she saw him clearly. Bought Rowland Hill's sermon on the Sunday Schools against the attack of Bishop Horsley,[2] who is, from all I hear of him, such a bishop as Suffolk parsons are clergymen. Scott thinks that evil spirits do work on our souls, and to me it is remarkable that he says the imagination is their great field. I have reason enough to believe him in the right. These are enquiries in which we have no other clue to guide us but Scripture, and surely

---

[1] This seems to have been an anticipation of table-turning.

[2] Samuel Horsley, born 1733, died 1806, Bishop of St. Asaph's, St. David's, and Rochester; celebrated for his controversy with Dr. Priestley.

there we find proofs without end of the agency of evil spirits; for my own part I have no doubt of it.

Bradfield.—As there was no church this morning, I had eleven poor women from the village to talk to upon their neglect of church. I read many passages on public worship and prayer out of Dodd's Commentary on the Bible, and explained, preached, and reasoned with them. One made a defence, and was inclined to prate. I took it coolly, and presently brought her to better reason. I doubt they liked a sixpence apiece better than my sermon, yet three of them cried. How much more docile and teachable are the poor than the rich! One might gradually do much with the poor, but very little indeed with their betters. God opens the hearts of the one, and hardens those of the others as a punishment for their pride and ingratitude.

The Duke of Bedford has asked Lord Carrington to the sheep shearing. Lord Egremont called, he remarks that the Chancellor, Lord Rosslyn, and Lord Grenville, &c. &c., all have in the late debates gone out of the way to abuse the Board of Agriculture, and remarks that keeping a Board only to treat it in this manner is preposterous.

7th.—My publications are very well adapted to take off the edge of all worldly infatuated admiration or dependence on the things of time in comparison of those of eternity. Washington's Letters have been advertised to the expense of 5*l.* or 6*l.*, and I do not believe that 100 are sold, and my enquiry into the cottage system for poor people will have no more effect on Government or the Legislature than if I had whistled 'Alley Croker.' So much the better perhaps for the good of my soul.

25th.—Mr. Hoole called and was let in. He has heard at a great table (he did not say where) a very so-so account of Lord Carrington—fidgeting, restless, dissatisfied, ambitious, avaricious, with a mere show of parts and knowledge. He has made immensely by the loan; and the richer he grows, so much the worse. The eldest girl said to Mr. H. when he called: ' My papa used to have prayers in his family; but none since he has been a peer.' What a motive for neglecting God! Also he is a dissenter and a democrat. A Unitarian he may be, but certainly no democrat. The Lord show mercy to him, and by interrupting his prosperity or lowering his health, bring him to repentance!

26th.—Yesterday I dined with the Duke of Grafton, and he asked me when the election of president and secretary of the Board was, for he heard there was an intention of turning Lord Carrington and me out. He said his answer was, as to Lord C., there were reasons which might account for that, but what can Mr. Y. have done? 'Oh, he is careless, and does nothing,' and so I dare say there are people to report and perhaps so think. Lord Somerville in revenge, I doubt not, hates everything belonging to the Board, and wishes to come in and sweep everyone clear away, in order to introduce creatures of his own, and this, uniting with Gifford's scandals and slander about the Board intending to pull down the club in the ' Porcupine ' and ' Anti-Jacobin

Review,'[1] gains the attention of fools, and mingled by the depravity of the world, is circulated and believed. But of all farces, that of my doing nothing is the most precious. What I have done through the whole session of the Board surpasses credibility, almost to myself, and nothing but rising at 4 A.M. in the morning could have enabled me to go through it. The first spare half day I have I will make a list of all I have done, and see if they will not acquit me to my own heart. Oh, did I serve my God as well as I have served the Board! Could I review my services to my Redeemer as satisfactorily, happy should I be!

27th.—Symonds and Hoole dined with us, and, as the former will see the Duke of Grafton to-day, I gave him a message card, on one side of which is '*Some use in rising at 4 A.M.*,' and on the other as follows: 'From January 20 to May 23 are 90 days, Sundays and vacation excluded, 50 Boards and Committees; 340 essays read, and every one commented on. Report to the House of Commons on Potatoes. Report to the Lords on Grass Lands. Enquiry into cottagers' land published, but drawn up for the Board. Memoir on Salt, from more than fifty authors. Ten new premises framed. Memoir on wastes, paring, burning, and arable land.'

If for such employment I am stigmatised for doing nothing, it shows that in order to please, it matters not what we do, caprice will be the only judgment.

---

[1] The *Anti-Jacobin*, or *Weekly Examiner*, was started by Canning, J. H. Frere, and others; the editor was W. Gifford. It ran from November 20, 1797, to July 9, 1798.

What conclusion is to be drawn from such cases? Serve God truly, and as to man trouble not thyself about him; let this be the golden rule, and it will bring peace at the last.

28*th*.—Lord Carrington fretting and worrying, and upon the full fidget about the newspapers' abuse, and the criticisms in the House of Lords upon the publication of the Board; swearing that he will allow no nonsense to be published, and this will be more absurd and pragmatical than ever. Oh! Mr. Pitt, Mr. Pitt, that thou shouldest have formed such a Board as this, and then permit it to frame such a constitution as should render it absolutely dependent on the folly and caprice of a president! What might it not have done had its laws been what they ought to have been!

Dalton, of Yorkshire, gave me a long account of his taking Hyder Ali when only the colonel of 500 horse—a soldier of fortune.[1] Lord Egremont came up from Petworth, where, he tells me, not a loaf for three days and a half, and a mutiny among the volunteers.

29*th*.—Dined yesterday at Lord Winchilsea's. There were the Duke of Bedford, Lord Egremont, Lord Romney, Lord Somerville, Mr. Calhoun, Mr. Northey, Mr. Conyers, and myself: much farming. Lord Romney gave Lord Egremont a guinea, to receive fifty when he produced a tench that weighed seven pounds.

Yesterday the Committee voted 50*l*. to my son for his labour in arranging &c., during thirteen weeks, the Reports from inclosed parishes to the House of Com-

---

[1] I print this as written, but can find no allusion in works of reference to the circumstance mentioned.

mons. I thanked them very awkwardly, and talked of gratitude, for it came on unexpectedly ; that readiness which is never at a loss I have not an atom of. My heart always speaks at a sudden ; whereas in many cases the head is most wanted. But the fault was on the right side, it was more than I expected.

June 6.—Charming weather for the country, now in its full beauty, and I am stoved up in this horrid place. Lord C. talked of adjourning the Board on Tuesday, which I hope much he will do. The 15th is the Sheep Show at Woburn ; it will be the 20th before it is possible for me to see Bradfield, and hardly then ; the longest day before a man gets into the country ! ! ! Let them turn me out of my secretaryship and I shall not regret it, but down all discontent ; it is God's will, and my duty is to be thankful for all.

It is a comfort which exceeds all others, that as age advances the end of life is viewed as a mere change of residence, and the mental eye fixed on heaven, with full confidence in the promises of God. I would not give this conviction for the wealth of the Indies, for the empire of the world. And what does one lose by religion ? I enjoy all such pleasures of life as are unattended by remorse, just as much, or more indeed, far more, than I did while I was a dissipated character. Reading, composition, serious conversation on any topic worth discussing, the rural beauties of Nature, and the pleasures of agriculture, friendship, affection, not love, as it is called, the whole of which I fear is founded in lust, and proves nineteen times in twenty the tyrant of the breast, and the fertile source of ten thousand miseries! Happy those in whom it terminates in a settled, quiet, tranquil friendship, sufficient to satisfy without the wanderings of the heart that lead to so much misery.

I was here (at Bradfield) three weeks at Easter after a severe confinement to incessant business; I am now again in the same deep retirement, the life of a hermit, after eight weeks of business and bustle. I feel how vast the benefit is to have these periodical retirements from the world in silence and solitude. Had I gone directly from London on my tour, plunging from one busy scene to another, my mind would have had no time to cool, none to settle into any calm and tranquil state for reflection, which is unfavourable to the growth of religion, of morals, nay, of talents to perform anything of consequence. A round of business or dissipation thus unbroken is mischievous to the heart, ties it to the world, and unfits it for every effort of regeneration and repentance, or of meditation and philosophy.

Lord Euston is going the tour of Suffolk, ordering returns to be made of all carts, waggons, horses, mills, and ovens; a step preparatory in the expectation of an invasion. But it is in everyone's mouth that with such a price of corn half the country would join an enemy. I must freely confess I dread the result. We have no hope but in the protection of the Almighty, who has hitherto so wonderfully protected us; and what has been the gratitude shown to Him?

Most melancholy is the reflection. Our rulers are truly infatuated, to have done nothing for the assistance of the poor, but leave them to such trying times without even showing a disposition to take any steps that could be effective. To do nothing to give relief, when land for the poor does relieve them so beneficially wherever they have it, is a cruel infatuation. To see poor rates at their present enormous height and the poor in misery—yet where they have land, to find rates 3d. or 4d. or 9d. in the £, and the poor in a state of ease and comfort—one would think should speak feelingly and powerfully—but no such thing. Men are governed by their stupid prejudices, and have too much pride to permit their eyes to be opened. Had an Act passed last session that had the effect of thus assisting the poor, instead of the pernicious system by rates, and some progress were now making in every county to carry it into execution, we should not hear such opinions advanced, because they would be groundless; the poor labourers, seeing such steps taken for their comfort and to free them from the ineffective thraldom of parish rates, would be patient and quiet. At present they see nothing done or doing for them, and have their hearts almost broken by penury—without resource—without hope.

In such a situation who would wonder to see men join an enemy in crowds? Heaven forbid that this infatuation of Government be not providential, and the means by which the Deity may mean to punish the nation for and by its sins!

The trumpeter of the Corps of Yeomanry came to me with a written engagement to forfeit 5s. the first absence and 10s. 6d. every successive one if we do not meet the first Friday of every month. I was always exempted on account of my necessary absence; however, as they expect to be called into actual service, I would not now retire when an invasion is expected, so I signed; but when the alarm is quite blown over—should that please the Almighty—I shall withdraw, for I am too old and too weak, and my pursuits too far off and too numerous to permit attendance.

September 7 [on tour, at Dunstable].—Breakfasted with Mr. Parkyn, and then went to meet a person who instructs people in plaiting straw, and I bargained with him at 30*s*. a week for a girl to be instructed—a month will do; that is 6*l*., and the journey there and back, about 4*l*., so for 10*l*. I shall be able to introduce this most excellent fabric among our poor. The children begin at four years old, and by six earn 2*s*. or 3*s*. a week; by seven 1*s*. a day; and at eight and nine, &c., 10*s*. or 12*s*. a week. This will be of immense use to them.

Got to Woburn by 2 P.M., sat down and wrote for two hours and a half, then dressed, but did not dine till nearly 8 P.M. The Duke of Manchester there with Lord Preston, Mr. Cartwright, and Edwards, the bookseller, who is putting the library to rights and showing how to make the catalogue. I was surprised to learn from him that a man could not lay out in one year more than 5,000*l*. judiciously in books; that Lord Spencer has been fourteen years expending 25,000*l*., and has the best library in England, perhaps better than the King's. He tells me the nation [France] bought L'Héritier's[1] library, and gave it to the Botanical

[1] C. de l'Héritier, born 1746, died 1800; botanist, and member of the Académie des Sciences.

Garden. Miss Knight,[1] authoress of the continuation of 'Rasselas,' whom I met at Kedington's, lent Dolmien's[2] 'Life at Naples,' through Lady Hamilton's interest with the Queen. He wrote to her from prison.

Did not get to bed till past 11 P.M. Such hours and fasting from 9 A.M. in morn to 8 P.M. at night did not agree with me. I waked at 4 A.M., and having a lamp, rose, washed, prayed, and sat down by candle-light to my notes and finished them.

Lord Preston swears; it hurts me to hear him. I certainly ought to convert such people and reproach myself, and confess the sin every day in my catalogue to God; but I go on and do it not. If I had wit I could laugh at it, but I have no more wit than a pig.

The following are selected from this year's correspondence:

From T. Symonds, Esq., describing Trinity College Establishment, Revenue, &c.

'Cambridge: March 20, 1801.

'You desire me, good friend, to send you a long letter from this place, but I could more easily find materials to write one to our friend Charles Cole, from his being perfectly conversant with every one here, and with almost everything. You observe very right, that landlords cannot come into a share of the wealth of their tenants but by a corn rent. This I have insisted

[1] Cornelia Knight, author of *Dinarbas*, a continuation of *Rasselas*, 1790, and other works.

[2] Celebrated French geologist. Accompanied Napoleon to Egypt; on his return was taken prisoner and confined at Messina by the King of Sicily; on peace being made with Naples was liberated.

upon of late frequently at Bury. The present state of the University is an indisputable proof of it. The pressure of the times is hardly felt by its members. Will you not think so, when you hear that the revenue of this College amounted to nearly 16,000*l.* last year, and that the eight senior fellows received more than 300*l.* each, and the junior half of that sum ? They have been obliged to raise, however, the price of the commons (as they are called) from fifteen to eighteen pence. But I sit down here every day for this sum to a dinner, which gentlemen of a thousand a year cannot give often with prudence.

'The papers, I presume, have informed you of the trial of our plate stealers last week.

'The whole business was ill conducted. The man who sold to the Jew the medals of King's College for 70*l.*, the plate of this for 300*l.*, and the plate of Caius for 500*l.*, pleaded guilty, and in consequence of a free pardon to appear against the Jew, who, though acquitted at these Assizes, will probably be hanged at the next. Grimshaw, the chimney sweeper, is the only victim at present. Your friend Simeon was not wanting in his visits to him. He told an acquaintance of mine " that he found Grimshaw's conversation delightful ; that he had grace to die ; and that the sooner he was executed the better, for fear this grace should evaporate." Should it ever be my lot to be condemned for execution, I will immediately apply to you for consolation. Simeon could work no conviction in the Jew ; this will not surprise you.

'I saw in the papers a list of the dancers at Lady

Carrington's ball; but, to my astonishment, did not discover your name. The papers have raised Lord C. to the degree of Viscount;[1] it would be too insulting for a man recently in business to step above the heads of our ancient Barons. I should have told you that we have here a young nobleman of unblemished character. I mean Lord Henry Petty, whose knowledge and abilities are such, both in writing and speaking in public, as to lead me to imagine that he cannot fail to make a distinguished figure in Parliament. By the bye, there seem to be some members of the House of Commons who are jealous of your Board.

'Yours sincerely,
'J. SYMONDS.'

January 24, 1802.—A great gap; but from coming to London in November to quitting it the following month I wrote journal letters paged to my friend.[2] Through the Christmas holidays a blank. I have subscribed to the Lock Hospital 5*l*. 5*s*., and go every Sunday. Wilberforce always there taking notes of Scott's sermons.

In the great business of my salvation I go on slowly, struggling hard, however, to advance, by freeing my imagination from sensuality and my heart from coldness. God give me grace to persist. I lay great stress on trying by every means to impress in my mind a constant sense of God's presence.

---

[1] Robert Smith, son of a banker at Nottingham; M.P. for that town from 1770 to 1796; supporter and friend of Pitt; raised to the Irish peerage in 1796, to the English peerage in 1797.

[2] Mrs. Orbell Oakes, the beautiful Betty Plampin of former flirtations, is 'the friend' henceforth constantly alluded to.

March 8.—At Wilberforce's last night till 10 o'clock, and was not in bed till quarter past 11 P.M. Though I was up before 4 A.M., and had no sleep in the day, or very little, the consequence was that in the night just past I slept very soundly indeed, and till 6 A.M. Dean Milner [1] there, and I had much conversation with him about W. while he and Mr. W. were out of the room. He first made an impression on Wilberforce's mind at Scarborough; he hinted on some person named being an enthusiast, but Milner (though not religious then himself) checked it with a firmness that made W. think. They afterwards travelled to Nice, and were there three months about the year 1783 or 1784. The Duke of Gloucester was then an infidel; the conversation M. had with him upon the journey had no other effect (indeed that was the capital one) but of making him serious in reading and considering the Bible, which he did with great industry and deep attention, bringing to it a *heart* open to conviction; his health was injured by application, but his eternal soul was saved. He afterwards broke off his intimacies with a social fashionable set, and particularly from dinners which hurt his progress in Divine impersonation. He fairly and openly told his friends the reason. Pitt never joked or laughed at him—some did, but he never; all were sorry to lose him. But he was in earnest, and carried his determination into effect to give himself wholly to the care of his soul in the first place, and next to

[1] Isaac Milner, 1751–1820, son of a poor weaver (brother of the no less remarkable Joseph Milner), Dean of Carlisle, and Professor of Mathematics at Cambridge.

perform his temporal duties by assiduity in business. The Dean remarked the great good his book is likely to do from this time to the end of the world. Many, many may be saved by it. He dictated an answer to some quotations from David which the Duke of Grafton gave me the other day in argument against original sin, the righteousness named 1,000 years before Christ. He replied as I had done on the spot to the Duke, that these men had the *spirit*, and then were righteous before God in *Jesus Christ* who saved from the creation.

The Duke of Bedford's death! How much I could write on that topic. I met Halifax at the Duke of Grafton's. He died with what is called perfect courage, collectedness, and resolution that is perfectly hardened in insensibility. A most tremendous, awful, horrible case! But very difficult to separate affection for the amiable temper and useful life from a just condemnation of his utter want of religion and piety.

From the Duke of Bedford[1]
in carrying out the plans of his late Brother

'Woburn Abbey: March 28, 1802.

'Sir,—The sudden and fatal event which deprived me of one of the kindest of friends and most affectionate of brothers, Agriculture of one of its firmest props, and Society of one of its best and most useful members, coming upon me too so soon after a former severe domestic calamity, left my mind in such a state of sad dejection as to render me wholly incapable of

[1] John Russell, sixth Duke, 'the great Duke of Bedford,' who did so much for agriculture, and in 1830 rebuilt Covent Garden Market at a cost of 40,000*l.* Died 1839.

writing to you on a subject deeply interesting to me, because it occupied the last thoughts of my much lamented brother. His zeal for that first and most interesting of pursuits, Agriculture, did not forsake him even in the last moments of his life, and on his death-bed, with an earnestness of mind expressive of his character, and with that anxious consideration for the interests of his country which occupied so many years of his well-spent life, he strongly urged me to follow up those plans of national improvement which he had begun, and from which he had formed the most sanguine hopes of success. He referred me to Mr. Cartwright and to you for explanations and details; with Mr. C. I have already had some conversation, and hope soon to have the pleasure of seeing you. I shall be in London in a day or two, and if you will favour me with a line in Arlington Street, to name the day and hour most convenient to you to call upon me, you will much oblige me. Should you be absent from Town I trust it will not be long before I have the satisfaction of seeing you at Woburn.

'Desirous as I am in every point of view to fulfil the last wishes of my departed brother, I feel that my humble efforts must be at such a vast distance from the exertions of his well-regulated and superior mind, that without the aid and advice of those most capable of assisting me, I should utterly despair of attaining the objects now so near to my heart.

'I am, Sir,
'Your faithful and obedient servant,
'BEDFORD.'

My Reply

'32 Sackville Street: March 1802.

'My Lord,—The melancholy event which has deprived your Grace of a brother so beloved was a stroke that affected every feeling of my heart; others more habituated to his merit on great occasions better knew than it was possible for me to do the powers of a mind that could fathom the most important subjects; but to me, sinking his great consequence in the country, he was a kind, most amiable, and indulgent friend, nor shall I ever cease to lament the loss of the best temper I ever met with; good humour seemed to spring from a perennial source in his bosom. Pleasing and happy it is for his lamented memory that all ranks and classes of the people have vied in the expressions of grief for the loss of so able, sincere, and unquestionable a patriot. It pleased him on several late occasions to converse with me on his plans of those establishments he meditated to connect with the employment of Mr. Cartwright. Probably that gentleman has explained all or most of them to your Grace. I shall be most happy to repeat them, and I am sure I need not add that veneration for the memory of one who commanded the regrets of a great nation, as well as the respect I owe to your Grace's character, will induce me most willingly to give you the little assistance that is in my power to lessen the loss we have all suffered.

'I rejoice in hearing of your Grace's determination to tread in those steps which proved so direct a path to a well-earned and most useful fame.

'From eleven o'clock to-day till four, and from twelve till three on Thursday, I am engaged with the Board, but will wait on your Grace at any other time you are pleased to appoint.

'I am, my Lord,
'Most respectfully your Grace's
'Much obliged and most humble servant,
'ARTHUR YOUNG.'

The Board has been busy in voting testimonies to the memory of the Duke of Bedford, a race who should express most strongly their veneration. The Bishop of Llandaff brought a dedication for the volume now ready—a medal ordered and a bust. These people are carnal and worldly, except, however, Mr. Wilberforce, who much promoted it, and spoke often in favour of it. His example is authority, or I should have considered the whole as a worldly-minded business, and bad. This Duke, with vast powers and immense influence, set an example to a town and populous neighbourhood in the country, and to a great circle of friends and dependents, of an utter neglect, if not contempt, of religion: all was worldly in his views; all his motives tending that way, and his example mischievous to religion and the souls of men. All this praise and veneration is therefore very questionable, and, I think, unlawful; it is looking at objects and judging of things with the herd, and therefore wrong; we cannot go with them but to do mischief. Of what consequence is religion to the world if farming and beneficence and good temper, and a life highly useful in a worldly view, is to outweigh the evils of irreligion, and so very bad an example in morals and want of piety? I cannot approve of it, much as I liked the man in all worldly respects.

Dr. Pearson talking of experiments observed that contrary experiments to good ones are nothing. 'I can get evidence for or against anything: for the existence of angels and devils,' &c. He is a great infidel, one of the gang of philosophers of the Royal Society, whose head, Sir J. B., is of the same mould, and whose influence is all on the same side, and does much mischief. The great, the wise, and the learned in this town, I fear, are nineteen in twenty infidels. Shocking! dreadful to think of!!

Dined at the Duke of Grafton's, Menil the Nimrod and Dr. Halifax there. I never fail to combat his Unitarianism, but do no good; yet his arguments are weak as water.

20th.—At the Farmers' Club. Carried with some difficulty a premium of fifty guineas for the best plough; several voted against it, because impossible to decide which of several should be the best! These folks can hardly know the right end of a plough.

25th.—Dined at the Bishop of Durham's; Price, the Vice-Chamberlain, there, and Mr. and Mrs. Bernard. I would have some serious talk, and therefore asked the Bishop if he had read Overton's [1] book? He had, and highly approved it. He met with it at York, and asked

---

[1] J. Overton, officer in the Excise; made telescopes, and had a private press, where he printed books, mostly theological. Died 1838. See *Annual Register* for that year.

the Archbishop if he knew anything of the author, and, to his surprise, found that he did not even know there was such a man, and knew nothing of him. The Bishop promised to send me his two charges and letters to the Deists. He was lately in company with Otto,[1] and made enquiries what that minister conceived would be the result of the present order of things in France relative to religion. Otto thought that it would end in the establishment of Protestantism;[2]

---

[1] L. W. Otto, Count of Morlay, was a German diplomatist in the French service, and lived 1752-1817. See Didot, *Biographie Universelle*.

[2] This was not, perhaps, impossible. See the following note from the *Daily News* Paris correspondent three or four years ago:

'An account of Napoleon I.'s visit to Breda in 1810 is now appearing, for the first time, in the *Débats*, and is deeply interesting. It will be seen that Napoleon I. at the zenith of his power was on the point of becoming a Protestant.

'The Emperor, after receiving several Deputies, went up to the Catholic Vicar, who had written a speech, and proceeded to read it. The Emperor, without replying, asked where were the Protestant ministers. Then M. Ten Oever, in his robes, followed by the entire Protestant clergy, was presented by the Prince de Wagram, and read an address. The Emperor remarked with satisfaction that the Protestant ministers wore their robes. Then, turning to the Roman Catholic clergy, he asked, "How is it that you are not wearing your frocks? What! I come to a Department [Holland had been annexed to France] where the majority are Catholics, who were formerly oppressed, and who have received more liberty from the King, my brother, and myself, and your first act is to show me disrespect! I have always found my Protestants faithful subjects. I have six thousand at Paris and eight hundred thousand in my empire, and I have no cause for complaint against a single one. Fools that you are! *If the Concordat had not been accepted by the Pope, I should have turned Protestant, and thirty million Frenchmen would have followed my example.* [The italics are my own.] You have calumniated Protestants, representing them as men teaching principles contrary to the rights of sovereigns. I have no better subjects. They serve in my palace in Paris. It was not Luther, nor Calvin, but the German princes who declined to submit to your fanatical this is remarkable and not improbable. The Concordat will not be executed. I questioned the Bishop about Paley: 'Mr. Y., I gave Dr. P. a living of 1,100*l.* a year for two great works, the " Horæ Paulinæ " and " The Evidences," and so I told him : " But, Dr. P., as to your Moral Philosophy I disapprove of it, and therefore do not mistake my motive " '! ! He is engaged in a work now at press on natural religion by the Bishop's recommendation.

27*th.*—Our third volume Part I. of the ' Communications ' is out, but I have yet heard nothing of the public opinion. The mere printing this thin quarto has been the whole business of the Board, that is, of the President, from last November ; nothing else done of any sort or kind. This is pitiable. He corrected the proofs and made them dance up and down to Wycombe, and wait as if time was of no consequence, and a whole Session will pass with this for its only employment. My ' Hertford ' is ready for printing, Pitt's ' Leicester,' Howlett's ' Essex,' and Plymley's ' Salop,' and all at a stand ; not one proof of the second part of the ' Essays ' at press in a fortnight, and nothing else thought of. He is as fit to be President of the Board as Grand Llama of Thibet ; such is the way that all public business is conducted. If I saw as much of the Treasury, have no doubt but similar though not equal neglect would appear. But what a table of cyphers to meet week after week and urge nothing to satisfy the public. The whole of this

yoke. The English were quite right to part company with you. You would like to set up scaffolds and stakes, but I will prevent you. All authority comes from God."'

flows from the most fastidious coxcombical pretension to purity of language: the time is spent in making phrases, as the French express it, which ought to be employed in devising and executing plans of improvement and pushing on the county surveys. Lamentable! A fine folly, however, has taken place; the President and two other members went to see Salisbury's botanical garden—there he agreed to hire six acres at rent and taxes 14*l*. an acre for Board experiments 1½ miles from Hyde Park Corner. I was not consulted, and 60*l*. paid for a lease before I knew a word of the matter; then I was ordered to view it, which I did, but no opinion asked. Next I was directed to draw up a plan of experiments, which I did, without corn, for myriads of sparrows from nurseries would eat all up. These were partly accepted and partly rejected, and potatoes scouted because *people are sick of the name of potatoes.* ' Suppose another famine, my Lord, what will those persons then think who are now sick of potatoes?'

It stands over for the Board. The whole idea is stark, staring folly; it will cost 250*l*. a year, and the harvest well deserved ridicule.

April 11.—Last Wednesday, Lord Carrington took me into his room and told me that his brother having the loan, he had spoken to him to write me down for 500*l*., and that the rise having been 4 per cent. he had directed it to be sold, and it would produce me 200*l*. clear of charges. I thanked him much. Such a thing never entered my thoughts, and consequently surprised me much. It was very kind and considerate, and I am certainly much obliged to him for it. Next evening he sent for me, and gave me a draft on Smith and Payne, 221*l.* 17*s.* 6*d.*, for the rise was 4½ per cent. I was thankful to God for this, and meditated much on it. If God had not been willing it would not have entered his head, and I find it comfortable to attribute everything to God, as, indeed, everything ought certainly to be attributed, and the more we trust entirely to Him the better I am persuaded it is for us. This is the first lottery for many years that I have been out of, but meeting with a passage in some of Scott's things against lotteries I would not put in, or have anything to do with it. If God pleases to give me money He has a thousand ways of doing it, and in these reflections I have had hard work to guard my mind against the temptation to consider it in the light of a reward which would be vile where there is no merit, no desert. I offend too daily and hourly to deserve anything but wrath at His hands, and this I cannot dwell on too much or too deeply. But for two years past of His infinite goodness He has made all money matters very favourable to me, and I thank Him for an uninterrupted stream of His bounty without let or hindrance, and this notwithstanding my sensual mind and many offences. I cannot be too grateful for so much goodness, and I pray Him to give me grace to be kind and charitable to others while He is so good to me. I think of these things with fear and trembling, lest they should throw my mind and conduct into an improper train.

Of late I have been ruminating on a short publication against the Deists, to consist merely of an attack on them to show the difficulties and absurdities of their system ; it will consist chiefly of extracts. I have read Bogue,[1] and Fuller and Berkeley's [2] 'Minute Philosopher,' and Leslie,[3] but none of them come up to my idea. It should be unmixed with a defence of Christianity, which should come in by way of appendix. I cannot get it out of my head, and shall certainly attempt it ; the worst is I must read their works (*i.e.* of the Deists, &c.), which is bad, but I shall not do it without prayer to God to fortify me against their sophistries and delusions.

Yesterday morning I hoped and expected to leave London, but Lord Pelham, Secretary of State, has sent us the returns of acres cropped last year from the clergy of the Kingdom, and so a Committee to-day, and to-morrow Good Friday ; for Saturday I have taken places Thus, after twelve weeks in London, I lose four days. Very unlucky, and very disagreeable, and for such nonsense as disgraces common sense. He wrote a circular letter to all the clergy of the Kingdom last June for this purpose, and from 10,000 parishes received accounts from about a half. Precious ones, to be sure ! A very probable matter that the farmers would give the number of acres sown with every sort of grain to the parsons ; such attempts degrade Government in the eyes of the people. What opinion can they have of men's abilities who expect thus to gain such facts?

[1] D. Bogue, D.D., *On the Divine Authority of the New Testament*, 1801.

[2] Bishop of Cloyne, *Alciphron; or, the Minute Philosopher*, 1732.

[3] C. Leslie, died 1722, author of *The Rehearsals: Tracts against the Deists and Socinians*, 4 vols.

I was in danger of returning to London without one entry in this Journal, but going up to wipe my dear Bobbin's book has thrown my mind into a fit of melancholy that I know not how easily to get rid of; yet will it go too soon? I have been whitewashing the house, cleaning about it, and keeping all things in pretty good order to do justice to the place as well as I am able; but my dear child's recollection brings forcibly to my heart the impression that it is the will of God I should have hardly any chance of this prosperity being kept in my family. My son has no children, nor likely to have any. Mary, no chance of marrying, so that my posterity ends with the next generation. The will of God be done, but human vanity and feelings will rise in the bosom, and they cannot rise without these unpleasant ideas forcing themselves into my mind. Bradfield has been ours 200 years, and I should have liked that my name and family might here have continued. But God has punished me for my sins; I can have nothing at His hands that I do not deserve. Blessed be His holy Name, be it my endeavour to submit to His will with resignation and cheerfulness.

Betsy and O. dined with me on Tuesday, but the day so bad I could not show her the round garden, which was got in very neat order. I have had a letter from the Duke of Liancourt in which he speaks of coming to England. I wrote to advise him against it, for he would, I fear, be very ill received. The Duke of Grafton read me a letter expressed in most indignant terms on the passage relative to him and his family in Mons. de

Liancourt's travels.[1] The new Duke of Bedford writes to desire me, in very kind terms, to go to the Woburn sheep-shearing ; asks it as a sort of favour. I had some very fine days on coming down, but of late the weather has been cold, damp, and melancholy, but I never come without wishing to live here constantly. I cannot help wishing it, but I hope without discontent—that would be black ingratitude to God. He fixes me where I am ; all, all things I am well persuaded come from His Almighty hand, and therefore a cheerful submission is one great article of a religious life. I brought down linen for the poor, but the number that want, and I cannot relieve, is melancholy : I think I have fixed straw work here, for above twenty-five have learned, and my splitting machines are all distributed. Some days since I sent off to Dunstable the first product of their work, and hope I shall have a good sale for the poor children.

June 1 : *London.*—I keep this Journal as I do everything else, lest good purposes be turned aside by trifles and want of resolution. This is the thanksgiving-day ; and last night was the Union masquerade, and the coaches are now (5 A.M. in the morning) rattling, and one fool in some monkey dress has walked by my windows.

A letter from the Duke of Bedford asking me to go to Woburn, which I shall do, and then I hope to Holkham, where Mr. Coke will take me in his coach—

---

[1] *Voyage en Amérique*, 2 vols. 1800. It seems that the French *émigrés*, after being most hospitably treated in England, showed little return in the way of graciousness. See *Letters of Maria Josepha Holroyd*; also the *Jerningham Letters*.

and there I am on my ground for the survey of Norfolk; but it is not yet decided whether I am to do it. It is a duty I owe to God to use the vacation in the best manner I can, but I can ill afford to travel at my own expense, determined as I am, if possible, to pay 700*l.* of debts.

I should like to make a long journey in enquiries concerning the poor; I know not what would be best, and have prayed to God to guide me, but I am utterly displeased with myself in my religious pursuits. My mind is sensual, and my progress slow; may the mercy of the Almighty be shed on me in grace to mend. I have planned a new work, 'Deism Delineated,' and made some progress, but do not please myself. It must be done gradually as I read, and my time is fully occupied with many pursuits.

Post to Chesterford, and having received a letter from the present Duke of Bedford requesting me to meet Lord Somerville and Mr. Coke at Woburn in order to consult upon the best means of carrying the late Duke's intentions into execution, especially in relation to the sheep-shearing, I set off accordingly, and got to Woburn at night, where I found Lord Somerville and Mr. Coke, and we considered the matter as well as the late Duke's proposals to breeders. At the meeting the Duke's attention was very pleasing, for he had great solicitude to arrange everything down to the minutest trifles in exactly the same manner as his brother had done on former occasions.

Before dinner, the first day, he came up to me and said, 'Mr. Y., I beg you will take your old seat, and preside at one end of the table, for which purpose I have ordered a servant to keep your chair.' Everyone remarked the extreme attention of the duke that all the business of the meeting should be well conducted.

12*th*.—Heartily tired of London, and the scenes I have endured at home. I left town, and took Betsy's new chaise, which I had bought for her (170 guineas) for Chesterfield, where her whole family were. It was a hurrying day.

Next morning, Sunday, to church, and in the afternoon, contrary to many feelings, to Baldock. No postchaise to be had, so went on in my whisky to Shefford, then post to Woburn by particular desire of the Duke of Bedford, to concert matters with Lord Somerville and Mr. Coke for the shearing business. It was 11 P.M. at night before I arrived; nobody there except they and Cartwright.

On the Thursday, with Mr. Coke and Mr. Talbot, in Coke's chaise to Brandon, and on Friday morning to Holkham.

Farmed on Saturday and too much on Sunday, so here have been two Lord's days profaned. How difficult it is to be in the world and preserve oneself uncontaminated by common practices! At church, however, in the morning.

The sheep-shearing the four following days, at which I had never been before. He does it handsomely; 200 dined on plate.

The dinner better than at Woburn, I think from vicinity to the sea, which gives plenty of fish.

At the Holkham meeting, had I entertained my

former feelings of pride and discontent, I should not have been too well pleased, for Mr. C. was personally civil and attentive; and yet he took not the smallest public opportunity of mentioning me, the Board, my report, or anything about it, though the occasion certainly called in reason for it. Once this would have mortified me, but now I value such matters not a straw. May God permit me to do my duty to Him, and as to what men think of me, I regard it less than the idle wind. I went to bed every night directly after coffee, between 9 and 10 P.M., and was up between 3 and 4 A.M.

[In London] at Mrs. Montagu's.—Sir Sidney not there; Ryder, the Privy Councillor, and his brother and Montagu, had been at Paris, and we had little conversation except on Bonaparte, &c. They contended that every scrap of land is cultivated and much that was waste. Sir F. combated the idea, and urged reports of prefects, speeches, &c., as proving rents sunk, price of land fallen, produce as four to six, population lessened, and the price of labour risen, &c. &c. The last no proof of decline.

Ryder, on corn, observed that the same fact of wheat being dearer in peace than in war is found in the French prices annexed to Arnold.[1]

They would not be introduced to Bonaparte. Fox had much conversation with him, and he plainly urged the fact that Wyndham was concerned in the infernal machine, asserting that he had the proof. Sir F. says that this proof was one George, being much

[1] Ambrose Marie Arnault, French economist, 1750–1812. See Vapereau.

with W., and afterwards going on the expedition to Quiberon. A party was taken amongst whose papers (on the arrests for the infernal machine) were letters on that conspiracy to or from George, which combination was Bonaparte's *proof*. The Government, [he says, is] the completest military despotism that ever was in the world.

At the theatre some Frenchmen finding Montagu was English, spoke much of me; and said they wanted of all things that I should come and examine France a second time under the new *régime*.

Dined with Swirenove, the Russian chaplain of the embassy, greatly employed by the nobility of that Empire in agricultural commissions. Patterson, bailiff to Lord Hardwicke, is going to Russia, and left me to make a bargain for him, which I did. He is to have 100 guineas first year, and increasing 20 yearly till 200 guineas; 60 for his son-in-law, and 20 for his daughter, and 25 for a ploughman. Count Rostopchin, at Woronowo, near Moscow, who has an immense estate, is the man. A Russian count there, Benwakin, I think, [he named] whose peasants pay him 30 roubles a year; but paper money so multiplied and at 50 per cent. discount, that all prices are greatly risen nominally. The Emperor's going to farm so largely has already had a great effect in turning the attention of the nobility to it. My annuity yesterday remitted from Ireland, 72*l*.[1] Thank God for that uninterrupted stream of His bounty which I have enjoyed of late years without let or

---

[1] See Chap. IV. 'Ireland,' for this curious bargain, by which A. Y., instead of a sum total of 700*l*., in 1776 was to receive 72*l*. per annum!

hindrance, and which my vile ingratitude returns so badly.

Lord Winchilsea called yesterday, and sat an hour with me. He is, I believe, one of the very best of the nobility, and a really respectable moral character, and benevolent to the poor.

August 22: *Bradfield.*—Here is a blank of many weeks, which shows once more how difficult it is to keep journal resolutions. After a long tour in Norfolk, which would have afforded much pleasure had not business occupied all my time, I met Betsy and O. at Harleston, on the 9th.

War much talked of. The militia calling out. These things, whatever the event, are certainly God's providences. His will be done. But when I consider the almost universal vice and iniquity of the kingdom, the amazing protection and blessings which have been showered down on us, and the vile ingratitude to God which pervades all ranks in an utter forgetfulness of Him, or contempt of His judgments, I must own I tremble at the thought.

I have lived some time without making a will, which has been very wrong. I am under such complex settlements that I do not understand what power I have; and Gotobed's draft was so full of law jargon, that I understand nothing of it. I wait no longer, but have made one plain and simple, and such as I hope, with the blessing of God, will not nor can be misunderstood. I have disposed of what I have to the best of my conscience, that is, if I was to die at Christmas.

Here is only 300*l.* to be made up by sale of timber, 'Annals,' &c. &c., but a farm auction would produce more than 900*l.*, and rents are always behind, some over due. I pray to God for better economy, and much hope, by a fresh and careful attention to my farm and 'Annals,' to bring things speedily to a better account.

I forgot 100*l.* due to me from the Board for Norfolk Report, so that I evidently leave enough for all demands, probably without cutting any timber.

I have never lived so well with Mrs. Young as for five weeks past.

War! To look into futurity is idle. The event is in the Lord's hand, and will depend on the number and piety of true Christians amongst us, and not be governed by fleets and armies. France is so unprepared at sea, that no war ever opened in that respect with better prospects. But this is the arm of flesh, and may mark the vanity of all trust in such circumstances.

The following letter to A. Y. may fitly close the chronicle of this year:

'Drinkstone: Dec. 8, 1803.

'Sir,—A letter from Lord Euston to Sir Charles Davers recommends that in case of invasion all horses and draft cattle that cannot be driven out of the reach of the enemy be shot; and that all the axle-trees or wheels of all carriages likely to fall into the enemy's hands be broken, the fullest assurance being given of complete indemnification, provided no horses, draft cattle, or carriages of any description fall into their hands through negligence or want of proper exertion on the part of the owners.

'All other stock is to be left for the use of the troops, unless there be evident danger it may fall into the invader's hands, in which case the measures formerly determined upon must be resorted to.

'I am, Sir,
'Your obedient humble servant,
'JOSHUA GRIGBY.'

CHAPTER XV

APPROACHING BLINDNESS

1804—1807

A great preacher—Arthur Young the younger goes to Russia—Cowper's Letters—Mrs. Young's illness—Dr. Symonds—Novel reading—Skinner's 'State of Peru'—Death of Pitt—Burke's publishing accounts—Literary projects—Approaching blindness.

February 24.—The sins of a journal are like those of life, much offence and a little repentance, minutes applied and months neglected. Last night, for the first time in my life, I was at a religious conversazione. Mr. Fry has it once a fortnight.

Mrs. Wilberforce and thirty more, I suppose, began with singing a hymn, and then a prayer, and ended in the same manner; the subject discussed was Providence. Scott, Macaulay, and Fry were the only speakers except myself, who threw in a word or two in a bad manner and not in unison; but I went without preparing the temper of my mind, and it proved to me a mere temptation to sin, as everything is sure to do when we trust in our own strength and do not pray for divine assistance. I like the thing itself much, and the recollection since it passed has produced in my mind a degree of humiliation which might not have been in it had I not gone there. I wished to touch on the state of the King's health, where the hand of God is so evident; but they would attend only to little and private things, and probably were right. They made every possible event, the most trivial, providential. Scott is a predestinarian, but impresses the necessity of attending to the *means* by which God acts as much as if the divine decrees were not universal. The next subject is Temptation.

May 22.—My dear friend [1] at Bradfield writes me in a most melancholy strain, on the ill success of her husband's farming. I doubt I shall lose largely by a scheme which was executed merely to keep him out of greater mischief.

The new Bishop of Bristol is in dress and manners much like what we call in Suffolk a leather breeches parson.

Somebody called on Mrs. Pelham, and found her lying on a sofa reading a novel, rouged as much as any Madame la Marquise. They thought she seemed to be too high flown to be asked to a sober party of whist. What a gradation of evil amongst the worldly even in the *respectable* (*soi-disant*) class.

An application from Phillips for another edition of the 'Farmer's Calendar.' He printed 2,000 of the fifth, and 1,200 sold in a month; they will all be gone before it can be reprinted. I had 100*l*. for that edition, 40*l*. more for this six months after publication, and in future 25*l*. each succeeding one.

How grateful I ought to be, but am not, to God for a success which has smoothed many difficulties, and enabled me much to lessen, in assistance to other cir-

[1] Mrs. Oakes.

cumstances, my debts. The sale is an extraordinary one.

What would be with me the result of moral reflections and trust in human means, in the power of a vile heart to cure its own iniquities? I have a conviction amounting to sensation in its truth, that everything but looking unto Jesus is weaker than water—vain and frivolous. This is the grand consideration, result, and object of religion in the soul, all beside is wide of the mark and without power and efficacy. Oh, my God, my God! write these truths in my soul, impress them in my heart, that by communion with Thee I may by Thy grace be purified, washed, and cleansed from every evil thought. Blessed be Thy Holy Name for keeping me from *acts* of sin. Oh! have mercy on my mind and take away every *thought* of it.

I shall have to experience another temptation, and should be preparing for it. I have little doubt but Lord Carrington will be again President of the Board. He likes not me, and I shall be much more uncomfortable than I have been with Lord Sheffield; but such changes, if they happen, will be from the Lord, for nothing is so idle as for a Christian to suppose that anything takes place by chance.

I do not mean to leave town till the Woburn meeting, but I am restless, and want to get away. This is a common folly, and ought carefully to be checked. It is the spirit that wastes half a life, ever looking to a future moment and never enjoying the present, which is that alone that is truly our own.[1]

[1] This recalls Goethe's line, 'Der Augenblick ist Ewigkeit.

There is not a more valuable lesson than to learn how to apply every portion of time to use, and not to suffer the expectation of, or waiting for, any future moment to make the intermediate ones tiresome or unpleasant. It is wasting life and time that is never to return.

Yesterday, at 7 P.M., I dined with Mr. Anson—a farming party : Duke of Bedford, Earl of Galloway, Earl of Albemarle, Lord Somerville, Sir Robert Lowley, Sir John Wrottesley, Mr. Coke, Mr. Motteaux, Mr. Child, Sir G. Pigot, Mr. Western, Mr. Wilbraham, all M.P.'s or in high life.

Nothing but a farming conversation makes the company of these people proper for me to have anything to do with; and that it is not to be conceived how little they know on the subject, considering it's a favourite pursuit. Such great fortunes and a life of luxury and bustle and motion are hostile to every kind of knowledge; and the conversation abounds with information for those who watch for and have a memory to retain it, yet it demands a good deal of knowledge previously digested and arranged to make a due use of it. A splendid house, one of the best in London; magnificent furniture, plate, servants, wines, and everything, equal to 30,000*l.* or 40,000*l.* a year, but he has no such income.

I have—I think I have—no envy of these doings. Such situations are so hostile to the religious principle that ought to animate the soul, that I should think of them with fear and trembling. I hate parties, and my heart condemns me whenever I go to them, in which

not a word ever occurs to give God the glory due to
His Holy Name, which is sometimes profaned but
never honoured, where Grace before and after meat is
discarded. And this is a sort of denial of Christ which
gives me no slight disquiet and remorse, and ought
entirely to banish me from all such company; it works
in me, and I cordially hope it will soon produce that
effect, for the pleasure I receive is little and the offence
to God I fear is much. 'Come out from among them
and touch not the unclean thing,' is applicable to more
cases than I have applied it to. I am determined to go
only to Woburn this year and not to Holkham; four
days of noise and bustle are too much, I will get away
in three; but a whole fortnight is horrible. I will get
to Cambridge by Saturday, and I hope Jane will meet
me there to spend Sunday, and perhaps Monday, with
Simeon, and make him promise to meet Fry at Bradfield. Yesterday and this day hurry, bustle, packing up,
paying bills, and recollection on the stretch lest anything
should be forgotten. Wrote to Cordell, the bookseller,
to settle with me for the Irish Tour. It has been years
out of print, and the last settlement in 1795. I have
half the sale; 154 were then left, my half, 30*l.* at least,
and it never came into my head before. Very careless
indeed, and in money to receive! Such busy days are
unpleasant because both mind and body are fatigued.

18*th* at Woburn. Came with Lord Sheffield yesterday. I detest this profanation of the Sabbath, but he
urged me so to accompany him that I yielded like a
fool. A great dinner, Lords Albemarle, Ossory, Ludlow,
Duke of Manchester, Sir H. Fetherstone, Sir R. Pigot,

the Wilbrahams, &c., twenty in all. Several apartments newly furnished, and many very expensive articles, clocks, &c., from Paris to the amount of 2,000*l*. Much done to the greenhouse, and everywhere a profusion of expense. The late rains have given a fine verdure, and the place in full beauty. Such a flow of worldly blessings as are seen in one of these very great residences makes me melancholy when I reflect on the immense temptation and dreadful responsibility that attaches. What have not these people to answer for if they forget the Giver in the profusion of His gifts? and where am I to go to find a great house and establishment with a society and conversation that shows the Gospel of our Lord to be held in reverence and affection?

This poor Duke of Bedford, whose nominal income is so enormous, will, I fear, involve himself with the same imprudence. Cartwright has built him a steam engine (700*l*.) for threshing and grinding : 12 per cent. interest in the least to be calculated, or 84*l*., and yet a one-horse mill, price 50*l*., would thresh all the corn that will ever be brought to this yard.

An extravagant duchess, Paris toys, a great farm, little economy, and immense debts, will prove a canker in all the rosebuds of his garden of life. The providence of the Almighty governs all, and will not permit an utter forgetfulness of Him to produce even the temporal happiness which is alone sought for.

I am tired of the whole, and long for the retirement and quiet of Bradfield after so many weeks of London, and this finishing of hurry and bustle. I would not have another week of it for a hundred pounds. What has a Christian to do with such scenes ? How a person of fortune and the world can be one I know not. They are never cool, and have no time for reading or thought. It is madness to continue in such a state, but to travel 120 miles in order to enter a fresh scene of it, and perhaps within earshot of such a profane beast and fool as that Captain G. I sat near last year—this would be insanity. What a spectacle at Woburn was that miserably swearing profligate, Major B., of Sussex, at the age of eighty-one, sticking to the last moment to worldly dissipation, and utterly regardless of what is to become of him hereafter. Like Lord Lauderdale, who declared that he feared nothing in this world nor in the next either! These people call themselves Deists; I think they must be atheists, or they are utterly in contradiction to themselves. It is a sin, and ought to be repented of, to go into such company. I feel myself here, looking on the tranquil bosom of the Ouse, as having escaped from a multiplicity of temptations, and that this is the first moment of my summer holidays, quiet and alone. This morning I had a letter from Jane, by which I find it is quite uncertain whether I shall meet her at Cambridge. She asks my directions, but had she thought, must have known that she could not receive an answer in time. I hope to hear Simeon [1] twice on Sunday, and much wish that she may be there, as I wrote before to request it; and she says she should like it of all things.

[1] Ch. Simeon, 1759-1836, an eminent divine of the Evangelical school. His works, consisting of 2,536 sermons, &c., were published in twenty-one volumes in 1832.

24th : Cambridge.—I dined here yesterday. Inquired for that great and good man, Simeon, but he was not to be in town till the evening. I walked behind Trinity and John's, &c., twice—a delightful day. Wrote and left a letter for him; at nine he came, and will certainly meet Fry at Bradfield. Thank God! I shall hear him twice to-day and Mr. Thomason once, for I shall go thrice to Trinity Church. I mentioned Fry's calculation of three millions of Christians; but he very properly thought it very erroneous. He thinks Cambridge a fair average, and in 10,000 people knows but of 110 certainly vital Christians—more than 150 can scarcely be from a seventy-fifth to a hundredth part therefore! There are, I am rejoiced to hear it, many very pious young men in the colleges.

Night.—I have been at Trinity Church thrice to-day. In the morning a very good sermon by Simeon, a decent one by Thomason, and in the evening to a crowded congregation a superlative discourse by Simeon on the twelfth verse of chapter iv. of the Acts : ' There is no other name under heaven,' &c. Vital, evangelical, powerful, and impressive in his animated manner.

Sunday, July 8 : *Bradfield.*—This day se'nnight took the Sacrament with Jane at Bury, suddenly, and therefore without any preparation, and got there in the Lessons. The week has been vile and miserable. Fry cannot come, but had a letter from Simeon, he will be here to-morrow! O Lord, of Thy mercy give a blessing to his presence, that conversation and prayer with him may give a turn to my mind! Were it not for what I think a firm faith in the Cross of my Redeemer, I should think that I was almost in the jaws of hell. But if I perish it shall be looking at the brazen serpent. Fiery serpents innumerable bite ; let me turn instantly to the Cross, and there see and trust to the blood of sprinkling. What should I have thought of this before my conversion ? Is it true and saving faith now to think and feel it—or rather to know it in my understanding than feel it in my heart ? I am full of apprehensions, and the only sign of spiritual life in me is some sense and feeling of my own iniquity and the plague of my carnal thoughts ; but if they were truly a load to me, would not the Lord ease me of the burden ?

10*th*.—Yesterday, Simeon came. His character singular. His piety—his strong expressions—his fervency in prayer—a powerful mind !

13*th*.—Simeon went this morning. I have been horribly negligent in not writing down many of his conversations. What he thinks of me I know not, but he spoke to Jane with great freedom and candour, and as became a good Christian.

His abilities are considerable, his parts strong, his ardour and animation uncommonly great. His eloquence great, and his manner impressive. His prayers admirably adapted to the cases of all who heard him. He came with a servant and two very fine horses, on which he places a high value. From his life and expenses must have a considerable income ; for his preferment is only expense, and costs him more than he receives from it. His fellowship is as good as 400 guineas a year to him. He must have a very good private fortune, from some circumstances, as I judge, which he dropped in conversation. He went to Cambridge from Eton and became a Christian on the third day, now about twenty-five or twenty-six years ago. During all which time he has never doubted of his future salvation. He is remarkably cheerful and has much wit, or something nearly allied to it.

I wrote to N. H., requesting his pulpit for Sunday, but he refused it; and after church apologised, saying it was not from himself, but he was *talked to*.

Oh! for the dumb dogs of our clergy who will neither preach the Gospel themselves nor let others do it. I told him that my request was to him a safe one, for I asked, of course, only for a regularly bred clergyman, and who possessed preferment in the national church. Very unlucky! Symonds dined here, and his conversation never does any good. He explained his chance for salvation in the merits alone of Jesus Christ, but denies original sin. This seems a contradiction; I would not think so for a thousand worlds! How can he be sensible of what he wants in the blood of the Saviour without knowing the utter depravity of his heart?

Tuesday morning, C. Coke, of Holkham, Allen, and Moore called on me to see the farm, and would have me dine with them at Moore's. Haunch of venison, &c. Mrs. M. young, and in the worldly sphere very agreeable; her dress horrid. She contrives to force out her prominent bust in a manner that must take no small attention in dressing, is very big with child, and thinly clad; such a figure is common in these times, but the fashion is contrived purposely.

Mr. Smirenove came last night to dinner, and

brought Count Rostopchin's snuff-box. It is turned in his own oak, lined with gold, and has a tablet containing the representation of a building dedicated to me. The inscription in Russian, *A Pupil to his Master*, set round with sixty-six diamonds. Query—Should not all such toys be turned into money and given to the poor? He was Prime Minister under Paul, and has 50,000*l.* English per annum.

On Monday I breakfasted, dined, and slept at Lord Bristol's; Lady B. and her sister, Miss Upton, sung Italian airs till twelve o'clock at night. They were many years ago a horrible temptation, now [they are] a frivolous waste of time, but ever a bad tendency on the heart. Pressed me greatly to stay; but I was engaged next day to dinner at Gooch's, and yesterday I dined at Betsy's. All this visiting is very bad for my soul.

Friday I dined again at Lord Bristol's, by desire of the Oakes, as they expected meeting none they knew, but there were several. Music in the evening, slept there; in the morning, at Bury, met Benjafield on justice business. He wanted to commit a woman for being a lewd woman, on the statute of King James, by which it can only be for a year; if this was executed, all the prisons in the county would not hold them, and the time is far too severe; nor do I conceive that the case comes within it. I declined, and desired they might be heard on Wednesday, as appeared the week before. I go on in repentance miserably, my heart is cold, and I am languid in devotion. Oh, could I sufficiently hate and abhor myself!!

November 2.—If I go ten yards from home it can

be only into the world, and therefore I never move but for mischief. I have every post a packet of letters from Lord Sheffield, filling the tables and for many hours employment every day. There seems to be no great reason for apprehending any famine, or even such a scarcity as before, but the price must be too high for the poor, without being half high enough for the farmer: I mean of wheat, the crop of which is full as bad as it has been for ten years past, but there is a stock in hand which will keep it down.

December 30.—I went to London on account of the Smithfield Club and there received the first Bedford medal of the Bath Society for an essay on the Nature and Properties of Manures, there being four other candidates. At London also I dined with M. de Novosilikoff, a particular friend of the Emperor Alexander, who is here on a political mission of great importance.

Davidson, who manages the Emperor's farm, and Smirenove were present; their plan at present is to have reports of their Governments made upon the same system as ours, of counties, and Mr. de N. talked much of the great advantage of my going. I would not offer myself, but said that the whole would depend on the sort of men employed. Since I came down I wrote to Smirenove, offering Arthur (by his own desire), provided the sum granted for the purpose was adequate.

De N. was out of town, so no answer yet.

The attention I give to all these worldly matters, though they do not sit at all close to my heart, yet occupy too much of my time.

I do not give enough to the far greater interests

of the eternal world; and I have been for months past, and am at present, in a dead, sinful state, remote from the only God of hope and consolation.

His mercy to me is great, for I have life and health. I am not in hell; but I find a horrible difficulty in coming to God, and a deadness of heart which hurts my prayers and plunges me more and more in sin and offence.

O Lord, of Thy mercy listen unto me. Oh! look with compassion on my wretchedness.

1805. *Jan.* 30.—The 19th I came to London; the 23rd breakfasted with Mr. Novosilikoff, and made my proposals of terms on which Arthur would go to Russia, having before received a letter from Smirenove announcing an entire approbation in Mr. N. of my son for the expedition. The terms were that he and his wife should go by land, getting out hence the beginning of March, in order to be at Moscow the beginning of May; that is, if out a year he should have a thousand pounds, and proportionably for a longer time, and all his expenses paid to, at, and from Russia. He came into it readily, and when the conversation was over, Mr. Davidson, who was present, said, 'Well, now it seems all settled, and it only remains to know where Mr. Y. is to be supplied with money for his journey.' Mr. de N. said Mr. Smirenove would be directed to advance it.

Reflecting afterwards on this conversation, I thought that some admission of the terms in writing should be obtained, as in case of deaths or revolutions they might be questioned; I therefore wrote to Mr. de N., recapitulating the terms on both sides and begging to know if I was correct.

No answer was returned; but Lord Somerville, calling on me two days after, mentioned in conversation that he had recommended a Mr. Green, who had farmed in Normandy, and been seven years in a French prison, of which he had published an account, to Mr. de N. to go to Russia to survey a government, hinting at the same time his knowledge that my son was in contemplation also. He said that G. had breakfasted with de N., who was much pleased with him.

All this awakens suspicions in my mind that, combined with the silence of Mr. de N., make it apparently necessary to know how we really stand, and I determined to write to Smirenove requesting that he would speak to Mr. de N., as any uncertainty was unpleasant, while my son was actually arranging his farm, &c., for his departure. This I have now done, and shall send it before breakfast, for no answer is yet come.

I do not like the complexion of the business, but think it likely that Green speaking French, which will save the necessity of Jane going as an interpreter, and perhaps his taking one or two hundreds instead of 1,000*l.*, may have induced de N. to think again of the matter.

I have prayed earnestly to the Lord that He would prevent the journey taking place if it would turn out in any way injurious to the state of their souls, putting the matter entirely in His Almighty hands, and determining to rest assured that if it does not take place, it will be the Lord's will, and that I should be thankful for His interference to prevent it.

The government of Moscow which A. was to have done is thirteen times as big as Norfolk. It would take two years to do it well without any doubt. A. is much disappointed, for he liked the thoughts of the scheme much.

I threw out in conversation with N. that if the business of the Board would permit, and they approved it, I would go over in June, and stay till November to assist in the work; that I should ask only my expenses. He seemed much to approve of this, but it was mentioned only as a contingency. Here the matter rests. I shall know soon what the event will be.

Many things have had a very lowering aspect of late, the 'Annals' with Phillips are certainly at an end. They do not answer with him, and he has demurred at settling the account, with 100*l.* or more due to me. This will be a loss of 180*l.* a year. My plan is to print four numbers a year on my own account, for the sake of selling old stock; by this I shall lose 40*l.* more. In Ar.'s (Arthur's) farm the rent will be sunk from last Michaelmas 20*l.* a year, and I am engaged to pay Noxford 20*l.* a year more tithe. This year the Exchequer annuity of 150*l.* a year ceases.

On the whole here is full 400*l.* a year loss of income, which will be very distressing if every expenditure be not pared down in a most economical manner. May the Lord's mercy give me grace to be steady and determined in this matter, for it is a most important one. I have very little to suffer personally in the reduction, for the expenses do not run that way, but comforts must be cheerfully lessened.

Feb. 3.—No answer came from Novosilikoff; I wrote therefore to Smirenove, who replied last Friday that N. was gone to St. Petersburg, that he had replied to my letter, and was surprised that I had not received it; that he approved of all the contents of mine, and had left orders with him to supply money.

This I despatched to A., who was become very uneasy and impatient. So now the business seems concluded and the die cast, but may the Lord prevent it taking place if it is to be productive of evil to the eternal interests of either! I pray for this, may He hear my prayers. I have little notion of comfort in anything that is undertaken without consulting God, opening the business to Him, and begging His direction how to proceed. I have had a letter from Orbell's[1] friend, who agrees to my terms of letting Ar.'s farm, so, thank God, that is settled.

17th.—Many difficulties have occurred relative to a post-chaise for them. Brown has examined my old one and sent an estimate of the repairs, 56*l*. Smirenove approved of it, but his second advice is that it would not do. He proposed one of his, and letters backwards and forwards. But yesterday I found one at Holmes's in Long Acre, built for a Mr. Lock to go to Malta, which will do exactly, and in which they may have bedding and sleep at full length; a journeyman said the price was 50 guineas. H. not at home, in the evening a letter, and 70 guineas named.

[1] Orbell Oakes, husband of 'my friend,' the beautiful Betsy.

I got up as always at 4 A.M., and have been reading and praying. Fry last Sunday alluded to an apostate from the truth, and Wilberforce asked him who it was, saying that of course he would not answer if the question was improper.

It was Townsend,[1] of Wiltshire, the traveller in Spain, who began his career quite in the style of Whitfield's energy and openness of declaring his principles in the fields or in barns, &c. The Lansdown folks told him they could never make him a bishop with such conduct or such principles; upon which he dropped the whole, giving out to his friends that he only suspended his conduct and meant to resume it at a better season. That never came, and he has continued an apostate from all religion, and from having 200 communicants at his church, has now only two or three besides himself and his clerk.

This miserably constituted Board of Agriculture is ever in a dilemma when a new president is to be elected. Lord S. will keep it no longer, and he is in a difficulty to propose another. He has written to the Duke of Bedford, and I fear in a way that may make the duke suppose that Government approves of it. Lord Carrington I suspected intended to come in again, but he assures me that he would not.

March 3.—I borrowed of Mr. Wilberforce, Owen[2] on 'Indwelling Sin,' to which are annexed two other

[1] J. Townsend, 1740–1816, English divine, and author of *A Journey through Spain*, 2nd edit. 1792.

[2] John Owen, D.D., 1616–1683, the great Nonconformist divine who accompanied Cromwell to Scotland. In 1817 A. Y. published *Oweniana* (or selections from his works).

essays on Temptation and the Mortification of Sin in Believers. The last work is incomparable, chapter ix. of it perhaps the most useful paper ever written. I have made many extracts from all three. The essay on Mortification I meditate printing a new edition of, being out of print, to which I could add notes that might be useful. The reading these treatises has had an effect on my mind which I hope, with the blessing of the grace of God, will produce a more serious attention to the state of my heart with God than reading any book has done since Wilberforce's.

April 20.—At Bradfield. Yesterday returned from Harwich. Arthur and Jane went on board the 'Diana' packet, Capt. Stewart, Thursday, the 18th, at 3 o'clock, and I have taken a long and melancholy farewell of them! Oh! may Almighty God give His blessing to the undertaking, and that we may all meet again in health and happiness. But when the fearful uncertainty of all earthly events is considered, such partings ought to be more melancholy than they are. She felt much, and has a cordial affection for me.

The undertaking, thus employed by a foreign sovereign to make a report of one of his provinces, is the first thing of the kind that has occurred, and will either give Arthur a great reputation, or sink that which he has gained. It is a very difficult work, however, to produce a good book from a very ill-cultivated province, and in the large experience of all our own reports we see that very few are well executed; the object has either been ill understood or poorly done, the surveyors deal in reflections instead of giving the experience of individuals, yet the husbandry of a county is made up of nothing else but private exertions. They do not half travel [over] the districts, and do not take notes of the practice of one hundredth part of those persons that might be applied to. Arthur goes with every possible advantage except languages, I hope he will exert them.

Bradfield is very melancholy without them. Jane was always cheerful, always affectionate and kind to me, ever pleased with my presence, and never parted from me but with regret. The loss of such a friend with much conversation and an excellent understanding nothing human can make amends for. It is a loss that ought to turn all my attention and all my heart to that better world where parting, sorrow, and death will find no place.

24th.—Last night I slept at Bury, at the Oakes', having walked there in the morning and dined with them. It raised my low spirits a little—but badly—for such company is mere dissipation.

On Monday morning, hankering after some sort of dissipation to divert my melancholy, I fortunately recollected that Jane had left Cowper's Letters, and that I had not read the third volume. I got it, and beginning knew not how to lay the book out of my hand, and before night read the volume through. There is an uncommon charm in his sentiments and his style; something that interests the heart wonderfully. The religious passages are peculiarly valuable, and a few struck me very much.

On the Sabbath he is extremely just. On turning

the mind from creation's beauties to creation's Author, the observation is fine; his remarks on the life of dissipation at Brighton, beautiful; on religion, page 106, on local attachments, on familiar communion with God, on natural music, terminated by a most sublime passage—' There is somewhere in infinite space a world that does not roll within the precincts of mercy; and as it is reasonable and even scriptural to suppose that there is music in heaven, in those dismal regions perhaps the reverse of it is found. Tones so dismal as to make woe itself more insupportable, and to acuminate even despair!' What a striking thought! But how many are there that will believe in neither hell nor devil, and what must their belief and feelings be who, closing their ears here, open them to the sounds of such a world as that! How many passages do we meet with in great authors which seem sufficient to strike a reader's mind to conviction and conversion; yet read by thousands, perhaps admired, without the smallest effect on the heart.

25th.—A Mr. Cole called here to ask about passports for Russia. He has hired 30,000 acres in the province of Minsk, which he is to have with 300 boors, paying half the profits as rent. He was advised not to take a grant of land, as it would cause a difficulty after it to quit Russia. I must caution Arthur about this, for he may entangle himself without being aware of it. In the melancholy, solitary moments I pass here, I have been thinking of the many blessings the Almighty has been graciously pleased to shower down upon me. First, He gives me great health, at sixty-four, as good as at any time for twenty years past, and much better than forty years ago. Secondly, He has been pleased to leave me two children. Oh, that He would call them to feel truly His faith, fear, and love! Thirdly, He has granted me an ample income very far beyond what I had, upon entering the world, the smallest reason to expect. I have many doubts of money ever being a blessing, but that is owing to the receiver and not to the giver, it certainly is that which might be made by grace a very considerable one. Fourthly, He has given me the power of being greatly useful to my country; it would be foolish not to reckon that which I know beyond the possibility of vanity deceiving me. Fifthly, He has given me a paternal estate and residence which I greatly love and never wish to change. I could go on and reckon many other things, but these are sufficient to call for a heartfelt and deeply abiding gratitude. I ought to be able to add, that I am miserable for want of feeling this as I should do; in truth I am in this respect a brute beast devoid of everything that marks the Christian and the penitent. O Lord, of Thy mercy soften this obdurate heart by the grace of Jesus Christ! Fill it with contrition for offences. Purify and renew it, bring it in holy faith to the foot of the Cross, and make it feel its iniquities, till it be changed and impressed with Thy holy image.

26*th*.—I read the concluding entry of yesterday, and it struck me that I had not thanked God for the friends He had given me, and this made me muse for a while. Had I wrote before I became serious, how warmly should I have thanked Him on this score!

How it is with others I know not, but with me religion has cooled, checked, or annihilated those feelings; real friendship cannot be felt by a Christian but to a Christian.

What surprises me much more is that I do not feel any very striking advantage from the society of Christians. This I attribute as a fault in myself, and dare say it is for want of more grace and prayer. I love their company, and, some hankerings apart, desire no other. I hope with God's blessing to improve in this respect—hitherto solitude has been my best friend. Here there are none to be acquainted with but a very few poor people who are never at their ease with me; and at London those I know are too much engaged to see many more than for a moment. Going to bed at nine o'clock prevents the society I might otherwise have there if it were followed up.

28*th*.—Symonds slept here the night before last and dined twice, which obliged me to postpone more business than I otherwise should have done. He told me one anecdote I had not heard before. In Lord Bute's administration, as his lordship told him himself, the King settled with him to give the Royal Society 500*l*. a year for ever, which was accordingly communicated, and to Lord Bute's amazement refused. On enquiry he found that the motive was an apprehension that he should become too popular if it was accepted! Was ever such folly heard of?

Another anecdote of Symonds. He dined last year at Sir C. Bunbury's, where he met the rich Mr. Mills, the brandy merchant, who bought Mure's estate, and who said he found my 'Annals' there, which were good for nothing. 'What, nothing good in them?' said S. 'No, nothing at all.' 'That is unfortunate with so many correspondents. But if the "Annals" are bad, have you read Mr. Y.'s travels?' 'Yes, and very poor stuff they are.' 'That is still more unfortunate, for I know that the Marshal de Castries and the late King of Prussia spoke in the highest possible terms of them, and books in French by respectable writers have been dedicated to Mr. Y. in consequence of that publication.' 'I can see nothing in them.'

The next day he wrote Symonds a letter with many apologies, as he understood that he had been talking to a gentleman who had contributed much to the 'Annals.'

So much for my rich neighbour.

Letters from London, and I am very sorry to find that my poor wife is much worse. Nothing but bad news. Sir J. Banks writes me that Sir J. Sinclair is to resume the chair of the Board under promises of good behaviour. My wife's miserable state is a much worse business.

May 22.—I am entirely alone and not without melancholy. Worldly people have a thousand resources, as I had once, but every atom of them leads to mischief, and I am a thousand times better without them. Lord Carrington the other day, speaking to Sir C. Willoughby about his son going to school, said, 'Oh, send him to a great one, which will give him a manly character fit for the world, make him a man of the world.' So it is with these people; Jesus Christ tells us to hate the world, and that what is in high estimation amongst men is abomination in the eyes of God; but worldly men declare, and think, and feel, and act, directly hostile to Scripture; they urge one another and impress as respectable everything that God abhors. Words cannot express a character more in contradiction to the Christian than that which is meant by a *man of the world*.

23rd.—I was awake at 2 A.M. and laid without sleep till 3 A.M. My thoughts were not edifying, so I jumped out of bed, and having prayed to the Father of mercies, I began with business. But the train of thought I had been in came again and interrupted me; it was upon the event of what would befall me as secretary to the Board. I have many reasons for thinking that several of the members do not like me, and should anything happen that gave them any handle, would be glad to get rid of me. This was not the case when I was one of themselves, but they know that I associate with religious people, go to the Lock (a very black mark), and read the Bible, and now and then words drop which I understand. Should Sir J. Sinclair become president or Lord Carrington, they might make it very unpleasant to me. Sir John is as poor as a church mouse, and would like well to have his lodging here. Should my family lessen, it would be quite unbearable, and if the idea was started, I must resist it, the question would probably be lost, and then I should resign; this would fix me in repose at Bradfield, and I should be to the full as happy as at present, but my family would not, and then—all this is very wild. I will have done with it for so much as I am persuaded that everything is in the hands of God; nothing can be greater folly than pretending thus to look forward, it is equally useless and uncomfortable.

June 3.—Since the last entry I have had letters from Jane and Arthur at Berlin, where they seemed to have stayed a week. They had been received with great politeness and attention by the Princess of Holstein, Prince Baratinsky's mother; had dined with her, and she carried them to her villa; they had dined also with the English and Russian Ambassadors, and been at Charlottenburg with Sir G. Rumbold.

I begin to be a little restless to get into the country.

15*th*.—Bradfield. I got here the 6th, earlier than ever before or since the institution of the Board, which is a great blessing. I have managed to escape both Woburn and Holkham.

I have missed Jane terribly, but I have endeavoured to turn it to a religious account. Poorly and weakly, but still better than not at all. The weather has been bad, which has caused my taking less exercise than is good for me, but blessed be God, my health is excellent.

I have stuck close to my great work the 'Elements,' and have gone through my own Norfolk report and the fourth volume of the Board 'Communications.' What an immense labour has it been, and for how many years to collect and arrange materials. I could not have conceived how much it is necessary to do before I can fairly say, Now all is before me and in order, ready to compare and draw conclusions.

I mean it to contain everything good that has ever been printed. Till all that is collected and before me, how can I know what is already done, and what wants to be added?

But the labour, when continued year after year, is what I never dreamt of when I began. I have worked hard at the first division—*Soils*, and brought it into some form; and it is a specimen of how much attention every division will demand. I have also began the second, on Vegetation. I fear making the work too voluminous, and that by-and-by I must curtail greatly. Success is pleasant, and I should fear that if it exceeded two large quartos.

Since I have been here I have read a little work of Flavel's,[1] 'A Saint indeed,' which is truly admirable; some [passages] in Marshall[2] on ' Sanctification,' and very many of Cowper's letters, all the religious ones.

18*th*.—Cowper is invaluable to a country gentleman that would enjoy his residence without the world's assistance. Reading his letters has made me more attentive to every beauty of this place, of which I was always so fond; there is something very amiable in the manner in which he converts every flower, tree, and twig to enjoyment, and I walk out better prepared for this pleasure from the perusal of that most agreeable writer. There is but one danger from which, poor man, his poverty secured him, and that is the mind insensibly running into speculation of improvement. I have

---

[1] John Flavel, Nonconformist divine, 1627-1662, author of numerous works.

[2] By Walter Marshall, 1692; frequently reprinted.

made many here, and the taste is very insatiable; this may without a guard lead to too much expense. But I endeavour to correct the wanderings of imagination, and to dwell on the beauties of every single tree, shrub, and spot, and to be content with them all as they are. The laburnum in the back lawn is more beautiful than I ever saw it, so entirely covered with rich clusters of its golden flowers, that I can admire it for an hour together. This enjoyment, however, is very poor and fading if we do not, with Cowper, turn our minds habitually to the great and beneficent Author of all these beauties. This sentiment is impressive and durable, and leads the mind to the richest contemplations. If for such a race the earth is thus clothed, what must heaven be?

A reading habit is a great blessing. I am sure I find it so, for though I have risen at 3 A.M. since I have been here, and not once been in bed at four, still I am not tired at night. A walk is a refreshment to be had in the country in a moment, but at London half a mile of street thronged and noisy, and then only a crowded park, with sights to wound or to tempt. I do not like snow, but a deep one and blustering wind here is preferable to calm sunshine in the streets of London.

But much as I like Bradfield even alone, I must leave it and get quickly into Essex. I could write the Report from materials before me, and from a long knowledge of the county, and produce a valuable work, but that would not be honest. I shall take their money, and will therefore travel as much in it, and give as much attention to it, as if I had no materials at all to work upon.

August 12.—Letters from Jane and Arthur at St. Petersburg. They give sad accounts of the treatment the English have received there if most specific agreements be not made beforehand for everything. I wish cordially they were well home again, and so do they, I believe.

October 20.—At Rayleigh. To keep a journal in this manner is nonsense, and worse than nonsense; besides, I have time to do better, and therefore ought to do it.

Three nights past I slept at the Earl of St. Vincent's, who, being a great character, forces a note. I had much inclination to have called on him, as I heard of Sir T. Leonard that he farmed, but I thought it would be a forward step, and so passed on to the Squire of the parish, Towers. He was in with the gout, but his sons told me that they had lately dined in company of Lord St. V., who mentioned my being in the country, and that he expected to see me. Whence this expectation came I have no conception. He received me politely, pleasantly, and cordially; kept me all day to dinner and to sleep, and desired me if ever I came near him again to be sure to make his house my headquarters. He showed me every acre, cow, ox, and pig, and talked sensibly enough on farming, as far as he knew of it. When he returned he told me he did not dine till 6 P.M., and as he should be out again, I should have a fire in Lady St. V.'s dressing room, and a pen and ink, and that I was my own master. Montague Burgoyne coming, he sent him up to me. At and after dinner much political conversation, for Burgoyne is a desperate politician. It was plain that Lord St. Vincent thought himself very ill used by opposition as well as by Mr. Pitt; he seemed to think that they made a great cry about him while it served their own purpose, but that when this would not answer, they cared little for him and forgot him, but he praised Lord Sidmouth greatly. Burgoyne, who wanted Fox in when Lord Sidmouth accepted, told Lord St. V. the only sin he ever committed was joining that lord, as he could not have made an administration without him. He said it was impossible to resist, the state of the country was such that his conscience would have condemned him; it was greatly to his personal injury, for he was, as commander of the Channel fleet, in the receipt of a good 25,000*l.* a year, which he gave up for a miserably paid Cabinet place then of only 3,000*l.* That the King urged him to keep the command with the Admiralty, and Lord Sidmouth agreed to it, but he would not do it, it would have been wrong. The King urged the precedent of Lord Howe, who kept both, and why should not he? But he was firm. He hates all religions, called Lord Barham an old canting hypocrite—all of them—and 'little Wilberforce too!' I said something against that, but not half enough. He remarked that the old hypocrite would soon, very soon, be removed. I hope in this he will find himself mistaken. He swears pretty much, not quite as sailors do, but he says grace before and after dinner; is not this hypocrisy? He has great spirits, a good understanding, and is very pleasant.

December 9.—My old friend Symonds being dangerously and in all probability fatally ill, I went yesterday to see him. I was there four hours. He dozed much, but when awake had the perfect use of his faculties, though not quite speech enough or recollection to explain himself as when well; my dear Jane took him to be a real Christian, though not without thinking he had bad notions on certain points. I ever doubted it, and thought I saw much in him of sound, good doctrine, but great deficiencies.

He utterly disbelieved original sin, which appeared always to me a fatal sign.

He talked to me of Naples, Bonaparte, &c., said he had something *particular* to say to me, upon which B. left the room. It was to tell me that Cocksedge would not give 40*l.* for a very well done map and survey of the Eldo estate, and that therefore he should take care that he should have nothing done to accommodate him, no part of the furniture should be his, &c. *This will be talked of,* and therefore mention the motive. What stuff to occupy the attention of a dying man! I took four or five opportunities, or rather made them, to turn his mind to Christ, but they passed, and he was silent, not one religious or serious word came out of his mouth, nothing of the kind seemed to be in his mind. He was in general quite easy and composed, and slept perfectly free from any apparent disturbance. Awful is such insensibility.

10*th.*—I was with him again yesterday, and through such a day of rain that I hope I shall not take cold. He was just the same, mentioned Casburn's account of the Blue Coat Hospital, and being washed four times a day;

talked of the water gods, smiled, and joked. I could not endure the moment passing without another attempt to turn his mind to more serious impressions. I asked C. if he had had any prayers said to and for him. No, he had not mentioned it, but two nights before he had prayed shortly for himself. I told him that there ought to be prayers in the room, and that C. could read them. He said, '*Yes, he could*,' and for the family also! It made no impression, and soon after closing his eyes as if for sleep, said, 'Your servant, I only keep you,' so I left him. I have fears that it is a sort of judicial blindness and insensibility of his state to have his senses and make no better use of them, I am much shocked.

11*th*.—Yesterday there again, but he was getting up to have his bed made, and White, the physician, thought I had better not go up.

January 10, 1806.—Peggy Metcalfe lent me 'Marie Menzikoff' as a true history, and I, like a fool, read much of it, after finding it a mere romance. I have not looked at anything of the novel kind for many years, but this French thing seized my attention and hurried me on. I wish she had been further before putting it in my hands. It has unhinged me, and broken my attention to better things, which shows strongly how pernicious this sort of reading is, and what a powerful temptation to vice such productions are sure to prove.

Oh! the number of miserables that novels have sent to perdition!

16*th*.—I have been looking over Dr. Johnson's 'Prayers and Meditations,' and, upon the whole, the feeling they have impressed is that of pity; he seemed by one passage to think his complaints nearly allied to madness, and often speaks of his morbid melancholy; his sloth seems to have been dreadful. What a contrast to the life of John Wesley!

His religion seems to have been against the very grain of his soul, and all the tendencies of his mind to have arisen from his understanding only, and never to have been truly in his heart. Company, and engagements, and indolence keep him from church from January to March; he scarcely ever got to it in time for the service, and he aimed in resolutions only at taking the Sacrament thrice in the year; he does not name a book (the Scriptures excepted) that was likely to give a right turn to his devotion. To study religion and to read the Scriptures was a matter for resolution, like rising early, but he does not seem to have been carried to the employment by the comfort, hope, joy, and consolation to be derived from them, they were never his pleasure. 'Tis well his mind was morbid, for he seems to me (from this work) never to have been really converted. Fasting, penance, and a gloomy superstition banished from his soul the felicities of piety founded in faith. But I must look it over again with more care. Yesterday morning I went to Flempton and called on Carter; with him I had some very proper conversation. He is far from the truly evangelical state, and his mind fully occupied with being satisfied with the opinions and conduct of the regular clergy in general; he has no affection, no regard for truly evangelical ones, a readiness to sneer at them, and with all a laxity in doctrines, a comprehensive *candour*, which gives me but an ill opinion of his doctrines. He is a very worthy respectable man in all worldly points.

My neighbour Gooch called yesterday. He has taken the curacy of Wattisfield of Plampin, who has evaded the curate's law. Gooch gave me twenty cases at least of rectors who decidedly cheat and impose on their curates by most unworthy evasions; but if a farmer cheats them of a turnip in tithe, they pronounce them all the rogues to be imagined. Most lamentable is this for those who should be the ministers of Christ's gospel.

But in no country that I have heard of is there such a set of clergy as in this neighbourhood. Dreadful!

I have been sketching out an essay on the defence of the kingdom in case of invasion, and yesterday added to it. The regularity with which I have made entries in my journal since I determined to write one line in it, shows the infinite importance of method and regularity in every pursuit and business of life. What is regularly undertaken will be regularly executed, but desultory endeavours at fits and starts perform nothing.

22*nd*.—Yesterday I went up into my dear Bobbin's room, in which I had not been for a year or more. I wiped the mould off her books, &c., with a heavy heart, and prayed to God that I might join her spirit in heaven. It made me very melancholy! She has been dead nine years, would therefore have been two-and-twenty had it pleased God to spare her. But what a world is this for a girl of that age!

23*rd*.—To-day I pack up and prepare, and to-morrow,

with God's permission, to London. May He protect me from all dangers! Mr. Pitt dead! This has struck a damp into my soul that I cannot shake off.

26th.—Arrived safely, thanks to the Lord. Yesterday I unpacked and set all my things in order. Mrs. Y. better than I expected, but I cannot perceive that warmth of gratitude to God which I hoped to find. I know not what to make of her state of soul! Pitt's death made a considerable sensation, and I wonder not at it. The providence of the Almighty has taken the two men perhaps the most necessary to our worldly prosperity in order to show us that it is on Him only we should depend, and to convince us that vain is the arm of flesh. May He protect us! Providence is better to depend on than a hundred Nelsons and Pitts if we consider them in any light except that of means in the hand of Him who governs the fate of nations.

Ministry not arranged. It is said that Fox is as much plagued with the apprehensions of some of his own people as with those of the Grenvilles. Grey First Lord of Admiralty! Is it possible? What a scheme!

Could not sleep longer for three nights past than half-past two or three; evil imaginations were generating. Plunged out of bed, but as I cannot get to bed before ten (at Lady Egremont's last night but one, and De Rees' last night) it makes me heavy. De Rees says that all foreigners agree as to the folly of our expeditions; that to the Mediterranean should have been in greater force to Venice, which would have preserved that city, and enabled the Archduke Charles to have stood his ground. It is obvious, if driven from the Continent, Venice at least would have been saved.

February 2.—I have seen Smirenove, he thinks his Emperor will have a great army on the Danube early in the spring, for preparations are active; they think, or have intelligence, that Bonaparte has ceded to Austria much more than Servia, probably large provinces, to cut Russia off from contact with the Turks. He has Trieste, and now his dominions embrace both shores of the Adriatic and join the Turkish Empire. This must be productive of great events, and I cannot but look forward to the destruction of that Empire which seems clearly advancing, and we all know how very important an epoch that will be towards the winding up of all things.

8th.—Mary dined with Lord Coventry, and met Mrs. Lyggon and Mrs. Nesbit, and heard that D. Moira will take nothing. He wanted to be Prime Minister, and the King would rather have had him. The Queen of Wurtemburg has written a letter to our Queen and to Lady Harrington in praise of the politeness and goodness of Bonaparte. De Rees in the evening; Fox was in powder, which made everyone stare.

14th.—Read much in Skinner's 'State of Peru,'[1] which has some curious things in it. I work every morning on my 'Elements,' but though I have been near thirty years reading and making extracts for this work (but with long intermissions), yet now I am arranging the chapters and sections I find numberless gaps to supply as I advance.

[1] Joseph Skinner, *Present State of Peru*, 1805.

15th.—Dined with the Duke of Grafton against my will, for I think it wrong to go to the house of a Unitarian, or have anything to do with them; the only defence of its lawfulness even that I know of is St. Paul's supposition of his converts being invited to a feast, and *if you are disposed to go*, &c., then do so. In the evening Walker, an engraver, who has been twenty years at St. Petersburg, and who brought letters from Jane some time ago, called. He gives but a bad account of Russia, and it is from every authority a very bad country to live in, in every respect that should make a country desirable, except the people being good tempered and very ingenious. England! England! thou art the first of countries! Oh! that thou wert grateful to Heaven for the multitude of thy blessings.

20th.—Lord Carrington half an hour, then Vancouver,[1] who has seen Vansittart[2] on his tour scheme, and who did not seem to approve of it at all, but desired him to have an interview at Tyrrwhitt's with Dr. Beke to hear his opinion, whom he esteems much, the greatest political arithmetician of the time. This is accordingly to take place. Vansittart told him the whole income of the public is 200,000,000 sterling. V. replied that it was three times as much. At night I went to the Lock and heard a most excellent sermon by Fry on Luke xi. 21, 22.

[1] 'There is now with us a Mr. Van Couver, of Vancouver's Island, who would entertain you very much. He is making an agricultural tour in Sussex.'—*Letters of Maria Josepha Holroyd*, p. 326.

[2] Nicholas Vansittart, Lord Bexley, sometime Governor of Bengal of great financial reputation.

22*nd.*—It was so fine a day that I took a walk to Kensington Gardens Gate. The Marquis of Hertford chatted with me for some time as he walked his horse, and wants a drainer for his estate in Ireland. I saw Marshall [1] also, and I never see and converse with him, but I think I see the haughty, proud, ill-tempered, snarling, disgusted character which he manifested in his connection with Sir John Sinclair. A thousand pities that so extremely able a man, for of his talents there can be no question, should not have more amenity and mildness. Government, however, should have promoted him without any doubt; and it is a blot in their scutcheon that they have not done it.

The funeral of Mr. Pitt. I think him a very great national loss, and did not go near any part of the business. Pomp and pageantry of all sorts do not accord with my feelings. A pamphlet published to prepare us for peace, 'The Relative Situation of France and England,' said to be by Wraxall.[2] I dread a peace politically, but as a Christian all is directed by Him who cannot err.

25*th.*—I have of late been uneasy lest Dodsley, the bookseller, should have lost much money by my 'Experimental Agriculture,' and called on Becket to know what became of him, and who he left. There I found that Nicoll was one of his executors, and now the only one left. I went to him and desired some information.

---

[1] W. Marshall, 1778–1817, a voluminous writer on agriculture, *Minutes of Agriculture*, &c. &c.

[2] Evidently alluding to Sir Nathaniel Wraxall, a voluminous writer in France, whose works are now forgotten.

On examining the list of his books he found there was but one single copy, and that consequently to suppose he lost by the work would be idle. 'I can tell you what he gave you for the copy, for here is one of the greatest of curiosities.' This was Dodsley's book for authors' receipts; in that he showed me William Burke's receipt for 6*l*. 6*s*. on account of Edmund Burke, for the copy of the 'Vindication of Natural Society.' That book, said Nicoll, was so much admired in France by d'Alembert, Diderot, &c. &c., that it made them mad, and really produced the Revolution.

'And now' (he added) 'I have shown you what Burke had for kindling the Revolution, let me also show you what he had for putting it out,' and then he pointed out his (Burke's) own receipt for 1,000*l*. for the profits of his famous volume. The [other] writings, &c., one other of his later pamphlets, were sold together for 300*l*. He seems, however, to have left it to Dodsley, and when the things were sold, to have taken what D. said was fair. Melmoth had a great deal of money of him, for his translations, &c.

At night letters to us all. Three came from Jane and Arthur. A sad account of the interpreter provided for him, who is an ignorant puppy of a nobleman who is too lazy to do anything. Of all the Governments I have heard of, it seems to be the most stupid, the most ignorant, and the most profligate: the fact, I dare say, is that the army alone is attended [to]. They had the news of the battle of Austerlitz, with a loss as they supposed of 40,000 Russians. Not a family at Moscow but must have lost a relation, yet a grand ball that night, and nothing but gaiety and festivity. They have no feeling. The governor took Jane into a window and told her that he was informed she disapproved of all her husband's farming ideas as much as anyone could do, and ridiculed all his schemes. Upon explanation it came from Marshall Romanzoff, who had it from a German baron that had been at Bradfield, who, admiring the number of experiments, Mrs. Y. told him that she detested them all, and that I had ruined myself by them. A true report I will answer for, for this was her conduct through life. Lamentable it was that no enemy ever did me the mischief that I received from the wife of my bosom by the grossest falsehoods and the blackest malignity; of just such anecdotes of her conversation I have had instances from every part of the world. But do such things rise from the dust? Oh! no, they come from God, and were far less than what I merited at His hands. I had such as I deserved, or much better.

27th.—I was up at four o'clock and kept the fast till 8.30 at night; and as I have a strong stomach that will bear it pretty well, I determined to take no snuff, of which I every day take much, and am almost uncomfortable if at any time I forget my box. This was more a fast with me than abstaining from food; but whether it was not done in a right spirit, or that I had thought about it too much, I know not, but I was dead, and sleepy, and sluggish in body and soul all day except at the evening sermon. Unluckily the night before the fast long letters from Russia, and an account that Arthur had been warned much as if he would be murdered, so determinately hostile to the object are all the Russian nobility.

March 1.—Yesterday was a most worrying moment, full of labour and anxiety. In the morning to Smirenove, to read him my letter to Novosilikoff. He advised me to call on Count Strogonoff, who is here on a political mission, and who treated with Arthur at St. Petersburg. Accordingly, as soon as I returned, I wrote to request he would name a time for my waiting on him, which he did, and fixed Sunday, 10.30. Oh, how the world values that day!

Then to copy fair my letter to Novosilikoff and inclose it to Arthur in his; this, with two hundred other things, kept me till dinner on the table to the chin in anxiety, for if I did not trust in the goodness and mercy of God's providence, I should be fearfully apprehensive of my son's personal safety, the hints he has had are alarming.

Their general conviction at Moscow, that he is come with full powers or intentions to emancipate the boors, have made them all hostile to the plan.

March 17.— Yesterday morning, at 4 A.M., I came down to pray according to custom, and it pleased God that I should pray with more than usual fervency. I then meditated a little and fell asleep. I awaked with a certain sweetness of frame that I noticed at the time, and a transitory idea crossed my mind that God had heard my prayers, and that what I felt might possibly be His grace, or an effusion in some small degree of the Holy Spirit in my soul. It struck me also that I should know if it was by the current of my thoughts and imaginations; for any proof of the Spirit unattended by good effects would be a mere fanatical idea. I took the blessed Sacrament, and in the evening Fry preached on the means of ascertaining whether a man has the Spirit or not—a very excellent sermon, and one well adapted to urge and assist self-examination. The day closed, and I was not sensible of giving way to any loose and wild imaginations.

23*rd*.—Thanks to the ever blessed God, I think that I spent last week in a more satisfactory frame of heart and mind than any for an age past—more upon the watch against sin—more in contemplation of the greatness and goodness of God; vile thoughts have intruded, but I dismissed them by struggling, and my prayers have been more fervent.

April 19.—I have only to-day and to-morrow in the country. Solitude agrees best with my soul. I read all day, and only divinity, temptations are distant. Wesley could not bear the country, from the hurry and bustle of his perpetual labours having given him habits quite contrary to it.

June 3.—I was up again this morning at 3 A.M., and by it escaped falling into evil imaginations. This is an evil I thus fight against and struggle to avoid. I think the Lord will hear my prayers and free me from this buffeting of Satan, this thorn in the flesh, which is a horrible disquiet to me.

4*th*.—I found the devil at work with me this morning, and jumped out of bed at twenty minutes before 3 A.M., dressed, and came down to prayers.

Paying debts formerly with me had but little effect

from the necessary contraction of new ones; but at present I have abstained steadily from all, so that though I want shirts, &c., and have only one coat, and that much worn, yet I order nothing, that I may endeavour effectively to get quite free as soon as possible.

17*th*.—A letter from Arthur, he has had a week's fever, and went back to Moscow, which recovered him. It was caused by want of sleep, owing to bugs, lice, fleas, &c., fatigue and vile food. They are horrid savages, and five centuries behind us in all but vice, wickedness, and extravagance. The interpreter behaves much better, which is comfortable.

18*th*.—The last Board for the season sat yesterday and adjourned till November. Mr. Coke was here, pressed me to go to Holkham; but I have long determined against it; there is not one feature which could carry a Christian there for pleasure, but a thousand to repel him, and this is so much the case with all public meetings that they are odious. The Norfolk farmers are rich and profligate; of course oaths and profanations salute the ear at every turn; and gentlemen and the great, when without ladies, are too apt to be as bad as the mob, and many of them much worse. I am never in such company, but the repugnance of my soul to it is so great, that much as I love agriculture I can renounce it with more pleasure than I can partake of it thus contaminated. I shall get to Bradfield as soon as possible, I hope on Saturday, and having much to do there, God send that employment may keep me out of all temptation.

July 13.—Every Sunday I hear sixteen or eighteen children read the Scripture and say their Catechism, and I pay for the schooling of all that will learn. They are sadly careless and inattentive, but still they come on. If it pleases God to turn it to account by their reading the Scriptures it will be well. The rest of the day I pass in reading; the spirit of visiting in the country among servants prevents much that might be done, but still I am not satisfied, and must find the means of doing more in the instruction of the parish poor.

14*th.*—I have been reading over my 'Inquiry into the Propriety of applying Wastes to the better Maintenance of the Poor.' I had almost forgotten it, but of all the essays and papers I have produced, none I think so pardonable as this, so convincing by facts, and so satisfactory to any candid reader. Thank God I wrote it, for though it never had the smallest effect except in exciting opposition and ridicule, it will, I trust, remain a proof of what ought to have been done; and had it been executed, would have diffused more comfort among the poor than any proposition that ever was made.

February 21, 1807.—To think of keeping a journal regularly is all in vain; the gaps in mine are terrible.

March 9.—Mrs. Wilberforce lent me Crichton's 'Diary of Blackadder,'[1] and gave me Dr. Owen on the 130th Psalm. I have read much of the former and find it a reproach to my whole soul, life, and conversa-

---

[1] J. Blackadder, lieut.-colonel, afterwards minister, died in prison 1685.

tion. What a Christian was there! and what a wretch am I? .

10*th*.—I am very much struck with 'Blackadder's Diary' and letters to his wife, so much so that I have prayed earnestly to God to enable me by His grace to have the same constant trust and reliance in His mercy and goodness that this excellent Christian had.

12*th*.—The Marquis Saloo, from Sicily, gave me many accounts of Bolsamo, and how much he referred in his lectures to his master, Arthur Young. If there be glory in this sort of fame, oh! my Father, let me have done with glorying save in the Cross of the Lord Jesus. I have been glorying in foreign and domestic fame for forty years in true fleshly vanity.

I have been seven weeks in London, and, blessed be the Lord, I have had only four or five invitations to dinner and accepted but two. There has been a great kick up in the Ministry. Tyrrwhitt, from Carleton House, called here, and tells me that Lord Sidmouth and his friends were actually *out*, but the Foxites made it up with the King, pacified him, and they were immediately restored; but Lord Howick and the rest are to give their opinion in the House of Commons, and the obnoxious clause to be left out. The King is ready to turn many out the moment there is strength enough to carry on business without them.

Called at Lord Egremont's; that detestable atheistical profligate kinsman —— was with him. Lord E. loud in the commendation of the *Dactylis glomerata*;[1]

[1] 'Cock's foot grass, considered valuable as a pasture grass in light soils.'—*Loudon*.

it succeeds so greatly with him on cold, strong, wet lands that oxen fatten where they could never be *kept* before, and it grows all winter. I was the first man in England that had five acres of this grass. I believe they had a root of it twenty years ago ; I had much, and recommended it greatly.

A letter from Tyrrwhitt, Carleton House, to inform me that Vansittart and Lord Grenville approve my plan, which I proposed to T. It is this : The Baltic and co. [country] around it being shut up or eaten up, and 400,000 men in our grainery [granary], should we this year have a short crop of wheat or a bad harvest, or a mildew, the supply being cut off, the price would rise beyond all experience; therefore I propose that the Government should supply money to enable the Board to give great premium for the culture of potatoes *for the use of cattle and horses*; without this object an alarm might spread and more mischief than good accrue. T. writes me they approve the idea, and will *advance* the Board 2,000*l.*, but I will have this explained ; it must not be to lend 2,000*l.* but to *give* it.

March 26.—I am very sure that I do not give to poor Christians so much as I ought to do, but I am in doubt whether I do not give more than I ought to do to others. Here is a German, Behrens, once a merchant in good circumstances, whom Sir John received papers from and sent to me. He translated a paper for the Board, and made known such poverty that I promised him a pair of boots ; but writing to him on the translation, I took occasion to enquire what religion he was of; he was educated a Lutheran, but I see plainly he has none. He shall have the boots, but I shall give him nothing else. I can do nothing for Christians if I give to all others that apply.

April 6.—At Bradfield. There is a poor fellow in the gaol condemned to die next Wednesday for forging or uttering bank notes. I heard some bad accounts of him, and as I came from Bury early in the morning, yesterday called to see him. I found that he had been attended by the minister, Mr. Hastead, and also by a Methodist, recommended by a brother of his. I had a good deal of conversation with him, and prayed with him. He was very ignorant, and had no feeling of religion till he was condemned, but has since been instructed and spoke properly enough, lamenting his want of faith at times, and at others being full of faith. I gave him the best instruction I could, and urged little more than (which is his only possible hope) faith in the Lord Jesus. He prayed aloud for some minutes, and more to the purpose than I should have expected. He thanked me much for coming, and as he begged me to come again I promised, and accordingly this morning went on purpose. It comforted him much. I prayed earnestly and fervently for him, and his amens and ejaculations seemed to come quite from his heart. I left him tranquil, and, blessed be a merciful God, I think he may without presumption hope strongly for pardon at the throne of mercy.

I am planting lands, and forming an experiment on the application of vegetable substances as manure.

29th.—London. At eight o'clock at night I received

the following note from Sir John Sinclair. I hurried away to the place named in the cover, Great Shire Lane, where I found Sir John; and Dr. Garthshore on the same errand as myself.

We signed a bail bond.

'My dear Sir,—A most extraordinary circumstance has happened to me. A rascally saddler, whom I employed at Edinburgh to furnish accoutrements to my regiment of Invincibles, brought me in so exorbitant an amount, that I refused to pay it; and instead of bringing an action against me at Edinburgh, he has arrested me for 750*l*. So many of my friends are out of town, that I must trouble you to give bail for my appearance.

'Sincerely yours,

'JOHN SINCLAIR.

'Tuesday.'

Sir John's regiment has been disbanded nine or ten years, and consequently this rascally saddler has been at least so long kept out of his money. What can these people think of themselves! To live quietly while thus depriving tradesmen of their right for such a number of years!

May 16.—This is the first fine day that has occurred since I left town; the lilacs are coming fast into blossom, and the fresh verdure of the grass and trees is highly pleasing.

August 29.—As the time approaches to go this Oxford journey, I dislike it more and more, and wish I had firmly rejected it. I am not in a situation at all comfortable here, and have only one maid—no man or boy—and only the carpenter to put my horse in the whisky; but with a little exertion all this could be arranged. Mrs. Y. going to the sea for seven weeks, and therefore seven weeks' peace here if I stayed. I am in a regular habitual application to my 'Elements,' and have made a good progress in them, so that if I kept here I should have gone through many meetings of the Board; and then if it pleased the Lord to take me, they would at least be in a state to be serviceable to mankind, and the great collection I have made in divinity would gradually be brought into order.

All around here is a region dead in iniquity and sins, as far as ladies and gentlemen are concerned. Amongst the Sectaries there is Christianity, and nowhere else, which is a horrible thing to think of. The clergy are, if possible, more dead than any others; many of them very profligate, many thoroughly worldly minded, but some of very respectable moral characters, but without a spark of vital religion.

I associate only with Mrs. O. Oakes. Having written till I am tired, I go once or twice a week to relax with the mild green (*sic*) of her soul, because I can be free and do as I like, and I try hard to make her a Christian, but hitherto in vain. If evil ideas at any time plague me, then I keep away, and, thanks to God, I have of late had an unusual command over my imagination, which for years plagued me terribly. Prayer is my refuge.

November 23.—The 17th, 18th, and 19th at Euston, and I had much conversation with the duke, in which I earnestly endeavoured to impress on his mind the fact, that by his tenets he placed himself entirely under the covenant of works, and that he must be tried for them, and that I would not be in such a situation for ten thousand worlds. He was mild and more patient than I expected.

He lent me, and I read it there, Priestley's Life, by himself. He asked me what I thought of it? My reply was that through the whole it was the recital of a man perfectly well satisfied with himself, not the confessions of a sinner lamenting what has been wrong in him. He seems to have had no feeling of the sort; as if, when tried by the test of his own merit, it would be a great injustice in God not to be satisfied with him, and that I had no conception of any man having it in his power to review or detail his life with any religious aspect without much self-condemnation, and beseeching God to try him in any way rather than by an appeal to his life or his own merit, but (if he be really a Christian) by the merits only of the blood of his Redeemer. He said it was my view of things, and not that of the doctor, whom he believed was undoubtedly a very good man. The conversation continued, but we were as far as the poles asunder. The duke has drawn up memoirs of his life, and he and Lady Augusta read to me that part which concerned his own administration, which is very satisfactory, as it consists much of original letters. He appears to much more advantage in it than I conceived he would have done, and it was certainly a wise step to leave such a memorial in justification of himself. Lord Templeton there one day. They seem to me to grow more and more economical, and to descend to minute attentions which are below their rank and fortune.

I do not feel comfortable, though he always receives me well, and desires me to come again. It is long since I was there before, and will be long before I go again; such visits, however, have very little of dissipation in them, and so much the better.

The less we like them the safer they are.

[Note, probably by Mary, Arthur Young's only surviving daughter]: '1807. It was upon this journey [into Oxfordshire] that Mr. Y. first perceived the approach of that dimness of sight which afterwards terminated in its total eclipse. His first suspicion arose from looking at the planet Jupiter, and perceiving what appeared to him to be two very small stars near him, at which he was much surprised, as he knew that the satellites were invisible to the naked eye, and nobody saw these stars but himself. This multiplication of bright objects increased the following year, till at last one lamp appeared to him to be five. Objects became by degrees more and more confused, and at last totally disappeared.'

(Total blindness appears to have resulted from the failure of an operation for cataract, as will be seen later on.)

CHAPTER XVI

LAST YEARS, 1808-1820

Gradual loss of sight—Illness and death of Mrs. Oakes—Daily routine—A disappointment—Riots—Death of Mrs. Young—Anecdotes of Napoleon—A story of the Terror—National distress—Close of diary—The end.

In February I was obliged to take a reader as my sight was failing fast.

February 27.—For some months past I have had the comfort of seeing my debts drawing to such a conclusion that I might consider myself as free; and I have certainly thought too much of it, and rested too much satisfaction in it, and not sufficiently been thankful to God for so great a blessing. If I am so ungrateful as not to thank God sufficiently for blessings, how can I expect to avoid misfortunes? My eyes! My eyes! Is not His hand upon me here, too, for the same reason?

What has been my gratitude to Him for their preservation during sixty-seven years? and what uses have I made of them?

April 4.—How employment can be carried further than with me I am at a loss to conceive. Notwithstanding the state of my eyes I am generally up at

4 A.M., though I do not call St. Croix [his reader] before five.

Last Tuesday I read the first lecture that was, I believe, ever read on agriculture in England, my subject 'Tillage at the Board.' The room was well filled, and several of much ability and more of rank; but the day was a bad one, which kept others away. I found that they were well satisfied.

So many years in the habit of incessant employment has made any idleness irksome to me. But my eyes force me to have time for contemplation; and I pray to God to enable me to fill it as a Christian ought to do whose conversation is in heaven; but my mind will run out too much on worldly objects, and sometimes on sinful ones.

How much in all things do I want washing in the fountain opened for sin and uncleanness!

May 13.—Much of my time has of late been lost by people calling on the malt business.[1] I am tired of sugar and malt before the question comes into the House of Commons, which will not be till Monday. I sent another letter to Cobbett last Monday, but he did not insert it. I care little about it, and I wish that I cared less, for these questions only connect one more nearly with the world than a Christian ought to be connected with it.

However, it is in my vocation, and my conscience is not at all wounded by the part I take, for I am well persuaded that the consequences of this measure will be mischievous and tend to scarcity, which is so

---

[1] *See* Hansard.

greatly to be guarded against for a thousand reasons. Sir John Sinclair spoke once against it in the House, and he tells me that Percival looked as black and indignant at him as if he had been talking treason.

July 25 : *Bradfield.*—I am tired of the thoughts of such a journal; had I kept it of late it would have been employed on my departing sight. I can see to write a little, but can read scarcely anything.

Praised be the mercy of God that enables me to pay a reader; St. Croix is with me. And I have been hard at work on my 'Elements' to get those papers into such order as to want as little as possible my own sight in the future progress of completing them. Whenever it may be the will of God to make me quite blind, oh! may I receive His dispensation with the submission of a Christian!

1809. *May* 16.—April twelvemonth I read my own lectures by means of Baker's great hand and black ink; but last month Mr. Cragg read the two, and one new one for me, for I am unable to do it; yet I can write a little, but cannot read when written. The Lord's will be done, and may He sanctify the affliction and turn all my attention to Himself.

Mrs. Oakes arrived at Bury last Sunday fortnight; and on Sunday se'nnight she broke a blood-vessel and brought up two spoonfuls, and on Saturday evening last had another smaller attack. My own fear and opinion is that it will end fatally. Her fatigue coming from Bath and Bristol, and at London, contrary to advice, has caused it. I have prayed most earnestly for her. Oh! may the Lord of all mercy hear and grant my petitions. My thoughts are all employed on the state of her soul. The long intimacy and friendship I have had for her, and the kindness and attention I have ever received from her, now lacerate the heart with wounds that sink deep; and my conscience reproaches me that I have not done all that I might have done to turn her heart more to God.

May 18.—I am very, very unhappy, and cannot think of her without wretchedness. In every worldly respect what a loss will she be to me! A placid, sweet temper, with a good understanding; that ever rec^d. [received] me with kindness, and attention, and preference, with whom I was at my ease, and where I could be at any time; a resource in blindness fast coming on that would have been great. The hope has fled and a sad and dreary vacancy, which freezes me, is in its place.

May 19.—Good news though not of better health. Hastead has been with her, to be sure, by desire, which shows an attention to her soul.

Poor thing! she has been bled twice more, and the blood as highly inflamed as ever; bleeding gives relief to her lungs.

The Duke of Bedford and Mr. Coke [have written] desiring me to go to Woburn and Holkham; but all great meetings, and anything like festivity, have for some years become so insipid and disagreeable that I shall have done with them wholly. They, like so many other things, are links of that worldly harness which it is high time for me to throw down for ever.

June 1.—Read the 'Edinburgh Review' on 'Cœlebs in Search of a Wife,' by Sydney Smith. Wretched stuff; false and frivolous, reasoning on cards, assemblies, plays,[1] &c.

June 3.—Yesterday, as the 'Edinburgh Review' was read to me, I was much struck with a reference to Necker on the finances, saying that 7,000 pedigrees of the nobility in the archives of the old Government were destroyed in the Revolution. It occurred at once to me that this was the exact number of *names* of *men* slain in Revelations. It is in the eleventh chapter: 'The tenth part of the city fell in a great earthquake, and 7,000, &c.' The commentators all seem to have reckoned France as the tenth part of the city; but of the names of men they knew not what to make, but 7,000 pedigrees answer to a wonderful degree, and the coincidence of numbers is truly amazing.

June 6.—Yesterday's letter bad. Poor thing, she has been bled eight ounces, and much inflamed; had been out twice, and I suppose took cold. She wrote herself, and there are some comfortable expressions relative to the state of her mind with regard to religion. I have little hope of her recovery.

July 4.—Betsy continues just the same, whether better or worse, the cough does not go, and therefore I conclude the case bad. But, thanks to God, her mind, I hope, goes on; she has the Testament read to her by all the four children.

July 6.—I work at the 'Elements' every day, and

[1] 'No cards, because cards are employed in gaming; no assemblies, because many dissipated persons pass their lives in assemblies. Carry this but a little further, and we must say—no wine, because of drunkenness; no meat, because of gluttony; no use, that there may be no abuse.'—*Sydney Smith on Hannah More.*

find every time they are read to me something to cancel, something to add, and much to reconsider and correct.

July 8.—The gradual declension of my sight in viewing the scenery of this place, but especially in knowing faces, makes me surprised that I can manage to write; I cannot read in the least degree, or know anything of the views in Lord Valentia's Travels.[1] It is a very great deprivation, but much better than feeling the torture of very painful distempers, so that I am very thankful to God for the less affliction. It was, I doubt not, very necessary for me to have some heavy one, and what I am likely to suffer is comparatively a mercy to what might have been the dispensation of the Almighty.

Mrs. O. the same, and the weather as unfavourable to her; I drank tea there on Thursday.

July 19.—Drank tea with her last night. [She was] bled in the morning, and going to have a blister. All her symptoms worse, I suppose she has caught cold.

August 4.—I have been so provoked, my dear Jane,[2] with so many of my letters miscarrying that I am determined to begin a book to use some safe opportunity of conveying it to you, for I know nothing so provoking as to write twenty letters for one or two that arrive safe. In your last you made many enquiries into what I was doing? How I passed my time, &c. &c. A very short account will answer this. I rise from four to five in the morning, pray to God for half an hour,

---

[1] *Voyages and Travels in India, Ceylon, &c.*, 1809.

[2] A pathetic interest attaches to this sentence. Here A. Y.'s fine bold handwriting (of late rather painting in black ink) ceases. A few desperate splashes, and we seem to see the pen despairingly cast aside and the journalising handed over to his secretary.

more or less, according as He affords me the spirit to
do it. At half-past five I call Mr. St. Croix, who comes
to me at six, and reads a chapter in Scott's Bible with
notes. I then dictate such letters as want to be written,
after which we sit down to my 'Elements of Agriculture,' which have been more than thirty years in hand,
and at which I have worked for two years past with
much assiduity, wishing to finish it before my sight is
quite gone. At half-past eight the servant brings me
the water to shave; from nine to ten we breakfast,
and sit down again to work for two or three hours,
as it may happen, as I take the opportunity of sunshine
for a brisk walk of an hour, very often backwards and
forwards on the gravel between yours and the round
garden. I wish much to have my thoughts during that
hour employed upon death and the other world, but
my weakness and want of resolution are lamentable,
so that I sometimes think on every subject except that
which I intend should occupy me. We then sit down
to work again, till the boy and his dicky arrive with
the letters and newspapers. When they are read we
work again, but usually catch half an hour for another
walk before dinner. When alone we dine at four, and
always at that hour in the height of summer, but if
any person be in the house, as it prevents an evening
work, five is the dinner hour. What is read afterwards
is usually some book not immediately connected with
work. At eight we drink tea and go to bed at ten,
but the Sunday is an exception; you know there is
service but once a day. At the church hour, whether
morning or afternoon (when no service), about thirty
children from Bradfield, Stanningfield, and Cuckfield

come to read in the Testament and repeat their Catechism, and undergo some examination from Mrs. Trimmer's 'Teacher's Assistant.' Whatever is well done receives a mark against the name; the girl or boy that has fewest marks receives nothing, the next a halfpenny, next a penny, and so on, all which does not amount to more than two or three shillings. I cannot boast much of their progress, though I pay for most of them as constant scholars. In the evening, between six and seven o'clock, forms are set in the hall to receive all that please to come to hear a sermon read, and the numbers who attend amount from twenty to sixty or seventy, according to weather and other circumstances. Such, my dear Jane, is the tenor of my life both in summer and winter while I am in the country.

December 1.[1]—Here is a pretty breach in the continuance of this book letter, but you are not to fail to remember that during this period I have sent off two letters to you, not short ones, which, from Smirenove's account of the conveyance, I hope may get to you safe. I have also received two short ones from you, and another from Arthur at Odessa, describing the severity of the winter, and an escape he had of being burnt in a Tartar combustion of old grass, but, most provokingly, saying not one word of his own intentions, or a syllable of what he is about. This is very mortifying to me, for what are frost and fire to me compared with his own plans and views? Nor does he say a word about coming to England; and the idea of the possibility of your coming in autumn is

[1] Still addressed to Jane Young.

now all past by, and I am precluded from the possibility of seeing you till next summer, by which time I shall have no eyes to see you.

April 9, 1810.[1]—The discovery lately made by your letter of the enormous expense of postage must limit my correspondence to private hands, and will not permit the communication of anything but topics the most immediately interesting to your future motions. My notes of the riots, therefore, are preserved for your eye by copying a letter to Mrs. Oakes:—

'I know not what reports may have reached you relative to the state of London, nor what newspapers you read, but I have been witness to such a scene as I hope, through the blessing of God, will not occur again. On Friday night the mob was extremely agitated in Piccadilly, especially near Sir Francis Burdett's, and they took the unaccountable whim of forcing everyone to illuminate. I lighted up as other people did, and when I went to bed left orders with the servant who sat up to be sure to keep the candles burning till daylight, instead of which, when others put out their candles, ours were extinguished also. At two o'clock the mob returned and broke many windows, and ours among the rest. The servant ran into my room and waked me out of my sleep to tell me the windows were smashing. We hurried the candles out again, and, upon examination, found the alarm exceeded the damage, for only three panes were broken. All Saturday passed in a very quiet manner, and in the evening the illumination was more general, but troops

[1] Written from London.

pouring into London from all quarters, we hoped to be secure without violence. The mob, however, were so determined, that by twelve o'clock we heard platoons firing in Piccadilly, and a few in other directions more remote, the Riot Act having been read. A person who saw much, and clearly, told me that orders being received by the commanding officer to fire with ball, about fifty cavalry fired twice over the heads of the people, that the whizzing of the balls might inform them what they had to expect; still, however, they were audacious, insomuch that the officer was forced to fire on them. In five minutes all Piccadilly was cleared. We afterwards heard a little more distant firing, and a party of horse scoured up Sackville Street, firing in a scattered manner at the flying mob; but, from the reports of the pieces, I believe with powder only. The reports relative to the mischief done are extremely vague and not to be depended on. Some say that one trooper was killed, others three or four; what was the loss suffered by the mob is, I believe, quite unknown, but certainly it was very inconsiderable. During Sunday the agitation of the streets threatened a bad night, but Government had brought in so many troops, that had we known it we need not have been alarmed. A train of artillery in the park, horses attached and matches lighted, two pieces of artillery in Berkeley Square, two others in Soho Square, and many more about the town, and doubtless many others of which I knew nothing, all ready at a moment's warning, with parties of troops scouring the streets, showed such a state of preparation as effectually awed the mob, notwithstanding the efforts of Sir F. Burdett to inflame them. He was at his house ready to resist the Speaker's warrant for commitment, and had the audacity to write to the sheriff to bring the *posse comitatus* to assist him in so doing, printing the letter in the Sunday's newspaper. They say he is still at his house, and that he will not be seized before the House meets this day. It really is a tremendous moment, for if they do not carry it with a high hand, as a means of prevention, we shall have an organised mob and great mischief will follow. It is expected that the gallery of the House will to-day be cleared by acclamation and a Bill brought in to suspend the Habeas Corpus Act, and the rascally authors, printers, and publishers of those inflammatory papers which have done so much mischief seized and imprisoned; but whether the Ministry, with such a violent opposition, will have resolution enough for this will depend on the influence the Marquis of Wellesley has among his colleagues in the Cabinet. I am much inclined to expect that good will result by drawing close to the Ministry all the honest men in both Houses, with all others that might be wavering; for it is a question now whether we are to be governed by Parliament or the mob. Many circumstances, however, are unfortunate, and not the least, that though the public revenue amounts to 62,000,000*l*., yet the expenses of the year will rise to above 80,000,000*l*., and must be made good by means that will occasion the necessity of having additional taxes. This will cause a yell for peace—and such a peace as must be ruinous if made. We have also one adversary armed at all points, and whose depth of policy is such as ought ever to create alarm and the exertions of all the talents the country possesses to oppose him.'

May 3, 1811.—I do not think that for the last twenty years of my life my general health has been better than at the moment when discontent, I fear, with the will of God, induced me to oppose that will. In the most mild and merciful manner He had nearly deprived me of sight without my feeling the smallest pain. Heavy as this dreadful deprivation is and must remain to me, I feel, in proportion to my convalescence, that even blindness itself may be a temptation; as a dispensation from God, it must have been meant as a calamity, and a calamity to be deeply felt. Is there not danger then that a mind which has been accustomed to look upon the favourable side of objects, should gradually so accustom itself to its new situation as to deprive it in a good measure of the misery which might be the direct intention of the Almighty? The capacity of continuing the attention formerly given to old objects by means of the eyes of others, may leave the mind almost as full of the world as when by sight I could enjoy its visible objects; this is a circumstance which ought undoubtedly to be guarded against, that is, prayed against. For a man of seventy to be struck blind and to continue worldly-minded, with his head and heart full of objects which, though not of sight, command attention, is to tempt God to send some deeper affliction in order to bring his heart home to its true centre. This is a subject which merits great attention, and may the Lord of His mercy enable me to consider it as I ought to do!

May 8.—Twelve o'clock at noon my dear friend Mrs. Oakes breathed her last, after a long severe illness, and many and great sufferings. Thanks to God she was attentive throughout this sad period, as I am well informed, to the state of her soul with God. Thus is terminated in this world a very intimate friendship of twenty-six years, with a temper so mild and cheerful, with manners so gentle and persuasive, that had it pleased the Almighty to have spared her, she would have been the source of great comfort to me in my melancholy state.

May 16, 1812.—At this time a new oculist appeared in town, a desideratum much wanted. The highest accounts were universally circulated of his skill and success, and the most unequivocal good effects attended his new attempts at removing cataract. I was unwilling to go to him, cherished no hope of my own case, and considered this calamity as the appointment of Providence, concerning which I had but one wish—that of submitting to it with the most unaffected resignation. But the persuasions of my friends, more sanguine than myself, and the high reputation of Mr. Adams at length prevailed, and a day was appointed finally to decide my state—to give some expectation of recovery or to destroy all hope.

The feelings of the mind may be subdued, but they cannot be destroyed. From the reluctance I showed to name the day even after resolving to go, the dread of hearing my doom, and the natural desire to enjoy a little longer the precious glimmering of hope, may be inferred. At length the long-wished-for dreaded morning came. The sun shone brightly as I walked to the house; I felt its warmth, and the thought that perhaps his light may still, ere long, 'revisit these sad eyes,' lent new interest to his cheering beams.

The man who has never had his mind enlivened and his senses cheered by contemplating the scenes of nature or the employment of his fellow creatures, would feel much less at the thought of learning whether this would ever be his fate or not, than he who, once having felt in every variety the extent of the blessing, loses it, learns by experience the sadness of the contrast, and goes with a throbbing heart to enquire if any hope exists of again enjoying that power he would gladly forfeit all his possessions to recover.

I was shown into a room, where I waited a few minutes (they were painful ones), and Mr. Adams appeared. 'I wish, sir, to be informed what is the state of my eyes,' looking very attentively at him. 'You have not, sir, undergone an extraction for cataract?'[1] 'That you must decide.' 'Why, yes, and I

---

[1] This is explained in a letter from Mary Young to her brother Arthur, dated March 27; no year added, but evidently written in 1811. The Duke of Grafton died March 14, 1811. 'It seems that the poor patient was very intractable, and that the operator said, "Indeed, sir, if you are not more patient I must leave you." . . . Mr. Wilberforce, with the best wishes imaginable, called [after the couching], and was shown up to his bedroom; and the very first words he said were, " So we have lost the poor Duke of Grafton!" then began and continued in his mild, soft manner a most pathetic dissertation on the duke's pious resignation, &c. &c., till your father *burst into tears*, which was, Phipps (the oculist) vowed, the worst thing possible, and which anyone knew in

fear unsuccessfully.' 'Is there any hope of recovery?' Mr. Adams started, and looked down with evident marks of bitter disappointment the first instant he saw me. 'I grieve, sir, to say that the eye itself is destroyed, the cornea gone, and there has been such an excessive discharge of the vitreous humour, that the coats are collapsed.' 'No chance, then, of course?' 'I fear, sir, *none*;' then, after a pause, 'I believe I am addressing Mr. A. Young?' I bowed. 'I have heard your case differently reported; it was the subject of much conversation, and excited unenviable interest last spring when it happened, and I had hoped that it would have been possible to relieve you, but I now see the contrary.' 'I am much obliged to you, sir, good morning,' I replied, and came away.

Mr. Adams was a young man, his aspect was pleasing and intelligent, and there was a sorrowful look when I departed that well became the sad occasion. There were two things worth repeating on that morning, one was his liberality in clearing his brother professor from the character of *carelesness*, which he endeavoured to do. I complained that I was sure I could not have been well prepared. But Mr. Adams replied that preparation was *not* necessary for extraction, that people of the worst habits had been treated in that way with no preparation and complete success; that the fault was not of the operator, but of the operation, which must always be liable to failure. Mr. Adams'

his lamentable state of inflammation was *destruction*. It flung him back, being only a week after the operation. Oh, Ar., as I greatly believe he will be entirely blind, do try to come to him.'

own method of removing cataract was not this ill-fated scheme of extraction. The second remark is this. It had become much the custom to use hot water for the eyes when weak or inflamed. The author of this memoir had been afflicted with a transient indisposition of them, and on application to Phipps, hot water had been recommended and used for a twelvemonth without effect.

Mr. Adams, on being questioned with regard to the expedience of its continuance, decidedly answered, that by increasing the relaxation, hot water would only augment the disease; prescribed the frequent use of the *citrine ointment* [1] (to be had at any druggist's) and *cold* water constantly. On the way home, I was for a few moments depressed. 'How happy,' I cried, 'are those beings who can see; no one can tell the misery of blindness, the dark gloom over that mind never cheered by the light of the sun, especially now with me, who am certain never to see again. If it were not for religion, I should wish to be the poor man who is to be hanged next Monday; but, thank God, I can consider the whole affair as His appointment, intended not for a curse but a blessing, and can reconcile my mind to it completely as His will. You will see,' I added after a pause [presumably addressing Mr. Adams], smiling, 'I shall be as cheerful and happy as ever,' and so I was.

1814.—This year I paid much attention to the 'Elements.'

My son came from Russia.

---

[1] 'Citrine ointment: a mercurial ointment, the unguentum hydrargyri nitralis.'—*Webster.*

1815.—Arthur, Jane, and myself went post to London the last day of January, Mary remained at Bradfield with Mrs. Young, who was unable to move.

About this time 'Baxteriana'[1] was published. Through the following spring I was, at various times, too apt to fall into reflections which tended, more than they ought to have done, to discontent; but in thirteen weeks to the present day I have not once entered the doors of any other person than those of Mr. Wilberforce, and I have not dined once with him, having been only at breakfast for the pleasure of hearing his Exposition and Prayer; for the conversation at and after breakfast has been entirely desultory, and not once on any religious question. And as to any Christian calling on me, John Babbington, from Peterborough, once breakfasted here, and is, I believe, never in town without calling. Mrs. Strachey, who was in town a month, was so kind as to call three or four times; Mrs. John Wayland twice, and here, I think, except Miss Francis,[2] dining once a week, is the whole amount of my communication with those whose conversation would please me.

It would be natural to suppose that a poor old blind man who, through the blessing of God, retains his health and strength might have received something more of friendly attention than this, but such discontent should be banished, for let me not a single moment forget the great mercies of God to me; and while many are on beds of torment from dreadful

---

[1] A selection from the writings of Baxter, by A. Y.
[2] This lady afterwards became assistant secretary to A. Y.

diseases, I am free from bodily pain. These are points that should give a perpetual spring of gratitude in my bosom, and if the neglect which I have been apt to think of too much turns my attention more to the Lord Jesus, it is a benefit and not a misfortune. Let me only take care to be looking unto Jesus, and then I shall esteem, in the manner it deserves, all that the world can do for me.

Monday, March 6, most execrable riots began in London, on account of the Corn Bill, then in the House of Commons, attended with circumstances proving decisively the abominable effects (sufficiently proved before) of printing in all the newspapers those violent and mischievous speeches which are made as much to the Gallery as to the House, and can be intended for nothing else but to inflame the people, which they have done to a degree of desperation. Petitions from a multitude of cities and towns pour in to the Houses every day they meet, and, in fact, the prayer of them all is to beg that they, the petitioners, may be starved, which would probably be the result of granting their desire. 600,000 qrs. of French wheat of an excellent quality have been poured into our markets to meet a crop generally mildewed; this has reduced the price on an average of the kingdom to 59$s.$ per quarter, and that average taken in so preposterous a way that the real price fairly ascertained would not amount to 50$s.$; 90$s.$ per qr. [quarter] would not pay the farmer in so bad a year. If importation was to be continued, at least half the farmers in England would be ruined, and wheat consequently must rise in a year or two to scarcity, and if importation should be prevented, by many probable events to famine. Country labourers throughout the kingdom are in the greatest distress, as I know from many correspondents. For want of employment they go to the parish, but these poor families never petition, even when starving, and a Legislature which attended not to their interest would deserve the abuse now vomited forth by towns. From thirty to forty houses at London have had their windows broken, many their doors forced, and everything in them destroyed; and after much mischief, with general anxiety and appehension, the military were called forth; but it was the last day of the week before their numbers were sufficient to secure any tolerable tranquillity.

Monday, March 13.—I breakfasted with Mr. Wilberforce: a file of soldiers in his house, because his servants had been violently threatened that it should be speedily attacked.

The bawler bearing[1] last week, in the House, read a denunciation in a petition from Carlisle against the Board of Agriculture, which made it necessary for me to hire a bedchamber elsewhere, as blindness would not permit an escape by the roof of the house.

I wrote to Mr. Vansittart, transcribing a resolution of the Committee of 1774, proposing to lay the millers under an assize. The Bill for that purpose passed the Commons, but was lost in the Lords.

In Mr. Vansittart's answer to me, he mentioned

[1] This must be a mistake of the French secretary. Surely Baring is intended.

the difficulties in the way, but observed that as Mr. Franklin Lewis had taken up the business of bread and flour in the House, he would mention to him what I proposed. From Lord Sidmouth's speech it seems they intend to remove the assize of bread, which will leave in case of scarcity the bakers without protection in case of riots, and also leave the millers in full possession of their rascality.

At Mr. Wilberforce's I met Miss Francis and Mr. Legh Richmond, who read to us, with Lord Calthorpe and General Macaulay, a most interesting letter from a Russian Princess, describing her conversion to vital Christianity by Mr. Pinkerton instructing her children, and her translating into Russian the 'Dairyman's Daughter,' and thanking Mr. Richmond for his other tracts sent her for the same purpose. Her English extremely good, and real Christianity, with expressions of the deepest humility, breathing in every line.

This was an eventful year, for my poor wife breathed her last after a long illness, and it gives me great comfort to be informed that she showed great marks of resignation and piety. My daughter was with her to the last.

May 12.—A few days ago, writing to Miss Francis, I used the expression, 'If a Christian was to call on me it should be entered in a pocket-book with a mark of exclamation.' Mr. Wilberforce saw this note, and yesterday morning Mr. Pakenham called on me, and introduced himself by saying that he came for some conversation with me, by desire of Mr. W. He was quite unknown to me, but I found that he was the grandson of that Lord Longford with whom I was in Ireland in 1776, forty years ago, which lord was in the Navy; and the present gentleman is also in that employment, about twenty-six or twenty-seven years of age; his father living and an admiral. I soon found that he was a firmly established Christian, ready to converse on the good subject, which he did with good sense and no inconsiderable energy.

He is in mourning for General Pakenham, and the Duchess of Wellington is his first cousin. Mentioning Miss Francis, he said he met her twice at Mr. Wilberforce's, and speaking in commendation of her, I told him that she was to dine with me at five o'clock, and that it would give me much pleasure if he would meet her; this he readily complied with, and came accordingly.

I have not had so much religious conversation for an age past; and had not Dr. Halliday from Moscow called between seven and eight, expecting to see my son, this conversation would have been uninterrupted. I wish he had come on some other day. Remarking that I had some apprehension of the ensuing war, because we should be, in fact, fighting for the restoration of the Pope, the Jesuits, and the Inquisition, Mr. P. replied, that Lord Liverpool had informed Mr. Wilberforce that Bonaparte was reconciled to the Pope, pretending to be a most dutiful son of the Church. It seems agreed by all that the first victory gained on either side will have most decisive consequences. I hope I shall hear more of this young man, whose determined avowal of his religious principles pleases me much.

May 15. — Breakfasted at Mr. Wilberforce's. General Macaulay there; he told me that in his late tour in France, travelling from Lyons to Geneva, he met with a Monsieur Michaud, who, speaking much of his farm and offering to show it, the general accompanied him to view it, and found everything in the highest state of management, and so much superior to all the rest of the country, that he enquired into the origin of such great superiority. The answer was, ' My cultivation is entirely that of Monsieur Arthur Young, whose recommendations I have carried into practice with the success you see.'

Much conversation about Bonaparte; the general is well persuaded that the allies will be entirely successful, as B. is, and must be, very badly provided to resist them, and that the first campaign will carry them to Paris.

May 17.—Last night, being at West Street Chapel, Mr. Gurney, after the sermon, came into the pew, when I told him he had not performed his promise, by calling, on which he came home with me, and gave us a long account of his life and conversion, beginning at four years old with a magpie which his father found in a nest, in a haunted wood, where he went at night in search of a reputed ghost, and which proved to be only a white pony. This magpie was, by a strange series of little events, his introduction to Drummond, the banker, and to procuring himself a school and college education, a knowledge of several of the nobility, and eventually, through Lord Exeter, the appointment to the Rectory of St. Clement Danes; and all this from having been no more than a poor country labourer's son, and one of *twenty-two* children. The detail was very interesting, from being not only well told, but, from the providence of God, clearly marked in many little circumstances, and attended by what to him were great events. These were so remarkable as to induce him to make many memoranda, and to think at times that they ought to be published, but on this point he does not seem to be at all determined. I urged it strongly as a sort of duty. He is uncommonly lively and animated in conversation, and contrived to talk with little interruption, from drinking tea and smoking several pipes, till twelve o'clock at night. I much hope that we shall see him often.

1816.—This was a very barren year, for the memoranda made are uncommonly few, but among them is the preparation for the publication of 'Oweniana.'[1] The extraction from my religious papers of those published under the titles of 'Baxteriana' and 'Oweniana' has greatly diminished the mass, but the remainder is considerable, and increases every year.

February.—Last Tuesday se'nnight Sir John Seabright, coming up to me, said: 'Mr. Young, the Archdukes of Austria desire to be introduced to you,' and the Archduke John, who Seabright said was the farmer, began a conversation on agriculture which, as many persons were around, was very short. Some

[1] A selection from the works of J. Owen, D.D., by A. Y.

days afterwards Mr. Ackerman, of the Strand, called to inform me that his Imperial Highness Archduke John desired to have more conversation with me, and in three or four days he called and made many enquiries into those points upon which, I suppose, he had most doubts, contrasting many circumstances with the system of Austrian peasants, who, by his account, are in general the proprietors of their little farms even to the amount of as little as three or four acres. In the conversation I took occasion to mention my son being in the Crimea, and intending to return to England by Vienna. In a most obliging manner he desired me to write to him to tell him to be sure not to pass Vienna without making himself known to him (the Archduke), as he would show him everything worth attending to in agriculture. The conversation was in French, for he speaks no English. It is a pity that he will go away without seeing anything of Norfolk or Suffolk.

Sir J. Sinclair just come from Paris. He saw Sylvestre[1] there, the secretary to the Royal Society of Agriculture, who told him that agriculture saved his life in the Revolution. He was in prison and brought to trial, and told that his life should be saved if he could show that he had ever done anything really useful to the Republic. He replied that he had unquestionably done good, for Arthur Young's 'Travels through France' contained much highly important information, and in order to spread it through the Republic in a cheap form, 'I published a useful

[1] A. F. Baron de, 1762-1851, celebrated agriculturist and member of the Institut.

abridgement,' he said, 'which has been much read, and has had important effects. I was pardoned and set at liberty,' and then, turning to Sir John, he said, 'Tell your friend, Mr. Young, that he was thus the means of saving my life.'

February 17.—The Board met for the first time last Tuesday, but had no business whatever before them. I suggested the propriety of sending a circular letter throughout the kingdom, in order to ascertain by facts the real state of the farming world. They approved the proposal, observing that not a moment should be lost, and I retired in order to draw out a letter with *Queries*. This they examined and altered to their mind; it was immediately despatched to the printer, and all the rest of the week has been employed in drawing out lists of persons from the reports, to whom these letters have been addressed, post paid, to the amount of 12*l.*, and many yet to despatch on Monday.

The replies have just begun to come in; by two valuable ones from Maxwell, near Peterborough, and from Page, of Cobham, the probability is that much important information will be gained, and a basis laid for a very interesting publication, but I greatly question whether they will permit any public use to be made of the information, and I suspect that it will disclose so lamentable a state of distress, that it may prove somewhat dangerous, or, at least, questionable to make it public. What are we to think of the infatuation of Government in laying on a property tax at such a moment, rather than borrow a few millions to avoid the necessity, one of the great evils resulting from our Government being in all money matters little better than a Committee of the Bank?

Answers to the circular letter of the Board, which was despatched throughout the kingdom the first week in February, flowed in rapidly till about April 10, and they describe such a state of agricultural misery and ruin as to be almost inconceivable to those who do not connect such a defect with the utter want of circulating medium; the ruin of the country banks, and the great want of confidence in those that remain, with an issue of Bank of England notes utterly insufficient to fill up the vacuity thus occasioned, has made the want of money so great as to cripple every species of demand.

It is difficult to pronounce what the consequence of the present ruined state of agriculture will prove, but I must confess that I dread a scarcity, which must have dreadful effects, coming at a period when such multitudes are almost starving for want of employment, even with such cheap bread. What must be their situation should it be dear? To my astonishment, Government seems utterly insensible of the danger, and has not taken one single step to prevent it, or to meet it should it come.

March.—Lord Winchilsea, who I have not seen for some time, called on me yesterday and mentioned his having been long absent in France, Spain, &c. He was at Marseilles when Bonaparte landed from Elba, in Provence; every circumstance was previously arranged. Messina, at Marseilles, kept everything quiet on his left, and the [garrison?] at Grenoble was prepared to receive him; of all this there was no doubt. Uncertain of what might be the event in France, his lordship embarked instantly for Barcelona; from thence he crossed Spain to Lisbon, and throughout the whole of his Spanish journey he did not pass through a town that was not in a state of ruin and desolation. He everywhere enquired the cause, and was always told 'that the French had done all the mischief;' with many expressions of cordial detestation. He would not have conceived a country to be in a more wretched and deplorable state.

April 24.—Miss Way and Miss Neve, daughter of the late Sir Richard Neve, both high Calvinists and constant hearers of Mr. Wilkinson, called on me the other day in order to converse on religion. They appear to me to be perfectly sincere, but seem wedded to the high Calvinistic notions of that preacher. Miss Way lent me two manuscript sermons of his full of predestination, and the impossibility of falling from grace; her sister took them in shorthand. This day Miss Neve called on me again, bringing with her a Miss Johnson, another Calvinistic lady, who, being in Italy with some relations, went to Elba to see Bonaparte, and had much conversation with him. He had told somebody, who told the Johnsons, that he wanted to see my 'Travels in France,' which he had often thought of reading, but came to Elba without them. Mr. Johnson had these 'Travels,' and took them with him to Elba and presented them to the Emperor, who expressed much pleasure at receiving them, and

Mr. Johnson afterwards heard that he had read them eagerly and with much approbation. His countenance indicates a steadfast, resolute, determined mind, and he is known to abhor all doubtful and hesitating answers that do not come immediately to the point in question. In the very short interview that took place he was standing with his hands in his breeches pockets clinking the money in them; but she observed that his nails as well as his teeth were dirty. He enquired, when they were in Provence, and especially on the coast, whether there were troops at Antibes or at Nice. This conversation took place on the Thursday, and he left the island on the Sunday following. He asked her name, and on the reply of Helen, 'Oh! I am to be sent to St. Helena,[1] this is ominous of my voyage.' The interview was very short with him, but with the Bertrands the conversation was rather longer.

I have finished reading the first volume of 'Gibbon's Miscellaneous Works,' published by Lord Sheffield. Of mere worldly production, it is the most interesting that I have read for many years, more especially Gibbon's own memoirs of himself. I have been acquainted with Lord Sheffield above forty years, and more than once met Gibbon at his house; and, if I remember rightly, the first time I was at Sheffield Place, which, I think, was in 1770, being invited by him on my advertising the intentions of the Eastern tour. Mr. Foster and Lady Elizabeth his wife, daughter of the Earl of

[1] Sir Walter Scott and other historians of Napoleon refer to a vague rumour that in 1814 and 1815 the Allied Powers had a secret design to remove Napoleon from Elba to St. Helena. He affected to believe the rumour, and frequently mentioned it.

Bristol, were there. I thought her a most fascinating woman—an opinion many times afterwards confirmed by often meeting her at Ickworth. I was not therefore surprised to find such advantageous mention made of her by Gibbon, but, alas! the whole volume has not one word of Christianity in it, though many which mark the infidelity of the whole gang. Lord Sheffield never had a grain of religion, and his intimate connections with Gibbon would alone account for it. Of course he took no pains to instil it into his family, and if Mrs. Clinton and Lady Stanley have any, they are not indebted for it to their father or to his friend. A great number of persons of high rank, extraordinary talents, and great celebrity thus passing in review, and all of them (Burke alone excepted) without the least suspicion of religion attaching to their characters, yield a melancholy impression on the mind of a Christian. Nineteen in twenty of the persons mentioned are gone to their eternal state, and of what account is it at present whether they were celebrated authors, splendid orators, great ministers, or successful generals or admirals? Whatever might be their worldly greatness how little are they to be compared at present to the case of a poor Christian whose employment was sweeping the streets! Without doubt the propriety of such observations depends entirely on Christianity being true; but what a dreadful situation is that man in whose safety is attached solely to the falsehood of that religion. The reflection makes my blood almost run cold, and old and blind as I am, and scarcely exchanging in six weeks a single word with more than one or two persons out of my family, I feel a comfort and consolation, and I will add a measure of happiness, not one atom of which would be found in my bosom if I were not most perfectly convinced of the absolute truth and importance of that blessed religion which forms the sole enjoyment of my life.

June.—Lord Winchilsea called here and chatted with me upon cottagers' land for cows, which he is well persuaded, and most justly, is the only remedy for the evil of poor rates.

1817.—The death of the Princess Charlotte this year created the greatest sensation ever known.

1818.—On coming to London in February, five-and-twenty claims for the premium on the [summary of] the state of the poor, the causes of their distress, and the means of remedying it, were received, and it afforded me continued employment for many weeks in reading and giving a character of them. Much the greater part of the authors who drew up these memoirs were of the same opinion as to the cause of the national distress, attributing it to the peace having thrown a vast number of men out of employment who were in the Army or Navy, or working in the manufactures immediately supported by military demands; and this evil concurring with a general stagnation from the failure of a multitude of country banks, had materially affected the industry of the whole kingdom. The remedies proposed were various, and many of them visionary; the most rational advised the issuing of Exchequer Bills in payment of various sorts of public works, such as canals, roads, harbours, fisheries, and many other employments. Such suggestions had been proposed to Government, but unfortunately the ministers in England have very rarely indeed listened to any such propositions. My friend Mr. Attwood, of Birmingham, in a work publicly addressed to me, wrote upon the subject with great ability, and most justly remarked upon dismissing at once both the Army and the Navy, and turning such numbers loose upon the public when it was perfectly well known that they could not find employment was highly mischievous. This ought to have been done slowly and gradually, as the expense would have been an evil far less deplorable than that which was insured by a contrary conduct. It was the beginning of 1818 before the kingdom was decidedly found to be in a reviving state, and in the mean time the infinite number of offences against the peace and property of the people arose to an alarming height in every part of the kingdom. The first week in January I received half a year's rents, and it was a great comfort to me to find that the tenants continued their regular payments without running the least in arrears, and this at a time when complaints on the non-payment of rents were very general over the greater part of the kingdom. I attributed this effect, which was very general around Bury and through all Suffolk, to the stability and flourishing state of our country banks, whose paper passed readily current, and formed a perfect contrast to the deficiencies and distress so generally felt in various other countries; nor can anything be more lamentable than for gentlemen of small estates finding their tenants running in arrears of rent.

This was much experienced in the counties of Cambridge, Huntingdon, and part of Bedford. Sir George Leeds informed me that he had farms in the former counties abandoned and lying absolutely waste.

Here ends the diary. Arthur Young died in Sackville Street on April 20, 1820, and was buried at Bradfield. The following letter from Mary Young to her brother in Russia gives some details about his last years. The letter (undated) apparently belongs to 1818: 'My father talks of going to Bradfield in June with Miss Francis and Mr. St. Croix. He is fearful lest Miss Francis (who is a granddaughter of Dr. Burney, and a daughter of Mrs. Broom by her first husband) will join the Wilberforces at Brighton, and leave him. When at Bradfield she sleeps over the servants' hall, with a packthread tied round her wrist, and placed through the keyhole, which he pulls at four or five times, till he awakens her, when she gets up and accompanies him in a two hours' walk on the turnpike road to some cottage or other, and they take milk at some farmhouse; and she distributes tracts (religious ones), and questions the people about their principles, and reads to them and catechises them. They return at half-past six, as that is the hour Mr. St. Croix gets up (his secretary), who finds it quite enough to read and write two hours and a half before breakfast. After breakfast they all three adjourn to the library till one, when Mr. St. Croix takes his walk for an hour; she and my father read, or write, or walk till three. Before she went to Bradfield, Mr. St. Croix had but one hour. She

ARTHUR YOUNG'S TOMB AT BRADFIELD.

has a table and great chair filled with books in all languages, as she reads in every language every day to keep them up—Greek, Latin, Italian, Hebrew, Arabic, German, Spanish, French, Dutch, &c. &c. &c.

'My father puts children to school at Cuckfield, Stanningfield, and Bradfield. Every morning, summer or winter, she inspects and teaches at these schools. Every Sunday they all meet in the hall and read, and are catechised; and every Sunday night a hundred meet, when St. Croix reads a sermon and a chapter, and my father explains for an hour, after which a prayer dismisses them! Last summer they went to church at Acton or Ampton every Sunday, each church ten miles out and ten home, besides teaching the schools and the meeting at night in the hall.

'He has taken out a licence for the hall, as there is an assembly of people which would have been otherwise liable to an information.

'Adieu, my dear Arthur. Are we ever to meet any more?

'Yours affectionately,
'M. Y.'

The following is added by Mr. St. Croix:—

'Mr. Young's benevolent exertions for the poor in his own and the adjoining parishes, and constant plan for welfare and relief of their necessities, was very beautiful, and I believe and fear very uncommon. To women this attention is natural.

'H. More truly says, "Charity is the employment of a female; the care of the poor is her profession;"

but to see this extend to the other sex, to witness the same solicitude for the distresses of the ignorant, unextinguished by business or by ingratitude, in a man of such activity of genius as Mr. Y., was indeed an impressive sight. At one time he established spinning matches; a cap was the prize, and several young girls contended for it, the best spinner being victorious. This occasioned industry and emulation, certainly; but even this was not without its attendant evil, and Mr. Y. finally abandoned it, from the dread of encouraging vanity, and appropriated the money to *winter feasts*.

'In this cold, unproductive season, there were amongst the poor constant endeavours and constant failure at repletion. Every Sunday after church a set of poor people, chiefly children, were invited, and a plentiful dinner provided for them, Mr. Y. waiting on them and carving himself.

'But this he was at last obliged to relinquish. The Sunday cooking was certainly a grand objection; and some neighbouring ladies who had (charity) schools remonstrated at the absence of the children, who were crazy if they were not allowed to forsake everything in order to attend Mr. Y.'s dinners. But another scheme, more extensive and more useful, succeeded this —namely, the introduction of straw-plaiting among the young cottagers.'

INDEX

ABERCORN, Marquis of, 347
Aldworth, Richard, 72
Allen, Alderman (father-in-law of Arthur Young), 32
— — (son of the above), 60
— Mrs., 36, 38
Althorp, Lord, 313
Amorette, Abate, 176
Anson, Mr., 394
Arblay, Madame d', 23 *note* 1, 32 *note* 3, 61 *note* 2, 100 *note* 1, 135 *note* 1, 196, 214, 216
Arbuthnot, Mr. (son of Viscount Arbuthnot), 66, 92, 97, 98, 124
Armstead, Mrs., 260
Ashby, Rev. George, 104 and *note* 2, 114, 129
Aspin, Miss, 15
Attwood, Mr., 471
Auckland, Lord, 314
Augusta of Saxe Gotha (Princess of Wales), 16

B., Countess of, 29
Baker, Whyman, 88, 111
Bakewell, Robert, 135 and *note* 3
Balgrave, Rev. —, 355
Banks, Sir Joseph, 150, 151, 163, 165, 167, 174, 201, 224, 321, 339, 350
Baroude, A. F., 464 *note*
Barrington, Dr. (Bishop of Durham), 254, 348, 352, 358, 376
Barry, James (painter), 115–118
Bayley, Butterworth, 59
Bedford, fifth Duke of, 172, 206, 244, 245, 246, 254, 256, 273, 276, 301, 313, 318, 330, 351, 360, 363, 372, 374, 375

Bedford, sixth Duke of, 372, 373 *note*, 374, 383, 384, 396, 444
Bentham, Jeremy, 247, 249, 308, 341
Bentinck, Lady Mary, 327
— Lord Charles, 328
Berchtold, Count Leopold, 167 and *note*, 168–170, 180
Bernard, Mr., 376
Berry, Edward, 323
— Miss Jane. *See* Young, Mrs. Arthur, daughter-in-law of Arthur Young
Bolton, M.P., Cornelius, 75, 80
Boswell, 191
Boulainvilliers, Comte de, 32 and *note* 4
Boyd, Hugh, 92–97
Bristol (Bishop of Derry), Earl of, 101, 102, 103–105, 113, 128–131, 228
— Countess of, 225, 227, 243
Brudenell, Mr., 18
Brunswick, Duke of, 355, 356
Bryant, Jacob, 245 and *note*, 291
Buccleugh, Duke of, 245, 256, 261
Bukaty, M., 159, 180 and *note*
Bulkeley, Lady Frances, 52
Bunbury, Sir C., 412
Burdett, Sir Francis, 345, 449, 451
Burgoyne, Montague, 418, 419
Burke, Edmund, 67, 93, 174, 232, 256–261, 302, 345, 428
— W., 257, 428
Burney, Dr. Charles, 23 and *note* 1, 51, 65, 92, 100, 101, 115, 144, 181, 194, 196, 197, 214, 232, 250, 299, 326
— Fanny. *See* Arblay, Madame d'

476   AUTOBIOGRAPHY OF ARTHUR YOUNG

Burney, Hester, 51, 100 note 1
— Sarah, 215 and note
Burrell, Sir Peter, 164
Burton, Colonel (afterwards Lord Cunningham), 67, 68
Bute, Lord, 192, 355, 412

CADELL (the publisher), 395
Cadogan, Lady, 313
Caldwell, Sir James, 69, 70, 75
Camden, Lord, 304
Canham, the elder, Bartholomew, 2
Canning, Mr., 327, 362 note
Carew, Pole, 202
Carnot, M., 307 and note
Carrington, Lord, 314, 315, 319, 333 note, 351, 356, 360, 361, 363, 370, 379, 393, 407, 413
Cartier, M., 157
Cartwright, Dr., 367, 373, 374, 396
Castiglioni, Count di, 176
Castries, Marshal de, 240
Catherine, Empress, 124
Charlemont, Earl of, 75
Chester, Bishop of, 97, 98
Chesterfield, Lord, 33, 34, 49
Chevalier, Rev. M., 14
Cibber, Mrs., 15
Clermont, Lord, 211
Clive, Lord, 49
Cobbett, William, 442
Cocks, Sir Charles (afterwards Lord Somers), 52
Coke, J. W., 212, 384, 385, 386, 400, 432, 444
Cole, Charles, 243, 245, 255, 290, 297, 304, 368
Colhoun, Mr., 363
Collier, Joseph and Mary, 27 and note 2
Cornwallis, Archbishop, 139
— Marquis of, 205
Cotton, Lady, 338
Coulter, Rev. Mr. (Master of Lavenham School), 7, 8, 23
Courtenay, Sir W., 192
Cousmaker, John, 103
— John de, 3, 126
— Miss, 102, 103
— —Anne Lucretia de. See Young, Mrs. (mother of Arthur Young)

Coventry, Lady, 20
Cowper's 'Letters,' quoted, 410
Coxe, Archdeacon, 236
Crewe, Mrs., 214, 233, 259, 260, 327
— Mr., 326
Crosse, Lady, 17
Cullum, Sir John, 104 and note 1, 114, 134
Cumberland, Duke of, 4, 6, 16 note 2

DANBY, Mr., 50, 55, 76
Darnley, Earl of, 245
Dartmouth, Lord, 236
Day, Thomas (author of 'Sandford and Merton'), 166 and note
Derry, Bishop of. See Bristol, Earl of
Doddington, George Bubb, 12, 161
Dolmein (geologist), 368 and note 2
Douglas, Bishop, 236, 304
Dryden (quoted), 35
Ducket, Mr., 172
Dundas, Lady Jane, 327
— Mr., 261, 327
Dundonald, Lord, 160
Dunstanville, Lord de, 245
Durham, Bishop of. See Barrington, Dr.

EDWARD AUGUSTUS, Prince. See York, Duke of
Egremont, Lord, 111, 179, 244, 245, 275, 299, 313, 315, 317, 324, 352, 358, 360, 363, 434
Elizabeth, Princess (daughter of George II.), 16
Ellerton, Mr., 50
Erne, Lady, 267
Estissac, Duchess d', 175
Euston, Lord, 365

FAWCETT, Sir William, 329
Fielding, Sir John, 69
Fife, Lord, 112
Folkes, Sir Martin, 2, 11
Folkestone, Lord, 59 note 1
Forbes, Mrs., 252, 253
Fordyce, Lady Margaret, 338
— Sir William, 147

INDEX 477

Forster, Lord Chief Baron, 75
Foster, Lady Elizabeth, 468, 469
Fox, Charles James, 202, 227, 233, 234, 259, 424, 425
— Henry (afterwards Lord Holland), 16, 134, 164
Francis, Miss, 457 and *note* 2, 460, 461, 472
Freeman, Miss, 20
Frere, J. H., 362 *note*
Fry, Mr., 391, 395, 398, 407

GAGE, Sir Thomas, 191
Garrick, 10, 15, 22, 31, 32
— Mrs., 245
George II., 16
— III., 112, 132, 138, 160, 178, 190, 224, 237, 268, 321, 322
George, Prince (afterwards George III.), 16
— — (afterwards George IV.), 192
Gibbon, Edward, 258, 259, 468
Gifford, W., 362 *note*
Gloucester, Duke of, 371
Gordon, Duchess of, 334
Gough, Captain, 5
Grafton, Duchess of, 139, 140
— Duke of, 139, 140, 141, 193, 201, 211, 239, 254, 305, 325, 361, 362, 372, 382, 426, 438, 454 *note*
Granby, Marquis of, 355
Gray, Thomas (the poet), quoted, 89, 90
Green, Valentine, 59
Grenville, Lord, 360, 435
Grey, Sir Charles (afterwards first Earl Grey), 327
— — — (afterwards second Earl Grey), 233, 234, 235, 424
Grigby, Joshua, 390
Guerchy, Comtesse de, 186, 187
Gurney, Rev. Mr., 462

HALIFAX, Dr., 372, 376
Hanger, Colonel George (afterwards Lord Coleraine), 192 and *note* 1
Harcourt, Countess of, 50 *note* 1, 358
— Earl of, 67, 75
Hardwicke, Lord, 338
Hardy, Professor, 238

Harte, Rev. Walter, 32 and *note* 5, 33, 35-43, 49
Harvey, Fenton, 20
Hastings, Warren, 164
Hawke, Lord, 241
Hawkesbury, Lady, 267
Hawksworth, Dr., 343
Héritier, C. de l', 367 and *note*
Hertford, Marquis of, 427
Hervey, General, 105, 106
— Lady Mary, 267 and *note*
Hesketh, Lady, 233
Hill, Rev. Rowland, 359
Hoar, Captain, 350, 352
Holdernesse, Lord, 56
Holroyd, John Baker (afterwards Lord Sheffield, *q.v.*), 58
Hoole, Mrs., 189, 198, 246, 250, 252
— John, 189
— Rev. Samuel, 189, 246, 251, 252, 361, 362
Horsley, Bishop, 359 and *note* 2
Howard, Sir Charles, 28
— John, 59, 60, 248
Howlett, Rev. —, 97, 285
Hunter, Dr. Alexander, 61 and *note* 3
Hutchinson, Rev. Mr., 336
Huthhausen, Baron, 173

INGOLDSBY, Dr., 19
— General, 4, 5, 6, 7
— Mrs., 6, 10

JABRÉ, General, 123
Jarvis, Lord, 267
Jefferys, Mr. and Mrs., 73
Jenkinson, Mr., 256
Jenyns, Soame, 244, 245
Jermyn, Sir Thomas, 2
Jobson, Rev. Mr., 337
John of Austria, Archduke, 463, 464
Johnson, Dr., 26, 27, 32 *note* 5, 285 *note* 2, 353, 421, 422
Joy, Mrs., 19

KALASKOWSKI, Count, 144
Kames, Lord, 84 and *note* 2
Keene, Mr. and Mrs., 3
Kennon, Mrs. Sidney, 10, 11, 12, 13

Kenrick, Dr., 27 and *note* 1
Keppel, Lord, 108
Kingsborough, Lord, 76, 77–80
Kinsman, Mr. (master of Bury St. Edmunds School), 7
Knight, Cornelia, 368 and *note* 1

LAFAYETTE, 191
Lamb, Mr. (King's Messenger), 45
Lambert, Captain, 29
Langford, Dr., 142
Latrobe, B. H., 172
Lauderdale, Lord, 314, 397
Law, Thomas, 229
Lawrence, Dr., 345
Lazowski, M. de, 119 and *note* 2, 120–124, 154, 175
Leeds, Duke of, 51
— Sir George, 472
Leigh, Mr. (Clerk of the House of Commons), 261, 262
Liancourt, Duke of, 119 and *note* 1, 120–123, 154, 259, 382
Liverpool, Lord, 339
Llandaff, Bishop of. *See* Watson, Richard
Lofft, Capel, 101 and *note* 1, 102, 276, 291, 317, 318
Longford, Lord, 71
Loughborough, Lord, 86, 98, 207, 208, 219
Louisa, Princess (daughter of George II.), 16
Luther, Mr., 179

MACARTNEY, Lord, 196
Macaulay, General, 460, 462
Macklin, Rev. Mr., 154, 267, 274
Macpherson, Sir John, 224, 225, 239
Macro, Mr., 170
Magellan, Mr., 150
Manchester, Duke of, 367, 395
March, Lord, 140, 141
Marlborough, Duke of, 26
Marshall, W., 427 and *note* 1, 429
Martin, Professor, 147
Massalski, Prince (Bishop of Wilna), 52
Mauduit, Israel, 255 and *note*
Medlicott, Mr., 71
Milbank, Lady, 350

Mildmay, Sir A. St. John, 348
Milner, Dean, 371 and *note*, 372
— Professor, 150
Miripoix, M. de (French Ambassador), 17
Moira, Lord, 243, 304
Moncrief, Sir Henry, 238
Montagu, Mrs., 233, 243, 244, 245, 312, 349, 358, 386
Montrose, Duke of, 245, 347
Mordaunt, Lady Mary, 52
More, Hannah, 233, 245, 246, 473
Mouron, M., 124
Murray, General, 171

NEPEAN, Mr., 341, 342
Neve, Miss, 467
Neville, Mr., 134
Newcastle, Duke of, 16
North, Lord, 60, 107, 201
— Rev. Mr., 344
Northey, Mr., 363

OAKES, Orbell Ray, 154, 266, 382, 388, 406
— Mrs. Orbell Ray, 266 and *note*, 270, 320, 321, 354, 359, 370 *note* 1, 382, 385, 388, 392, 438, 443, 444, 445, 446, 453
O'Connor, A., 317 and *note*
Oliver, Right Hon. Silver, 74
Onslow, Dr., 191
— General, 4, 15, 16, 191
— Lady, 20
— Mr. Speaker, 4, 20, 28
Orde, Mrs., 245
Orford, Earl of, 60, 206, 207, 233
Orwell, Lord, 16 *note* 1
Ossory, Lord, 331, 332, 395
Otto, L. W., Count of Morlay, 377 and *note* 1
Overton, J., 376 and *note*

PAKENHAM, Mr., 460, 461
Paley, Dr., 378
Parkyn, Mr., 367
Partridge, Rev. S., 280
Patulle, M., 36, 40, 42
Pearson, Dr., 376
Pelham, Lord, 381
Peterborough, Bishop of, 147
Peterson, Lady, 20

INDEX 479

Petty, Lord Henry, 370
Phillips, Sir John, 17
Pigot, Admiral, 193
Pitt, William, 134, 137, 161, 166, 201, 203, 219, 221, 254, 255, 306, 314, 315, 327, 345, 346, 363, 371, 424, 427
Plampin, Betsy. *See* Oakes, Mrs.
— Captain John, 154, 423
Polignac, Prince and Princess de, 162 and *note*
Pope, Alexander (quoted), 136 *note* 1
Popple, Mr. (Governor of Bermuda), 13
Porteus, Bishop, 178, 179
Portland, Duke of, 51, 326
Potemkin, Prince, 102, 125
Poulett, Mr., 246
Preston, Lord, 367, 368
Priestley, Dr., 99, 150–153, 439

QUEENSBERRY, Duke of, 192

RADNOR, Lord, 161
Richardson, Samuel, 192
Richmond, Legh, 460
Roberts, Dr., Provost of Eton, 142
— Lewis, 91 and *note* 1
Robertson, Messrs. (of Lynn), 22, 23
Rochefoucault, Counts de la, 119–121, 154
Rochester, Bishop of, 4, 28
Rockingham, Marquis of, 42, 50
Roper, Dr., 52
Rose, George (President of the Board of Trade), 132 and *note* 1, 137, 221, 241, 242
Ross, Bishop, 160
Rosslyn, Lord, 360
Rossmore, Lord, 347
Rostopchin, Count, 387, 401
Ruggles, Th., 194 and *note* 1
Rumford, Count, 323
Ryder, Lady Susan, 327, 328
— Mr., 327, 386

ST. VINCENT, Earl of, 418, 419
Sambosky, Rev. —, 124, 125
Saunderson, Dr. Nicholas, 14 *note* 1

Scott, Rev. Thomas, 349, 359, 391, 392
Seabright, Sir John, 463
Sheffield, Lord, 132, 220, 245, 258, 344 and *note* 2, 393, 395, 402, 407, 468, 469
Shelburne, Earl of (afterwards Marquis of Lansdowne), 67, 69, 102
Shelley, Mr., 20
Sheridan, R. B., 164 and *note*, 234
Shipley, Mr., 59 *note* 1
Sidmouth, Lord, 419, 434, 460
Simeon, Rev. Charles, 369, 395, 397, 398, 399, 400
Sinclair, Sir J., 159 and *note* 3, 160, 219, 220, 224, 241, 242, 243, 245, 247, 256, 299, 314, 315, 316, 413, 414, 437, 443, 464
Smirenove, Mr., 387, 400
Smith, Sydney (quoted), 445 *note* 1
Somers, Lord, 359
Somerville, Lord, 245, 315, 316, 318, 347, 361, 363, 384, 385, 404
Souga, Anthony (Austrian Consul), 169
Spencer, Lord, 313, 367
Stafford, Lord, 161
Stanhope, Lady, 313
— Philip, 33
Stanislas, King, 119
Stonehewer, Mr., 193, 346
Sturton, Sir Thomas, 344
Sutton, Dr. Robert, 8 and *note* 2
Symonds, Professor John, 103, 114 and *note* 1, 120–124, 129, 140, 144, 146, 154, 160, 184, 192, 201, 210, 236, 239, 253, 283, 295, 304, 344, 355, 362, 368, 400, 412, 419–421

THORNHILL, Major, 78, 79
Thurlow, Lord, 161
Tillet, Mr. de, 170
Tomlinson, Mr., 22
— Mrs. (sister of Arthur Young), 20, 22, 126
Tour du Pin, Count de la, 257
Townsend, Rev. J., 407 and *note* 1
Townshend, Lord, 136
Trant, Mr. and Mrs., 73
Tuam, Archbishop of, 75

Turner, Miss, 15
Turton, Dr., 264, 273, 274

VALPY, Dr. Richard, 106 and *note* 2, 133, 297
Vancouver, 426 and *note* 1
Vansittart, Nicholas (afterwards Lord Bexley), 426 and *note* 2, 435, 459
Vary, Mr., 140, 141, 193
Vassy, Governor, 4
Voltaire (quoted), 39

WAKEFIELD, Edward, 75 and *note* 1
Washington, General, 189, 191, 360
Watson, Richard (afterwards Bishop of Llandaff), 97, 123, 124, 147, 150, 177-180, 236, 237, 254, 375
Way, Miss, 467
Wedderburn, Alexander (afterwards Earl of Rosslyn), 97 and *note* 1
— Colonel, 16 *note* 1
Wellesley, Marquis of, 451
Wentworth, Lord, 245
Whitbread, Samuel, 52, 59, 161
Wight, Alexander, 84 and *note* 1
Wilberforce, William, 201, 287 and *note*, 288, 289, 297, 307, 325 and *note*, 326, 345, 348, 359, 371, 375, 407, 454 *note*, 457, 459
Wilkes, John, 10
Willes, Mr. Justice, 52
Willoughby, Sir C., 351, 413
Winchester, Earl of, 245
Winchilsea, Earl of, 244, 315, 351, 363, 388, 466, 470
Windham, William, 161
Wollaston, Dr., 277
Wurtemburg, Queen of, 425
Wyndham, M.P., Mr., 259

YELDHAM, John, 47
York, Duke of, 16, 266, 327

York, Mrs., 245
Young, Rev. Dr. (father of Arthur Young, writer of the Autobiography), 2-6, 8, 9, 10, 13, 14, 24
— Mrs. (mother of Arthur Young), 3, 22, 24, 28, 56, 57, 61, 77, 81, 126
— Arthur (son of Arthur Young), 51, 139, 143, 299, 317, 318, 323, 352, 363, 382, 402, 403, 406, 408, 415, 418, 428, 429, 432, 448, 456, 457, 464
— — (last descendant of Arthur Young), 127 *note*
— Mrs. Arthur (wife of Arthur Young), 32 and *note* 3, 46, 81, 142, 146, 319, 339, 389, 413, 424, 429, 438, 457, 460
— — — (daughter-in-law of Arthur Young), 323, 397, 398, 399, 404, 409, 415, 429, 446, 448, 457
— Bartholomew (grandfather of Arthur Young), 2
— Elizabeth ('Bessy') (second daughter of Arthur Young), 51, 146, 181, 189. See also Hoole, Mrs.
— Elizabeth Mary ('Elisa Maria') (sister of Arthur Young), 1, 15, 19, 20. See also Tomlinson, Mrs.
— Rev. Dr. John (brother of Arthur Young), 2, 9, 57, 107, 127, 132, 138-143
— Martha Ann ('Bobbin') (youngest daughter of Arthur Young), 110 and *note*, 158, 159 *note* 2, 184, 185, 263-284, 286, 287, 290, 294, 295, 298, 323, 382, 423
— Mary (eldest daughter of Arthur Young), 43, 184, 382, 425, 440, 454 *note*, 457, 472

SMITH, ELDER, & CO.'S NEW BOOKS.

THE LETTERS OF ELIZABETH BARRETT BROWNING. Edited, with Biographical Additions, by FREDERIC G. KENYON. In 2 vols. With Portraits. Second Edition. Crown 8vo. 15s. net.

DEEDS THAT WON THE EMPIRE. By the Rev. W. H. FITCHETT. With 11 Plans and 16 Portraits. Crown 8vo. 6s.

THE STORY OF THE CHURCH OF EGYPT: being an Outline of the History of the Egyptians under their successive Masters from the Roman Conquest until now. By E. L. BUTCHER, Author of 'A Strange Journey,' 'A Black Jewel,' &c. In 2 vols. Crown 8vo. 16s.

THE LIFE OF SIR JOHN HAWLEY GLOVER, R.N., G.C.M.G. By Lady GLOVER. Edited by the Right Hon. Sir RICHARD TEMPLE, Bart., G.C.S.I., D.C.L., LL.D., F.R.S. With Portrait and Maps. Demy 8vo. 14s.

THE AUTOBIOGRAPHY OF ARTHUR YOUNG. With Selections from his Correspondence. Edited by M. BETHAM-EDWARDS. With 2 Portraits and 2 Views. Large crown 8vo. 12s. 6d.

THE WAR OF GREEK INDEPENDENCE, 1821-1833. By W. ALISON PHILLIPS, M.A., late Scholar of Merton College, Senior Scholar of St. John's College, Oxford. With Map. Large crown 8vo. 7s. 6d.

TWELVE YEARS IN A MONASTERY. By JOSEPH MCCABE, late FATHER ANTONY, O.S.F. Large crown 8vo. 7s. 6d.

STUDIES IN BOARD SCHOOLS. By CHARLES MORLEY. Crown 8vo. 6s.

FRANCE UNDER LOUIS XV. By JAMES BRECK PERKINS, Author of 'France Under the Regency.' In 2 vols. Crown 8vo. 16s.

A BROWNING COURTSHIP; and other Stories. By ELIZA ORNE WHITE, Author of 'The Coming of Theodora' &c. Small post 8vo. 5s.

THE POEMS OF ELIZABETH BARRETT BROWNING. New Edition. Complete in 1 volume. With Portrait and Facsimile of the MS. of a 'Sonnet from the Portuguese.' Large crown 8vo. bound in cloth, with gilt top, 7s. 6d.

*** This Edition is uniform with the Two-volume Edition of Robert Browning's Complete Works.

THE GREY LADY. By HENRY SETON MERRIMAN, Author of 'The Sowers,' 'With Edged Tools,' 'In Kedar's Tents,' &c. New Edition. With 12 Full-page Illustrations by ARTHUR RACKHAM. Crown 8vo. 6s.

MARCELLA. By Mrs. HUMPHRY WARD. Cheap Popular Edition. Crown 8vo. bound in limp cloth, 2s. 6d.

FRIENDSHIP'S GARLAND. By MATTHEW ARNOLD. Second Edition. Small crown 8vo. bound in white cloth, 4s. 6d.

NEW NOVELS.

DEBORAH OF TOD'S. By Mrs. HENRY DE LA PASTURE, Author of 'A Toy Tragedy,' 'The Little Squire,' &c. Crown 8vo. 6s.

THE MILLS OF GOD. By FRANCIS H. HARDY. Crown 8vo. 6s.

IN KEDAR'S TENTS. By HENRY SETON MERRIMAN, Author of 'The Sowers,' 'With Edged Tools,' &c. FIFTH EDITION. Crown 8vo. 6s.

ONE OF THE BROKEN BRIGADE. By CLIVE PHILLIPPS-WOLLEY, Author of 'Snap,' 'Gold, Gold in Cariboo,' &c. Crown 8vo. 6s.

JAN: an Afrikander. By ANNA HOWARTH. Crown 8vo. 6s.

London: SMITH, ELDER, & CO., 15 Waterloo Place.

SMITH, ELDER, & CO.'S PUBLICATIONS.

BY LORD ARMSTRONG, C.B., F.R.S., LL.D.
With Autotype Plates. Imperial 4to. £1. 10s. net.

ELECTRIC MOVEMENT IN AIR AND WATER. With Theoretical Inferences. By LORD ARMSTRONG, C.B., F.R.S., LL.D., &c.

'One of the most remarkable contributions to physical and electrical knowledge that have been made in recent years. . . . The illustrations are produced in a superb manner, entirely worthy of so remarkable a monograph.'—TIMES.

GABRIELE VON BULOW, Daughter of Wilhelm von Humboldt. A Memoir Compiled from the Family Papers of Wilhelm von Humboldt and his Children, 1791-1887. Translated by CLARA NORDLINGER. With Portraits and a Preface by Sir EDWARD B. MALET, G.C.B., G.C.M.G., &c. Demy 8vo. 16s.

'Miss Nordlinger's excellent translation gives English readers an opportunity of becoming acquainted with a very charming personality, and of following the events of a life which was bound up with many interesting incidents and phases of English history.'—TIMES.

ISABELLA THE CATHOLIC, QUEEN OF SPAIN: her Life, Reign, and Times, 1451-1504. By M. LE BARON DE NERVO. Translated from the Original French by Lieut.-Colonel TEMPLE-WEST (Retired). With Portraits. Demy 8vo. 12s. 6d.

'Neither too long nor too short, not overladen with detail nor impoverished from lack of matter, and is at the same time ample and orderly enough to satisfy the ordinary student.'—DAILY TELEGRAPH.

POT-POURRI FROM A SURREY GARDEN. By Mrs. C. W. EARLE. With an Appendix by Lady CONSTANCE LYTTON. Eighth Edition. Crown 8vo.

'Intelligent readers of almost any age, especially if they are concerned in the management of a country household, will find these pages throughout both suggestive and amusing.'—TIMES.

NEW AND CHEAPER EDITION OF 'THE RENAISSANCE IN ITALY.'
In 7 Volumes, large crown 8vo. with 2 Portraits.

THE RENAISSANCE IN ITALY. By JOHN ADDINGTON SYMONDS.

1. THE AGE OF THE DESPOTS. With a Portrait. Price 7s. 6d. Ready.
2. THE REVIVAL OF LEARNING. Price 7s. 6d. [Ready.
3. THE FINE ARTS. Price 7s. 6d. [Ready.
4 & 5. ITALIAN LITERATURE. 2 Vols. Price 15s. [In December.
6 & 7. THE CATHOLIC REACTION. With a Portrait and an Index to the 7 Vols. Price 15s. [In the press.

THACKERAY'S HAUNTS AND HOMES. By EYRE CROWE, A.R.A. With Illustrations from Sketches by the Author. Crown 8vo. 6s. net.

☞ NOTE.—The Edition of the Work for sale in this country is limited to 260 copies.

THE ANNALS OF RURAL BENGAL. From Official Records and the Archives of Native Families. By Sir W. W. HUNTER, K.S.C.I., C.I.E., LL.D., &c. New, Revised, and Cheaper Edition (the Seventh). Crown 8vo. 7s. 6d.

'One of the most important as well as most interesting works which the records of Indian literature can show.'—WESTMINSTER REVIEW.

FROM GRAVE TO GAY: being Essays and Studies concerned with Certain Subjects of Serious Interest, with the Puritans. with Literature, and with the Humours of Life, now for the first time collected and arranged. By J. ST. LOE STRACHEY. Crown 8vo. 6s.

'Undeniably clever, well-informed, brightly written, and in many ways interesting.'—TIMES.

COLLECTED CONTRIBUTIONS ON DIGESTION AND DIET. With an Appendix on the Opium Habit in India. By Sir WILLIAM ROBERTS, M.D., F.R.S. Second Edition. Crown 8vo. 5s.

London: SMITH, ELDER, & CO., 15 Waterloo Place.

SMITH, ELDER, & CO.'S PUBLICATIONS.

MY CONFIDENCES: an Autobiographical Sketch addressed to my Descendants. By FREDERICK LOCKER-LAMPSON. Edited by AUGUSTINE BIRRELL, Q.C., M.P. Second Edition. With Two Portraits. 8vo. 15s.

THE LABOUR PROBLEM. By GEOFFREY DRAGE, M.P. Demy 8vo. 14s.

THE MAMELUKE OR SLAVE DYNASTY OF EGYPT, 1260-1517 A.D. By Sir WILLIAM MUIR, K.S.C.I., LL.D., D.C.L., Ph.D. (Bologna), Author of 'The Life of Mahomet,' 'Mahomet and Islam,' 'The Caliphate,' &c. With 12 Full-page Illustrations and a Map. 8vo. 10s. 6d.

COSMIC ETHICS; or, the Mathematical Theory of Evolution: showing the full import of the DOCTRINE of the MEAN, and containing the PRINCIPIA of the SCIENCE of PROPORTION. By W. CAVE THOMAS, F.S.S. 8vo. 10s. 6d.

THE SPAS AND MINERAL WATERS OF EUROPE. With Notes on Balneotherapeutic Management in various Diseases and Morbid Conditions. By HERMANN WEBER M.D., F.R.C.P., Consulting Physician to the German Hospital and to the Royal National Hospital for Consumption, Ventnor, &c.; and FREDERICK PARKES WEBER, M.D., M.R.C.P., Physician to the German Hospital. Crown 8vo. 6s.

₊ The purpose of this book is to give a description of European Mineral Waters and Spas, and to indicate the complaints for which the Waters are likely to prove beneficial.

THE BROWNINGS FOR THE YOUNG. Edited by FREDERIC G. KENYON, late Fellow of Magdalen College, Oxford. Small fcp. 8vo. cloth, 1s.; or with gilt edges, 1s. 4d.

THE APOSTOLIC GOSPEL. With a Critical Reconstruction of the Text. By J. FULTON BLAIR, B.D. 8vo. 12s. 6d.

RENAISSANCE FANCIES AND STUDIES: being a Sequel to 'Euphorion.' By VERNON LEE, Author of 'Euphorion, Antique and Mediæval in Renaissance' &c. Crown 8vo. 6s. net.

A SHORT HISTORY OF THE RENAISSANCE IN ITALY. Taken from the work of JOHN ADDINGTON SYMONDS. By Lieut.-Col. ALFRED PEARSON. With a Steel Engraving of a recent Portrait of Mr. Symonds. Demy 8vo. 12s. 6d

HYPNOTISM, MESMERISM, AND THE NEW WITCHCRAFT. By ERNEST HART, formerly Surgeon to the West London Hospital, and Ophthalmic Surgeon to St. Mary's Hospital. Second Edition, Enlarged, with Chapters on 'The Eternal Gullible,' and Note on 'The Hypnotism of Trilby.' Crown 8vo. 5s.

JOHANNESBURG IN ARMS, 1895-6. Being the Observations of a Casual Spectator. By CHARLES G. THOMAS. With Illustrations. Crown 8vo. 2s. 6d.

OFF THE MILL. By the Right Rev. G. F. BROWNE, D.C.L., Bishop of Stepney. With 2 Illustrations. Crown 8vo. 6s.

FIFTY YEARS; or, Dead Leaves and Living Seeds. By the Rev. HARRY JONES, Prebendary of St. Paul's, Author of 'Holiday Papers,' 'East and West London,' &c. Second Edition. Crown 8vo. 4s.

RECOLLECTIONS OF A MILITARY LIFE. By General Sir JOHN ADYE, G.C.B., R.A., late Governor of Gibraltar. With Illustrations by the Author. Demy 8vo. 14s. net.

London : SMITH, ELDER, & CO., 15 Waterloo Place.

SMITH, ELDER, & CO.'S RECENT BOOKS.

HISTORY IN FACT AND FICTION. By the Hon. A. S. G. CANNING, Author of 'Lord Macaulay: Essayist and Historian,' 'The Philosophy of Charles Dickens,' &c. Crown 8vo. 6s.

'An intensely interesting book. . . . I do not think that I ever saw the difficulties of the Eastern question in so clear a light as I did after reading the short chapter which Mr. Canning devotes to it.'—PALL MALL GAZETTE.

THROUGH LONDON SPECTACLES. By CONSTANCE MILMAN. Crown 8vo. 3s. 6d.

'Altogether a very pleasant and companionable little book.'—SPECTATOR.

AN ACCOUNT OF THE LIFE AND WORKS OF DR. ROBERT WATT, Author of the 'Bibliotheca Britannica.' By JAMES FINLAYSON, M.D., Physician to the Glasgow Western Infirmary and the Royal Hospital for Sick Children; Hon. Librarian to the Faculty of Physicians and Surgeons, Glasgow, &c. With a Portrait. 8vo. 3s. 6d.

SIR CHARLES HALLÉ'S LIFE AND LETTERS. Being an Autobiography (1819-60), with Correspondence and Diaries. Edited by his Son, C. E. HALLÉ, and his Daughter, MARIE HALLÉ. With 2 Portraits. Demy 8vo. 16s.

'The volume is one of the most interesting of recent contributions to the literature of music. . . . A strong sense of humour is manifest in the autobiography as well as in the letters, and there are some capital stories scattered up and down the volume.'—TIMES.

THE MEMOIRS OF BARON THIÉBAULT (late Lieutenant-General in the French Army). With Recollections of the Republic, the Consulate, and the Empire. Translated and Condensed by A. J. BUTLER, M.A., Translator of the 'Memoirs of Marbot.' 2 vols. With 2 Portraits and 2 Maps. Demy 8vo. 28s.

'Mr. Butler's work has been admirably done. . . . These Memoirs abound in varied interest, and, moreover, they have no little literary merit. . . . For solid history, bright sketches of rough campaigning, shrewd studies of character, and lively anecdote, these Memoirs yield in no degree to others.'—TIMES.

PREHISTORIC MAN AND BEAST. By the Rev. H. N. HUTCHINSON, Author of 'Extinct Monsters,' 'Creatures of Other Days,' &c. With a Preface by Sir HENRY HOWORTH, M.P., F.R.S., and 10 Full-page Illustrations. Small demy 8vo. 10s. 6d.

'A striking picture of living men and conditions as they once existed. . . . It combines graphic description with scientific accuracy, and is an admirable example of what a judicious use of the imagination can achieve upon a basis of established facts.'—KNOWLEDGE.

A YEAR IN THE FIELDS. Selections from the Writings of JOHN BURROUGHS. With Illustrations from photographs by Clifton Johnson. Cr. 8vo. 6s.

'The book is an excellent example of its kind, pleasant, chatty, and readable. . . . Fresh and graphic, instinct with country sights, scents, and sounds.'—LAND AND WATER.

'The book is pleasant reading, and Mr. Burroughs is a true lover of Nature.'—ATHENÆUM.

THE MONEY-SPINNER, and other Character Notes. By H. SETON MERRIMAN, Author of 'The Sowers,' 'With Edged Tools,' &c., and S. G. TALLENTYRE. With 12 Full-page Illustrations by Arthur Rackham. Second Edition. Crown 8vo. 6s.

'We have many bad books, and many goody-goody books, but few good books; this is one of them.'—Mr. JAMES PAYN, in the *Illustrated London News*.

SELECTED POEMS OF WALTER VON DER VOGELWEIDE THE MINNESINGER. Done into English Verse by W. ALISON PHILLIPS, M.A., late Scholar of Merton College, and Senior Scholar of St. John's College, Oxford. With 6 Full-page Illustrations. Small 4to. 10s. 6d. net.

'There is in the outpourings of the famous Minnesinger a freshness and a spontaneity that exercise an irresistible charm. . . . Mr. Phillips deserves thanks from all lovers of poetry for bringing him before the world again in so acceptable a form.'—TIMES.

A HISTORY OF THE HEBREW PEOPLE FROM THE DIVISION OF THE KINGDOM TO THE FALL OF JERUSALEM IN 566 B.C. By CHARLES FOSTER KENT, Ph.D., Associate-Professor of Biblical Literature and History, Brown University. With Maps and Chart. Crown 8vo. 6s.

* This Second Volume completes the Work.

London: SMITH, ELDER, & CO., 15 Waterloo Place.

Lightning Source UK Ltd.
Milton Keynes UK
UKHW020630200721
387437UK00002B/104